D0085538

New Approaches to Semiotics and the Human Sciences

# Semiotics and the Human Sciences

Roberta Kevelson
*General Editor*

Vol. 13

PETER LANG
New York • Washington, D.C./Baltimore • Boston
Bern • Frankfurt am Main • Berlin • Vienna • Paris

# New Approaches to Semiotics and the Human Sciences

*Essays in Honor of Roberta Kevelson*

*Edited by*
William Pencak
& J. Ralph Lindgren

PETER LANG
New York • Washington, D.C./Baltimore • Boston
Bern • Frankfurt am Main • Berlin • Vienna • Paris

**Library of Congress Cataloging-in-Publication Data**

New approaches to semiotics and the human sciences: essays in honor
of Roberta Kevelson / William Pencak and Ralph J. Lindgren, editors.
p. cm. — (Semiotics and the human sciences; vol. 13)
Includes bibliographical references and indexes.
1. Semiotics (Law). 2. Semiotics. 3. Kevelson, Roberta. I. Kevelson,
Roberta. II. Pencak, William. III. Lindgren, Ralph J. IV. Series.
K213.S46 302.2—dc21 97-12496
ISBN 0-8204-3814-6
ISSN 1054-8386

**Die Deutsche Bibliothek-CIP-Einheitsaufnahme**

New approaches to semiotics and the human sciences: essays in honor
of Roberta Kevelson / William Pencak and Ralph J. Lindgren, eds.
–New York; Washington, D.C./Baltimore; Boston; Bern;
Frankfurt am Main; Berlin; Vienna; Paris: Lang.
(Semiotics and the human sciences; 13)
ISBN 0-8204-3814-6

The paper in this book meets the guidelines for permanence and durability
of the Committee on Production Guidelines for Book Longevity
of the Council of Library Resources.

Printed in the United States of America.

# Contents

## Semiotic Theory



## Appendices

# Introduction
# The Semiotic World of Roberta Kevelson

**William Pencak**

It is appropriate that this collection of essays honoring Roberta Kevelson includes representatives of seven nationalities (American, Chilean, Scottish, English, Hungarian, Dutch, and Canadian) and seven disciplines (Law, Philosophy, Communications, Political Science, Art/Video Creation, History, and Economics). Two of us (myself and Bob Ginsberg) were colleagues of Bobbie's at Penn State. Thomas Sebeok and John Deely first met her through the Semiotic Society of America, an organization of which she was elected president in 1996. John Brigham, Dennis Brion, Robin Malloy, Paul Ryan, Bill Scott, and co-editor Ralph Lindgren know her principally from the Round Tables she has organized since 1987 through the Penn State Center for Semiotic Research. Rolando Gaete, Bernard Jackson, and Willem Witteveen are primarily associated with her through the International Association for the Semiotics of Law, another anti-institutional institution where she was present at the creation and to which she has remained faithful ever since. Marcel Danesi has worked with her through the International Association of Semiotic Societies and is now embarked with her on new publication and conference projects involving semiotic centers in Canada.

Other aspects of this collection are as fitting, and celebratory, as the eclectic nature of the disciplines, ethnicities, and academic connections of the contributors. It appears in the first series Bobbie began with her most frequent publisher, Peter Lang: Semiotics and the Human Sciences. This volume honoring Bobbie was requested by Peter Lang editor Chris Myers, who, with his predecessor Michael Flamini, has been Bobbie's most frequent collaborator in the publishing world. I regard this request as a symbol of the mutual admiration and affection that develops only too rarely between authors and publishers in the age of post-modern scholarship. Having worked with these wonderfully competent gentlemen (a word I use sparingly, and with care) myself, I can only praise their willingness to let authors speak in their own voices in an era where so many academic presses think style is something that comes canned in a manual by way of Chicago. Nor do they believe that innovative thought can only emerge from a years-long process in which work is revised *ad nauseam* according to the dictates of supposedly impartial referees, a sure process for perpetuating variations on existing themes. Under such spirit-dampening circumstances, I doubt very much I could have obtained essays like these from world-renowned scholars. For in keeping with Bobbie's championing of freedom and unconventionality, I specifically asked them to write the most thought-provoking and unconventional pieces they could.

The very fact that a publisher would produce such an eclectic collection is worthy of the highest praise. A short while ago, in my capacity as editor of *Pennsylvania History*, I had the good fortune to bring to publication a collection of essays honoring another superb scholar, Richard S. Dunn, Professor of Early American History at the University of Pennsylvania. Yet this personal serendipity masked a tragedy. Despite Professor Dunn's contributions to his own university, his creation and long-term directorship of the Philadelphia Center for Early American Studies—the most dynamic center for study in this field in the world—and his kindness and effectiveness in helping not only his own graduate students but a host of young scholars, no press was willing to publish the collection of essays which scholars of his stature have deservedly anticipated as the capstone of extraordinarily distinguished careers.

Once upon a time, state universities existed so that people who could not afford the costly higher education only offered at expensive private schools could have something approximating a fair chance in life. Now that tuition is nowhere free, as those who run the world not only expect to profit from the skills, inventions, and discipline of college graduates but expect them to pay for the privilege of acquiring such training themselves, the university press is turning itself into a symbol of this deplorable institutional setting. Instead of fulfilling its original purpose of bringing to light scholarship which is not commercially viable, the academic press is expected to turn a profit.

For some reason, books which have a tightly-knit theme earn money, and those which resemble scholarly journals in exploring a field or range of topics from diverse perspectives do not. I suppose that is because academics now are so specialized that they are uninterested in the world beyond their supposed competence—except, of course, as filtered through *The New York Times*, CNN, and comparable mass viaducts. Hence, the constant subjects of conversations with colleagues that begin: "Have you read..." and "Did you watch..."

In fact, the effort to narrow the scholarly focus which originates in economic pressure has turned back upon the scholarly world itself. At conferences, where one would think it enough to hear a variety of interesting papers, commentators bore us to death by searching for uninteresting unities in papers which stand (or do not) quite nicely on their own. So in thanking Peter Lang Publishing, Chris Myers, and my distinguished colleagues for the opportunity to publish this book, I proclaim that its unity lies in its reflection of the diverse, iconoclastic, and outrageously interdisciplinary "New Directions" in "Semiotics and the Human Sciences" which Bobbie Kevelson has fostered throughout her career.

But there is a greater unity. As Bobbie noted in the interview published in this book: "The greatest thing about semiotics is the recognition that . . . . We are open to the world; the self is a dynamic sign in play that continually creates something genuinely new. Semiotics can keep freedom alive—it is experimental and anti-authoritarian." All of these essays are about how people are continually recreating the world in defiance of the expected, the orderly, and the dictates of the powers that be.

Several, addressing issues of legal semiotics which have occupied much of Bobbie's attention, deal with the crisis of justice in late twentieth century America. John Brigham writes about efforts to develop alternatives to courtroom justice that is increasingly failing to satisfy popular demands for legitimacy. Denis Brion notes that juries' refusal to accept law handed down from the judges and other authorities has in fact been a creative force maintaining freedom in Anglo-American society. Robin Malloy warns us that if we deny people—such as working-class Whites—human dignity and the participation in the dialogue which constructs law and justice, this act of exclusion can only lead to resentment and violence. Robert Ginsberg urges us to rethink pornography, arguing that we can hardly condemn sex-crimes while trying to eliminate a therapeutic tool which can prevent them. Paul Ryan suggests how Peircean semiotics can help people "learn to learn" both the skills needed to acquire new jobs and the means of conflict resolution to work creatively, and harmoniously, together once they have them.

Three of the papers take a more historical approach to how law and society are dynamically, kaleidoscopically constructed. Rolando Gaete, taking a leaf from Bobbie's Seventh Round Table theme, "The Eyes of Justice," examines how both the icon and the reality of Justice as a woman, sometimes blindfolded, holding scales, has been preserved as a (nevertheless changing) Classical image which has served to blind us to the injustice behind the mask. Bernard Jackson takes us on a journey through the ages showing that what some would argue for as the unshakeable foundation of justice—*lex talionis*, "an eye for an eye"—is in fact a shifting concept mediated by millennia of exegesis, social change, and metaphorical modification. My own essay shows how songs of the American Revolution demonstrated that the patriots were psychologically preparing for revolt through verse, constructing an outlaw space through play, a metaphorical state of nature, in the manner of the English Robin Hood ballads Bobbie analyzed in her 1977 book *Inlaws/Outlaws.* Play in the form of crossword puzzles, the search for the definitive signfier and perfect pattern, Utopia on the printed page, is the subject of Scott and O'Donnell's essay illustrating that there are tastes in crosswords that symbolize the shifting and diverse self-constructions of European nations.

Four of the essays are theoretical arguments for the open universe championed by Bobbie and her fellow semioticians. Marcel Danesi displays Language before us as an ever-changing, immensely complicated adventure recreated thousands of time a day in societal interaction and nuances of meaning. Borrowing from Bobbie, Willem Witteveen uses the terms "Great Webs and Tapestries and Fabrications" to describe a semiotics of law that refuses to accept the claims of positivism and natural law adequately to define our legal universe. John Deely expands the semiotic universe to include animals and our interaction with them, arguing that whereas our humanity lies in our knowing use of signs, our solidarity with creation rests in our common sign-usage. And it is appropriate to end with Thomas Sebeok's summary of his own effort to force us to rethink what is the "self" we imagine ourselves to be—a product of innumerable interactions with micro-organisms and the environment in ways we can only reflect on sporadically and inadequately.

If semiotics frees us from a determined fate and deterministic universe, it also humbles us by making us realize our unfathomable dependence on the dead and the unborn, on contexts cosmic and microcosmic, on ceaseless creation. Although she would chide me for trying to find "the" or "a" meaning of a short story that simply "is" intriguing and beautiful, I would like to think that Bobbie summed it all up, years before she had heard of semiotics, in her wonderfully enigmatic piece "Leeward Bound." The interview with which the collection concludes shows how Bobbie has practiced as well as preached her philosophy, gloriously expanding her own self and thought in a perpetual process of semiotic self-creation.

Ralph Lindgren's contribution to this collection has been to make our variously typed and word-processed texts into an attractive volume with an index. He brought to this artisanal task the same care and decency that was evidenced in his participation at the many Round Tables and his essays which appear in many of their proceedings. We are deeply grateful to him. I am also thankful to Jeff Brendle, a former student of Bobbie's, for help with these mysterious computers.

# Chapter One
# Remedial Practices and Legal Form: An Essay in Constitutive Theory

**John Brigham**

> It is time to explore new ways to deal with such family problems as marriage, child custody and adoptions outside the formality and potentially traumatic atmosphere of courts.
>
> Chief Justice Warren E. Burger[1]

A remedial urge is the social practice behind informalism, the "alternative" to law that has been such a preoccupation around the legal profession since the 1970s. In the last 25 years, groups advocating this orientation have spawned a new profession. Groups such as The Society for Professionals in Dispute Resolution (SPIDR) and the National Conference on Peacemaking and Conflict Resolution, took the practice in a professional direction following the activism of the 1960s. In this period, informalists built centers, like the National Institute for Dispute Resolution (NIDR) in Washington, D.C., they drew millions of dollars from foundations like Ford, Aetna and Hewlett, and became a force in law. From these institutions they went forth to proselytize. Unlike activists in the previous decades, informalists in the 1980s were closely linked to legal institutions—courts and the legal profession. It is in this sense that the movement has been a movement in law.

As a legal form, informalism made disputes its business. Just as medicine claimed illness, informalists worked to heal conflict. From within the movement, the remedial urge is not a political demand or a vision of social processes, but the discovery of something latent, a fact of life. The "process of disputing"—the natural and seemingly inevitable eruptions in the social fabric—became a preoccupation for those who mediated and disputes became an elemental aspect of social life.[2] According to practitioners of the remedial arts, men and women have disputed from the Biblical Cain and Abel to contemporary Israel and Palestine. Nature is posed against the inevitable counter arguments that link disputes to professional interests and particular configurations in social history. Working under the shadow of a Biblical tradition, as well as a legal one, the peacemakers, according to this movement, will inherit the earth.

However, informalism or alternative dispute processing is, of course, a movement constructed by men and women following their sense of what needs to be done. The construction of disputes, or the disputes paradigm, serves the remedial urge and is neither particularly natural nor inevitable. The shyness about agency seen in the legal academy and attributed to Realism, is also characteristic of informalists operating from remedial premises in law. Law offers a cover for politics and informalism makes use of it in various ways. Unlike most movements in politics where publicity is expected, informalism would prefer not to be seen as a movement. Presenting themselves as the inevitable response to natural phenomena rather than a political process, informalists try to mask the representation of interests. But, informalism is more accurately associated with politics than nature. Informalism is a movement that may indeed have become an "industry."[3]

Informalists operating under the remedial impulse need disputes to work on. That is, there have to be disputes before there can be remedies. Toward this end, informalists developed a framework from anthropology and conflict theory that made disputing central. The anthropologists built on the work of Karl Llewellyn and Edward Hoebel, Max Gluckman, and P.H. Gluckman.[4] These scholars applied the principles of American jurisprudence to other societies, which they called primitive. They also developed a case approach like the one that the American law schools had instituted fifty years before. Rather than reflecting the body of precedent associated with English law, cases were viewed as the conventional response of ordinary people dealing with inevitable social problems. In conflict theory beginning in the 1960s, scholars incorporated the practices of arbitration into a more intellectually sophisticated picture of social processes. In the work of Vilhelm Aubert, an important early sociologist of law, for instance, conflict became a building block for a new theory of social control which incorporated the perception that disputes were natural.[5] With these tools in the academy as a basis for an energetic scholarship, the orientation to disputes could build its empire.

The movement has had some critics and they have helped to highlight the political aspects of informalism. British scholar Maureen Cain and Hungarian Constitutional lawyer Kalman Kulcsar, published an influential article during the academic frenzy over disputes in the early 1980s. They responded to the sudden growth of informalism and the prominence of the remedial urge. Cain and Kulcsar titled their work "Thinking Disputes: An Essay on the Origins of the Dispute Industry."[6] They argued that the assumptions of academics, when instituted in a movement practice, constitute an ideology.[7] They further articulated the ideology as a way of calling attention to the politics of this activity and associating ideas and actors. The ideology of informalism, in their view, includes a belief in *universality*, whereby disputes are everywhere in human society, *functionalism*, whereby disputes and their remedy serve as vital parts of society, *settlement practices*,[8] where the critique of courts leads informalists to new institutions.[9] Universality, functionalism and settlement practices are some characteristics of the orientation to disputes that are shared by a large group.[10] The practitioners might acknowledge these characteristics at the same time that they would deny the movement nature of their activity.[11]

Remedy supplants other social practices traditionally associated with disputes, like law. Informalists present remedy as a righteous crusade and a trump to other forms in law, like the claim of right. In the world of labor negotiation, where informalism flourishes as arbitration, dispute resolution processes are available as alternatives to strikes and labor violence. Informalists offer remedy as a higher social practice than the fights and rights of the litigation process. Viewed within the ideological form this seems attractive enough. But in the context of politics, problems have arisen. For example, in the last decade African-Americans have challenged Feminists on a number of issues. One of the most provocative is the "myth of the Black rapist" which places African-American men in forefront of violence against women.[12] The initial informalist response to issues of race and rape was remedial, that they are subject to settlement rather than the basis for calls for justice. In fact, the clash between informalist ideology and contemporary concern for domestic violence has led to significant amendments in the articulated practice, that is, to places where the ideology of mediation did not seem appropriate.

When informalism sits in the place traditionally left for law in theories of public authority we say of this social practice that it constitutes a community in law. The form is different from the right asserted by Gays in the controversy over the Baths in San Francisco and it differs from the rage against pornography, both discussed in my book *The Constitution of Interests*.[13] Because informalism is so close to law in a professional and institutional sense, it is akin to Realism in law school. Some of the features of law's magisterium, like the robe and the gavel, are clearly jettisoned in favor of the urge to resolve rather than judge. But, the lawyer and his professional forms are very much in evidence. And, along with the professional orientation of the participants, many of whom are lawyers, movement practice is depicted as standing against the uninformed.[14] This key feature of modern legal ideology was described by Peter Goodrich as "institutional" whereby ". . . the profession also stands between justice, lady and queen of all moral virtues, and barbarism."[15] Programs from court diversion to institutional grievance procedures are advanced by members of the legal profession, court administrators and attorneys in private practice.

Out of the attacks early in the century on the inherited legal process, often called formalism, legal activists articulated a range of alternatives. Reformers like Dean Roscoe Pound in his 1906 speech, "Popular Dissatisfaction with the Administration of Justice,"[16]desired greater efficiency and access. Informalism grew from these reforms. The informalists depicted legal actors and their processes in a highly critical fashion. The old form, the ground that launches informalism is epitomized by embattled courts and battling lawyers with their own institutional interests in the forefront. Thus remedial interests made the legal shark and the court bureaucracy a foil. These are the opposition against which informalists propose to make their contribution. Like Realism, informalism is associated with law schools and, like Realism, it operates from denial of a traditional legal form. In the process, conflict resolution became a central aspect of law and came to represent remedial practices. Thus, remedy and informalism, mediation, conflict resolution, disputes processing and alternative dispute processing or ADR along with delegalization, constitute a movement when looked at from the perspective of law and law reform.[17]

The present analysis highlights the extent to which the movement depends on a distinctive remedial practice which puts forth settlement as the overriding concern. It is far better, in this framework, for mother and daughter, Egypt and Israel, even the tobacco industry and the American Cancer Society to "settle" than to come to fight for a right. The movement ideology is remedial due to this commitment to reaching a resolution. This becomes a priority and "getting to yes" is elevated to a matter of principle.[18] The Holy Grail of agreement becomes an article of faith in the movement. Here, as a form of conflict management, informalism occupies in history the soil tilled by the progressive revolt against formal processes in the courts.

## Law Reform as Form of Law

The remedial orientation manifested as informalism constitutes a form of law in a number of senses. Practitioners place the importance of a remedy in opposition to the legal process. They characterize the law in formal terms. Much as the Realists have done, they depict their own activity in opposition, as informalism. In the guise of institutional practices like "mediation," informalism claims to be different from the legal process. Mediators disavow procedural rules and sometimes even theories of practice.[19] On the surface they affect a militant casualness, in dress—shorts, golf shirts, even Birkenstocks in certain contexts—and style of speech. In the case of Howard Bellman, a regulatory negotiator charged with bringing industry and environmentalists together on the matter of a federal nuclear waste dump the form of presentation is illustrative. During negotiations in 1990 he offered the following summation.

> I think the formal process is going to expire either in a few hours or after this next meeting. The informal process was going on a hell of a long time before we started and is going to continue, I presume, for decades, as a matter of fact, kay.[20]

The casual style, as presented in a portrait by Prof. Christine B. Harrington, asserts the opposition of informal and formal and suggests an alternative to traditional professional practice.

Informalism is grounded in an assessment of law by lawyers. Lawyers may not have thought of elevating the importance of remedies first, although there are a number of instances, like plea bargaining and settlement conferences where remedy is the operative feature of law. Lawyers have appropriated informalism to become its primary benefactors and some of its foremost advocates. Lawyers like former Chief Justice Warren Burger brought it to the courts. Lawyers like Joel Handler sold it to the foundations. Handler, who teaches at the UCLA Law School and was President of the Law and Society Association from 1991–1993, consulted with the Ford Foundation in the early 1970s when the Foundation helped to set up NIDR. And lawyers like Janet Rifkin make it more acceptable to the public. Rifkin, professor of Legal Studies at UMass, Amherst, has held a number of positions in the American Bar Association and participated actively in the dispute resolution community. Her most recent creation is an "Internet Mediation Process." In addition, the prominence of legal authority in some communities, like academic social science that relates to law, leads many who have only a passing association with the profession, to embrace informalism.

This is paradoxical since the ideology of "informalism" or alternatives to court is based on a critique of traditional legal forms. Lawyers inevitably bring the movement close to the state apparatus even while informal procedures and remedial interests eschew the state's traditional forms. Remedial practice, informalism and the alternatives movement, seek to build a community around the absence of both rage and right. Yet, as a movement practice, remedy is closely associated with institutions of law. Thus, informal alternatives to law become intricately connected to courts, the bar and the law schools. The form appears in a variety of settings from plea-bargaining to family mediation and the debates generated take pride in their orientation to procedural rather than substantive issues.

Prof. Harrington's work on mediation and informal justice shows the movement character of informalism, how it is rooted in law reform,[21] and parallels with the Progressive changes advocated in the first few decades of the 20th Century. Those movements were associated, through Dean Pound, with Sociological Jurisprudence,[22] an approach to law grounded in positivism and linked to Legal Realism and the intellectual precursor to Law and Society. The Progressive period in legal reform was driven by a framework for public authority aptly characterized as "the Corporate Ideal." In a book carrying this title, James Weinstein offered two theses running counter to prevailing opinion with regard to the role the state plays in the interests of business.[23] The first is that the liberal state had been established by the end of the First World War and the second is that the liberal corporate social order was developed by those with political hegemony, the corporate financial establishment. The pressure for change may have come from the bottom but the reforms were put in place by liberal leaders. They were elite efforts to stem the tide of socialism and expand the political economy. The social theory of this framework holds that the liberal state requires federal intervention and that it cannot survive in a truly laissez-faire order. According to Weinstein, the ideology of federal intervention does not capture the nature of American liberalism. Rather, liberalism promotes the idea that the state is in opposition to capital.

This opposition, like that between the formal and the informal, is one way that beliefs can be organized to maintain their dominance. One of the specific reforms brought by corporate liberalism was workmen's compensation. The reaction to entrepreneurial greed served those who would stabilize the economy. In the early 19th century, recourse to damages was through the courts based on laws that kept recovery low and made it difficult to establish responsibility for working conditions, such as the fellow servant rule, the assumption of risk, and contributory negligence. Labor attacked these defenses and didn't generally support workman's compensation. Compensation laws were suspect as to amounts and most unions opposed government regulation on the theory that government was controlled by business. Workmen's compensation might also reduce loyalty to the unions.

At the same time, a mounting attack on courts was being thwarted by industrialists. One aspect of labors new look at politics from 1905–1908 was a fear that increasing use of court injunctions against labor would move the American Federation of Labor to political action to limit the judiciary. When Carnegie contributed to the AFL appeal in the Buck's Stove and Range Case he warned that he would not give "the slightest countenance to attacks on the Supreme Court."[24] In the area of legal reform as well as industrial struggle, the courts were the enemy. For instance, in 1911 the New York Court of Appeals held in *Ives* v. *South Buffalo Railroad Co.*[25] that the "conservative" compensation act of New York (relying on private insurance) was unconstitutional. In New York, an amendment backed by Theodore Roosevelt was passed to reverse *Ives* decision. As President Roosevelt often told big business, social reform was truly conservative. By 1920 every state but six in the south had workmen's compensation and the federal government had a program for civil employees.

In the end, the more radical alternatives presented the greatest threat to the legacy of the National Civic Federation reformers. Their "politics of social responsibility" was a basis for the emerging corporate system. Their reforms clouded class identification during a period when Socialists like Victor Berger were elected to Congress and seventy-three Socialists were elected Mayor. The Federation has an "Industrial Economic" Department look into socialism. Support for research into the extent of the menace came from liberal business leaders and reformers like Jane Addams. The reaction linked the "informal" with the harsh and final as Scott Nearing, an economist, was fired from the University of Pennsylvania in 1915. Though it failed to destroy the socialist movement, National Civic Federation activity set limits. By moving to the left it absorbed some of the issues of social reformers which Socialist strategy was based.

By analyzing the constraints of legal form in the movement for informalism we draw out the tension in critical realism. That is, we see the underside and implications for a movement in law even in the words it uses. Grant McConnell saw a number of paradoxes in Progressivism. Although linked to rural Populism, Progressivism was an urban movement. Although speaking for the masses, it was hostile to organized labor. For

McConnell this same tension was characterized in the paradoxical support for private power through the critique of itself.[26] This analysis of progressive interests and ideologies rests on a view of law that is quite complementary to the one offered here. The law does not nor can it simply "contain" private interests. The law must be understood as constituting those interests. Only at this depth of analysis can we hope to understand the way law and legal institutions determine politics.

Characteristic of the reforms instituted in this period, the self-defined "better" classes were making an effort to transform the values and limit the power of the immigrants who had come to dominate the urban landscape.[27] Harrington's analysis of this phenomena draws on comments by Reginald Heber Smith to the Committee on Small Claims and Conciliation which "hailed small claims courts as socialization agents worth more to the cause of Americanization than any amount of talk."[28] Lower costs and an expansion of access would perform the socialization function all the more comprehensively and, most important—in the argot of the time—more efficiently. Although the movement expressed an affection for the "less formal" it was also highly "professional," the new code for gentry control.

Contemporary academics have infused remedial practices with forms of law that reflect their reformist tendencies. Like Realism, remedial practices are nurtured by conservatives and liberals alike. We see this in Mark Kelman's book, *A Guide to Critical Legal Studies*,[29] and in Richard Posner's recent survey of the law and literature movement. The interest in informalism, in a practical sense, "comes out" of the epistemological critique in Legal Realism.[30] The heart of contemporary Realism and the foundation for the alternatives movement is the indeterminacy position. This is a characteristic of Critical Legal Studies where governance by rules is made to look impossible because cases require human intervention in the form of interpretation. The CLS position draws on modern conceptions of language and elevates practice and convention over the traditional formal exegesis. Similarly, on the need for purposive intervention, CLS, drawing from Law and Society, draws attention to the law in action and thereby focuses on its essentially political character.

The Realist view of conflict is another aspect of its position with affinities to ADR. Conflict is more natural than order and the fact that failures of normative order may be embraced by left and right alike is a source of support for the Realist position. For the Crits, "the idea that state power is often exercised on behalf of those who capture influence in battle certainly seems to be the common wisdom of the 1980s."[31] While they profess to avoid a faith in pluralism because of its failure to recognize the influence of entrenched interests, they are also reluctant to accept the state capture frameworks of the first Realist period. In this avoidance of the determinative, their epistemological skepticism makes them less radical than their predecessors and much more like the informalists who deny the role of institutional coercion entirely.

The continued interest in grand theories and the inevitable pull toward structural explanations ultimately separates the academic realism of Critical Legal Studies from the institutional realism of alternative dispute processing. In the case of Law and Economics, the market orientation to bargaining is similar to the operative framework driving informalism, but the doctrinal payoff for Law and Economics goes in a different direction from the practical changes sought by the alternatives movement. As part of their position in the academy, Crits project a theoretical cynicism. This clashes with the optimism of informalists. They don't put much stock in the benevolence that may or may not be part of the Rule of Law,[32] but certainly is a feature of informalism. The alternatives movement is less self conscious about the power that rests in even the least formal institutional arrangements than either the Law and Economics or Critical Legal Studies Movement. They seem to have trouble recognizing the more ordinary psychological convention that acknowledges transference—of the sort commonly practiced by mediators—to be a form of manipulation. A telling feature of academic discussion of informalism is the propensity to maintain that this movement is organized around an "alternative" practice. Informalism, in positing itself in opposition to law, resists the incorporation of law into the "alternatives" framework.[33] With regard to law reform as a form of law, however, there are a number of respects in which facets of law are central to the mediation "alternative."[34] Historically, it also appears that from the mid 1980s a more sophisticated presentation of informalism developed that more fully acknowledged the extent to which the movement was a part of the legal process. To observe this development in movement practice we turn first to the earliest articulations of the informalist creed and then to the critiques as they emerged from the application of informal processes in the area of family law.

## The Pound Conferences

Three historic speeches reflect the concerns of the alternatives movement and link them to the law: Roscoe Pound's 1906 address to the American Bar Association; Chief Justice Warren Burger's speech to a 1976 conference which sought to build on the concerns expressed by Pound; and a 1976 speech by Prof. Frank E. A. Sander at the same conference where the Chief Justice keynoted. Sander is an influential contributor to the ideology of informalism working out of Harvard Law School. These speeches and two conferences are the basis for examining what my colleagues have aptly called "the production of ideology."[35] Like other phenomena which relate laws' forms to its social life, the speeches in conference settings, with their links to people actually meeting, developing strategies, and generating support to institutionalize their position, are evidence of law *in* society.

Roscoe Pound's speech, "The Causes of Popular Dissatisfaction with the Administrations of Justice,"[36] which is quite famous in law reform circles, was given at a conference of the fledgling American Bar Association held in St. Paul, Minnesota in 1906. The Association, formed in the late Nineteenth Century, had only just reached a place of prominence, but not yet national significance when it put on the conference for two to three hundred members.[37] Pound himself was relatively unknown. Born Nathan Roscoe Pound in 1870 on the Nebraska frontier, by the time of the conference, the 36 year old had acquired a Ph.D. in Botany from Nebraska and done a year of law study at Harvard. He had taught Botany, publishing 15 professional papers and practiced law, where five of his papers had been published, including "The Decadence of Equity."[38] He began teaching Roman Law at the University of Nebraska in 1895 and was Dean of the law school from 1903. Historically, the conference and its speaker placed alternatives to the inherited legal system on the national agenda.

Pound's "sociological jurisprudence" was the driving force of the speech and in its claim for a place for social science in the national legal establishment. It predated Justice Louis Brandeis' sociological brief in *Muller v. Oregon*[39] by two years but was basically part of the same movement. Just as Brandeis would link academic scholarship to the record in a case before the Supreme Court and be acknowledged in the opinion for the usefulness of this technique, Pound is known for having expanded the empirical foundations for understanding courts. In this he differs somewhat from later Realists such as Jerome Frank and Thurman Arnold for whom the analytic critique of process and theory has more affinity with some of the more vocal contemporary manifestations of Realism.[40]

He begins by grounding dissatisfaction with the legal process in the fabric and history of Anglo-Saxon law. From its roots in the early contests over royal sovereignty in the Middle Ages, to democratic resistance in Nineteenth Century America, the various problems to which Pound alludes depict the growth of the law. From the claim of equal justice for rich and poor to concern over corruption by judges in courts which served as a newly institutionalized Renaissance expression of the technologies of governance, Pound depicts dissatisfaction as an engine for growth. In America, especially in the early 20th Century, some of the dissatisfaction was a democratic resistance to control of courts by conservative interests. Pound's work is a response to those forces which, like the reform orientations discussed earlier, met redistributive demands with institutional refinements.

The speech depicts courts as overburdened and inefficient. Initially, it was not simply the flood of cases that bothered Pound, but how they were handled. According to Pound, the system of courts in America needed attention in three different respects: multiple courts, concurrent jurisdictions, and a waste of judicial manpower. Commentators note that this system of classifying reflected the botanists training and was a style Pound would employ throughout his scholarship.[41] Pound denounced the "mechanical" operations of the law, foreshadowing the mechanical jurisprudence which was to become such an important foil for Realism and which suggests links between Pound and the Realists rather than a strong separation.

While the details get lost in the historical picture, the image of an overburdened court system persists. This image of the legal system seems to be as enduring as de Tocqueville's dictum that everything in America inevitably ended up in litigation. Pound spoke in a language that appears remarkably fresh.

> Judicial power may be wasted...by rigid districts or courts or jurisdictions, so that business may be congested in one court while judges in another are idle. Uncertainty, delay and expense, and above all, the injustice of deciding cases upon points of practice—have created a deep-seated desire to keep out of court, right or wrong, on the part of every sensible business man in the community.

Indeed, the freshness of Pound's words are as much a function of the success of the movement attached to this position as it is to the speaker's ability to anticipate developments in the law. In laying a foundation for the contemporary "litigation crisis" mentality, as well as informalism, this picture is among the most compelling depicting American courts. Yet, except in the broad sense, it is not entirely clear how law reform and the critique of the administration of justice becomes a foundation for the alternatives movement.

One of the particularly creative parts of Pound's speech condemned "the sporting theory of justice" where he said lawyers tended to seek private advantage instead of searching for truth and justice.

> With the passing of the doctrine that politics, too, is a mere game to be played for its own sake, we may look forward confidently to deliverance from the sporting theory of justice.

This depiction of "the sporting theory" was ultimately embedded in Realism through the work of Jerome Frank in *Courts on Trial*. The depiction of the fight for its own sake or empty contest aspect of the American system became the basis for informal alternatives such as mediation and arbitration.

The legacy of Pound's speech is important to the alternatives movement. The speech continues to be published in pamphlet form by The American Judicature Society of Chicago, a group that traces its formation in 1913 to the speech. And, according to John Wigmore, this was "the spark that kindled the white flame of progress."[42] Although not initially well received—a resolution at the conference calling for mass printing of the speech was defeated—the speech is an icon of court reform. Wigmore, who observed the speech, was a Dean at Northwestern University Law School and he brought Pound to Evanston, the first step in a journey from the frontier to the citadel of legal power.

A conference in 1976 tied to the Pound speech came during preoccupation with the bicentennial of the Declaration of Independence that generated a rhetoric of renewal. The keynote address was given by then Chief Justice Burger who applauded Pound's effort "to bring rationality and order to the economic and social chaos caused by the industrial revolution, by the subsequent growth of our cities and by the waves of immigration."[43] The bicentennial conference sought to mobilize the leadership of the bar and the judiciary and it is a key source of interest in the ideology of informalism. The conference was billed as "The National Conference on the Causes of Popular Dissatisfaction with the Administration of Justice." It was held at St. Paul, Minnesota in the same hall where Pound had initially spoken seventy years before. Sponsors included the American Bar Association, the Conference of Chief Justices and the Judicial Conference of the United States. Proceedings were published in the Federal Rules Decisions, the official agency publication.[44]

Warren Burger opened the 1976 conference with an "Agenda for 2000 A.D." which included a call for reform in the direction of alternative dispute resolution or "ADR." Amid an extraordinary number of references to the Pound oration, the Chief Justice emphasized the need for fundamental change. No minor tinkering, as Pound had initially pointed out, would do.[45] Change was important to the Chief Justice although one had to admit that he was a quite solidly situated baron of the bar. Change would be the necessary response to the massive changes the country would be facing. Burger, in his speech, looked to institutional structures developed in response to Pound as a way to measure the success and health of the official normative order. The National Center for State Courts, the American Judicature Society, the Judicial Conference of the United States, the American Law Institute and the Institute of Judicial Administration.

Expansion of the federal judiciary is one of the keys to institutional reform suggested by Burger, but the structural element of Burger's presentation is also reflected in the alternatives movement. In the guise of alternatives, ADR is a largely a lawyer's movement closely linked to the institutional establishment.

Another concern borrowed from Pound and the Progressives and made to work in the interest of the judicial establishment at the conference is efficiency. Although not "an end in itself . . . it has as its objective the very purpose of the whole system—to do justice."[46] Small litigants, he said, "are often exploited by the litigant with the longest purse" who can use delay to his advantage. But the small guy, especially if he has been judged guilty or condemned to die is less salient in the argument when the issue of efficiency is taken to bear on appeals and the jury system. In anticipating the charge that the conference was stacked in favor of those who would reduce access to courts, Burger cited as the first of his fundamental changes, the need to find ways to "resolve minor disputes more fairly and more swiftly than any present judicial mechanisms make possible."[47] The Chief Justice suggested that non lawyers might be brought in for neighborhood or community disputes and that, "It is time to explore," he said, " new ways to deal with such family problems as marriage, child custody and adoptions" outside "the formality and potentially traumatic atmosphere of courts."

During the 1976 Conference, Professor Sander, who was to become a key activist in the alternatives movement, drew images from an academic past in a talk titled the "Varieties of Dispute Processing."[48] This presentation came as organized interests were arrayed around new institutions championing alternative ways of resolving disputes. Informalism had risen to significance as an instrument of liberal reform.

## Family Mediation Alternatives

At the height of the contemporary informalist movement, activists made the family a featured object of reform, along with consumer, environmental, and business disputes.[49] Robert Mnookin and Lewis Kornhauser, law professors who were early supporters of the alternatives movement in family situations, described informalism in the area of domestic relations as " an alternative way of thinking about the role of law at the time of divorce."[50] The alternative would be a new perspective. Rather than viewing law as "imposing order from above," they saw mediation "as providing a framework within which divorcing couples can themselves determine their post dissolution rights and responsibilities." The academic foundation for moving from courts to informal appendages was the belief in mediation as leading to a form of "private ordering" or what Lon Fuller called the "law" that parties bring into existence by agreement.[51] While media support, in the form of dramatic presentations of law's failure such as the popular movie *Kramer* v. *Kramer*, with Dustin Hoffman and Meryl Streep, broadened support, a community of attentive and interested mediation professionals came increasingly to represent an institutionalized force in the law.

Prof. Frank Sander's keynote address at the "First ABA Conference on Alternative Means of Family Dispute Resolution," in June of 1982 was titled "Family Mediation: Problems and Prospects."[52] Sander had chaired the American Bar Association's Special Committee on Dispute Resolution and helped to organize the conference which took place in Washington, D.C. and was funded by a special committee set up by the bar association and various foundations. It received support and programmatic assistance from newly established groups like the National Institute for Dispute Resolution, funded by the Ford Foundation and Hewlett Foundations. Sander's address, with its specific concern for family mediation, is a good example of movement discourse. It epitomizes a focus on remedial action as it is structured by a view of the legal system. The most obvious thing about the discussion of "alternatives" is its disputes focus. It is infused with a discursive practice familiar to those who are around courts or define themselves in terms of lawyers and courts. It is not that the law is the only place we find disputes, but rather that disputing is a term of art for a particular movement. Disputes are the social reality on which remedial practice in law is based. As it is used by Sander, the disputes paradigm is a practice for the movement. From disputes as a phenomena in social life, the movement has built a structure of understandings that transform the social phenomena into a highly organized aspect of political culture.

Sander pays homage to Lon Fuller, as a legal theorist interested in alternatives and he plays down the issues of court congestion that the Chief Justice introduced as the basis for his interest in alternatives to court. Sander presents "reports from the field" in the form of commentary from "litigators" and the search is for a better way with the skill of the intermediary interposed as a new path away from the "donnybrook" toward "civilization." The family environment is linked to the movement in terms of characteristics to which informal processes are addressed, like intensity of feeling and the existence of continuing relations. The inevitability of disputes demands an institutional response.

A characteristic of this speech is its heavily procedural and institutional orientation. Although it deals with conflict in the family, the real detail and the passion is linked to the various forms for channeling that conflict rather than about substance of the conflict. The listing of institutional forms is impressive. Just in terms of those linked to courts Sander gives examples of "small claims mediation, court-annexed arbitration for routine middle-sized claims, medical malpractice screening tribunals, and the mini-trial used in large and complex litigation."[53] This attention to institutions and the separation of process from substance, while not unique to the legal profession, is a skill more finely honed among lawyers than among most of the citizenry.

At a more superficial level, we can see that the authority for the discussion is in the legal profession. The author is a Harvard professor, the bibliography is overwhelmingly from law reviews or about law, the authorities from whom Sander draws his material are either in law or part of the growing paraprofessional community in dispute resolution. The community draws from law and the social sciences. It relies on the institutions of the law, particularly law reviews, but approaches the material from often critical social research. This symbiosis has been central to the emergence of the alternatives movement.[54]

Closely linked networks pursuing shared goals are important considerations for establishing that remedial practices like the disputes focus and the substantive/ procedural split are carried by a political movement. Shared practices associated with the legal profession identify law as a problem and the informal alternative is offered as part of a strategy with significant consequences for how power is wielded in America. The Third National Conference on Peacemaking and Conflict Resolution in 1986 carried an impressive list of supporting organizations, headed by The William and Flora Hewlett Foundation.[55] Even greater evidence of links with the law can be found in the SPIDR conference held in New York City in 1987 where the Opening Plenary Session is addressed by Margaret Shaw, Director of the Institute of Judicial Administration and Peter S. Adler, Director of the Program on Alternative Dispute Resolution, Hawaii State Judiciary. In both of these conferences there are sessions on Family Mediation and an "issues" sessions devoted to the family, but only a few years after Sander's call, the family as a center of mediation practice seems to be in decline.

Critics of informalism in the family mediation area have been among the most vocal in opposition to the remedial orientation. In an essay in *The New York Times*,[56] Professors Lenore J. Weitzman, Herbert Jacob and Mary Ann Glendon presented the position that women fare worse under no-fault divorce and the essay drew responses from practicing lawyers who argued that the process of divorce, like criminal prosecution, goes to trial less than 10% of the time. The NOW Legal Defense and Education Fund's 1984 pamphlet "Divorce Mediation: A Guide for Women," has a more extensive treatment of the subject. Written by attorneys Judith Avner, from the Family Law Project, and Susan Herman, from the Institute for Mediation and Conflict Resolution, the work represents the perception that feminists need to respond to the growth of informal alternatives.

The pamphlet begins with a caution that divorce mediation should be carefully examined and scrutinized because women are often the most vulnerable partner in a divorce. Describing "subtle prejudices" that often relegate women to an inferior status such as economic dependency and the desire to avoid conflict, the authors warn that these may hurt a woman in the mediation process. Stressing that divorce mediation is a voluntary process, the authors distinguish it from going to court additionally on the basis of its lack of formality. Some states, like California, mandate mediation in cases of divorce and others, like Massachusetts, encourage the parties to work with court officers to try and resolve differences before going in front of a judge.

Based on a question and answer format, the pamphlet leads women through the possibilities, concluding with the proposition that the appropriateness of mediation will depend on the women's situation. At about the same time, the Family Law Project of the University of Michigan Law School offered the following concerns to the participants at a Conference on Women and Mediation at New York University. First, the parties should be of relatively equal bargaining power for mediation to be desirable. Second, because women "feel greater responsibility for the quality and success of a relationship and family life" they might be misinterpreted as blameworthy. Third, women, feeling the treat to custody of children may be willing to bargain away nearly everything else in the interest of maintaining a position as the primary caregiver. The caveats shift to dire warnings where there is violence in the family. They reflect the view which became more common in the middle of the 1980s that where there is violence in a relationship mediation is not appropriate. The authors hold that "Mediation provides no deterrent to the assailant and even gives him a protected right to speak his mind about his wife, who because of the peculiar characteristics of victimization, will often agree with him when he enumerates her many failings."[57]

In this critique, informalism intersects with feminism. It is a clash that seems inevitable but for the absence of attention to the issues in documents like Sanders' speech.[58] By 1987 "cautions" were being raised to the extension of mediation into family disputes.[59] And by the end of the decade the warnings had become a chorus.[60] Here, a relatively enthusiastic movement discourse has given away to the more guarded product of the political process. Judge Richard Posner's consideration of family law and the application of economic analysis to family relations links family mediation to academic thinking and indirectly to another of the movements we have discussed.[61]

## Difference and the State

A facade of folksy informality and therapeutic conviction masks the institutional structures supporting informalism and makes it difficult to assess transformations in the nature of law. Here, the law that looks accessible, human, therapeutic, even friendly, is produced by people well within the state.

Informalists also mix informality with the language of social science which gives presentations a complex passivity. From Bellman again,

> Now it seems to me that we can end this with some sort of a bundle of input that all of you may or may not fully like . . . but hopefully is a consensus as initially defined.[62]

The terms "bundle of input" and "consensus" emerge as non technical terms of art that help define a separate practice and situate it in opposition to traditional legal practice.

In discussing remedial practices in law I have drawn on elements of social relations in order to suggest some of the distinctive interests we need to take account of in order to understand informalism. These relations as well as some analytic similarities have linked informalism and remedial practices to Realism. Here, the analysis is expanded to indicate some of the implications of this movement for various arms of state power. In particular, the expansion of a form of power where efficiency is more salient than justice and remedies more highly prized than rights portends a legal form that is constructing claimants out of citizens.

Three aspects of state control as social practice deserve note in the context of this attention to informalism. The first is direct corporate sponsorship and its correlate the various indirect attachments characteristic of the Harvard Negotiation Project and its would be competitors. The second is foundation support which is sometimes an aspect of the indirect attachments but also exists on its own as part of the cultural environment in which remedial practices thrive. One example here is the National Institute for Dispute Resolution with substantial support from the Ford Foundation. Finally, in the only slightly removed arena of the academy there is the life of institutions, careers and professional relationship that facilitates this aspect of informalism.

The foundation connection involves a telling conjunction of financial interest, careerism and the material dimension of intellectual fashion that drives foundation decisions. The National Institute for Dispute Resolution was set up in the 1970s with funds from the Ford Foundation and received substantial support for the next twenty years. Its apparatus is actively involved in professional associations like the unaffiliated Law and Society Association and the more guild associated American Bar Foundation. In its academic attachments, the Institute commissions research drawing attention to the issues as movements operatives would have them discussed. In the etiquette of the contemporary academy, the conclusions can not be stipulated, but it remains perfectly acceptable to set the research agenda and create the setting for its presentation. The Fund for Research on Dispute Resolution was administered by NIDR under a separate board chaired by Sanford Jaffe and with Joel Handler and Felice Levine, long time Director of the National Science Foundation's Law and Society Program, as members. The Fund operates on the edge of the academy drawing interest in its agenda with a budget of nearly $2 million. Recent grants fuel the alternatives movement and provide a form in which academics may cast their work in order to get funding.

In the Harvard Program on Negotiation, the home base of such movement figures as Fisher, Sander and Susskind, we have the more fully developed corporate influence over knowledge long bargained and managed in private universities. The primary mechanisms are consulting and a special institutional relationship in which the time of university faculty is directly purchased by corporate patrons. Here, the setting is either the corporation itself or the ivy covered walls themselves where traditional bastions of gentry academicians, like the Harvard Faculty Club, may be rented out to corporate visitors who pay for the status of dining there under the auspices of the Program on Negotiation.

On the other side, it is hard not to see institutional aspects of Owen M. Fiss' comment in *The Yale Law Journal*, "Against Settlement."[63] The work comes from a leading advocate of proceduralism, an alternative to informalism and it is institutionally based in the scholarship and forms associated with a particular law school. Perhaps not coincidentally, the article begins as a critique of a report by the Harvard Overseers, and Derek Bok's call for attention to "the new voluntary mechanisms."[64] Linking the movement to all sorts of developments central to consideration of informalism as a very successful movement in law, such as well funded institutes, sections of the ABA, and new rules of civil procedure, Fiss holds that the received ". . . account of adjudication and the case for settlement rest on questionable premises."[65]

In a context of knowledge production such as these it makes little sense to characterize the state as in opposition to economic interests. The state and the economy, in relations like the three above and in this case through the development of the ideological practice of remedy and informalism in law, become mutually constitutive. And, we have the intermingling described by Prof. Sally Falk Moore and the "interlegality" at the core of Bonaventura de Sousa Santos' cartographic analysis of the contemporary state of the law.[66] Santos draws attention to " different legal spaces [as] non-synchronic" thus resulting in "uneven and unstable mixings of legal codes."[67] These codes reach in and out in cultural space and resonate as layers of meaning through which legality presents itself. The fragmentation which results, noted both by Macaulay [68]and Santos[69] becomes anything but chaotic and in the guise of the informalism examined here, the practices that manifest themselves as a remedial system significantly dull the capacity of law to be wielded against the interests of those it constitutes, however imperceptibly.[70]

What Christine Harrington and Sally Merry have called "ideological production" and what Cain and Kulcsar identify as the reasons for the growth of this movement amount to a complex social and intellectual configuration that masks the interests served by the movement and in this case its links to the institutional apparatus from which it putatively sets itself apart. The economic support and elite enthusiasm that fueled informalism obviously come from its attractions. Informalism fits nicely into the penetrating modern mechanisms of social control uncovered in all their post-modern ambiguity and seeming innocuousness as against the brutal past by scholars such as Michel Foucault, Dario Melossi and David Garland.[71] And, as a characteristic of all the movements discussed as part of law's politics, informalism is essentially a legal form. Informalism cries for remedies, for peacemakers and conciliators. This is an analog to the traditional institutions of lawyers and courts in a somewhat romanticized for. And, in addition, it constructs the legal formalism of "qualitative interchangeability"[72] in which disputants, like voters and consumers, become atomized in a system that provides for them but which they can not escape.

Through this attention to a movement based in the state's institutions that extends the reach of the law by drawing on a conception of its inefficacy and limits we have a microcosmic evidence of the construction of family and personality by law. Here, the ultra realism of the remedial form commodify husbands and wives, landlords and tenants into parties to disputes. The family, the schools, and the social welfare bureaucracy,[73] all major instruments of indoctrination to public norms, have either embraced or been depicted as embracing the ideal of a system for resolving disputes. The movement works through conventional institutions where people can learn the specifics of appropriate degrees of conformity and the propriety of peace. The ultimate power of the state over the demands placed upon its bureaucratic shoulders is in the construction of demand in relation to these institutions. Instituting a new therapeutic discourse and thus allowing experts to interpret needs in a fashion that functions as the old institutions is the characteristic contribution of informalism.[74]

# Notes

1. "Agenda for 2000 A.D.—A Need for Systematic Anticipation,"*Federal Rules Decisions* 70 (1976): 23–35, 34.

2. Susan Leeson assured me of this quality and described disputes as "always having been around" in commenting on a panel at the Western Political Science Association in 1986.

3. Maureen Cain and Kalman Kulcsar, "Thinking Disputes: An Essay on the Origins of the Dispute Industry," *Law and Society Review* 16 (1981–1982): 375–402.

4. Max Gluckman, *The Judicial Process Among the Barotse of Northern Rhodesia* (Manchester: Manchester University Press, (1955); P.H. Gulliver, *Social Control in an African Society* (London: Routledge and Kegan Paul, 1963); Karl Llewellyn and Edward A. Hoebel, *The Cheyenne Way* (Norman: University of Oklahoma Press, 1941).

5. Wilhelm Aubert "Competition and Dissensus: Two Types of Conflict and of Conflict Resolution," *Journal of Conflict Resolution* 7 (1963): 26.

6. *Law and Society Review* 16 (1981–82): 375.

7. The concept is used here after the fashion suggested by Alan Hunt, "The Ideology of Law," *Law and Society Review* 19 (1985): 11 and developed by the Amherst Seminar, "Special Issue: Law and Ideology," *Law and Society Review* 22 (1988).

8. Richard L. Abel "A Comparative Theory of Dispute Institutions in Society," *Law and Society Review* 8 (1974): 217

9. Cain and Kulcsar also suggest that in the ideology of disputes the parties are seen as qualitatively identical, like the consumers in the marketplace they are interchangeable but for quantitative differences, like more money or more power, and that the conceptual practice of identifying disputes provides a comparative foundation. "Dispute Industry," 380.

10. They are also adhered to in a manner Cain and Kulcsar call ideological idealism.

11. Compare Abel, *Politics of Informal Justice* with the Special Issue of the *Law and Society Review* on disputing.

12. Angela Davis, *Women, Race and Class* (New York: Vintage, 1983).

13. New York: New York University Press, Forthcoming.

14. Peter Fitzpatrick, *The Mythology of Modern Law* (London: Routledge, 1992).

15. "Without the interpreters, in other words, justice would have no tongue." Peter Goodrich, *Languages of Law: From Logics of Memory to Nomadic Masks* (London: Weidenfeld and Nicolson, 1990), 90.

16. Roscoe Pound, "The Causes of Popular Dissatisfaction with the Administration of Justice," *American Bar Association Reports* 29 (1906): 395.

17. My work on these questions draws heavily from Christine Harrington who introduced me to the field and with whom I continue to share the inquiry into this movement. See her *Shadow Justice* (Westport, CT.: Greenwood Press, 1985).

18. Roger Fisher and William Ury, *Getting to Yes: Negotiating Agreement without Giving In* (New York: Penguin, 1983).

19. For discussion of practitioner rejection of this theoretical orientation, see Christine B. Harrington, "Howard Bellman: Using 'Bundles of Input' to Negotiate and Environmental Dispute," *When Talk Works: Profiles of Mediators* (San Francisco: Jossey-Bass, 1994), 105–147; Originally "'Bundles of Input': Negotiating the Nation's First Nuclear Waste Dump—A Profile of Howard Bellman," Paper for the Harvard Program on Negotiation (May 17, 1991).

20. Harrington, "Bundles of Input," Original, 37.

21. Christine B. Harrington, "Delegalization Reform Movements: A Historical Analysis," in Rick Abel, ed. *The Politics of Informal Justice*, Vol. I (New York: Academic Press: 1982)

22. *Ibid.*, 36.

23. James Weinstein, *The Corporate Ideal and the Liberal State 1900–1918* (Boston: Beacon Press, 1968).

24. *Ibid.*, 48.

25. 201 NY 271.

26. *Private Power and American Democracy* (New York: Knopf, 1966).

27. Amy Bridges, *A City in the Republic* (Cambridge: Cambridge University Press, 1984).

28. Harrington, *Shadow Justice*, 44.

29. (Cambridge: Harvard University Press, 1987).

30. See Brigham, *The Constitution of Interests*, Chapter 3.

31. *Ibid.*, 247.

32. As with the gentry introduced into legal theory by Douglas Hay and E. P. Thompson because, ultimately, their grace under the Black Acts is seen as an aspect of legal power and system stability, rather than benevolence. Douglas Hay, et al., *Albion's Fatal Tree: Crime and Society in Eighteenth-Century England* (New York: The Free Press, 1975).

33. Laura Nader described the limitations of what she called "binary thinking" in the law reform literature. See "The Recurrent Dialectic between Legality and Its Alternatives: The Limitations of Binary Thinking," *Univ. of Pennsylvania Law Rev.* 132 (1984): 621.

34. For an interesting account of this problem and an alternative to the traditional framework pitting informalism against rights, see Craig A. McEwen, Lynn Mather and Richard J. Maiman, "Lawyers, Mediation, and the Management of Divorce Practice," *Law and Society Review* 28 (1994): 149–186.

35. See Sally Merry and B. Christine Harrington, "Ideological Production," *Law and Society Review* 22 (1988): 709–735.

36. The address was published in *ABA Reports* 29 (1906), 395 and an abridged version was republished in *ABA Journal* 57 (1971): 348.

37. Arthur L. Harding, "Professor Pound Makes History," in Harding, ed. *The Administration of Justice in Retrospect: Roscoe Pound's 1906 Address in a Half-Century of Experience* (Dallas: Southern Methodist University Press, 1957).

38. *Columbia Law Review* 5 (1905): 20.

39. 208 U.S. 412 (1908).

40. John Henry Schlegel, *American Legal Realism and Empirical Social Science* (Chapel Hill: University of North Carolina Press, 1995). Schlegel says very little about Pound.

41. Harding, "History," 8.

42. Introduction, *Roscoe Pound...The Causes of Popular Dissatisfaction With the Administration of Justice* (Chicago: American Judicature Society, no date).

43. Warren Burger, "Agenda," 84.

44. *Ibid.*

45. Pound's example of tinkering was eliminating law Latin and French. Burger's tinkering included the Administrative Procedure Act and the merger of law and equity.

46. Burger, "Agenda," 92.

47. Burger, "Agenda," 93.

48. Like Sander's work in general and that of his colleagues Roger Fisher and Larry Susskind, the speech indicates newer dimensions of informalism. Frank Sander, in M. Feeley and R. Tomasic, eds., *Neighborhood Justice* (New York: Longman, 1982).

49. Christine B. Harrington, "An Overview of the Dispute Resolution Field," A Report to Christine B. Harrington, "An Overview of the Dispute Resolution Field," A Report to the Ford Foundation, MS, May 1986, 4.

50. Robert H. Mnookin and Lewis Kornhauser, "Bargaining in the Shadow of the Law: The Case of Divorce," *Yale Law Journal* 88 (1979): 950.

51. Lon Fuller, "Mediation—Its Forms and Functions," *Southern California Law Review* 44 (1971): 305–339, 353.

52. Frank Sander (Sander II), in J. A. Lemmon, ed. "Successful Techniques for Mediating Family Breakup," *Mediation Quarterly* 2 (1983): 354–363.

53. Sander II, (1983) 355.

54. The community came out in the late 1980s to review the book *Dispute Resolution* by Sander, Stephen B. Goldberg and Eric D. Green. Legal InfoTrac reported reviews in all the major law journals, fourteen in all. See reviews by Simon Roberts, *Modern Law Review* 53 (1990); Barbara Yngvesson, *Law and Social Inquiry* 13 (1988); Richard Delgado, *Law and Social Inquiry* (1988); Sally Engle Merry, *Harvard Law Review* 100 (1987); Carrie Menkel-Meadow, *Judicature* (1986); Warren Burger, *ABA Journal* (1985); Austin Sarat, *Law and Society Review* (1988).

55. From the Academy of Family Mediators, American Arbitration Association, ABA Special Committee on Dispute Resolution, American Sociological Association Section on Peace and War to Wayne State University's Center for Peace and Conflict Studies and Woodbury College's Washington County Mediation Project for a total of fifty sponsors.

56. “The Home Section,” November 7, 19.

57. *Family Law Project* (1984), 6.

58. For a discussion of some of the scholarship on violence in the context of domestic disputes and feminism see Jo Dixon, “The Nexus of Sex, Spousal Violence, and the State,” *Law and Society Review* 29 (1995): 359–376.

59. Howard S. Erlanger, Elizabeth Chambliss, and Marygold S. Melli, “Participation and Flexibility in Informal Processes: Cautions from the Divorce Context,” *Law and Society Review* 21 (1987): 585.

60. Trina Grillo, “The Mediation Alternative: Process Dangers for Women,” *Yale Law* Journal 100 (1991): 1545.

61. Posner, “The Ethical Significance of Free Choice: A Reply to Professor West,” *Harvard Law Review* 99 (1986): 1431.

62. Harrington, “Bundles,” 37.

63. “Against Settlement,” *The Yale Law Journal* 93 (1984): 1073–1090.

64. Derek Bok, “A Flawed System,” *Harvard Magazine* (May-June 1983): 38.

65. Fiss, “Against,” 1075.

66. “Law: A Map of Misreading,” *Journal of Law and Society* 14 (1987): 279–302.

67. *Ibid.*, 298.

68. “Images of Law in Everyday Life: The Lessons of School, Entertainment and Spectator Sports,” *Law and Society Review* 21 (1987): 185.

69. Santos, “Map,” 298.

70. This point has been driven home in scholarship in the last decade. In Lauren B. Edelman, Howard S. Erlanger and John Lande, “Internal Dispute Resolution: The Transformation of Civil Rights in the Workplace,” *Law and Society Review* 27 (1993): 497–534, “internal dispute resolution” refers to efforts within firms to deal with rights grievances. The findings are that remedial processes such as these “tend to recast discrimination claims as typical managerial problems . . . [possibly] undermining legal rights by de-emphasizing and de-politicizing workplace discrimination.”

71. Michel Foucault, *Discipline and Punish* (New York: Pantheon, 1977); David Garland; Dario Melossi, *The State of Social Control* (New York: St. Martin's, 1990).

72. Cain and Kulcsar, "Disputes Industry."

73. Samuel Bowles and Herbert Gintis, *Schooling in Capitalist America* (New York: Basic Books, 1976); John Brigham, "Bad Attitudes: The Consequences of Survey Research for Constitutional Practice," *The Review of Politics* 52 (1990): 582–602.

74. Nancy Fraser is more critical of the struggle between rights and needs discourse. See *Unruly Practices: Power, Discourse, and Gender in Contemporary Social Theory* (Minneapolis: University of Minnesota Press, 1989).

# Chapter Two

# Chaos—What Judges and Juries Do[1]

**Denis J. Brion**

## Introduction

The 1995 murder trial of the former professional football athlete O. J. Simpson, as sensational media event, was an unqualified success. As a process for determining whether Simpson was the perpetrator of the murders of which he was accused, the trial succeeded only in generating deep and passionate controversy. As a process for achieving justice, however, it is my intention to argue that the verdict was predictable and that, even if Simpson was the killer of his wife and her friend, this verdict was altogether just.

I want to offer this argument by addressing a larger subject, the matter of patterns of Chaotic Order in the judicial process in the United States—in common law judicial decisions and in jury verdicts in criminal trials. In other words, I want to talk about the law, but not in a traditional way—not by describing doctrine as a coherent structure of determinant principles and rules or by offering a critique of the substantive thrust of doctrine. Instead, I will describe what particular individuals—judges and jurors—do in performing their roles in the judicial process.

There are three principal elements to my analysis. The first two will be relatively brief—a description of the pattern of the results that courts reach in common law disputes as Chaotic in nature, and an argument for the connection between Chaotic patterns in natural systems and Chaotic patterns in the actions of individuals within human social systems. I will then offer a more extended analysis of the phenomenon of jury nullification, the traditional power of the criminal jury to refuse to return a verdict of guilty despite a clear violation of the formal law. I will offer a description of particular instances of jury nullification as also following a pattern of Chaotic Order, and an argument that the fact of this Chaotic pattern strongly undercuts the principal objection to the jury nullification power.

## What Judges Do

### Common Law Doctrine

I will define the common law as those several doctrinal areas—contract, tort, and property—developed by judges in the appellate process. I will further define doctrine as the outcome of the traditional project of legal academia—describing, through the process of induction, the structure of principles and rules necessitated by the body of results that courts reach as they carry out their functions of resolving disputes and explaining their reasoning. A growing body of critical analysis demonstrates that doctrine exhibits several strong characteristics. First, it is evolutionary in nature; the substance of doctrine changes, often radically, over time.[2] Moreover, it is heterogeneous—doctrine does not fall into a fully coherent and complete rational structure, and it fails to do so because of the recurrence of various conflicting underlying themes in the judicial opinions on which doctrine is based. In addition, doctrine is non-determinant—doctrine forms a weak basis for predicting the outcome of particular disputes.

I want to focus on the heterogeneity of doctrine, in particular, the phenomenon that it falls into pronounced substantive patterns. In property doctrine, four themes recur. The first might be called Individuality[3]—property conceptualized as instrumental to the interests of the autonomous individual; in William Blackstone's seminal formulation, it is "that sole and despotic dominion which one man claims and exercises over the external things of the world, in total exclusion of the right of any other individual in the universe."[4] This theme dominates in United States legal doctrine.[5] The second might be called Communality—the contours of ownership are determined within the matrix of values of the immediate community.[6] The third might be called Sociality—the contours of ownership are determined within a hierarchical structure of political society.[7] The fourth might be called Natural Order—the contours of ownership are subject to the implacable play of natural forces.[8] This same four-theme pattern is replicated in the other common law areas. In contract doctrine, the themes might be called Transactional,[9] Paternal[10],

Adhesional,[11] and Relational.[12] In tort doctrine, they might be called Causational,[13] Pure Accident,[14] Utilitarian,[15] and Duty of Care.[16]

What is significant about these patterns of themes is that, necessarily, the structure of principles and rules that can be derived by induction from the results that come about when judges resolve the disputes brought before them is not the determinant of these results. That is, although these principles and rules derive from these several themes, there is nothing in these principles and rules themselves that determines how a court selects from among them in order to reach a result.

What is further significant about these patterns of themes is their striking similarity to Chaotic Order. Briefly put,[17] the "new science" of Chaos rejects the Newtonian concept of a clockwork universe in which the outcome of a process is exactly determined by its initial conditions, with results proportional to the magnitude of initial conditions. Chaos instead understands that such outcomes are not predictable in detail and that small changes in initial conditions can have a radical effect on outcomes. What is predictable is that a process will lead to one of several possible orders, with these several possibilities functioning as basins of attraction. The particular outcome is not predictable; the pattern of outcomes, however, is predictable.

To describe Chaos in this way, however, is to describe it in exactly the same terms that the foregoing discussion described the judicial process of dispute resolution—it is not possible to predict, from the substantive contours of doctrine, how a court might resolve a particular dispute; one can predict, however, that the outcome will fall somewhere within a larger pattern, with the four themes acting as if they were Chaotic basins of attraction.

Is, however, this similarity simply a coincidence? Let me turn to an argument that there is a connection between the dynamics of natural systems and the patterns of what people do—in particular, appellate judges deciding cases.

## The Human World

This argument begins with the proposition that this four-theme pattern is not random. To the contrary, it maps onto the principal cosmologies that anthropologists have identified as the bases on which individuals, and homogeneous cultures, organize and explain their Worlds[18]—Individualism, Hierarchy, Communalism, and Atomized Subordination. Transactional contract, Causational tort, and Individuality property map onto the cosmology of Individualism. Paternal contract, Utilitarian tort, and Sociality property map onto the cosmology of Hierarchy. Relational contract, Duty of Care tort, and Communality property map onto the cosmology of Communalism. And Adhesional contract, Pure Accident tort, and Natural Order property map onto the cosmology of Atomized Subordination.

These anthropological cosmologies serve as cognitive filters, as perceptual controls that admit, filter out, and supplement our perceptions in order to make perceptive experience cognizable.[19] In making our experience cognizable, we make a World. And the function of Worldmaking is what makes humans unique among organisms.

Define the Cosmos as all of creation, and the Environment as those elements of the Cosmos with which an organism interacts significantly.[20] The non-human organism exists only in the Environment, a dyadic milieu of action and reaction. Humans, however, transcend the Environment through language, creating a World—a milieu which provides an explanation for the Cosmos: "All men in all cultures know what is under the earth, what is above the earth, and where the Cosmos came from."[21] The World imposes meaning in the Environment; it thus is a triadic milieu, a milieu of "aboutness".

The anthropological cosmology is the set of deeply fundamental values that determine the particular substance of the World-as-explanation.[22] Each cosmology embodies an alternative way in which we experience the Environment. In the cosmology of Individualism, we experience nature as a cornucopia;[23] in the cosmology of Atomized Subordination, we experience nature as capricious; in the cosmology of Hierarchy, we experience nature as tolerant; and in the cosmology of Communalism, we experience nature as fragile.

We have yet to understand fully the nature of consciousness. It seems to be clear, however, that it involves the mechanism that provides the connection between the dynamics of natural systems and the dynamics of human action. Gerald Edelman's Theory of Neuronal Group Selection[24] posits that groups of neurons, rather than individual neurons, interacting throughout the brain, form the neural correlate of perception. These neuronal groups[25] are connected to one another and to receptors for sensation, and thereby form neuronal maps. These maps are mutually connected through "re-entrant signaling"—selecting, and giving different emphasis to, sensory experience[26] They are, in essence, maps of meaning.[27] This process dynamically builds up a picture of the world that is generalized and individual. And this world changes with the experience of the individual—"the brain is an apparatus for constructing categories in the light of experience"[28]

In consequence, the primary function of the brain is to create categories, abstractions, and generalizations. The world does not have predetermined structures. Our structuring of the world is our own. Our brains create structures in light of our experiences. And this process—and its consequences—are dynamic across the individual's lifetime.

Descriptions of the cognitive realm are strikingly similar to this description of the neurophysiological realm. The cognitive process of language is a process of metaphor.[29] Meaning, understanding, and rationality arise from and are conditioned by the patterns of our bodily experience, and imagination is the link between cognitive structures and bodily structures.

Quantum physics recognizes that it is impossible to distinguish between the observer and the observed.[30] Thus, what we know of reality is a mental construct, one that arises from an interaction with the Environment. Because, however, language is a process of social interaction, then meaning, understanding, and rationality, though they are attributes of individuals, are constructed within, and through the processes of, the social order. Thus, a conception of property is a construction of the social order. And, as a mental construct, it will necessarily correspond to a conception of the natural order, because consciousness arises from the processes of the brain, which is a natural system. As such, the conceptions that it generates will correspond to human experience with the Environment—these conceptions, that is, will follow a pattern of Chaotic order.

In consequence, the World that each of us creates is a mental construct of meaning. It is generated through language—the Peircean triadic linguistic sign. And it arises from the choice that the individual makes, whether by advertence or by inadvertence, among alternative cosmologies. Thus, the World is synthetic and contingent. And, because each cosmology is incomplete—there is no meta-cosmology—the World is non-enduring.

The judicial process, because it is a process of determining the meaning of the facts of a dispute, is quintessentially a milieu of Worldmaking—"If these are the events that transpired between the parties to this dispute, shall the institutions of society ratify or condemn their acts?" As a process of Worldmaking, it proceeds from the choice of cosmology, a choice that determines the outcome to the dispute. Thus, the process of reasoning by which appellate courts resolve disputes is not deductive—it does not proceed from an *a priori* reified structure of principles and rules. Instead, the reasoning process follows the mode of non-linear abduction[31]—it is the abductive choice of a cosmology that generates the Result that determines the Rule to be applied to the Case, thereby justifying the Result.

We have looked, then, at what appellate judges do, and have seen that the deep values that underlie the Results seem to fall into a pattern of Chaotic Order. We have also seen that this pattern can be explained in terms of a connection between the processes of human consciousness and the processes of natural systems. Now consider another salient actor in the judicial process—the jury.

## What Juries Do

### Background

The standard account of the jury process holds that it is the function of the jury to determine the facts based on the evidence and testimony presented to it, and then to reach its verdict by applying instructions—propositional statements of law delivered by the judge—to the facts that it has found. The formal structure is deductive—"If you find facts *x*, then you must decide *y*."

The reality of what juries do, however, blurs this picture of deductive formality. This is the consequence of the phenomenon of jury nullification. This may be defined as the power of a jury, in a criminal trial, to decide, on the basis of community values or conscience, not to apply the law, as given in the court's instructions, to the acts of the defendant, in order to avoid an inequitable or unjust result.[32] The power to nullify is a power only of leniency. It is not a power to define a crime or to find guilt of a greater crime.

Jury nullification is the consequence of the limited power of the courts to intervene in the verdict of the jury. In a civil action, a court can, in limited circumstances, enter a judgment notwithstanding the verdict.[33] In a criminal action, however, as a consequence of the 1896 decision of the United States Supreme Court in *United States v. Bell*,[34] a court cannot intervene into a verdict of acquittal.

Two prominent cases illustrate the long history of the phenomenon of nullification. The first is from England, *Bushell's Case* (1670).[35] Two Quakers, William Penn and William Mead, were tried for preaching to an unlawful assembly. They admitted to the facts but challenged the legality of the indictment. Several members of the jury, including one Bushell, refused to return a verdict of guilty, despite being imprisoned and fined by the trial judge. On appeal, the Chief Justice of the Court of Common Pleas affirmed the right of the jury to give its verdict "according to its convention."

The second case is the prosecution of John Peter Zenger in the New York Colony in 1735.[36] The defendant, a printer, was tried for criminal sedition—publishing without official authorization. Zenger's attorney argued that the jury had "the right beyond all dispute to determine both the law and the facts." The jury voted to acquit.

Jury nullification is a matter of both federal and state jurisprudence. The position of the United States Supreme Court has changed over time. In *Georgia v. Brailsford* in 1794, the Court strongly supported the power to nullify.[37] In *Sparf and Hansen v. United States* in 1895, however, the Court's position had changed to grudging acceptance of the power to nullify, and strong disfavor of its exercise.[38] Because of its contemporaneous decision in *Bell*, however, courts have no practical means to prevent its exercise.

In this century, the Supreme Court has continued to acknowledge the nullification power.[39] And, in a substantial number of cases, the Court has firmly established a role for the jury as the source of community common sense and conscience,[40] a role that is altogether consistent with the power of nullification.

The issue whether a criminal jury has the power to nullify thus seems to be well settled. What is a matter of some dispute, however, is whether the jury is to be informed of its power to nullify. The Supreme Court has not directly addressed this issue.[41]

In state jurisprudence, this issue has been given varying treatment. Provisions in two state constitutions directly address the matter. The Indiana Constitution provides, "In all criminal cases whatever, the jury shall have the right to determine the law and the facts."[42] The Maryland Constitution provides, "In the trial of all criminal cases, the Jury shall be the Judges of Law, as well as of fact, except that the Court may pass upon the sufficiency of the evidence to sustain a conviction."[43] In the other states, the uniform judicial position is that the trial courts can not instruct the jury that it has the nullification power.

Thus, in judicial doctrine, in academic commentary, and in general political discussion, jury nullification is a considerably controversial matter. The anti-nullification[44] position contends that nullification fosters disrespect for the formal law and generates legal anarchy. The pro-nullification position contends that it allows for greater democratic participation in the process of creating law and results in a law in application that more accurately reflects community values.

## Phenomena

Turn now to several prominent examples of "what juries do". The first case is the prosecution of O. J. Simpson. He was charged with the murder of his estranged wife and a male friend of hers. Defense counsel, in summation, strongly urged nullification. Although experienced prosecutors considered that the evidence of guilt was overwhelming,[45] the jury returned a verdict of not guilty.

In post-trial interviews with the press, the individual jurors repeatedly asserted that race was not a factor[46] and that their verdict was based solely on reasonable doubt of guilt.[47] There is, however, a subtext to their statements. After the verdict was read, one of the African-American jurors appears to have given the black power salute to Simpson.[48] Many juror statements revealed that they had concluded that the police and prosecutors were lacking in integrity,[49] and that their "reasonable doubts of guilt" were based on this lack of integrity and on the fact that the police investigators had both the opportunity and the means to manufacture evidence against Simpson.[50] Significantly, however, their doubts could not have been based on any evidence that the case against Simpson had been manufactured. All this provides a strong basis for surmising that the jury was unwilling to return a verdict of guilty not because they doubted that a case of guilt had been established,[51] but instead because of the general and antecedent corruption of the police.[52]

The second case is the penalty phase of the prosecution of Susan Smith. In November 1994, ten days after reporting the kidnaping of her two young boys,[53] Susan Smith, their young mother, who was separated from her husband, confessed to drowning them in a lake. In the period leading up to her 1995 trial for capital murder, a portrait of Susan Smith emerged in the press that pictured her as self-centered, calculating, unfeeling, unfaithful, and manipulative.[54]

Capital murder is now tried in two phases: guilt and penalty.[55] In the first phase, she was quickly found guilty of murder. Under South Carolina statutes, in the sentencing proceeding, "the jury . . . shall hear additional evidence in extenuating, mitigation, or aggravation of the punishment".[56] Among the ten defined aggravating circumstances are:[57]

(9) "two or more persons were murdered by the defendant by one act";
(10) "the murder of a child eleven years of age or under".

Thus, there was a strong basis for the jury to return a sentence of death.

Using lay, rather than expert, witnesses [family, teachers, clergy, neighbors], however, her attorney masterfully depicted her as a victim of incest by her stepfather, the insecure, often suicidal product of a devastating home life, the victim of her husband's unfaithfulness, and now suicidal again over the enormity of her crime. The jury rejected the strong prosecution plea for the death penalty, and returned a verdict for a sentence of life in prison.[58]

The third case involves Dr. Jack Kevorkian, a retired pathologist and outspoken advocate for the right of the terminally ill to take their own lives with the assistance of a physician. Since 1990, Kevorkian has been present at the deaths of more than thirty people in the State of Michigan.[59] This has taken place in a contested cultural climate. The American Medical Association—the pre-eminent professional association in medicine—is strongly opposed to physician-assisted suicide.[60] Two federal courts of appeal have recently held, however, that mentally competent, terminally ill adults have a right to assistance in ending their lives.[61] And there is considerable anecdotal evidence that hospital personnel engage in acts that amount to "mercy killing"[62] and that at least some physicians, in a much less public way than Kevorkian's, assist terminally ill patients in suicide.[63] Moreover, opinion polls indicate that a substantial portion of the general public favors physician assisted suicide.[64]

Under Michigan law, suicide assistance is a felony. Kevorkian has been prosecuted three separate times for assisting in suicide. The jury each time has returned a verdict of acquittal.

In the first trial, Kevorkian was prosecuted for assisting in the 1993 death of Thomas Hyde, who was suffering from Lou Gehrig's Disease. The prosecution went forward under a Michigan statute that made it a felony to assist a suicide.[65] The jury returned a verdict of acquittal in May 1994.[66]

The second trial also proceeded under the Michigan statute. Kevorkian was prosecuted for assisting in the 1993 deaths of Merian Frederick, who was suffering from Lou Gehrig's Disease, and Dr. Ali Khalili, who was suffering from cancer. This trial, too, ended in acquittal, in March 1996.

The third trial was based on the common law.[67] Kevorkian was prosecuted for the 1991 deaths of Marjorie Wantz, who was suffering from pelvic pain, and Sherry Miller, who was suffering from multiple sclerosis. This trial ended in acquittal in May 1996.

The fact that Kevorkian did assist in the suicides was uncontested in each trial.[68] Defense counsel argued strongly at summation for the jury to reject the definition of assisting a suicide as a felony.[69] It appears that the juries have acquitted because Kevorkian is motivated by the desire to end suffering—a matter of *ends* [70]—even though he intends to achieve this end by terminating the life of the "patient"—a matter of *means.* Yet, according to the letter of the law, Kevorkian has committed a crime—the end does not justify the means.

Again, as with the themes that underlie common law doctrine, we can see a pattern in these verdicts. The first element of this pattern consists of verdicts in which the jury appears to conclude that the act for which the defendant is being prosecuted is not deserving of punishment—the act itself is not a crime. This is exemplified by the three verdicts in the prosecutions of Jack Kevorkian as well as *Bushell's Case* in 1670 and the prosecution of John Peter Zenger in 1735. Other examples, I would argue, are the acquittal of the defendants in the first [Simi Valley] prosecution of the police who beat Rodney King,[71] and Southern juries who acquitted white defendants for lynching and other violence against African Americans during the Jim Crow era.[72]

The second element of this pattern consists of verdicts in which the jury appears to conclude that there is lacking an indispensable prerequisite to the State's power to prosecute, moral authority.[73] This element is exemplified by the verdict in the O. J. Simpson prosecution. Anecdotal observations of urban judges and prosecutors seem to provide other examples from the routine of the urban criminal justice system.[74]

The third element of this pattern consists of verdicts in which the jury, although it does not reject the State's definition of the act for which the defendant is being prosecuted as criminal, nevertheless seems to conclude that who defendant is mitigates the act. This element is exemplified by the refusal of the jury in the penalty phase of the Susan Smith prosecution to impose a sentence of death. It is also exemplified by all-white juries who acquitted white defendants accused of lynchings of blacks during the Jim Crow Era, and by present-day juries in urban ghettos who refuse to convict fellow denizens of the ghetto.[75] The latter examples in particular demonstrate an underlying justification of community solidarity.[76]

## Taxonomy

These several examples of what juries do in reaching a verdict can, as can our previous examples of what judges to in resolving a dispute, be mapped onto the several anthropological cosmologies:

1. The jury rejects the definition of the act as criminal. This is exemplified by the Kevorkian verdicts, and embodies the cosmology of Individualism.
2. The jury denies that, in the particular circumstances, the State has the

moral authority to prosecute. This is exemplified by the O. J. Simpson verdict, and embodies the cosmology of Hierarchy.

3. The jury concludes that who defendant is mitigates the act. This is exemplified by the Susan Smith sentence, and embodies the cosmology of Communalism.

Our taxonomy is complete if we consider that a verdict based on nullification, however frequently it might occur, is nevertheless somewhat exceptional, and thus add to our analysis the typical verdict; thus:

4. The jury substantially follows the instructions of the judge. This is exemplified by probably the majority of verdicts, and embodies the cosmology of Atomized Subordination.

## Consequences

### The Nature of Justice

The principal arguments against jury nullification are based on the fears that it fosters disrespect for the formal law and that the rational order of the law will be disrupted. These fears are based on the assumption that there are only two possibilities for the law, rigid structure and a yawning abyss of nihilistic disorder. And this assumption in turn is based on the deeper assumption that the law achieves justice only to the extent that doctrine is rationally ordered and determinant.

As every able trial attorney understands, however, successful litigation is the art of telling stories.[77] It is not the facts themselves that are of central importance but instead the meaning of those facts. And narrative arrays facts so as to give them meaning. Thus, counsel for Susan Smith "told the story of her life" and thereby was able to save her from the death penalty. And the jurors, involved in a complex process strongly sensitive to initial conditions, responded to the story that they were told.

Thus, the jury process achieves justice to the extent that it proceeds within, and takes into account, the community in which the dispute is situated. That is, the jurors must ascribe meaning to the relevant facts through a cosmology that reflects the values and context of that community. The pattern of outcomes that this process yields will comprise a Chaotic Order—it will not be random—precisely because the process follows the abductive mode of determining the Result on the basis of values and context rather than the deductive mode of proceeding from a prior structure of rules embodied in the instructions. And the Supreme Court has implicitly ratified this process in its recognition that the jury serves as a mirror of community values and a safeguard against the arbitrary exercise of power.[78]

Implicit in my argument seems to be the proposition that any exercise by a jury of its power to nullify is necessarily just. And I would argue that the verdicts in the prosecutions of O. J. Simpson, Susan Smith, and Jack Kevorkian are just. In the Simpson case, the long record of misconduct of the Los Angeles Police Department in particular and the well-publicized incidents of misconduct by other urban police forces in general seriously undermined the moral authority of the State. Horrific as Susan Smith's deed is, who she was within her family and her community justified her escape from the death penalty. And, unappealing as Dr. Kevorkian might be as a person, it is clear that his community specifically, and the society at large generally, do not believe that physician assistance of suicide is a criminal act.

At the same time, however, several verdicts that we have considered are deeply troubling. In the Rodney King episode, what is so striking about the videotape of his beating is not the fact of it—after all, there seems to have been a need that he be put under some form of restraint. Rather, what is so striking is the energetic participation by several of the officers on the scene and the vehemence with which they proceeded. The scene conjures up what might be done to a rabid dog—the overt message of the text of their actions proclaims the victim as not one of us, a mere outlaw. The beating was inhumane. And the verdict in the first prosecution of the police officers, rendered by a jury drawn from a community similar to that of those officers but altogether alien to the victim's community, seems tacitly to repeat that message—what these officers did was not wrong because the victim had no standing within that community.

The Jim Crow juries are altogether similar, drawn from the subcommunity of the accused with total exclusion of members of the subcommunity of the victim. And the message of their verdicts is similar, though more complex—what these accused did is not a wrong because it was done to an outsider, a non-person; and even if it were wrong, we must stand behind one of our own against the outsider.

Thus, the common thread in the acts of nullification that are disturbing is the narrow embrace of the community from which the jurors were drawn. These juries did not meet the thrust of the Supreme Court's criterion of representativeness[79]—they did not reflect the community of both accused and victim. I would argue, then, that the failure of a jury to follow the formal law does not thereby render its act of nullification unjust. And an act of nullification is just if it properly accounts for the community of both accused and victim.

## The Nature of Law

It must be clear that I am not taking a traditional approach to the law. Under the traditional view, the law is an artifact, an objectivized thing. In concept, the law is a complete, determinate, rational structure of rules and principles; and, to the extent that it falls short of this ideal in practice, the paramount function of the processes of the law is to work toward its achievement.

Walker Percy, the novelist and Peircean semiotician, imagined a scenario in which a Martian visits Earth in order to make a survey of the status of science on earth.[80] The Martian would find that earthly scientists are preoccupied with the substance of their theories—formulating them, testing them, and refining them, all in order to arrive at ultimate scientific truth. What would be of interest to the Martian, however, would not be the substantive content of earthly science but instead what scientists *do* —their ongoing practice of formulating an endless succession of theories.

Similarly, what I find to be of interest in the law is not doctrine but instead what particular individuals who determine the outcomes to disputes—jurors and appellate judges—do when they resolve those disputes. Consistently with the Legal Realist tradition,[81] I consider that what they do is the law. In this view, doctrine is an epiphenomenon of the law. In consequence, law and science both are aspects of what it is that humans quintessentially do—make their World. And World-making is the process, carried out in the crucible of language, of ascribing meaning to reality and thereby creating an explanation for the Cosmos.

Under the alternative view that I am taking, the characteristics of doctrine that are problems under the traditional view—its inconsistency, its instability, and its indeterminacy—are simply consequences of the nature of the law. If law is, like science, the consequence of the human experience with the Environment, and if, like science, it is one of the ways in which humans make their World, and if we cannot make complete, enduring Worlds, then the substance of doctrine, understood as the consequence of what decision makers do by way of resolving disputes, will necessary present an inconsistent and constantly changing pattern.

This pattern, however, will not be random, but instead "classically" Chaotic. Although on a micro-scale outcomes of particular disputes are not strongly predictable, on a macro-scale the larger pattern into which these outcomes will fall is altogether predictable. Thus, because its Results are not random, the judicial process is not thereby capricious. In consequence, the instability of doctrine is not so much a problem as it is a symptom of the circumstance that law is a core part of the never-completed process of World-making. Similarly, jury nullification is not disrespectful of the formal law, because the formal law is not *the law.* And, nullification cannot disrupt the rational order of the law because rational order is beyond the power of humans to achieve.

# Notes

1. An earlier version of this essay was presented in the First Encounter on the Semiotics of Law at the Third Latin American Congress on Semiotics, "Chaos and Order", Sao Paulo, August 31–September 3, 1996. The Frances Lewis Law Center of Washington & Lee Law School provided generous support in the preparation of this essay. James P. DeRossitt IV and Kara D. Schrum provided able and energetic research assistance.

2. A trenchant description of this characteristic of doctrine is set out in Morton J. Horwitz, *The Transformation of American Law*, 1780–1860 (1977) [hereinafter "Horwitz"].

3. The terms Individuality, Sociality, and Communality are developed in Ronald Garet, "Communality and Existence: The Rights of Groups", 56 *S. Cal. L. Rev.* 1001 (1983).

4. 2 William Blackstone, *Commentaries* *2.

5. The leading case is *Pennsylvania Coal Co. v. Mahon*, 260 U.S. 393 (1922), in which the Court, in invalidating a statute regulating the mining of coal, conceptualized the land as a resource to be commodified by, and exchanged among, rights-bearing individuals for the purpose of maximizing their individual utility.

6. E.g., *Penn Central Transp. Co. v. City of New York*, 366 N.E.2d 1271 (N.Y. 1977), in which the Court, in upholding an administrative act that prevented the owner of an architectually significant building [Grand Central Terminal in New York City] from modifying it in order to increase the economic yield of the land, conceptualized the value of individual parcels of land as arising from the interactive actions of landowners in a particular locality. This conceptualization is exemplified by the Old Order Amish [Mary Douglas & Aaron Wildavsky, *Risk and Culture* 102–125 (1982)], many Native American cultures [see, for example, W.C. Vanderwerth, *Indian Oratory: Famous Speeches by Noted Indian Chieftains* 121 (1972) (quoting Chief Joseph)], and traditional Islamic societies [Lawrence Rosen, *The Anthropology of Justice: Law as culture in Islamic society* (1989)].

7. *Penn Central Transp. Co. v. City of New York*, 438 U.S. 104 (1978), in which the Court, in upholding an administrative act that prevented the owner of an architectually significant building from modifying it in order to increase the economic yield of the land, conceptualized the right to property as properly subject to the expertise-based decisions of the State taken in order to maximize societal values.

8. *Just v. Marinette County*, 201 N.W.2d 761 (Wis. 1972), in which the Court, in upholding a land development-limiting regulatory statute, conceptualized the exercise of the property right as properly limited by the need to protect the

integrity of natural biotic systems. *Keystone Bituminous Coal Ass'n v. DeBenedictis*, 480 U.S. 470 (1987), can also be read as appealing to this conceptualization.

9. This is the dominant theme in common law contract doctrine—two autonomous individuals, of equal bargaining power, meeting for the moment in the marketplace in order to carry out a self-interested exchange. See John D. Calamari & Joseph M. Perillo, *The Law of Contracts* 1–21 (3d ed. 1987) [hereinafter "Calamari & Perillo"].

10. In the late eighteenth and early nineteenth centuries, the judiciary actively policed the terms and conditions of contracts, refusing to enforce terms and conditions that violated common norms of substantive fairness and good faith dealing. For a concise description, see Horwitz, note 2 above, at 161–173. These concepts survive in the Uniform Commercial Code, in provisions that deal with good faith [§1–203], unconscionability [§2–302], course of dealing [§1–205], and course of performance [§2–208].

11. Courts will uphold the validity of "contracts of adhesion"—bargains that are not negotiated between parties with equal bargaining power, but instead imposed by one party on another, to the advantage of the one and the disadvantage of the other, with an appeal to a broader social policy, such as utility, as justification. Calamari & Perillo, note 9 above, at 418–424.

12. An alternative to the self-interest concept of transactional bargain is to conceive of the bargain as an undertaking of mutual benefit, in which each party has regard for the interests of the other, and the undertaking itself functions as a milieu of synergy that creates benefit beyond the immediate exchange interests of the parties. This alternative is incisively explicated in Ian R. Macneil, *The New Social Contract: An Inquiry into Modern Contractual Relations* (1980).

13. This is the dominant theme in common law tort doctrine—imposing liability on the individuals whose acts negligently cause injury to others. See W. Page Keeton et als., *Prosser & Keeton on the Law of Torts* 160–234 (5th ed. 1984).

14. According to this theme, there are instances of harm that fall into the realm of "pure accident" for which no individual can be held to be responsible. *Id.* at 162–164.

15. A theme that is becoming more prominent understands the law of tort as a process for determining who ought to bear the cost of a harm on the basis of minimizing the costs of accidents and thereby maximizing societal wealth. The seminal case is *United States v. Carroll Towing Co.*, 159 F.2d 169 (2d Cir. 1947), in which Circuit Judge Learned Hand set out the famous cost-benefit based "Hand Formula" for determining liability. This theme is incisively explicated in Guido Calabresi, *The Costs of Accidents: A Legal and Economic Analysis* (1970).

16. A prominent theme, particularly during the nineteenth century, defined actionable harm in terms of a violation of a duty of care owed by each person to all others. See *Winn Dixie Stores, Inc. v. Benton*, 576 So.2d 359 (Fla. Dist. Ct. App. 1991); *Drake v. Lerner Shops, Inc.*, 357 P.2d 624 (Colo. 1960).

17. See generally, John L. Casti, *Complexification: Explaining A Paradoxical World Through The Science Of Surprise*( 1994); James Gleick, *Chaos: Making a New Science* (1987).

18. The concept of cosmologies is explicated in Mary Douglas, "Introduction to Grid/Group Analysis", in *Essays in the Sociology of Perception* 1 (Mary Douglas ed. 1982) [hereinafter "Douglas"]; Michael Thompson, et al., *Cultural Theory* (1990) [hereinafter "Cultural Theory"].

19. Douglas at 1.

20. The taxonomy Cosmos, Environment, and World comes from Walker Percy, *Lost in the Cosmos: The Last Self-Help Book* 85–126 (1983). This taxonomy provides an incisive explication of the difficult cosmological categories of firstness, secondness, and thirdness in the pragmatism of Charles Sanders Peirce.

21. *Id.* at 100–101.

22. The cosmology can be understood as the particular substantive content of the Ground in Peirce's conception of the linguistic sign: 1. sign—"A sign or representamen is something which stands to somebody for something in some respect or capacity. . . . The sign stands for something, its object. It stands for that object, not in all respects, but in reference to a sort of idea, which I have called the ground. . ." 2. ground—"If a sign is other than its Object, there must exist, either in thought or expression, some explanation or argument or other context, showing how—upon what system for what reason—the Sign represents the Object or set of Objects that it does." Charles S. Peirce, *Collected Papers* (1931–58) [hereinafter cited as "CP" followed by volume and page number]. CP 2:230. In Peirce's pragmatism, the genesis of values occurs in our experience with the Environment. This experience generates knowledge. And this knowledge forms the substantive basis of our World. CP 5:187; 6:73.

23. *Cultural Theory*, note 18 above, at 26–29. Similarly, we understand human nature in alternative ways: 1. Individualism—humans are invariably self-seeking and thus not malleable in the sense that their fundamental nature can be altered by the imposition of coercive incentives. 2. Atomized Subordination—humans are fundamentally unpredictable. 3. Hierarchy—humans are born sinful, although they are redeemable by morally good human institutions. 4. Communalism—humans are born good, but are corruptible by morally bad institutions. *Id.* at 33–37.

24. Gerald M. Edelman, *Bright Air, Brilliant Fire: On the Matter of the Mind* (1992); Oliver Sacks, "Neurology and the Soul", *The New York Review of Books*, Nov. 22, 1990, at 44; Oliver Sacks, "Making Up the Mind", *The New York Review of*

*Books,* April 8, 1993, at 42; Daniel Goleman, "Brain May Tag All Perceptions With a Value", *The New York Times*, 8 Aug. 95, at C1; John R. Searle, "The Mystery of Consciousness: Part II", *The New York Review of Books*, Nov. 16, 1995, at 54.

25. There are typically perhaps a hundred million such groups in the brain, with between 500 and 10,000 neurons each. "Neurology and the Soul", note 24 above, at 48; "Making Up the Mind", note 24 above, at 44.

26. "Making Up the Mind", at 43.

27. *Id.* at 48.

28. *Id.* at 48.

29. George Lakoff & Mark Johnson, *Metaphors We Live By* (1980); Mark Johnson, *The Body in the Mind: The Bodily Basis of Meaning, Imagination, and Reason*(1987).

30. See, e.g., Jim Baggott, *The Meaning of Quantum Theory* 30–33 (1992); Alastair Rae, *Quantum Physics: Illusion or Reality?* 9–14 (1986).

31. Charles Sanders Peirce, "Rule, Case, and Result", CP 2:372–388 ; Umberto Eco, *Semiotics and the Philosophy of Language* 40 (1984); Felicia E. Kruse, "Toward an Archaeology of Abduction", 4 *Am. J. Semiotics* 157, 164 (n. 1) (1986); John Dewey, "Logical Method and Law", 10 *Cornell L. Q.* 17 (1924) [the Logic of Consequences and the Logic of Antecedents].

32. This is based on a model nullification instruction in Alan Scheflin & Jon Van Dyke, "Jury Nullification: The Contours of a Controversy", 43 *L. & Contemp. Probs.* 51, 54–55 (Autumn 1980) [hereinafter " Scheflin & Van Dyke"]. The discussion of jury nullification in this section is a condensation of the extended discussion in Scheflin & Van Dyke.

33. Fed. Rule Civ. Proc. 50(b).

34. *United States v. Bell* , 163 U.S. 662 (1896) [a verdict of acquittal is a bar to a subsequent prosecution for the same offense under the Double Jeopardy Clause of the Fifth Amendment to the United States Constitution].

35. 124 Eng. Rep. 1006 (C.P. 1670).

36. *A Brief Narration of the Case and Trial of John Peter Zenger* (J. Alexander ed. 1963) [cited and discussed in Scheflin & Van Dyke, note 32 above, at 57].

37. 3 U.S. 1 (1794).

38. 156 U.S. 51 (1895).

39. *Morissette v. United States*, 342 U.S. 246 (1952) [acknowledging the power to nullify].

40. *Duncan v. Louisiana*, 391 U.S. 145 (1968) [jury as safeguard from government oppression]; *Witherspoon v. Illinois*, 391 U.S. 510 (1968) [rejecting the exclusion of jurors who harbored any doubt about imposing the death penalty; the jury links contemporary community values to the system of justice]; *Jenkins v. Georgia*, 418 U.S. 153 (1974) [jury determines community standards of obscenity]; *Taylor v. Louisiana*, 419 U.S. 522 (1975) [jury as hedge against the exercise of arbitrary power].

41. A federal Court of Appeals has upheld the refusal of a trial judge to give a nullification instruction [*United States v. Dougherty*, 473 F.2d 1113 (D.C. Cir. 1972) [2–1 decision].

42. Ind. Const. art. 1, §19.

43. Md. Const. art. 15, § 5. The approved instruction provides: "whatever I tell you about the law . . . is not binding upon you as members of the jury and you may accept it or reject it. And you may apply the law as you apprehend it to be in the case." Scheflin & Van Dyke, note 32 above, at 83.

44. These arguments, however, seem to ignore the fact of prosecutorial discretion, which introduces just as much "legal anarchy" through decisions whether or not to prosecute based on "politics". *Id.* at 87.

45. Richard Price, "For the Public, the Deliberations Go On", *USA Today*, Oct.6. 1995, p. 4A.

46. Julia Campbell, "Hispanic Juror Says Race Not an Issue", *The Houston Chronicle*, Oct. 10, 1995, p. A3; Timothy Egan, "The Simpson Case: The Jury", *The New York Times,* Oct. 5, 1995, p. A1.

47. Patricia Holt, "O.J. Simpson Jurors Speak Out", *The San Francisco Chronicle*, Jan. 23, 1996, p. B4; "Juror Disliked Fuhrman from the Beginning", *Greensboro News & Record*, Jan. 17, 1996, p. A1; "2 Simpson Jurors: In Civil Suit, We'd Find O.J. Guilty", *Orlando Sentinel*, Jan. 17, 1996, p. A1; Sergio R. Bustos, "Jurors Explain Verdict", *Fort Lauderdale Sun-Sentinel*, Oct. 5, 1995, p. 12A.

48. George Gordon, "O.J. Juror: He Killed His Wife", *The Daily Mail*, Oct. 5, 1995, p. 1; Timothy Egan, "The Simpson Case: The Jury", *The New York Times,* Oct. 5, 1995, p. A1.

49. "2 Simpson Jurors: In Civil Suit, We'd Find O.J. Guilty", *Orlando Sentinel*, Jan. 17, 1996, p. A1; Julia Campbell, "Hispanic Juror Says Race Not An Issue", *The Houston Chronicle*, Oct. 10, 1995, p. A3; Adam Pertman, "Jurors Saw Ineptitude, Plot By Police", *The Boston Globe*, Oct. 5, 1995, p. 1.

50. Patricia Holt, "O.J. Simpson Jurors Speak Out", *The San Francisco Chronicle*, Jan. 23, 1996, p. B4 [prosecutorial manipulation]; "Juror Disliked Fuhrman from the Beginning", *Greensboro News & Record*, Jan. 17, 1996, p. A1; "2 Simpson Jurors: In Civil Suit, We'd Find O.J. Guilty", *Orlando Sentinel*, Jan. 17, 1996, p. A1; Mark S. Miller & Donna Foote, "How the Jury Saw It", *Newsweek*, Oct. 16, 1995, p. 37; George Gordon, "O.J. Juror: He Killed His Wife", *The Daily Mail*, Oct. 5, 1995, p. 1; Michael Fleeman," Jurors Break Silence On Case", *The Durham (NC) Herald-Sun*, Oct. 5, 1995, p. A1; Lorraine Adams, "Simpson Jurors Cite Weak Case, Not "Race Card", *The Washington Post*, Oct. 5, 1995, p. A1; see [Judge] Harold J. Rothwax, "Guilty!", *Greensboro News & Record*, April 14, 1996, p. F1.

51. "2 Simpson Jurors: In Civil Suit, We'd Find O.J. Guilty", *Orlando Sentinel*, Jan. 17, 1996, p. A1 [would vote in favor of civil liability].

52. Richard Price, "For the Public, the Deliberations Go On", *USA Today*, Oct. 6, 1995, p. 4A.; see Timothy Egan, "The Simpson Case: The Jury", *The New York Times*, Oct. 5, 1995, p. A1 [the vehemence of the denial by one juror that race was a factor in the verdict suggests that the issue struck a nerve; another juror re¨vealed a strong emotional basis for the vote]; see Lorraine Adams, "Simpson Jurors Cite Weak Case, Not 'Race Card'", *The Washington Post*, Oct. 5, 1995 [a juror statement hints that it was the police who were on trial— for example, that Mark Fuhrman is a racist does not go directly to his credibility]; "Simpson Jurors Speak Out On How They Reached a Verdict", Primetime Live (ABC), Oct. 4, 1995 [Transcript No. 422] [one juror thought that his hotel room was bugged, and admitted that a race-based verdict is not wrong—"whites do it"]. See Phil McCombs, "For O.J., The Trials Are Far From Over", *The Washington Post,* Nov. 11, 1995 [to a member of the African-American community, Simpson is not a hero].

53. Three-year-old Michael and 14 months old Alex. *U.S. News & World Report*, Nov. 14, 1994, p. 17.

54. For a description of the deep animosity overtly directed by the local community toward Susan Smith in the days immediately after her confession and arrest, see, for example, Gary Lee & Barbara Vobejda, "In S. Carolina, An Angry Arraignment", *The Washington Post*, Nov. 5, 1994, p. A1.

55. *Gregg v. Georgia*, 428 U.S. 153 (1976).

56. S.C. Code Ann. §16–3–20(B) (Law. Co-op. 1976).

57. *Id.*, §16–3–20 (C)(a).

58. For juror statements that their decision was based on the alternative picture of Susan Smith presented by her defense attorney, and for descriptions of the markedly changed attitude of the local community, see Stephanie Saul, "Jurors Cite Smith's Troubled Past in Decision to Spare Life", *The Los Angeles Times*, July 29, 1995, p. 16; Craig Whitlock, "Life Sentence Came After Little Debate", *The Raleigh News & Observer*, July 29, 1995, p. A1; Brian McGrory, "After Smith Trial, S.C. Town Begins to Heal", *The Boston Globe*, July 30, 1995, p. 3.

59. Edward Walsh, "Jury Acquits Kevorkian in Two Suicides", *The Washington Post*, March 9, 1996 [twenty seven as of early March 1996].

60. Edward Walsh, "Kevorkian Critics Left With Dilemma", *The Washington Post*, May 18, 1996, p. A3.

61. *Compassion in Dying v. Washington*, 79 F.3d 790 (9th Cir. 1996) [Washington statute that criminalizes physician assistance in suicide of terminally ill patients violates the due process clause]; *Quill v. Vacco*, 80 F.3d 716 (2d Cir. 1996) [similar New York statute violates the equal protection clause].

62. David A. Asch, "The Role of Critical Care Nurses in Euthanasia and Assisted Suicide", *New Eng. J. Med.*, 23 May 96, at 1374 [as many as half have done so].

63. Mark Strasser, "Assisted Suicide and the Competent Terminally Ill: On Ordinary Treatments and Extraordinary Policy", 74 *Ore. L. Rev.* 539 (1995); Note, "Don't Ask—Don't Tell: The Secret Practice of Physician-Assisted Suicide", 44 Hastings L. J. 1291(1993).

64. Ed Garsten, "Kevorkian Faces Murder Charges Under New Michigan Ban", CNN News Report, Transcript No. 497–1, Aug. 17, 1993; Don Terry, "As He Hoped, Kevorkian Is Charged in a Suicide", *The New York Times*, Aug. 18, 1993, p. A12.

65. The statute [1993 Mich. Pub. Acts, No. 3; Mich. Comp. Laws Ann. §§ 752.1021–1027], which has since expired, provided: 1. Under § 7(1), it is a felony to provide the physical means for suicide or participate in a physical act by which another commits suicide. 2. Under § 7(3), the act does not apply "if the intent is to relieve pain or discomfort and not to cause death, even if the medication or procedure may hasten or increase the risk of death." 3. Under § 7(5), § 7 is repealed as of six months after a commission report provided for by § 4 [within fifteen months of 25 Feb. 93, the effective date of the act].

66. Yale Kamisar, "The Reason Kevorkian Was Acquitted", *The Recorder*, June 13, 1994, p. 8; Edward Walsh, "Jury Acquits Kevorkian in Two Suicides", *The Washington Post*, March 9, 1996, p. A1.

67. In 1920, the Michigan Supreme Court held that assisting in suicide is homicide. *People v. Roberts,* 178 N.W. 690 (Mich. 1920)]. The Court modified this in 1994 from homicide to a common law felony. *People v. Kevorkian,* 527 N.W.2d 714 (Mich. 1994).

68. In the first trial, there was some confusion over whether the assisted suicide had taken place within the prosecuting jurisdiction. Tamar Lewin, "Side Issue May Decide Kevorkian Verdict", *The New York Times*, April 29, 1994, p. A14.

69. Judy Pasternak, "Kevorkian Acquitted In Suicide Case", *The Bergen (NJ) Record*, May 3, 1994, p. A1 [first trial]; CNN "Burden of Proof", Feb. 12, 1996, Transcript No. 96 [defense counsel Geoffry Feiger in advance of the second and third trials]; ABC "World News Sunday", March 31, 1996, Transcript No. 613, pp. 11–12 [second trial].

70. Phil D'Ameri, "Dr. Jack Kevorkian Is Acquitted In Michigan", NPR All Things Considered, May 2, 1994 [first trial]; Edward Walsh, "Kevorkian Acquitted In Suicide", *The Washington Post*, May 3, 1994, p. A1 [first trial]; Donald W. Nauss, "Kevorkian Acquitted in Two More Suicides," *The Palm Beach Post*, March 9, 1996, p. 1A [second trial]; "Kevorkian's Latest Acquittal May Silence Prosecution", CNN News Report, Transcript No. 1360–6, May 14, 1996 [third trial]. Gail Donaldson, a nurse, who was a juror in the first trial, observed afterwards, "I don't think it's our obligation to choose for someone else how much pain and suffering they should endure." "Kevorkian Eyes Suicide Centers", AP Online, May 3, 1994, 05:30 ET.

71. The community in which the officers were tried and from which the jurors were drawn is geographically remote from Los Angeles [Rodney King's community], substantially populated by 1970s "white flight" from Los Angeles, populated by a large number of people involved in police work, and populated by a very low proportion [1.5%] of African Americans. Leef Smith, "Jury Was Asked to See Events as Police Did", *The Washington Post*, April 30, 1992, p. A25; Sheryl Stolberg, "Juror: Acts Prior to Tape Mattered Most", *The Memphis Commercial Appeal*, May 1, 1992, p. A1; Nina Bernstein, "Bitter Division in Jury Room", *Newsday*, May 14, 1992. The many statements of the jurors in the aftermath of the verdict reveal a strong identification with police and the value of the work that they do, and a conceptualization of Rodney King as someone depersonalized, entirely alien, and possessed of a generally dangerously threatening character—that is, these statements reveal a striking "we-they" attitude. Leef Smith, "Jury Was Asked to See Events as Police Did", *The Washington Post,* April 30, 1992, p. A25; "Jurors Tell Their Side of Story After L.A. Police Trial", *Agence France Presse*, May 1, 1992; Nina Bernstein, "Bitter Division in Jury Room", *Newsday*, May 14, 1992; Bob Sipchen, "Analysis Backs Jury in Rodney King Trial", *The Los Angeles Times,* Sep. 24, 1992, p. E2.

72. In the Jim Crow Era, white juries would not convict white defendants, often on the grounds that there was no moral wrong in the killing of an African-American. A likely example is the history of the June 1963 murder of Medgar Evers. Juries refused to convict Bryan de la Beckwith in February 1964 and April 1964

[deadlocked 6–6, and 8–4 to acquit]. In 1990, he was re-indicted on a finding of jury tampering, and, in 1994, he was found guilty.

73. In a passionate essay arguing a normative basis for nullification by African American jurors, Paul Butler advocates this basis in justification of nullification. "Racially Based Jury Nullification", 105 *Yale L. J.* 677, 705–714 (1995).

74. For example, see Matthew J. Moran, "Ensuring Verdicts Based on Law", *Chicago Daily Law Bulletin*, March 18, 1996, p.6.

75. Paul Butler advocates this basis as well— though a young African-American has violated the drug laws [which is a wrongful act], it is a victimless crime, and incarceration will serve no useful purpose, while acquittal will allow his community to try to take him under its wing. note 73, *supra,* at 718–722.

76. Here, the juror would see that the act is morally wrong, but would vote to acquit out of community solidarity. However much the novels of John Grisham are considered to fall short of great literature, in his book*The Chamber* (1994) there is a good description of this attitude of solidarity. There is, however, a difference beween the attitudes of "Jim Crow" jurors and jurors from an urban ghetto. Both might engage in nullification out of communitarian solidarity with a wrongdoer. In addition, however, the Jim Crow juror might also acquit on the basis that visiting harm on the outsider is not morally wrong. The urban ghetto juror would not acquit on that basis, but might acquit on the basis that the State lacked the moral authority to prosecute. The difference lies in the one being in a position of social power and the other being in a position of social powerlessness. The mixed attitudes of racism and solidarity that the Jim Crow juror might hold are incisively described in Harper Lee, *To Kill A Mockingbird* (1960).

77. For example, Sally Frank, "Eve Was Right to Eat the 'Apple': The Importance of Narrative in the Art of Lawyering", 8 Yale *J. Law & Fem.* 79 (1996).

78. See the cases cited at footnote 40 above.

79. As developed in *Witherspoon v. Illinois*, 391 U.S. 510 (1968).

80. As Walker Percy puts it, the Martian would find to be of interest the universal practice of scientists of making assertions about the world, while the scientists themselves are interested in the content of those assertions. Walker Percy, "Culture: The Antinomy of the Scientific Method", in *The Message in the Bottle* 215–242 (1975); "A Theory of Language", *id.* at 298–327.

81. "What these officials do about the law is, to my mind, the law itself." Karl Llewellyn, *The Bramble Bush* 12 (1930). I am a Realist only in part, because I do not agree with the second, normative, element of Legal Realism— that law ought to be instrumental to the development and functioning of the economic order. The descriptive and normative aspects of Legal Realism are incisively described in Laura Kalman, *Legal Realism at Yale, 1927–1960* 3–44 (1986).

# Chapter Three
# Benign Racism: Class Conflict in White America—Reading the Signs of Discontent

**Robin Paul Malloy***

The O. J. Simpson trial has caused Americans to reassess the continuing problem of race and racism in American society. While many important aspects of this problem are now being discussed and debated in the context of the Simpson criminal trial, one particular part of the problem remains generally unexplored. This is the problem of racism exercised by elite, power- holding, White Americans against the working class poor and low-income members of their own race. This problem is important to understand and to deal with because the on going conflict within White America will make it impossible to build a national consensus on civil rights. It is also important because its consequence fuels an ever expanding distrust of government and of the exercise of State power. If, as Americans, we are to make progress on a national civil rights agenda we must first come to grips with the fact that racism and class conflict are much more complex than the initial analysis of the O. J. Simpson trial would suggest. We must also recognize that many of the semiotic messages sent out by the Simpson trial, in fact, facilitate the benign racism and class conflict of powerful Whites against less powerful members of their own race. This essay offers one way of thinking about the issues raised in the O. J. trial. It is a perspective which has not been explored by the media. It is offered to challenge us to think more critically about the hidden messages of racism and class conflict within the O. J. trial.

To examine the Simpson trial from the point of view of benign racism and White class conflict consider five different aspects of the case:

1. *Trial venue*. The open discussion of this issue and the decision to hold the trial in downtown L.A. focused on the fact that suburban working class Whites could not and cannot be trusted to do justice in America (e.g. Rodney King trial). The suburbs are, after all, the places where people engaged in "White Flight" go in search of crime free streets, schools that seek to provide a safe environment for learning, and shopping centers that provide ample parking while sparing customers of the need to trip over every conceivable social problem on their way in and out of the store. Whites in these areas cannot be trusted to do justice nor can Whites who merely aspire to such lifestyles. These Whites must be excluded from the process of justice. White working class justice is no justice. Their exclusion makes the process open.
2. *Jury selection*. Reports on the jury selection process and on the changing composition of the jury throughout the trial emphasized the clear message that White jurors are incapable of rendering justice in a decision involving a Black man even when that man is a successful and idolized hero of White culture, even White working class beer-drinking culture. But, these Whites are not objective; justice may be blind but She is not White and not working class.
3. *Coloring the court room*. Throughout the trial one element of media comment and celebration was the diversity of race and gender in the court room. A Japanese-American judge, African-American lawyers, Jewish lawyers, women lawyers, this was all cause for elite Whites to pat themselves on the back. Elite Whites applauded their generosity for making this all possible. But the undertone of their self congratulatory message was justice might actually be done, but only because everyday Whiteness, middle and working class Whiteness, had been minimized. In the theater of contemporary law courts, White is the symbol of impurity and injustice: the mosaic of diversity must color it in. The court room had to appeal to the viewing audience; T.V. programming no longer merely reflected reality it created a new reality. Like the White Television programing executives that dictate our television

programs, the White cultural elite delivered a show suitable for massive consumer consumption, a show with all the appropriate casting.

4. *Mark Fuhrman*. A man for whom there can be no excuse is presented as a symbol of justice dressed in White, most certainly working-class polyester White. The iconic image of Fuhrman is that he represents White America in that only White cops act the way he does and then only against "non-Whites." Fuhrman is offered by Blacks as a revelation to White America. To low-income Whites he is, of course, no such revelation. For many of them have their own first hand experience with rogue cops and they certainly know that some cops are racists and plant evidence or shade their police reports because police of all colors do this to people of all colors— only elite Whites are surprised by Fuhrman. Only elite Whites would envision or present Fuhrman, through the media, as an exclusive Black/White phenomenon because it frees them from the guilt of generally being above the law in their own daily conduct.
5. *The verdict response*. Note the preparations for the reading of the verdict. In anticipation of a guilty verdict all of America was told to expect Black Americans to riot and protest. In the event of an acquittal Whites were expected to go home and accept the outcome of the judicial process. Likewise, after the verdict Black Americans were free to cheer and celebrate; White Americans that complained were labeled racists... imagine the consequence of a White celebration in the event that the verdict would have been guilty. Because elite Whites accept their system, they imagine that all Whites do. Excuses are made for others but not for poor and working class Whites.

The messages of the Simpson trial reflects similarly situated messages circulating throughout our broader society. This is a serious and disturbing problem. The question raised by these messages is how it is that they have become accepted by elite Whites who make up a major portion of our national power structure? These messages are accepted by elite Whites because they both facilitate their power and confirm their goodness while separating them from the consequences of their own exercise of power. Elite Whites know that they exercise considerable (perhaps disproportionate power) in America. Refusing to acknowledge their own central role and complicity in the negative consequences of their exercise of power, they buy into simplistic arguments offered by critical race scholars which posit that all Whites hold power and benefit from their Whiteness in the institutional structures of American life. This allows elite Whites to acknowledge White power while at the same time using class distinctions to separate good from bad exercises of that power. In this way elite Whites exercise power for "good" purposes against Whites who exercise or benefit unfairly from the "bad" exercise of power.

This conflict can easily be seen in the generation of elite Whites that I would refer to as the "Woodstock Elite." These are the primarily middle and upper middle class White kids of the Woodstock generation who attended good universities during the sixties, invented the fashion of over-priced casual clothes, and drove across the country in little cars while spending mom and dad's money in between drug parties, protests, rock concerts, and expressions of sexual freedom. From their privileged position they took pity on themselves, rebelled against their parents for expecting them to grow up, get a job, and pay their own bills. They also had the audacity to villainize poor and working class White kids who were drafted into service during the Vietnam war. These Woodstock Elitists now control our schools, our universities, our government agencies, our not-for-profit foundations and a variety of other social institutions. Undoubtedly, their own feelings of guilt combined with their access to power lead many of them to become active on behalf of disempowered minorities. And, part of proving their credentials of "goodness," in the continued exercise of power and privilege, involved the stamping out of injustices perpetrated by Whites of ill will.

Members of the Woodstock Elite can be found behind every "good" university speech code... after all free speech was meant for the benefit of "good" people. They are also supporters of limited notions of democracy where the idea of community and participation is naturally extended only to those people of "good" (similar) will. But a key distinction between elite and other Whites, which the elite have failed to recognize, is that working-class poor and low-income Whites do not feel and have no reason to feel guilty about past injustices done to Blacks or others. Working-class poor and low-income Whites are against racism and unfairness and unequal treatment because it is wrong, not because they feel guilt over the past exercise of power in the hands of people that have also used it against them. Ask poor Whites, self-made successful Whites, and immigrant Whites, and they will tell you that hatred, poor treatment by the police, injustice, intolerance are everywhere in America. You don't have to be Black to experience these things nor White to commit them.

Working-class poor and low-income Whites have no power and they know it. This is why they despise elite Whites who pretend the opposite. This is why they reject the messages of the O. J. Simpson trial and why they reject the messengers of White power holders. This is why they resist a national agenda on civil rights (established and imposed by others) and this is why they increasingly gravitate toward political candidates that offer almost any agenda as long as it includes less government.

In the wake of the O. J. Simpson trial we must acknowledge that benign racism and White class conflict exists. We must work to construct a positive and inclusive environment in which hard-working, poor, and low-income Whites are included in the national dialogue rather than excluded. A failure to do this will hinder the progress of civil rights for all people.

* I am deeply indebted to Bobbie Kevelson for her many years of friendship and guidance. She has taught me much and has proven herself as a wise, and gentle friend. I can only hope that the suggestive nature of the issues raised in this short essay are useful to get us thinking about the complexity of the racial and class-based messages that fill our society. I hope that, in some small way, this essay will contribute to this volume which is dedicated to such a prolific and profound scholar as Roberta Kevelson.

# Chapter Four
# In Favor of Pornography

**Robert Ginsberg**

The arguments against pornography are well known. No need to repeat them here. Arguments in favor of pornography are rare. Pornography has had to make its case largely as the defendant against the prosecution: a negative procedure. The social presumption is that pornography is bad. Hence, to speak out against pornography is socially approved. It wins votes. Discourse against pornography, often angry and accusatory, plays a powerful role in public moralizing and political action. Discussion of the merits of pornography thereby is eclipsed by the commitments taken by the parties to social controversy. Study of the pornography debate is appropriate to understanding the symbolic uses of the topic made in discourse for programmatic ends. But pornography should be studied for its own merits, independent of presumptions and programs.

One of the jobs of philosophy is to test unpopular positions by arguing them out. That way they are easier for others to refute, or else they appear in their unanticipated soundness. The philosopher should see that opposed positions on problems be given fair reasoning, even if the philosopher gets into arguing for what that thinker does not believe, for we cannot say we have found the truth if we have dismissed out of hand the unpalatable candidates for the title. I take as my duty, then, to speak on behalf of pornography itself. So all parties to the debate should be pleased by the present undertaking. The course of the argument, even if not sound, should throw light on social policy, legal power, and even human sexuality.

If I am mistaken then I will have done you the service of espousing and exposing arguments that you, who are more enlightened, may carefully correct with solemn reasons and humane principles. I will make some room here to respond to your critical questions and objections.

The merits of pornography number at least six, to wit: 1. It is good for people. 2. It is educational. 3. It is of aesthetic value. 4. It is of value to the economy both domestic and worldwide. 5. It stimulates international understanding and goodwill. 6. It enlarges the scope of human freedom.

I will develop some of these points, especially no. 3, at length, while others, notably no. 6, I will give in a quick sketch. I invite other scholars, including you, to fill in the case where needed for each argument. Despite these, and other, merits, pornography in most cultures is morally denounced and made illegal.

The core to pornography, too often forgotten, is in its making accessible sexual experience by vicarious means. The "graphic" of "pornographic" refers to writing or pictures. These in the classic sense are substitutes for the presence of live human beings as sexual subjects. Any sexual activity involved in the pornographic experience is between the material and the enjoyer, not between the models or persons depicted and the enjoyer. Pornography, in other words, does its sexual work by imagination. That is its great humanizing value. It allows the individual to experience many kinds of sexuality, including unacceptable acts, without really engaging in those kinds.

A parallel case is the murder mystery or the western adventure where the reader enjoys, say, shootouts, by second-hand experience of them, without engaging in shooting anyone. The murder mystery is an enjoyable, and sociably acceptable, substitute for murder. The pornographic work may similarly be an enjoyable substitute for some other kind of illegal, undesirable, or monstrous behavior. No one really gets hurt in the fiction book; the reader does not engage in the acts portrayed. No one really gets hurt in the pornographic representation, and the enjoyer of it does not really do the acts depicted. The acts depicted may be the last things in the world you would will to do, yet that does not preclude your enjoyment of their representation. Pornography is a kind of escapist fiction.

A big mistake in denouncing pornography is to take it at the face value of its content. Thus, if disgusting, anti-social, or oppressive acts are depicted, the facile assumption is that pornography is thereby disgusting, anti-social, or oppressive. Your enjoyment of it, though, may be positive, uplifting, liberating, without thereby committing you to those acts. The opposite result should be appreciated: pornography, like murder mysteries, may well assist you not to commit undesirable acts by the very savoring of them through imaginative means. Pornography may defuse feelings, may make feelings diffuse, that otherwise might erupt into antisocial behavior.

Pornography serves individuals for their sexual pleasure by means of graphic material. Therefore it is a human good. Human beings as sexual beings have rights to their sexuality, including sexual pleasure, assuming that only consenting adults are involved in the act. Enjoyment of pornography, while it can be indulged in by couples and even social groups, is classically a solitary activity. Since no other person need be involved, no one's consent need be solicited. The social value of pornography is evident from its harmless character in serving the sexuality of members of society. Pornography is chosen by those individuals for their interest or gratification. It therefore has an instrumental role in their freedom of pursuing experience, and should be protected.

Doesn't pornography degrade those it depicts, especially women? And shouldn't pornography be banned as corruptive of the morals of minors? Wouldn't pornography unlimited by law flood the market place and the media, leading to a squalid society, swamped by sexuality? These grave challenges are answered on behalf of pornography as liberating women and men from sexual oppression, as providing educational material, and as protecting society from criminal acts such as abuse of children. A healthier, more tolerant, less obsessed society may result from freedom of pornography. On the other hand, suppression of pornography, especially by law, may play a role in sexual oppression of women and men.

## Good

Pornography is good for you. Well, it is good for me, and by extension I can see how it can be good for others. People do enjoy pornography. This is a striking fact. This enjoyment usually occurs in private. Privacy is crucial to much of sexuality as an intimate dimension of human experience. Part of the pleasure in enjoying pornography is the secrecy of the experience which may involve socially stigmatized materials. If you are discovered, even by someone who knows you well and respects you, you might hear: "What? Do you really enjoy *that?* Shame on you!"

That it is forbidden adds to the pleasure. Most of our sexual desires are forbidden—by ourselves as well as by society. Sexual responsibility as a human being means not giving in to most of your desires. Internal psychic repression is the price you pay for maturity, morality, and sociability. Freud analyzes this burden on our humanity in his book, Discomfort in Culture (*Das Unbehagen in der Kultur*, 1930).

Pornography to the rescue. It makes civilized life bearable. It works by allowing a safe outlet for forbidden feelings. Obvious isn't it? Yet many people denounce pornography because of the presence of those bad feelings rather than applauding the value of the safe outlet. Pornography allows us to indulge in what we do not indulge in. And, for the most part, what we should not indulge in. The shamefulness of some of the experiences rubs off on the vicarious enjoyment of them. Even in undiscovered secrecy, you might feel guilty about the pleasure. "Dirty books," like tobacco, alcohol, and other drugs, may have been the forbidden pleasures of adolescence. A residue of shabbiness may accompany the adult's indulgence in pornography. The portrayal of sexual acts thought to be undesirable, such as _____, or even _____, may liberate these feelings without acting them out in reality. This contributes to a well-rounded personality, honest with itself, unashamed of most of its feelings, even those attached to shameful deeds, and restored to a fuller emotional energy once the checks and guards against the forbidden have been breached in the soul. Pornography does not transport the user beyond that person's established personality. Instead, it facilitates a conciliation of the personality, making it more at home with itself, including its powerful sexual drives. And some of the sexual content of pornography may not be shameful, forbidden, or undesirable.

For each person, pornography has one of three forms of experience:

1. pleasure which is not marked by shame or guilt,
2. pleasure marked with some shame or guilt which is bearable without ruining the pleasure, and
3. disgust occasioned by what the individual cannot pleasurably entertain in feeling.

Everyone is turned off by something or other. Sexually explicit material which turns your stomach is by definition no longer pornography. Aren't definitions wonderful? If you can't enjoy it at all, then it cannot be pornography. Someone else may find it enjoyable. Hence, the same material may change its status when experienced by different people. This teaches us something about the problem of identifying what is pornographic and suggests something about individual rights. For some people, traditionally called prudes, all sexual material is unenjoyably disgusting. Yet people who are prudish about sexuality in life may find that the vicarious sexuality which pornography provides is pleasurable. For others, a lot of what may disgust you may give them some pleasure.

The line between these three forms of experience may change with your experience and age as well as with shifts in social mores. What you would not have enjoyed in college without shame, you might now find pleasant without inhibition. Other things may strike you now as too nasty to contemplate. You may even take pleasure in being censorious of some sexual feelings. Often by vehemently denouncing the sexual preferences of others, such as _____, we strengthen our hand in keeping the lid on the same proclivities within ourselves. A paradoxical delight occurs in being affronted by what unknown to you attracts you and then suppressing its influence over you. Some vicarious sexual experiences may lose their interest to you, while new doors to pleasurable experience await your opening them. In sum: pornography is a lifetime of self-discovery amid pleasure.

Pornography is an appropriate accompaniment of an active and evolving sexual awareness. You are awakened by it to sympathetic responses in your feelings that correspond to behavior with which you had been unfamiliar. This may be what family, church, and society fear most about pornographic freedom. They think that you might be seduced by it into becoming a pervert. But becoming a pervert is your business as an adult, not society's. The user is not seduced by the material used by choice. Instead, the user takes responsibility for choosing. Someone who loves jazz may come to enjoy symphonic music. So the same person, having appreciated one mode of sexual activity may discover second-hand the joys of another kind. The music lover not only increased the field of that person's pleasure but intensified the whole domain of music for that person. Likewise, pornography does not just add to your erotic thrills; it allows you to extend the horizons of your humanity. Pornography is your safest guide to your sexual self-awareness. Regard pornography not as a corruptor of your values and behavior, but as strengthening your character, helping you to deal with your proclivities while not harming others.

Suppose, for the sake of argument, that you were beset by desires for what you regard as disgusting, anti-social, perverse sexual activity. You would be on the verge of doing something dastardly, shattering social ties, or else by struggling with yourself to resist, you could shatter your peace of mind. As doctor of philosophy, I would prescribe the therapeutic aid of pornography. You would thereby master the temptation by giving in to it. But only in the imagination. What you renounce in action you obtain in imagination. Nice deal. Thus, you do not have to invest considerable psychic resources in guarding against this pleasure. It is harmless. Enjoying it within your feelings means that you are no longer driven to harmful enactment in reality. You have rendered your anti-social desire socially harmless. You will have used pornography to prevent your desires from seducing you into regrettable action. Pornography is not the fodder for a class of depraved and immature persons but the fillip to the emotional health of many people of different sexual predispositions and peculiarities. Pornography is socially valuable as well as a good for individuals.

A healthy society is the consequence of improved emotional conditions among its members. Vicarious enjoyment of what you forbid to yourself but which others in society choose for their sexual activity leads to a tolerance for those others, assuming that the acts in question are consensual private acts between adults that are non-destructive to yet other parties. These four provisos should be understood to apply to everything I say in favor of sexual activity: it must be

1. reserved to adults,
2. based on their informed consent,
3. conducted in private,
4. not directly harmful to others.

Point no. 4 is derivable from the others, but worth insistence.

The psychological blocks that people maintain to deny themselves some sexual pleasures give rise to social and sometimes sexual restrictions meant to inhibit others. Thus, we may regard an act, say, as so degrading if we did it that we forbid others, as well as ourselves, to do it. Sexuality as resource for forbidding. Social injustice finds a convenient excuse in sexual "deviance," that deviously used word.

A flourishing pornography will cause the scales to fall from the eyes of the public. Though people of different sexual inclination need not embrace, they will come to respect to one another. We all share the same great sexual motions of the soul; hence, we need no longer be foreigners to one another. Pornography exposes us to the richness of human sexuality and so helps us to appreciate the loving experiences of others. Just as your personality comes to permit itself to consider the forbidden and even take pleasure in it, so our society can come to accept the unusual in sexual behavior—and in human behavior generally. Pornography, then, is a valuable key to a healthy and democratic society.

## Education

A vital means of sustaining the mental health of individuals is education of the emotions, just as an harmonious society is strengthened by education in tolerance. The first educative virtue of pornography lies in self-discovery. Thus, the art fulfills the Delphic command to Know Thyself and is appropriate as a philosophic quest. Let yourself be exposed to a variety of sexual experience—in imagination. Your emotional reactions can then be given free reign—in privacy. Keep fear, punishment, ostracism out of the experience. Be an honest monitor of your feelings. Note what gives pleasure, shame, or disgust. You have now found what delights you and what repels you. It is an instructive experiment in sexuality which does not involve doing anything to or with anybody. This exercise in imagination may help you decide which objects and methods of excitation you will permit yourself in reality, which you will forever relegate to the imaginary realm, and which you are willing to test further in pornography or in life to see if they are appropriate for you. Be the honest mentor of your sexuality.

I am not claiming that you can invent your sexual desires regardless of who you are, nor that you ought to accede to those desires you find yourself stuck with. Instead, you will find helpful to your decisions and behavior as responsible human being to find out just what the range of your desires can be. Don't be afraid of yourself.

The second educative merit of pornography consists in the insight it gives into the desires of others. Pornography fulfills the novelist's creed of showing us the secret springs of the human heart. I like that eighteenth-century phrase because a spring is wound up, under tension, and jumps up with sudden power. It has to be kept down or given a little relief, but it is coiled to take its own way. Yet it remains largely unknown to us. We live with secrets that drive us hither and thither but which do not disclose themselves to us. While we can gain some self-knowledge about what makes us tick, we do not know what makes other people run. Their drives are a mystery to us, and their behavior may strike us as belonging to members of another species. Pornography gives harmless release to those secret springs which we may share, so that in becoming better known to ourselves we can come to know the desires of the mysterious other.

Take the case of a ______ who is unconvinced of the healthiness or dignity of the acts of ______ practiced by others. We can argue the case on abstract grounds, urging the familiar reasons that good biological, mental, and social causes support such behavior, that on ethical and legal grounds the acts, though distasteful to some, are permissible so long as our four provisos apply, and that personal satisfaction and mutual ecstasy are the frequent consequences of such acts. But the intellectual arguments, as you may find them in a textbook on sexuality, may do little to remove the emotional conviction of the ______ that the acts of ______ are beastly, foul, depraved, vicious, unnatural, corruptive, inhuman, degrading, sinful, cursed, indecent, dangerous, harmful, sick, and vile.

Now enter pornography which eschews argument as it aims at enjoyment. But like the fine arts, pornography teaches us much about people and their values in the course of pleasing us. To be widely read in pornography is to become learned about what you don't like but which others do like. Thus, the ______ may see the forbidden acts depicted in appealing ways, evidently desired by other persons, and perhaps arousing sexual desire of the _____. (Figure 1) Though the ______ has not abandoned that person's preferred brand of sex, yet that person has uncovered in experience an area of sexuality whose traces the ______ shares with other people who lead quite a different sexual life. The _____, while standing firm for one mode of sexuality, has come to understand something of humanity.

Fear and hatred often take as their object what we have only in mind without having encountered it in life. When the details of an allegedly disgusting act are experienced in imagination and partly enjoyed, the horror we may have had for its participants may diminish. Some kinds of sexual deviants, like _____, are not monsters but decent human beings. We can learn to not label people as ______ or _____, as if they were a special kind of animal, hence sub-human, and instead we can respect them as people whose sexuality, like their religion, is their own business.

But some sexual practices injure third parties or are not engaged in voluntarily by adults. We rightfully forbid these in practice. We may better understand the perpetrators of such acts by our sampling of pornography. See what they do in fantasy so that we can counter such deeds in reality. While we use pornography to please us, we may also study it as a warning about what pleases others.

Among the many pleasures of pornography is that it satisfies your curiosity. Everyone wonders at times how______ would go about doing _______ with ______, while ______. Haven't you wondered about this? Pornography shows us. (Figure 2) Pornography shows us many things of anthropological interest and of practical value. A liberated pornography contributes to the scientific advance of a free society. The physiology of sexual response, the psychology of sexual desire, the inventiveness of sexual fantasy would be amply available to scientists through the documentation of pornography. The study of pornography should be a requirement for sexologists, criminologists, and psychologists.

Pornography supplements textbooks on sexuality by opening the behavior to the student's experience. It is also the experimental supplement to sexual handbooks. Pornography is the illustrated guide to how to do it. Pornography might be encouraged as a learning resource for adults. Universal sex education with a clinical approach is appropriate to children such that they receive sexual information without being excited sexually. But excitement, the arousal of desire, the stimulation of deep sources of pleasure are crucial to a person's attitudes toward sexual facts. To have just the cold facts without any emotional involvement may be detrimental to adult personality and social relations. You would be missing something essential if you studied art without opening yourself to aesthetic feelings.

## Aesthetics

A serious and humane art of pornography is possible. I say "possible," although in several respects the art is being actualized, because pornography is a persecuted art. The experiences it now makes available are not quite the ones it would make available were it to be socially respectable. When art students may take a course of study to prepare them for a career in pornography then we will see beautiful results. Hence, this is a preliminary discussion of a field that does yet allow of definitive analysis. I have to imagine what I analyze. Though I will usually speak of what pornography is, for the most part I will be aiming at what pornography would be, if given due recognition and social appreciation.

The art of pornography does not exist in the same sense that an art of painting or even of portrait painting exists. The pornographic is not limited to a single medium. It may be visual, literary, or dramatic. An art of pornography does exist in the same sense that we have an art of the comic, for the pornographic deals with a subject matter in various media which it constructs in such fashion as to arouse a designated range of feelings: the sexual ones. The pornographer as artist will then be a dramatist, or novelist, or painter, or photographer, or practitioner of some other established art. As artists, pornographers might ply their trade in several of the arts or conjoin a few of them into a hybrid art. We might also say that in the art of cinema will be an art of pornographic cinema, and so on for the other major arts.

Pornography as a candidate for such a position must be defended against two charges. (1) Pornography cannot be a fine art within the various arts that play host to it, because it is a crude skill, like the "art" of thievery, or the "art" of prostitution, consisting of traditional rules and tested techniques but incapable of achieving distinction in the human quality of the subject matter treated or in the methods of treating it. Rather than an art, which means a field of aesthetic objects, acts, and experiences, pornography is a disgusting business. (2) If pornography were to be legally permitted and socially valued as an art it would sap the other arts of their aesthetic powers by giving its users a cruder experience. Though sexual expression would be liberated, beauty would be lost in the process. The non-pornographic parts of the arts would suffer, since people would no longer be receptive to the beauty of a nude portrait or a love scene in a traditional novel, when they can see more explicitly in pornography the bodies and acts that draw forth more powerful feelings. We would no longer have the patience for or the interest in aesthetic treatment of love.

The two charges are variations of the same view that sexual excitement is antithetical to genuine aesthetic experience so that pornography and art are permanently irreconcilable.

I argue that the pornographic experience can be an aesthetic experience and not a crude one, that the free exercise of pornography will be beneficial to the established arts, and that an art of pornography is possible and desirable.

The root of the opposition to pornography as aesthetic is this presumption which underlies much talk about the subject: the pornographic is disgusting in its arousal of sexual feelings, while art aims at the wholesome pleasures. Many kinds of disgust occur, and more work on the subject is needed in aesthetics, especially if we are to keep abreast of political and artistic developments. We can raise this question for the anti-pornographer about the object of the disgust. Do you mean that the acts depicted are themselves disgusting? If the answer is positive, then we press further to ask if all acts represented by pornography are disgusting in themselves rather than only some. If the answer is all, then the respondent has ruled out the art of lovemaking along with the art of pornography. To contend that human sexuality itself is disgusting is itself a disgusting attitude. The more reasonable answer is that some of the acts portrayed by pornography, such as ______, are themselves disgusting, while others are not; in fact, some other acts, such as _____, are beautiful.

If the disgust adhering to pornography is not simply to be in the acts portrayed, then it might be assigned to the portrayal of them. Suppose the portrayal were accomplished by the barest transformation of the subject matter, say, by a videotaping of acts seemingly performed by people unaware of the recording. While those deeds that were categorized as inherently disgusting would appear as disgusting, the beautiful things would remain beautiful. But such a neutral role for the portrayal may be challenged, since any portrayal, including a documentary video, involves aesthetic principles of selection and order which govern the product.

What of the beautiful things? The anti-pornographer might argue that the beautiful acts of sexuality are rendered disgusting by their portrayal in pornography. That could happen, and it would be an artistic failing, but art is also capable of portraying what is beautiful beautifully, and even of rendering the disgusting beautiful. Ample evidence of the first case is offered by paintings of landscapes, still lifes, and portraits, while under the second instance we have beautiful paintings of death, disease, and destruction.

How come a photographer can capture the beauty of a model in the photographer's art, while the pornographer who uses the same model and the same instrument of art is destined to create something disgusting when representing a beautiful sexual act engaged in by that model? What mysterious substance creeps into the camera to make the second product revolting? And at what point does the photographer pursuing that art in capturing the beauty of the subject degenerate into a pornographer snapping dirty pictures? The answer may be offered that the noxious ingredient consists in making public what requires privacy for the preservation of its beauty. The erotic statuary of _____, which is not regarded by the art-world as pornographic, disconfirms this point, since many intimate scenes are beautifully portrayed which in principle would be spoiled if third parties were to be on the real scene to view them.

Public policy has insisted that pornography has to be disgusting. You had better be disgusted by it, or else something is wrong with you. This not only dictates what your reactions should be but causes them to be what should be. If you were to examine allegedly pornographic material in the courtroom or the lecture hall, your disposition to appreciate it will be quite different from what it would be if you were making the examination alone and unbeknownst to others. Not merely will your attitude differ; you will have different experiences as if you had been considering different objects.

With reason it can be urged that the disgust occasioned by pornography is due to the immorality of the pleasures involved. This moral disgust interferes with the aesthetic enjoyment, overriding it in an uncanny fashion. What you would like to enjoy, if you had your way, you must not enjoy, and the energy of your disgust may be proportional to your inclination to enjoy. The process is reversible. Though you have invested energy in being disgusted by something in public, if you are able to enjoy it in private then much of that energy is converted into pleasure.

Circular reinforcement occurs in the psycho-dynamics of pornography. When you feel the forbidden can be attractive you are more appalled by it; when you can enjoy the forbidden you are all the more pleased. If we were to remove the "forbidden" label from pornography, it could turn out to be quite pleasant to us publicly, though not to the extent our moral training leads us to fear, while its private power would be largely weakened. The public vs. privacy dimensions of pornography are crucial. Suddenly confronted with pornography in public, you are likely to be disgusted, ashamed, or outraged. Even if you did not have such reactions, you would probably blush.

The label of immorality traditionally applied to sexual practices, such as ______ or _____, and especially ______, was a self-protective act of society which felt threatened. The fear was that too much sexual freedom enjoyed by individuals weakens the cohesive power of institutions. The culturally approved life-styles lose conviction when alternative sex-styles are openly permitted. But open diversity of sex-style is good for individuals and leads to less uptight, more tolerant, less conflicted, more harmonious, less fearful, more understanding society. Liberated pornography is not dangerous to society; it advances and strengthens the bonds of community. If that were accepted, then we would agree that pornography is not immoral. When it is no longer felt as immoral, pornography in large part will cease to be disgusting. Then the art will be seriously developed.

Art consists in working around to delicate or profound feelings with techniques and imaginative devices that suspend excitement and increase it so that pleasure is drawn out and enhanced. Thus, the true artist in pornography takes the scene, let us say, of a ______ and a ______ who are engaged in ______ with ______, a scene all too familiar to the users of pornography, and makes the scene freshly exciting.

While I have cited the example of a ______ and a _____, the examples would do just as well with a ______ and a _____, a ______ and a _____, a ______ and _____, or any combination of these and in any number of participants. You can imagine your own examples throughout this chapter. Much of the arguments against and for pornography hinge on the examples chosen.

One of things which caused pornography to be outlawed is its exposure of the whole range of forbidden sexuality in which people engage, and this is also one of the things that makes pornography so educational and so humane.

When pornography is made freely accessible, the rush to accommodate the market will produce crude materials aimed at immediate excitation. But once the general public has had a good taste of legalized representation, they will demand refinement. The artful pornographer will give the pleasure that the crude pornographer can no longer provide. The initial rudimentary—and rude—works will be soon neglected as the art progresses. Excellence will be insisted upon in pornography just as it is in other arts.

The fear may be justified that by removing hindrances to pornography everything may turn pornographic overnight, including advertising, television, and scholarly books. But soon after the initial wave of pornographizing, the prevalence of sexually explicit material in daily life will be self-canceling. Most of the sexual appeals will have little effect, just as you may not have your appetite stimulated by the many billboards, ads, shop windows, and jingles touting food that you encounter during the day. A small proportion of the pornographed materials will be re-experienced as works of art in the fields of literature, photography, cinema, etc., which deal with erotic material though without provoking sexual response. Connoisseurs of pornography tell me that the blatant pornography fails after a while to be stimulating, while the high-class fancy pornography becomes appreciated for its aesthetic worth.

An art of liberated pornography would increasingly fuse sexual and aesthetic experiences in the course of finding new ways of satisfying sexual desires. Success in the second soon is transformed into success in the first. Such an art of pornography would be self-transcending since its goal continually recedes yet is approached with increased skill. Where brute sexuality is, there aesthetic eroticism shall be. The link between pornography and art is imagination. The great philosophic studies of the faculty or power of imagination unfortunately overlooked the presence of pornography and its kinship to art.

If free exercise of pornography brings about a diminished scope for its existence, what it will leave behind is an invigorated art of the erotic, an art that seeks arousal of feelings of beauty connected to sexuality rather than causing sexual stimulation. The art of the erotic does exist, though its subject matter and its modes of treatment are limited by the need not to be mistaken for pornography. Eroticism is socially acceptable, whereas pornography is not. The erotic is beautiful, positive, while the pornographic is dirty, disgusting. Some arguments against pornography have redrawn the definitional boundaries of sexual representation so that only the vicious material, such as _____, is found in the territory of pornography, while any nice stuff falls outside that territory. By definition, then, pornography is evil. That ends the debate before it begins. But some of that nice stuff, containing approved sexual acts, such as _____, meet my definition of vicarious experience of sexual feelings. Over the years, I have noticed how some materials, such as ______ and ______, initially regarded as pornographic, have passed over in the view of critics and general public to the territory of the erotic. You could build a great catalogue of valuable works of art that once were banned as pornographic. Is this due to a reassessment of a mislabeled work, to a maturation in attitudes, or to a strategic shift in definition?

A distinction has crept into popular discourse between “soft porn,” which might be tolerated under special conditions as dirty though not dangerous, and “hard core,” which should be banned as harmful. The terms also have been used to differentiate between the mild eroticism, say, of underwear advertisements and the pornographic. In *franglais,* “le hard” refers to authentic pornography. “Pornography” as a multisyllabic word of Greek origin becomes awkward with frequent use, as you have seen in this chapter. It is given a cute trim as “porn,” echoing “corn,” which makes it sound like a popular treat. “Let’s have pop corn at a porn flick,” sounds like fun. “Porno” is another popularizer, as in “porno star.” Such terms take the fright out of the label “pornography,” making the subject more familiar, less forbidding (and less forbidden). “Kiddie porn” is a questionable turn of phrase that makes child abuse cute-sounding.

I am not convinced that liberated pornography would wither away as sexuality becomes banal. The incalculable element of genius may revive sexual imagination. But if only an art of the erotic remains, then it might as well be identified as pornography, for it would stimulate the imagination to enjoy sexual feelings, granted that those feelings would have been highly aestheticized. In place of the disgust attached to our sexual desires that prevent them from turning to disruptive behavior, beauty might attach itself to those very feelings, integrating them with respectable social attitudes. Pornography will have made its contribution to the humanization of sex.

Pornographic freedom will spell a renaissance in the arts. The motion picture as work of fine art may proceed fully with the scenes which it only now borders on. These would really be adult films, as artworks for the mature person, rather than the "adult films" played in pornography theaters, which sometimes are called "art theaters." The dance will have new life when nudity will be the order of the day. The taboo now in force is an absurd negation of the foundations of the art: appreciation of the human body in space and motion. For each art you can imagine the opening of creative frontiers thanks to pornography.

All this talk of art might be dismissed as rationalizing the use of pornography as instrument of sexual experience. What difference does it make if you peep through a window at an act of ______ or see a pornographic film, composed with artistic techniques, in which the camera, peeks through the window at the same act? It is not experienced as the same act. The real event is one thing; you are present in time and proximate space. You are a participant. You could be discovered—and punished—as a voyeur. The pornographic event is quite another thing; you are somewhere else, say, in a darkened theater or your own home, and at a different time. You could be discovered, but only as a user of pornography. What do you get out of the film that you don't get out of the real window? Safety, for one thing. Release from shame, guilt, and other moral self-reproaches. A more comfortable setting. Finally, a thoroughness, heightening, and accessibility of the act in imagination that enhances your enjoyment.

People may make pornographic use out of works of art which have erotic elements. Though those works were not constructed to arouse sexual desires in the audience or readers, yet those persons may neglect the context to concentrate on the sexuality and by dint of imagination become excited. Thus, you might get quite excited over ______' s nudes, if you tried hard enough, though they were painted as monumental rather than seductive. When I was a student in Paris in 1960, a street vendor offered me a packet of photos for 5 francs. "All nudes!" he insisted, glancing furtively over his shoulder. They turned out to be pictures of paintings in the Louvre—all nudes.

We should not insist that the pornographic experience must be either a sexual experience devoid of aesthetic feelings or else an aesthetic experience with muted erotic appeal. It can be both sexual and aesthetic, something artificially contrived and biologically directed. We enjoy beautiful sunsets and beautiful paintings of sunsets. It is possible to talk about the objective aspects of the sunset framed by our selective and artistic vision which makes it correlative to our enjoyment.

The art of love has always had room for the sharing of aesthetic experiences, and the arts have always had room for beautiful treatment of love. Lovemaking is aesthetic activity of the highest order. Sexologists rather than aestheticians have illuminated this art, whose stages may include attraction, foreplay, and ecstasy, and in which the beloved increases in beauty in the course of the love act. All the senses are intimately called into play, while imagination, memory, desire, and inspiration find a place. If love is graced with beauty, while the acts of love can be performed with art, then the sharp line between "real" sexual experience and aesthetic erotic experience should not be drawn. The aesthetic dimension to love is no incidental accompaniment but a key component of the erotic activity. The greater the aesthetic experience in the sexual act, the finer is the sexual act in human worth. We have no reason, then, to withhold the title of art from pornography because it arouses sexual desire.

In the case of any object, any act, any portrayal, any occasion, how are we to draw the lines between the pornographic, the erotic, the sexual, the aesthetic, the pleasurable, the beautiful, the disgusting, the obscene, the salacious, the prurient, etc.? Some of the lines shift with time and place and age. In the 1970s, a motion picture that had been banned in Pennsylvania as pornographic was licensed across the river in New Jersey. Or was it the other way around? In one culture a person who ______ or ______ in public would not be noticed, whereas in another culture that would be sexually exciting to passers by. The books that we once read surreptitiously in college as pornographic, such as ______, ______, ______, or ______, are now available in paperback in the college bookstore. The divisions between intense sexual excitement, refined erotic beauty, and moral disgust shift like the wave lines on a beach. Attempts to fix a legal demarcation for pornography are like drawing on the sand to mark the boundary of the land and the sea.

Much is revealed by the quip of the U.S. Supreme Court Justice that though he could not define pornography he knew it when he saw it. This suggests that definitions miss something in the objects, and that the response of the individual determines the pornographic status of the object. Another person would see it differently. While differences occur between objects, differences occur in definition and in application, but also in experience. And experiences change. Now you see it, now you don't.

I attended the oral arguments before the Supreme Court in the 1980s dealing with pornography cases. The Attorney General of the state of _____ complained to the Court, in decorous language, that material the state wished to ban showed a ______ and a ______ whose ______ were so close together that evidently they were starting the act of ______, which the state had ruled is pornographic. (Figure 3) If showing the act of ______ is wrong, then showing people ready to begin that act is also wrong, ran the argument. I was surprised that the Justices did not ask, "What, pray tell, is wrong with the act of _____, in the first place?" Or to put it in more judicial terms, "What prevailing state interest is served by acting against the portrayal of the act in question?" By repeatedly trying to rule pornography out of bounds, we have imposed unnecessary limits on the play of aesthetic possibilities as well as on the play of sexual imagination. Forbidding pornography is immature.

## Economics

The argument presented so far may strike you as too idealistic, painting a glowing picture of responsible, educated, and pleased people living in a tolerant, pluralistic, and peaceful society. What is lacking is a sense of reality: those brute facts of economic structure and of human motivation that might convert the noble world aided by pornography into a base scramble for sexual enslavement. If the virtues of pornography are publicly acknowledged so that the art is elevated in respectability and open to universal adult accessibility, then the number one industry of advanced societies would shift from the military to pornography. Everyone will want to get into the act. The act of producing or marketing pornography, that is. Mass production, uninhibited by moral denunciation, legal restraint, or postal regulation, will flood the market with crudity. Advertising will clog even respectable magazines and television programs with tantalizing sexual views. This is partially a description of American society now, even though pornography is officially denounced.

If pornography were permitted as more of a regular business, then the whole community would benefit from it economically. Reputable manufacturers and dealers could carry out the services that recently have been in the hands of shady operators in run-down neighborhoods. A national chain, say, Pornography Unlimited, might provide well-lit, safe, capacious stores in every city and shopping mall. Materials would be organized by genre, specialty, and level of explicitness. Such a store would cater to everyone's fantasies. Every fetish, deviance, and desire would be addressed: a dream palace for the sexual imagination. In other kinds of shops, such as bookstores and video stores, special sections would be proudly marked as Pornography: Adults Only. Once sexual materials can pass through the mails like other personal products, pornography would become the leading mail-order industry. Electronic and cable pornography would be among the most popular forms of entertainment. At modest price, an individual would be able to call up on a screen at home any form of sexual practice for enjoyment.

Marketing would be limited to adults. The windows of pornography shops would be blocked out so that no passerby could take offense by a display of objectionable material and no child would see what is going on. This is the present practice in Paris where "sex shoppes" fit discreetly into quiet streets.

Once capital investment is made by high-class business in the field, the mighty industry will have need of hundreds of thousands of workers, ranging from pornographers to salespersons, consultants, product testers, accountants, and economists. Liberated pornography may be the best thing that happens to a capitalist economy. Since the raw materials of the industry are natural resources of any country, that is, human sexuality, and since the products are manufactured at home for distribution domestically and abroad, pornography fulfills the great desideratum of any economic theory: profitable, long-term self-sufficiency of business. Pornography may be the panacea for such economic ailments as unemployment, inflation, stagnation, deflation, monopolies, high interest, shortage of capital, recession, and deficit spending.

A tax could be levied on pornography, not as a penalty for its use, as in the case of such poisons as tobacco and alcohol, but as an entertainment. The fund could be reserved for support of victims of sexual abuse, for research on sexuality, and for universal early sex education. A sexy way for the state to support public benefits, which is better for the character than lotteries, numbers games, and betting casinos that feed on addiction to gambling.

The field of publishing will get a much-needed shot in the arm, turning out the classics of pornography, such as ______ and ______. Writers, illustrators, designers, translators, researchers will have new professional opportunities. The profits could support little reviews, the reissue of ordinary classics, and the works of new writers.

The visual arts will develop as high-quality pornography is marketed. Breakthroughs in visual exploration in art have at times been related to our visual experience of sex. Sexual accessories, including clothing, will find a new open market. With a booming business in pornography, positions will be opened in advertising offices, libraries, museums, and universities.

Do not fear that such an open market will flood society with an undesirable product. The product is desired. It is demanded by consumers. Millions of people regularly spend money on it. While earlier in this century pornography was an illegal business in almost all countries, today in several countries it is tolerated, with tight restrictions, although laws against "pornography" still exist on the books. Customers in the United States spend an enormous amount of money on pornography, although shops may be hard to find in many locations. Open up the market and healthy competition will occur among producers and among vendors, the commodity would be improved with high production values, the discriminating buyer will have greater variety, at lower cost, and within easier access. These are the classical conditions of a favorable economy.

The market will not boom endlessly. After a generation or so, the expansion will likely cease as pornography becomes a normal feature of life. At the point of saturation, capital and personnel will have to be diverted into the other industries that have prospered during the boom. The pornographic industry will be the stable broad base for a diversified and dynamic economy.

Even before the market nears domestic saturation, it will expand into the rest of the world. Profits from abroad injected into the home economy will boost all productive activity. "Made in ______" will be the stamp of assurance on pornographic materials received by appreciative people throughout the world. How much more pleasant it will be to win the hearts of people through sex rather than weapons. While clandestine pornography industries and some open ones exist in several countries, and a brisk international trade has always existed in the commodity, the untouched markets cry out for planned development. When free societies allow liberated pornography then the products will have global appeal, just as do denim clothes, padded athletic footwear, rock n' roll music, and carbonated flavored water.

Some countries will continue to forbid pornography, but curious, mature, and educated citizens will find access to it. People on missions of humanity will smuggle pornographic videos and books behind the lace curtains that keep the multitudes in the dark. In a few minutes of electronic transmission, entire libraries of pornographic classics can be sent anywhere on the globe. You may verify this by dialing ______ on the ______ line.

In time, all countries all likely to establish home industries in pornography to preserve their economic independence and domestic accord while getting a piece of the international action. Or else the world will truly become a free market. Liberated pornography has an historical role to play in liberating the world market. If vicarious sex can cross freely over borders then so can the rest of entertainment products. The free circulation of ideas comes along too. Pornography, then, would be the toehold in liberating the world.

## International Understanding

Extending the world market to handle pornography is not merely a step to sell a product for profit, but it is a way of giving everyone what they want for a modest price. And what they want is sexual pleasure through secondary materials. In the course of taking that pleasure, people all over the globe will come to share understanding, to discover the abundance of human experience, and to take vicarious sexual enjoyment from one another. People from different parts of the earth, with varying physical features, brought up under different sexual codes, fearing each other as potential enemies, as if creatures not of a common humanity, may see each other as they are, thanks to the medium of pornography. For we human beings are engaged in much the same activities, and those activities in which we differ may yet prove of interest to the other party.

Understanding a culture requires understanding its sexual patterns. Pornography, along with eroticism, shows the inside story of sexual attitudes. Thus, Japan is a fastidious and formal culture with strong inhibitions against public display of sexuality. In private, the Japanese enjoy a refined and extensive pornography, as exemplified by ______ and _____. In Italy, strong moral ties to family and church also limited public display of sex, but a lighthearted evasion of those prohibitions occurs. When I visited Pompeii in 1961, the pornographic frescoes were hidden from view behind locked panels; the obliging guards offered to unlock the covering for a slight consideration.

One vision of peace on earth is that all people share the same bed. Pornography comes close to that ideal by showing everyone everywhere everyone's bed and what goes on it. A long, strong taboo has barred lovemaking between people of different nationalities, colors, ethnic origins, and religions. Showing such loving pornography should weaken that divisive and cruel ban.

Thanks to pornography, superstitions evaporate, mistrust dissolves, fear is flushed away between peoples. The world recognizes itself as one sexual community with room for all feelings. The path to world peace is through world pornography.

## Freedom

The happiness and well-being of people throughout the world is aided by pornography; this leads to an increase in their freedom. Three senses of freedom are involved: the political and social freedom of persons within communities, the freedom of communities to fulfill their goals, and the freedom of individuals to fulfill themselves.

Restrictions on pornography in some countries now constitute one of the chains of incipient tyranny. Censorship imposed on pornography may carry over against freedom of press, freedom of speech, and academic freedom in the dissemination of information and experience. Artistic liberty will be affected, as well as free competition in the economy. The laws against pornography may be as outdated as the laws against blasphemy that have been repealed or are disregarded. Under the totalitarian regimes of Communism, pornography was outlawed and freedom of sexual expression was suppressed. Erotic love was to be replaced by solidarity with comrades. Sexual experimentation by individuals was anti-social.

During my visit to post-Communist Russia in 1993, I was struck by the public absence of sexuality. I did not see erotic features on posters, magazine covers, television programs, or the multitudes of statues. But in the Moscow metro entrances, counter-culture newspapers were being sold with pictures on the front page of ______ in a state of ______ . This attracted the great interest of Russians, who seemed to have no interest in the ordinary newspapers such as *Pravda.* Although the illustrations struck me as less explicit than magazines and tabloids at American newsstands, the police obliged the vendors of these papers to cease displaying and selling them. The offense could no longer be to the state, and surely it was not to religion. Was the offense to public morality? Or did the new freedom of expression threaten the authoritarian status of the police?

Tyranny is opposed to sexual freedom as an excess of individualism, an indulgence between persons in private which slips out of state control. Under Communism, the public was offered sports, pageantry, medals, cheap liquor, and cigarettes in place of sexual expression.

Censorship is undesirable, especially when its advocates declare as their intention the protection of the public from itself. This parentalization keeps people down by denying their maturity and responsibility. The people need protection from censorious regulations. The proposed remedy for the supposed evil of pornography is more dangerous to the liberty and well-being of the community than the unchecked evil ever could be. Zealous censors will find pornography where none exists, and they will ban valuable works of information and art because they may in part be pornographic. An attack on pornography may be part of a campaign to injure people whose sexual desires are disapproved.

The worst that could occur when pornography is rampant is that people will enjoy themselves. The worst that can happen when censors have free reign is that speech will be silenced, education shortchanged, manners subjected to repression, the arts stifled, "deviants" persecuted, and rights eroded. Legal limits on pornography, and the moral negativism that accompany them, generate unhealthy attitudes toward sexuality while paradoxically encouraging the illegal trade in pornography.

The case for access to pornography could be made in terms of human rights, namely, the right to know, to right to communicate, the right to experience, and the right to seek happiness. I would add that human beings have a right to sexuality. This does not mean that we may practice any kind of sexual act in public, or on unwilling persons, or on non-adults. It does mean that we adults may express ourselves sexually with one another as we wish, in private and with consent. Sex is significant to selfhood. This is a good part of who we are, of how we relate to others, of how we grow. Vicarious sexual experience stands under the umbrella of this right. While the broader right to sexuality does not extend to the enactment of all practices, the right to pornography allows second-hand experience of such practices. Freedom of imagination and of feeling go with the right.

Pornography, like obscenity, often has played a powerful role in political and social protest, especially in France, where *épater le bourgeois* is a perennial goal of the *avant-garde*. Pornographic elements have been worked into cartoons, posters, manifestoes, graffiti, and chants in order to liberate strong sentiments in opposition to oppressive systems. Open sexuality, and the pornographic representation of it, helps break down social and political control. Salacious and witty, scathing and disarming, provocative and instructive, pornography can be a radical weapon for change by striking new notes in consciousness. Thus, it is a form of symbolic speech to be protected. It is an effective way of showing that "the emperor has no clothes."

## Interconnections

The several lines of argument above may be fitted together as follows. A society that does not liberate pornography is not fully free. Pornography provides each state with a measure of self-reliance while participating in a global market. Pornography supports the harmony within a state as sexual groups become better appreciated. It cleanses the emotional life of the citizens, relieves them from costly psychic repression, and gives them a fuller—if indirect—sex life. It contributes to the atmosphere of liberality that extends into the arts and communication generally. The society is liberated to put its energies into other tasks, while counting upon harmony among its people. The freedom of the individual is increased. The wonderful variety of sexual experience that lies within everyone's imagination is freed for the enlightenment and enjoyment of individuals. They come to know themselves and to be more fully themselves, while simultaneously exploring bonds of feeling that connect them to others. To the freedom of thought, of inquiry, of teaching, which are great principles championed as the birthright of all human beings, recognition may now be added of the freedom of emotional experience, of sexual excitation, and of erotic expression.

## Disadvantage

Only one major disadvantage to pornography need concern us here: a flourishing pornography would likely contribute to a diminution of erotic appetite and activity. Pornography will lose its appeal when it is easily available on a daily basis. That it is no longer forbidden but even socially approved would weaken its attractions. Sexual behavior too will likely be more mundane, though probably more varied, once fear, mystery, superstition, and taboo have been dissociated from much of it. Sexuality will pose fewer problems for individuals and communities, so that matters sexual will have less tension, excitement, or fascination for people. Looking at pornography might become of no greater significance in a person's life than looking at food in a store window. Sex would not be such a big deal.

The way to preclude such a disadvantage is to outlaw pornography. The ignorance, inhibition, and disgust caused by such a prohibition may assure an intensity of sexual experience. Some wags might argue that we should publicly outlaw pornography so that a few may continue to enjoy it privately. This was the situation in Victorian England, which produced such elegant pornographic works as ______ and ______. But it would be more just to make pornography available to everyone for its beneficial effects even if in the long run it leads to a general lowering of sexual intensity. The march of civilization, as Freud argued, entails a clamping down on sexuality so that people can handle other pressing problems in their reality, such as killing one another. To forbid pornography is reactionary; it doesn't save civilization but slows its progress. Though cognizant of the value of retaining turbulence in the sexual life by means of censorship, I cast my vote nonetheless for the tranquility of a free and pornographic world.

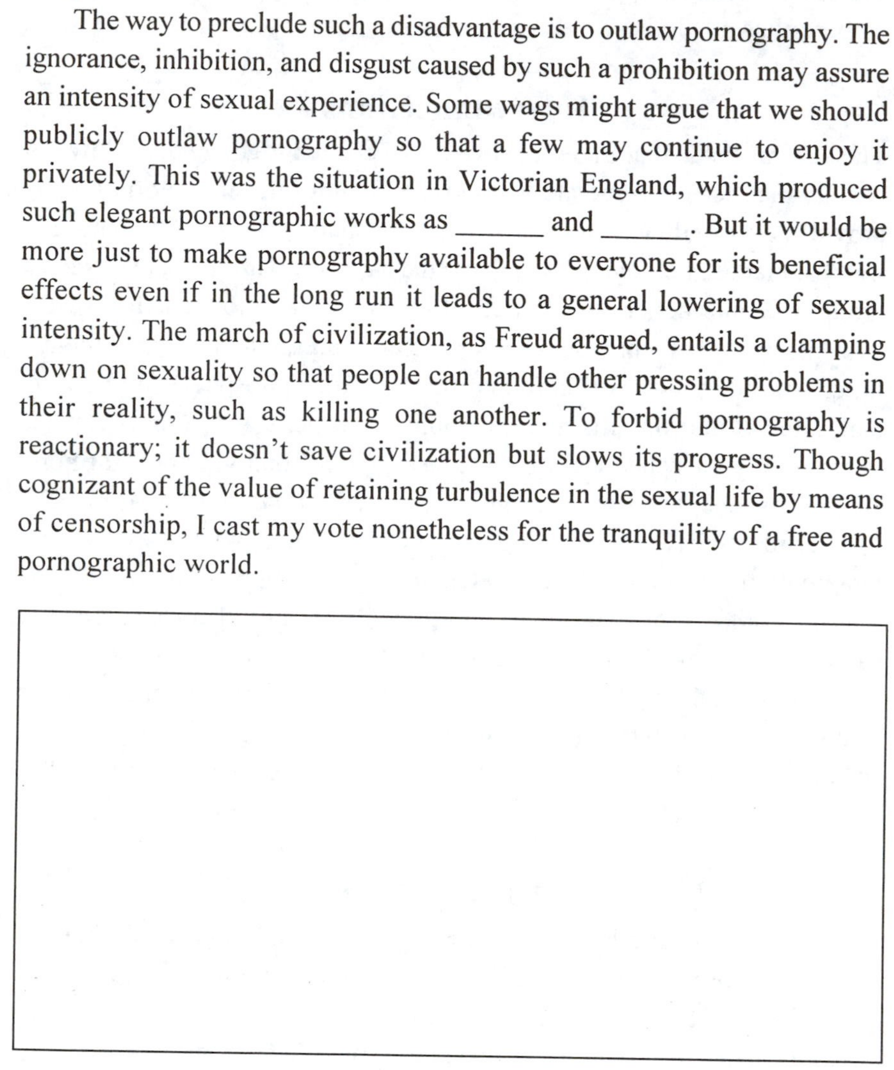

Figure 1, 2, 3, etc. Pornography in its visual form is addressed to the imagination of the viewer. All rights to reproduce strictly reserved.

## Questions

Dear reader, since you have listened so patiently to these arguments, holding in suspense your objections, counter-arguments, and questions, let me take time to listen to your questions. I will offer brief answers.

Reader. Thank you for the opportunity. I thought you had completely forgotten that readers existed, so preoccupied were you in the flights of fancy you call reasoning. You have created such a bag of foolish claims that they can easily be shot down. I will try to control my raging disgust at what you have done and raise polite if pointed questions. If, for the sake of argument, we suppose all this rot to be sound, then doesn't it nonetheless fail because of the danger of corrupting children?

Author. Pornography should not be marketed to children. Because they are not adults. They are not adult sexually and should not be targets of sexual arousal. Otherwise, some of their freedom would be abused, and their growth as persons could be harmed. Today, pornography does get into the hands of children. That is the cost of respecting an adult society. To keep sensitive materials out of the hands of adults so that children won't inadvertently get hold of them is to cheat adults of *their* freedom and further growth. To keep a society at the level of childhood does not make enough of a world for children to grow up in.

The best antidote to any pornography that gets into the hands of children is to provide free, universal, mandatory sex education from the earliest ages. The illustrated facts of sex can be presented in a clinical fashion to build a healthy awareness of human sexuality. The subject should be demystified for youngsters. Nowadays, secrecy, fear, disgust, and shame are associated with sexuality. Children who are well sex-educated will have a fighting chance against being exploited by pornography as well as being sexually abused.

A decent comprehensive sex education will make better citizens, for people will grow up with tolerance of the sexual preferences of others. But one reason that adults want to withhold sex education from children, as well as their access to pornography, is the intolerance with which the adults regard others, such ______ or ______, who are excoriated as deviants. Another reason that sexual information is denied children is the wishful thinking that children are not sexual beings but little angels. Sex is for adults, while children have a life of play, according to that view. This shared myth is a mark of immaturity on the part of society. All human beings are sexual. And children are human beings. Sex education is not just giving children information about what adults do and what they could one day be as adults; it also helps the human being, which is that growing child, in self-understanding.

I will relate an incident for your judgment that occurred while I was visiting Denmark in 1962. I had approached a kiosk in Copenhagen to buy a newspaper or post cards. A Danish family were in front of me asking the vendor directions. The father held his little son on his shoulders. While the adults talked, the son's finger traced the sexual couplings of the figures in the photographs that were displayed on the counters and panels of the kiosk. Kiosks provided many public conveniences, selling stamps, tobacco, maps, phone cards, and pornography. The child exhibited no shame and no excitement. The parents and the elderly kiosk-keeper were not horrified. Only I was embarrassed. Would the child have been better off by being chastised for his interest? Would the child have been better off by not being subject to public access to pornography?

But I stand by the proviso that governs all my arguments here: pornography is to be restricted to use by adults in private.

Reader. What about the use of children as models in pornography? Isn't child pornography a monstrous abuse to be rooted out?

Author. Yes. Sexual exploitation of children is criminal. Since they cannot fully exercise their responsibilities, the state must protect them from being sexually used by others. Laws are on the books for this purpose. Photos, films, and videos of children engaging in sexual acts are evidence of criminal activity and should be subject to seizure.

Reader. What of other forms of child pornography that do not involve models, such as stories or drawings? Shouldn't that stuff also be outlawed?

Author. Since children were not criminally abused by serving as models for the material then it is not evidence of a crime committed.

Reader. What of artistic pictures of naked children that are not offered for sexual arousal? Shouldn't these be outlawed as taking advantage of those children?

Author. While the child is not engaged in sexual acts, yet the child has been deprived of privacy. The child may suffer for this now or in later years. The old joke is that we are all embarrassed by photos of us taken in infancy lying bare upon a bear rug. While bear rugs have been outlawed to protect the dignity of the bears, I wonder if such photos should be banned to protect our dignity. Yet beautiful photos of nude children, as by ______ or ______ , that have appeared in art museums and art books, eschew erotic arousal while teaching us to appreciate the aesthetic dignity of childhood. The nude child has long been a subject in visual art. Cupid or Eros is the classical example. Entering the Luxembourg Gardens in Paris, that high point of French civilization in which I am most at home, you will encounter nude stone boys, cherubs, putti), cupids, call them what you will, carrying flower holders.

Reader. But pornography is the theory, and rape is the practice. Isn't that sufficient danger to stop pornography?

Author. The slogan should be revised: pornography is the substitute for the practice of rape. Enjoyment of anti-social and criminal acts in the medium of pornography does not mean that the enjoyer will seek their enjoyment in reality. The opposite is the likelihood. If you can enjoy it safely second-hand, then why risk doing something harmful and criminal in reality?

Sexual abuse portrayed in pornography does not necessarily cause increased sexual abuse in society. Sexual abuse in society might well decrease by liberating pornography to portray such sexual abuses, but also by expanding sex education. Pornography is essentially harmless. The harms we must fight against are those in behavior.

I am not aware of empirical evidence that pornography, which has been around for millennia, is a cause of sexual crime. How such causality might be established is a puzzle. Anti-pornographers *want* the causal connection to exist so that pornography can be justly banned. While you can cite instances of individuals who confess to having committed a sexual crime following their enjoyment of a pornographic depiction of that crime, we may wonder if the individuals were going to commit those crimes anyway. Even if pornography in some cases contributes to causation, we would have to balance the cases against those in which pornography is a cause of people not committing the acts. How you would establish that kind of causality is also puzzling. Millions of people use pornography involving enjoyment of harmful acts, yet they do not commit such acts. Isn't that the clincher?

Return to the parallel with murder mysteries. Some murderers have claimed to have been inspired by fictional portrayals of murder. We may still doubt that the fiction rather than the propensity of the person was the cause of the murder. But millions of non-murderers enjoy murder mysteries.

We need public programs that enforce the prohibitions against rape and murder as monstrous acts unacceptable to humanity, but pornography and mystery stories should be left alone.

Reader: Pornography fuels the cultural bias that women are primarily sex objects for men. This attitude is to be combated for the safety, dignity, and fulfillment of women. Pornography is the last refuge of a sexist society.

Author. Since most societies are patterned to devalue women, we must change their structures as well as their attitudes. Sexism remains a major systemic evil of humanity. Let us track it to its core, which is a false moral judgment, and clean it up. Actions should be political, social, economic, educational, and personal. The public expression of sexism should be denounced at every occasion. But don't throw pornography out as the baby with the bath water. Much of it is degrading to women. Yet some of it may increase appreciation of women as sexual subjects, that is, as persons with responsibility, choice, preference, desire, and joy in matters sexual. This recognition of women as sexual subjects rather than as sexual objects or non-sexual beings can be advanced by pornography as well as sex education.

Pornography is an admirable field for women contributors, since they may humanize the sexual representation of women. Women are now involved creatively in the production of videos meant to please the imagination of women as well as men. The availability of pornography through home video allows women greater access to it, whereas in the old days pornography shops were a male reserve. The bright new chapter in the history of pornography will be written by the female sensibility. Feminism needs to get into the act instead of siding with the censorious tradition of anti-sexual expression which is embedded in male-dominated societies.

Granted that some pornography does give enjoyment by depicting the degradation and commodification of women. Better that individuals savor that pleasure in private than abusing women in reality.

The chief mistake in discussion of pornography is to equate enjoyment of its content with enjoyment in reality of the same acts. But once you get it through your head that pornography works through the imagination rather than getting the viewer to engage in the acts, then you will cease to attack it as you fight against harmful acts.

Reader. Yet people are really engaged in the acts that are shown the viewer. Thus, the act of ______ by _____, involving the ______, is staged by real people for the benefit of that viewer. Pornography thereby degrades its participants by prostitution. They are the victims of what you are trying to excuse as a victimless crime. Sometimes pornographic models are raped, beaten, drugged, and enslaved in order to perform. To clean out that underworld culture of pornography we need to outlaw pornography.

Author. Rape, assault, drugging, and enslavement should be vigorously repelled by law, morality, and social programs. Such coercive and harmful deeds should be outlawed in the pornography industry just as in any other human activity. To clean out the underworld culture of pornography, we need to liberate pornography. Only consenting adults should engage in its production. Competition in a free society and public standards for the safety and health of participants would improve working conditions and chase criminal activity from production. Like other forms of entertainment, or sports, and other activities involving bodily contact, licensing might be required to prevent abuse, disease, and coercion.

An enormous change has occurred in the history of pornography that does require further reflection. In the past, pornographic works could be produced without live models. Drawings, paintings, stories did not carry with them the sense that anyone was engaging in the acts so that the user could enjoy them. The work sprang entirely from the mind of the pornographer. Photography and film introduced live people seemingly engaged in the acts. Sometimes the acts were simulated. Thus, in many mildly pornographic videos shown in the 1980s in American hotel rooms as pay-for-play adult movies, the participants appear to be engaging in _____, though they were not. An occasional uncut frame reveals the simulation. The producers and distributors could defend against the charge of offering pornography, while offering customers a convincing illusion of it.

All that has changed. When you walk into any pornography shop in America, you will find endless magazines and videos depicting in unmistakable actuality people engaging in _____. Hence, we have a new care, that did not exist in the nineteenth century, for the health and well-being of those who choose to make a business out of such sexual performances. The user of pornography now knows that people have performed these depicted acts for the user's gratification. This leaves less to the imagination. The phrase, "So-and-so leaves nothing to the imagination," was a journalistic convention once used when reporting that So-and-so had appeared nude. The experience of modern pornography is still guided by imagining the acts rather than by engaging in them.

The next step, you might say, is direct viewing of live sexual activity, but this may well be a form of prostitution in which the client participates in the activity as it is taking place. That staple of burlesque, the old-fashioned striptease, and the current forms of sex shows are not pornography, although videotapes of these would be. When as a college student in Chicago in the l950s I once slipped into a burlesque house in the Loop, I observed that between the acts on stage vendors would go up and down the aisles hawking packs of photos of the performers. The pictures were pornography, while the stage show was performance.

But the medium is now at hand that makes possible realistic visual pornography without prostitution by performers. Customized Virtual Reality is the electronically manipulated simulation of human beings who will engage in whatever acts you choose. The fulfillment of all the dreams of the Id on the screen of the imaginagion.

Reader. You argue from a universal point of view with an ideal of humanity in mind, but the world is organized into quite different cultures and local communities. What is acceptable as eroticism in one place may offend most people in another place as disgusting. Therefore, should not the prevailing community standards of decency be decisive in outlawing pornography?

Author. No. Because all communities are subsumed under the human community. People have rights as human beings that may not be vetoed locally or regionally. Moreover, local communities no longer exist in the narrow sense of a shared territoriality and a restricted communication. We are citizens of the world community. We cross provincial boundaries and national boundaries with ease. The world's newspapers, magazines, and books may be flown in to our newsstands and bookstores.

I used to commute by train from Washington to Philadelphia. On the train I would pick up newspapers of Washington, Baltimore, Wilmington, and Philadelphia to see how they treated a news story. On the way home, the papers on board would include Boston, Hartford, New York, Newark, and Trenton. Though I was sampling the perspectives of several communities, to what community did I belong while on the train?

Cable television and electronic transmission give us worldwide access to cultural expressions. We may form multiple communities as electronic interest groups. I belong to the community of those who would change communities for the better. Prevailing community standards may be intolerant of groups who deserve freedom of expression. Just as Thoreau had claimed in matters of righteousness to be a majority of one, so we may each claim in sexual matters to be a minority of one, for each of us is unique. You, as well as I, are deviants from some exact pattern of sexual feeling.

Yet we must protect the majority from offense. The principle of privacy does just that in our case for pornography. The local community cannot take offense at practices, or the depiction of practices, that they do not encounter. If it is out of sight, then it does not affront.

Reader. But people may take offense in knowing that others are enjoying forbidden experiences even if in private.

Author. Too bad. The offense suffered is self-inflicted. It is not inflicted by the behavior of the non-conforming individuals. The harm, if such exists, suffered by the censorious party weighs less in the balance of fairness than the harm that would be inflicted on the non-conformists by curtailing their freedom and interfering in their privacy. That others dislike what you feel and what they suppose you do at home is not grounds for them to cut short your feelings and stop your private activity. Disgust ought not to outweigh privacy. We have to learn to live with a burden of disgust that we feel toward others.

If you grant the public the right to outlaw your private sexual activities, including vicarious ones, because the public claims to be injured by *knowing* that you are engaging in them, then what is to stop the same interference into your private thoughts, feelings, prayers, and conversations?

Reader. You dress up pornography in fancy aesthetic clothes, but isn't it basically an appeal to prurient interest and therefore should be banned?

Author. Nothing is wrong with appeal to prurient interest. We have an interest in seeing that pornography is not banned, since we all have prurient interests. But pornography has other appeals, as well, including aesthetic and educational aims, that I have sketched above.

Reader. My final objection comes down to this: pornography has no redeeming social value because it stimulates sexually.

Author. *That* is its redeeming social value.

# Chapter Five
# Peirce and Work

Paul Ryan*

This paper is a report on using Peirce's categories to structure a program for training workers. I offer this paper to honor Peirce scholar Roberta Kevelson because of the deft insistence in her 1994 keynote address to the Semiotic Society of America that pragmatism itself will only grow as it learns by doing.

## The Context

Downsizing in the defense industry has been estimated to result in the loss of over two million jobs (Rifkin 1995: 38). In the spring of 1994, I was invited to design a core curriculum for workers displaced from the defense industry by a company called ETI which is responsible for retraining and placing some of these workers. ETI's clients lost their jobs due to layoffs by Pratt-Whitney and Hamilton Standard in East Hartford, Connecticut. ETI has had similar retraining contracts with IBM and Pan Am. My invitation was triggered by the publication of my book, *Video Mind, Earth Mind* (Ryan: 1993) in a series on semiotics and the humanities edited by Roberta Kevelson. In that book, I articulated the Earthscore Method, based on my cybernetic adaptation of Peirce, whereby videographers could create a shared perception of ecological systems (Ryan 1993: 379–393). The question posed by this invitation was whether the Earthscore Method, specific to video work in an ecological context, could be generalized for other workers. I thought it could and set about designing a program based on the same method.

I called the program Success Skills which I defined, after Aristotle, as habits of right reason and ease about work to be done. The Success Skills program shapes and supports habits that enable people to find new jobs and thrive in what is being called the new world of work, where everybody is seen as in business for themselves in one way or another (Bridges: 1994). In February and again in April of 1995, I ran two Success Skills workshops for ETI clients in Connecticut. Subsequently, I taught others how to conduct the workshop and two have been conducted successfully without me. Based on testimonials, focus group reports, job club activity, and job placement rates, ETI considers the Skills curriculum a genuine success with a promising future. Currently, with my ETI associates, we are redesigning the workshop for students in School-to-Work Programs. Discussion is also under way about adapting the program for welfare-to-work clients.

The necessary skills for success in the 1990s and the next century have been identified by The Secretary of the United States Department of Labor's Commission on Achieving Necessary Skills, known as the SCANS skills (United States Department of Commerce: 1992). There is evidence of a consensus about the identity and value of the SCANS skills. As identified in a report by the American Society for Training and Development (Carnevale: 1990), these skills include the three basics of reading, writing, and computation as well thirteen others. These, informally known as the "soft" skills, are the focus of the Success Skills program. They include: being an effective member of an organization, leadership, interpersonal relations, negotiations, teamwork, self-esteem, goal setting and motivation, career development, creative thinking, problem solving, listening, oral communication, and learning to learn.

To build a coherent training program, I analyzed each of these skills in terms of three generic life skills. Each participant profiles his or her own capacity to perform these generic skills using a questionnaire. Based on these profiles, participants then organize themselves into recombinant teams of three or more and follow a carefully choreographed sequence of exercises over a forty-eight hour period. Each exercise is grounded in the generic skill sets and activates one of more SCANS skill. At the end of the workshop, a Success Skills Club is formed to sustain the ongoing task of shaping productive work habits.

The three generic skill sets are based on three fundamental categories identified by Charles S. Peirce (1931–35). For Peirce, the purpose of thinking is to establish effective habits. This understanding makes his categories well suited for a training program designed to shape good work habits. Strictly speaking, a pure understanding of the categories of firstness and secondness does not involve habits or skills. However, I think my use of Peirce here is justified in that I have identified skill sets that reference firstness and secondness. As a practicing artist (Ryan: 1993), I can claim that the skills of an artist, for example, reference firstness. Likewise, zen practice cultivates skill in firstness. Sherlock Holmes, as presented by Sebeok, is portrayed as skilled in abduction (firstness), induction (secondness), and deduction (thirdness) (Sebeok 1981: pp. 17–53).

To adapt Peirce's categories for non-academic users I dehyposthesized firstness, secondness, and thirdness into "the first set of skills", "the second set of skills", and "the third set of skills". I found that my habit of explaining what we were doing using Peirce's hypothesized designation of categories only confused people. Prior to this dehyposthesation, as someone tutored by Gregory Bateson in logical types (Ryan 1993: 174–196), I had always seen Peirce's categories as antithetical to set theory. However, recent reading in "fuzzy logic" convinced me that this dehyposthesation, if understood in a fuzzy set sense, was legitimate (McNeil and Freidberger: 1993).

By basing Success Skills on these three broad generic categories, I believe I have developed a program that can make a serious contribution to creating a highly skilled and flexible workforce. Existing programs that effectively teach reading, writing, and computation can be integrated into Success Skills. The Skill Standards initiative, developed by the National Alliance of Business, will make it possible to design and deliver high performance Success Skill programs for any industry. Industry-specific skills can be analyzed in terms of the three generic skills and an appropriate program developed to combine SCANS skill training with industry-specific needs in any area of the country.

For example, the retail industry has developed Skill Standards that include two specific skills: 1) listen and ask open-ended questions; 2) acquire and apply product knowledge (*American Management Association,* June, 1995: 28). The Success Skills program already includes training in listening and questioning in terms quality of emotion, specific facts, and overall pattern. Emotion, fact, and pattern each reference one of the three generic skill sets. A salesperson with this training would satisfy the listening/questioning standard. To address the standard of acquiring product knowledge, I would develop a Success Skills module that taught people to examine a product in terms quality, fact, and pattern. The common ground between customer and product, created by addressing both in terms of the generic skills, would make it easy for a salesperson to apply his product knowledge by matching a specific customer's need with a specific product. Moreover, a Success Skills participant would also understand, through the Myers-Briggs indicator and through the performance assessment (more on these later), just how his or her own preferences and performance skills figured into his or her habits of right reason and ease about selling.

By building specific training based on generic skills, the program can maintain commitment to a flexible workforce. Flexibility is uncommitted potential for change (Bateson 1972: 502–513). The global marketplace is unpredictable. We need a flexible workforce that can respond to it quickly. Consider an acrobat on a high wire. In order to maintain his balance he must be free to move rapidly from one position to another. Rigidity in any part of his body will cause him to fall. A healthy economy needs a workforce that is not trapped in rigidly outmoded skills. By grounding the learning of very specific skills in a balance of the three generic skill sets, the capacity to learn new skills is built into the Success Skills program.

As mentioned, participants use a questionnaire, which is a self-assessment instrument to profile generic skills. (Readers of this paper are encouraged to take the time to take the questionnaire, presented as an appendix.) Participants use their profiles to organize teams with complementary skills during the workshop. There are no right or wrong answers. There are, instead, judgments to be made about one's own abilities that draw a picture of personal skills. The more accurate the picture, the better will be the fit with teammates. Participants are encouraged to as honest as possible. If unsure, they are instructed to make their best guess.

In the workshop, teams are organized based on these fundamental skill sets. As a member of these fundamental or generic skill teams, participants are given exercises that activate specific SCANS skills in the context of work search. Each of these specific skills has been analyzed to see how it makes use of the more generic and fundamental skill set profiled. Based on this analysis, team exercises have been developed that combine generic with specific skills. For example, a problem-solving team of three people will be organized with one person who is strong in each of the three sets. The strong second (to use Peirce's categories) will analyze the problem, the strong first will imagine a solution, and the strong third will apply the solution to the problem. People then switch roles and analyze another problem. Now the strong first can analyze the problem with the advantage of having seen how a strong second analyzed a problem. The other two have a similar advantage in facing their respective tasks. Taking turns in this manner will enable people to learn from each other on a regular basis.

## Teamwork and the Talking Stick Protocols

Readers will note that the questionnaire in the appendix is structured so that options are intransitive, as in the child's game "paper, rock scissors". This intransitive use of Peirce's categories is key to the workshop. McCulloch has argued that the non-hierarchic circularity of preference inherent in intransitive choices is at the core of humans' logic of survival (McCulloch 1965: 40–45). I have argued elsewhere that this non-hierarchic way of making choices is also at the core of the choice-making that engenders art (Ryan 1993: 395–404). A Cézanne, faced with what he fondly calls *those little blues, those little browns, and those little whites* (Lacan 1978: 110), allows himself to choose white instead of blue even though he has chosen blue over brown and brown over white. There is no hierarchy of choice. Rather a heterarchy of choice takes place, a circularity of preference that is the basic circuitry for making art. Working as an artist using video while reading Gregory Bateson, Warren McCulloch, and Charles Peirce, I was able to invent a relational circuit that has served me in my art-making as a figure of regulation for intransitive composing with firstness, secondness, and thirdness. One of the yields from this effort has been the creation of a non-verbal art of behavior called Threeing. Normally when three people get together two combine and extrude the third. Threeing provides a choreography based on the relational circuit that precludes such exclusion.

This non-verbal art of triadic relationships, analogous to T'ai Chi or Yoga, provides the model for the protocols of the talking stick at the core of the success skills workshop. The talking stick protocols allow three people to work together in a formal way, taking turns using the three generic skill sets to accomplish a task.

## The Tricolor Talking Stick

The cooperation necessary to work together in threes does not come naturally. The Tricolor Talking Stick Protocols are designed to prevent certain problems from arising within the group, so the group can learn together, intransitively, as a team, with optimal results. The problems are:

1. Two or more people talking at the same time.
2. Someone dominating the group or manipulating the conversation.
3. People being left out.
4. Confusing as to the roles people are playing in conversation. Is someone throwing out a suggestion, reacting, or mediating?
5. Confusion between helping and competing. If I think I am helping you and you think I am competing with you, pain and confusion will result.
6. Failure to consider a topic or situation in a comprehensive way.
7. A vague or arbitrary decision-making process.
8. Relational tensions accumulating so the group splits apart.

I will describe the protocols in detail and then explain how they preclude the eight problems stated above.

The talking stick is a round, fifteen-inch length of wood with a diameter of between one and three inches. The stick is painted with three five inch bands of solid color: yellow, red, and blue. The red band is in the middle of the stick.

Each group of three gets one stick. The stick is passed around among the trio. Each member indicates the role he/she is playing in the conversation with the other two by where they hold the stick. Holding the yellow band indicates that one is exercising the first skill set. the red band the second skill set, the blue the third. Sometimes the emphasis is on the role the person is playing: initiator (yellow), reactor (red), mediator (blue). Example: Yellow throws out an idea, red reacts, and blue mediates. Sometimes the emphasis is on what the person with the stick is paying attention to: feelings (yellow), facts (red), or patterns (blue). Example: Yellow listens for emotion and feeling as someone presents an idea, red listens for the specific facts, and blue listens for the reasoning behind the idea and the overall context.

Let me provide a further example. Participants are asked to develop their best alternative to getting a "job" in the industrial sense. Each person presents his/her alternative to a group of three for feedback. The group then questions the person about their alternative by moving down the ladder from the person's alternative as stated (blue) to red (facts supporting that alternative) to yellow (mood, intuition that helped generate the alternative). This is a non-confrontational style of inquiry and the phrasing of the questions should reflect a non-advocacy approach. In fact, the exercise suggests using certain types of phrases to make sure the inquiry is not mistake for confrontation.

**Blue**: If I understand you correctly you are saying that If.....then.....Am I right?
Can you show me how you got from the "if" to the "then"? I did not follow you.

**Red**: What are the facts behind your statements?
How could you verify these facts?

**Yellow**: How do you feel about the alternative you've developed?
What was you mood as you thought about what you could do?

Confrontation, however, is possible within the talking stick protocols. Often it can be healthy. With a talking stick, participants can combine the three non-confrontational generic roles with advocacy or adversarial roles. Confrontation or non-confrontation is indicated by the way a person holds the stick. In the non-confrontational roles of yellow, red and blue, the stick is held vertically. To indicate confrontation the stick is held horizontally with the ends pointing at the two people in confrontation. Basically at any point in the exchange among the three, one member of the team can directly challenge another by laying the talking stick on a horizontal line between the two of them and addressing that person in the type of adversarial statement described below. The person addressed directly can then turn the stick around and respond. The third party can also enter into this exchange if one of the two points the stick at him or her. Three times back and forth between two parties is a reasonable limit. Then the stick must be pointed at the third party or pointed upward by one of the people arguing. By pointing the stick upward, that person is either going into yellow with a fresh initiative or asking the third party to go into yellow with a fresh proposition that might resolve the argument. The trio then works through the fresh proposition in the three roles. If they fail to reach consensus, then the decision-making procedure, shown below, comes into effect.

Inquiry and cooperation take place with the stick pointed up. Questioning from an advocacy position is a symmetric confrontation with the stick horizontal, which is often more productive if someone willingly presents to others the reasoning, facts, and feeling associated with his or her position. Certain introductory statements can go a long way toward making the confrontation formal and clear enough to be productive. Here are some samples of proper confrontational phrasing:

"Here is how I understand the context in which I am stating my argument..."

"Here is how I define my terms."

"I am assuming..."

"Here's what I think, here's how I came to think this way..."

"I came to this conclusion because..."

"Here are the facts I 'm basing my argument on."

"Here are some examples of how I think what I'm proposing will effect what we are talking about."

Decision-making is also part of the Talking Stick Protocols. Briefly, it works as follows. When three people work together on an exercise, each has a domain determined by the generic skill set indicated by his or her color on the stick. In one's own domain, one's decision cannot be overridden by the two other members of the triad unless a predesignated fourth party (a facilitator or other workshop member) agrees with the other two. Then three can override one. However, if the fourth party does not agree with the two then the decision made by the one in charge of the domain stands. Experience in actual work situations with this method has been positive. No one feels his or her decisions will be overruled in an arbitrary chain of command. Moreover, some people come to see the two others plus the fourth party as a safety net, allowing them to entertain risky decisions, knowing they have a triad of consultants to rein them in.

I said that The Talking Stick Protocols are designed to prevent certain problems from arising in small groups so that the group can work together with optimal results. I will now indicate how the protocols resolve the eight problems stated above.

1. Two or more people talking at the same time.
   The person who holds the stick talks. The others listen. Each person gets a turn. The stick is exchanged in an order appropriate to the exercise. Simple.
2. Someone dominating the group or manipulating the conversation.
   Taking turns with the stick in different roles allows for a sharing of leadership and prevents any one person from becoming entrenched in fixed position of power.
3. People being left out.
   Normally when you get three people together, two tend to combine and push out the third. Two is company and three is a crowd. Some cultures have interpersonal tactics that neutralize this tendency. For example: in parts of China if A asks B a question in the presence of C, B will answer the question facing C as if C had asked. The point is not to exclude the third party. The talking stick insures that three can work cooperatively by taking turns in three different roles. When there is a fourth or fifth party, they can await a turn in the trio, play a backup role, or start a new trio.
4. Confusion as to the roles people are playing in conversation. Is someone throwing out a suggestion, reacting, or mediating? The

three colors on the talking stick can be used by the participants to clearly indicate what role each is playing.

5. Confusion between helping and competing. If I think I am helping you and you think I am competing with you, pain and confusion will result. In normal interpersonal relationships, we often confuse each other about the manner in which we are relating. I may think you are in a symmetric relation to me like two boxers going toe to toe. You may think I am in a complementary relation to you, as a student to a teacher.
   This confusion can be emotionally difficult and counter-productive for the group. In the talking stick protocols, all complementary, asymmetric relationships clearly take place when the stick is held vertically. All adversarial, symmetric relationships take place when the stick is held horizontally.
6. Failure to consider a topic or situation in a comprehensive way. The three basic roles indicated by yellow, red, and blue provide an approach to everything that is relevant to a topic or situation. Just as any color can be created from yellow, red and blue, so any topic can be approached in a comprehensive way using the three skill sets.
7. A vague or arbitrary decision-making process.
   While the decision-making procedure in the talking stick protocols can be used to override one person, that overriding happens according to a formal procedure that respects his or her point of view. No one can position him/herself to make an arbitrary decision. Nor is a two against one coalition ever allowed to have decision-making power.
8. Tensions in relationships accumulating so the group splits apart. The principal reason why tensions accumulate and tend to split relationships apart is that participants get caught in an escalating pattern of reacting to each others' reactions. Sometimes this happens in a confrontational symmetric fashion such as in a shouting match or a fist fight. At other times the escalation takes place in a non-confrontational, asymmetric way. An example

would be two people who avoid confrontation at all costs and, eventually, separate because they can no longer communicate.

The Talking Stick Protocols preclude these escalating patterns in three ways:

1. Escalations happen more readily when there are only two parties involved. The protocols involve the constant presence of a third party mediator.
2. The role of reactor is legitimate and clearly marked as such. Through constant rotation however, participants are never stuck in a reactionary role.
3. Escalation happens when people get locked in confrontation or non-confrontational patterns. The protocols require a constant shifting back and forth between these two ways of interacting. One way serves to preclude the other from going too far. Relationships become sustainable.

The Talking Stick Protocols are used throughout the workshop, which has a sequence of four parts.

*Part One:* The first two days' participants learn to work together based on their performance profiles using the talking stick protocols. In these first two days care is taken that everybody is clear on the generic skills and the protocols. The talking stick protocols are seen as training wheels for cooperation based on the generic skills. Training wheels come off only when the whole group is proficient in the protocols.

In the course of using the talking stick the following six SCANS skills are incorporated: learning to learn, listening and oral communication, interpersonal relationships, teamwork, and leadership. Hence all sessions are consistently exercising at least these six SCANS skills. At least eighty per cent of the time is spent in exercises. In addition, two SCANS skills, creativity and problem solving, are featured on the second day, Tuesday.

*Part Two:* Wednesday is devoted to applying the generic skills to the world of work. Thursday the generic skills are linked to Myers-Briggs profile of personal preferences and applied to the self. Monday of the next week is devoted to negotiating a relationship between self and the world of work. Taken together these three days address the issue of career development, a SCANS skill, for the participant. In the course of these three days the six SCANS skills built into the Talking Stick protocols are continually exercised. Creativity and problem solving are also called as needed. In addition, participants learn about being a member of an organization, negotiating, self-esteem, goal setting, and motivation. In the first five days of the workshop, all SCANS skills will have been practiced, many of them cumulatively.

*Part Three:* This part is formatted as a series of All-for-One sessions. Each participant is on the hot seat for three continuous hours. The participant simulates a job interview and raises other issues that pertain to his or her work search. The purpose of these sessions are threefold: 1) To provide a fullness of peer feedback for each participant based on trust levels established over five days of working with formal protocols. 2) To provide the opportunity to reinforce the SCANS skills and the generic skills in a pressure situation. 3) After working with the three generic skills as a member of different teams, the All-for-One allows all individuals to reappropriate from the group these generic skills for their own personal use in their own way.

*Part Four:* The last session of the workshop is devoted to organizing the Success Skills Club. The Club meets for three hours each week over ten weeks following the workshop. Members of the workshops elect a leader and three advisors each, representing strength in one of the generic skills. One hour of the weekly meeting is devoted to general business of the club under the direction of the leader and his advisors. Two hours of the

> meeting are given to mini all-for-one sessions with teams of four. Members of the four person team have a half-hour to present whatever they need to the team of four for feedback in their job search. Issues are selected by participants. The Success Skills club is designed to help stabilize the SCANS skills in the context of work search.

How the SCANS skills are integrated with the generic skills is shown in the following chart.

| SCANS: | FIRST SET | SECOND SET | THIRD SET |
|---|---|---|---|
| *membership* | | | |
| *Experience of membership in Success Skills Program based on three generic skill sets . Examine Corporate Culture formally and informally for* | | | |
| | tone and feel | facts of situation | Overall patterns |
| *leadership* | | | |
| | take initiative | respond realistically | mediate |
| *interpersonal relationships* | | | |
| *Talking Stick Protocols exercise a range of relational skills such as symmetric and complementary interaction, including a third party and recognizing one's preferred role in relationships without getting stuck in preferred role. Three primary roles are keyed to three sets of skills.* | | | |
| *negotiations* | | | |
| | invent options | focus on interests | reference standards |
| *teamwork* | | | |
| *Cooperate with others to accomplish tasks using talking stick protocols. Please see interpersonal relationships above. Example, figuring out how analogies from nature apply to dealing with new world of work.* | | | |
| *self esteem* | | | |
| | attending to stream | isolating | disarming |

| of consciousness | pathological critic | critic |
|---|---|---|

*goal setting and motivation*
*Highlighted by the All-for-One sessions, motivation stimulated by constant feedback from group regarding*

| emotions | discussion of specific obstacles | context |
|---|---|---|

*Goal setting (subset of motivation) stimulated by Storyboard of Career path, developing your Best Alternative to a Negotiated Agreement, and the All-for-One exercises which are all structured according to the three skill sets.*

*career development*

| focus on self | focus on world | negotiate self/world |
|---|---|---|

*creative thinking*

| collage | elements | pattern |
|---|---|---|
| dreamer | realist | critic |

*problem solving*

| analogy | defining problem | applying analogy |
|---|---|---|

*listening*

| for tone | for facts | for pattern |
|---|---|---|

*oral communication*
*Inquiry*

| about quality | facts | patterns |
|---|---|---|

*Advocacy using*

| defined terms | statements of fact | if...then thinking |
|---|---|---|

*Learning to learn*

*The figure of regulation that organizes the three skill sets in every exercise is the relational circuit. The relational circuit provides a formal, self correcting, approach to learning to learn.*

Learning to learn in Success Skills can be understood with reference to Gregory Bateson's theory of learning (Bateson 1972: 279–308). To understand Bateson's theory of learning in the context of the workplace the following breakdown was developed.

*Zero Learning*: IBM accountant loses job because Hudson River Plant closes. He gets a Job in IBM accounting in Yonkers.

*Learning I:* IBM accountant loses job at IBM. He goes to Digital and learns that IBM's style of accounting was only one way of accounting. By reviewing the larger set of skills called "general accounting", he is able to move from the IBM way to the Digital way. Note that he does not stay in the set of skills called accounting, but uses that set to move from one specific area of accounting to another. He then returns to the level of zero learning in the Digital context. If he were to stabilize at Learning I, it would mean hanging out a shingle and doing accounting for anybody who knocked on his door.

*Learning II:* Former IBM accountant, now freelance accountant, realizes accounting is only one set of ways to deal with money. He goes to business school and gets training as a fiscal manager, a set of skills that subsumes accounting and includes other things like forecasting. He then hires out as a fiscal manager.

*Learning III*: The business school itself has a new curriculum for enabling people to learn a new set of money skills that change fiscal management and accounting for the better. Once they learn these skills, they return to Learning II or Learning I activity and do it better than others.

The method I have developed can be understood in Bateson's terms as a cultural instance of Learning III. I know he says that's rare, but it does occur: a group of people can learn to learn. His paper just focuses on the individual. My assumption is that once people learn this way of learning, then they can accelerate their learning of any other thing to be learned. What this means in practical terms is that we spend the first block of time teaching people this triadic method, then we format every workforce skill so that it can be learned in an accelerated way, based on the fact that everybody knows the method.

I'm suggesting that this new method can itself be considered Learning III in a formal way. It enables people to communicate better in every context, whether Learning I or II. We can teach this way of learning to learn and map out how people can use it in the various communication skill contexts that they work in.

Let me use a comparison. The classroom is a way people can learn together, a culturally invented form of Learning III. Once everybody knows the format which includes literacy, and the protocols, any kind of learning can be plugged in with books, etc. So using the triadic method we don't have to give people a fish each time they do something new and good and hope they invent a new way to learn. We have already invented the way. We invite people to go from where they are to Learning III in a formal way, and then back to where they want to be with their skill level.

## Peirce and Jung

One of the interesting things about using Peirce's categories is that they give Success Skills an open architecture that allows the program to interlink with other effective programs. For example, the Myers-Briggs Character Typology of Preferences has been integrated into Success Skills. Myers-Briggs is a widely used and respected tool in the training field. In contrast to the *performance* profile presented in the appendix, people using Myers-Briggs profile their patterns of *preference* using a questionnaire. This questionnaire, or indicator, is then analyzed in terms of sixteen different possible character types. The types are based on combinations of whether one's preference profile indicates extroversion or introversion, intuitiveness or sensing, thinking or feeling, judging or perceiving. Insights derived from this analysis are woven into training.

The Myers-Briggs terminology can be misleading and the complexity of the full system forbids a complete explanation here. Our main concern is to appreciate the difference between the Myers-Briggs system based on Carl Jung and the pragmatic system of triadic relationships based on Charles Peirce. Jung developed his four orientating functions, the four preferences cited above, from empirical observations made over many years. He defined a function as "a particular form of psychic activity that remains the same in principle under varying conditions". Jung stated: " I distinguish these functions from one another because they *cannot be related* or reduced to one another" (Myers and McCaulley 1985:12, *my emphasis* ). Behind Jung's fourfold distinguishing of functions is his more basic distinction between perception and judgment:

> Perception includes the many ways of becoming aware of things, people, events, or ideas. It includes information gathering, the seeking of sensation or of inspiration, and the selection of the stimulus to be attended to. Judgment includes all the ways of coming to conclusion about what has been perceived. It includes decision making, evaluation, choice and the selection of the response after perceiving the stimulus (Myers and McCaulley 1985: 12).

In contrast to Jung, Peirce was able to unify perception and judgment through his notion of a "perceptual judgment". He argues that if your eyes see something vague, your mind will try to resolve that vagueness into something you can identify as either this or that. You make judgments about what you perceive as part of your ongoing way of being in the world. It is a continuous process. For example, if you are in a strange neighborhood at night and you see a figure at a distance coming toward you, your mind may activate itself to judge if the figure is a man or a woman. Based on the "prejudice" that women are less of a physical threat than men, you will activate a habit, a safety procedure, based on your judgment. This kind of judgment does not easily fall into the two categories of "Thinking Judgment" and "Feeling Judgment" developed by Jung precisely because a perceptual judgment is not separated from perception. However, Jung's categories of judgment are separated from perception. Peirce "related" what Jung could not.

By distinguishing between perception and judgment, Jung was following an understanding common in European philosophy, which was most firmly established by Immanuel Kant. We know that Peirce studied Kant closely. He appropriated Kant's fundamental insight that "concepts are empirically meaningful only if they contain schematic possibilities for their application to sensible experience.... However, Peirce's pragmatic appropriation...radically alters Kant's understanding of the schema. Such a schema is no longer a product of productive imagination as distinct from the understanding of the faculty of judgment. *Rather, both understanding and imagination are unified and transformed into a creative function of habit...*" (Rosenthal 1994: 26. *My emphasis.* Rosenthal has a very useful discussion (p. 21 ff.) of how Peirce's understanding of habit incorporates both perception and judgment.)

## Implications of Theoretical Differences for Empirical Data

One way to explore the implications of Peirce's incorporation of perception and judgment for the training field is to look at some of the anomalies in the empirical data collected using the Myers-Briggs Type Table. Can these anomalies be explained by a revision of the Myers-Briggs Jungian theory along the lines laid out by Peirce?

—Myers and MaCaulley pointed out that the large number of J types (Judging Types) in religious work was unexpected (Myers and MaCaulley 1985: 43). "Judge not that you might not be judged," said Jesus. If judgments are understood as integrated with perception and necessary for habits of virtue, this would not be surprising.

—Because "creativity in the arts requires highly differentiated use of tools and materials, one might expect artists to prefer sensing perception rather than intuition." But in contrast to this expectation, ninety-one per cent of fine artists prefer intuition. (Myers and McCaulley 1985: 41) If, as Aristotle tells us, art is a habit of right reason and ease about something to be made, then there is a continuous flow from the "right reason" of the imagination through the process of making and using materials. The relationship between intuition and sensing is itself critical to art. This relationship can be understood in pragmatic categories. In these categories no choice is forced between sensing and intuition, just as no choice is forced between perception and judgment.

—Another unexpected result of the Jungian approach: N's, or intuitives, occur more frequently than in Myers estimates (Myers and McCaulley 1985: 47). This may be because the Intuitive function as described by Jung—a subdivision of perception which includes perception of patterns, relationships, and future events—cannot really be separated out from judgment functions. Perceiving one pattern means I have made a judgment favoring that pattern rather than another. If I anticipate future events, I have made a judgment that the flow of present events will unfold in a certain way. Because judgment and intuition are so related in experience, it may be that respondents cannot separate them out when they take the indicator. As a result, respondents answer more frequently as intuitives because that "type" actually includes a judging function.

In short, some anomalies within the Myers-Briggs indicator may result when the artificial separation between perception and judgment must, perforce of people's experience, be conflated in their self-description. Obviously, much more work needs to be done to see if this line of inquiry is fruitful. This is obviously an undertaking beyond the scope of this paper, which can only be suggestive.

## Implications of Theoretical Differences for Success Skills

Imagine designing Success Skills based on Jung's theory. The separation of perception and judgment in the theory would play out in the program. Success Skills is a workshop designed to help people find a job and, in the process, activate the new habits of work identified as SCANS skills. Insights gained through perception are not habits. Judgments are not habits. A whole set of exercises would be needed to help participants gain insights, using time that could go directly to habit taking. More time would have to be given to processing insight gained in preparation for judgment rather than uniting perception and judgment in habit-taking thorough exercises. Pragmatism, with its focus on practical affairs—i.e., getting a job— and its emphasis on habit-taking —i.e., learn SCANS skills—appears the more appropriate theory on which to base Success Skills.

Yet the Myers-Briggs theory has much to recommend it for job seekers. Most salient is the fact that participants can profile their personal preferences against vocational patterns based on the pool of empirical data about participants generated by the Myers-Briggs. Also, the extrovert and introvert distinctions are useful for those in job search apart from the judgment and perceptual classifications. There is also extensive useful experience to report on from the career counseling experience with Myers-Briggs.

The question thus became how could we work with both theories in Success Skills. The triadic pragmatic approach has an open architecture that, in principle, should be able to accommodate the wealth of intelligence accumulated by the Myers-Briggs effort. Moreover, pragmatism evaluates concepts by their results. So by pragmatic criteria, if the Myers-Briggs theory strengthens the program it should be included. The purpose of Success Skills is to provide a workable program for people who want to use the SCANS skills in their job search. Optimum workability is key. Purity of theory is irrelevant unless contradictions in theory result in confusing the participants and undercutting their job search. This is certainly a possibility and should not be ignored.

To insure workability and avoid confusion, the program maintains a clear distinction for the participants between the performance profile that goes with the pragmatic approach and the preference indicator that goes with the Myers-Briggs. The key use of the Myers-Briggs theory for the participants in the workshop is to assess their own personal preferences. That assessment will then be compared with their performance pattern. The *expectation* of match between Myers-Briggs and the pragmatic method can be seen in the appended chart. (See Appendix II.)

## Conclusion

I wrote this paper in the spirit of Roberta Kevelson's insistence that pragmatism itself learns by doing. What I have learned through my efforts in the field of worker training is that Peirce's approach, incorporated into protocols of intransitive triadic relationships, can be adapted for worker training. Moreover, Peirce's approach can incorporate other effective training tools such as that of Myers-Briggs. My experiences with Peirce and work also created renewed hope that some of my earlier efforts to use my cybernetic adaptation of Peirce for education and responding to the ecological crisis can be revisited and reinvigorated with the tools developed in the workshop (Ryan: 1993). In fact, I am currently working with The American Forum for Global Education, developing a workshop on sustainability for New York City High School teachers using the Earthscore

Method. I am also discussing redesigning curricula according to the Earthscore Method with colleagues at The New School for Social Research in New York City.

My application of Peirce to work also raises questions. What is the relation between Fuzzy Logic and Peirce's Continuum? Can the relation between skills and firstness and secondness be articulated in a clearer way? How will the questionnaire stand up to empirical testing? How can the questionnaire be refined to include the tenfold sign classification of Peirce? Can the questionnaire be used effectively in the academic world? What will the empirical data show my projection of the correlation between the Myers-Briggs preference indicator and the Peircian performance profile? Can Peirce's approach actually be of significant use on a large scale in the new world of work? Can such uses of Peirce maintain a continuity with the rich world of Peirce scholarship exemplified by the work of Roberta Kevelson?

## Appendix I: The Performance Profile Questionnaire

Please note that the questions are organized around themes. The theme is stated as a question and then the person has three either/or choices to make. What is unusual about this questionnaire is that options appear not once, but twice. For example:

What motto would you choose for your softball team?

| | | | | |
|---|---|---|---|---|
| a | Fight for Victory | or | b | Play Smart |
| a | Play Smart | or | b | Enjoy the Game |
| a | Enjoy the Game | or | b | Fight for Victory |

It takes a minute to get used to this repetition of options. Some people are more comfortable reading the whole group of options before they make any choices. Others are more comfortable making their choice as the options appear. You are never asked to repeat a choice between the same two options. All questions must be answered for the profile to be as useful as possible. You are asked to circle the number and letter to the left of the choice you make between the two options offered (a or b).

As a detective would you be better at:

| | | | | |
|---|---|---|---|---|
| 1a | finding evidence of the crime | or | 1b | figuring out who is guilty |
| 2a | reading a suspect's mood | or | 2b | finding evidence of the crime |
| 3a | figuring out who is guilty | or | 3b | reading a suspect's mood |

You are on a team preparing a report about a product for a potential market. Do you think you would be better at:

| | | | | |
|---|---|---|---|---|
| 4a | researching the product | or | 4b | researching the market for the product |
| 5a | researching the market for the product | or | 5b | presenting the report |
| 6a | presenting the report | or | 6b | researching the product |

Your team is dividing up tasks. Do you think you would be better at:

| | | | | |
|---|---|---|---|---|
| 7a | analyzing a problem | or | 7b | imagining a creative solution |
| 8a | imagining a creative solution | or | 8b | applying a creative solution |
| 9a | applying a creative solution | or | 9b | analyzing a problem |

In negotiations that you take part in, are you better at:

| | | | | |
|---|---|---|---|---|
| 10a | inventing options | or | 10b | focusing on your interests |
| 11a | using objective criteria | or | 11b | inventing options |
| 12a | focusing on your interests | or | 12b | using objective criteria |

Are you better at:

| | | | | |
|---|---|---|---|---|
| 13a | institutionalizing change | or | 13b | initiating change |
| 14a | initiating change | or | 14b | resisting change |
| 15a | resisting change | or | 15b | institutionalizing change |

Do you consider yourself better at:

| | | | | |
|---|---|---|---|---|
| 16a | discussing facts | or | 16b | discussing overall patterns |
| 17a | discussing possibilities | or | 17b | discussing facts |
| 18a | discussing overall patterns | or | 18b | discussing possibilities |

In conversation, do you think you are better at:

| | | | | |
|---|---|---|---|---|
| 19a | initiating a discussion | or | 19b | playing devil's advocate |
| 20a | playing devil's advocate | or | 20b | mediating a discussion |
| 21a | mediating a discussion | or | 21b | initiating a discussion |

If you were asked to resolve a conflict where both sides seemed near right and were of equal strength, would your best effort be to:

| | | | | |
|---|---|---|---|---|
| 22a | flip a coin | or | 22b | suggest arm wrestling |
| 23a | suggest arm wrestling | or | 23b | reason about the conflict |
| 24a | reason about the conflict | or | 24b | flip a coin |

Your amateur theater group is casting the Marx Brothers. Would you give a better performance as:

| | | | | |
|---|---|---|---|---|
| 25a | the "reasonable" Groucho | or | 25b | the emotional Harpo |
| 26a | the troublemaker Chico | or | 26b | the "reasonable" Groucho |
| 27a | the emotional Harpo | or | 27b | the troublemaker Chico |

Do you think you could write a better essay about:

| | | | | |
|---|---|---|---|---|
| 28a | the past | or | 28b | the future |
| 29a | the present | or | 29b | the past |
| 30a | the future | or | 30b | the present |

In an amateur theater company, do you think you would be better:

| | | | | |
|---|---|---|---|---|
| 31a | doing the lighting | or | 31b | directing |
| 32a | directing | or | 32b | acting |
| 33a | acting | or | 33b | doing the lighting |

Walking in the woods with your still camera, you come across an abandoned rusted car in a meadow. If all of the car were in a good light, could you take a better picture of:

| | | | | |
|---|---|---|---|---|
| 34a | the rusted roof | or | 34b | the exposed engine |
| 35a | the car in the meadow | or | 35b | the rusted roof |
| 36a | the exposed engine | or | 36b | the car in the meadow |

Using a still camera with good light for all the shots, do you think you could take a better picture of:

| | | | | |
|---|---|---|---|---|
| 37a | a particular gnarled branch | or | 37b | the tree as a whole |
| 38a | the bark of the tree | or | 38b | a particular gnarled branch |
| 39a | the tree as a whole | or | 39b | the bark of the tree |

You have been asked to analyze a movie. Do you think you would do a better job analyzing:

| | | | | |
|---|---|---|---|---|
| 40a | close-ups of faces | or | 40b | the action sequences |
| 41a | the action sequences | or | 41b | the overall plot |
| 42a | the overall plot | or | 42b | close-ups of faces |

You have just been in a minor auto accident. Nobody is hurt. Do you think you would be more articulate about:

| | | | | |
|---|---|---|---|---|
| 43a | the facts of the accident | or | 43b | who was at fault |
| 44a | who was at fault | or | 44b | your feelings |
| 45a | your feelings | or | 45b | the facts of the accident |

If you could live forever, which role do you think you would perform better?

| | | | | |
|---|---|---|---|---|
| 46a | a child | or | 46b | a parent |
| 47a | a parent | or | 47b | a grandparent |
| 48a | a grandparent | or | 48b | a child |

## Key to Scoring:

Circle the answers you gave in the lists below.

| 1st Skill Set | 2nd Skill Set | 3rd Skill Set |
|---|---|---|
| | 1a | 1b |
| 2a | 2b | |
| 3b | | 3a |
| | 4a | 4b |
| 5b | | 5a |
| 6a | 6b | |
| 7b | 7a | |
| 8a | | 8b |
| | 9b | 9a |
| 10a | 10b | |
| 11b | | 11a |
| | 12a | |
| | | 12b |
| 13b | | 13a |
| 14a | 14b | |
| | 15a | |
| | | 15b |
| | 16a | |
| | | 16b |
| 17a | 17b | |
| 18b | | 18a |
| 19a | 19b | |
| | 20a | |
| | | 20b |
| 21b | | 21a |
| 22a | 22b | |
| | 23a | |
| | | 23b |
| 24b | | 24a |
| 25b | | 25a |
| | 26a | |

| 1st Skill Set (continued) | 2nd Skill Set | 3rd Skill Set |
|---|---|---|
| | | 26b |
| 27a | 27b | |
| | 28a | |
| | | 28b |
| 29a | 29b | |
| 30b | | 30a |
| | 31a | |
| | | 31b |
| 32b | | 32a |
| 33a | 33b | |
| 34a | 34b | |
| 35b | | 35a |
| | 36a | |
| 36b | | |
| | 37a | |
| | | 37b |
| 38a | 38b | |
| 39b | | 39a |
| 40a | 40b | |
| | 41a | |
| | | 41b |
| 42b | | 42a |
| | 43a | |
| | | 43b |
| 44b | | 44a |
| 45a | 45b | |
| 46a | 46b | |
| | 47a | |
| | | 47b |
| 48b | | 48a |

Add up the number of circles in each skill set:
1st Skill Set Multiply by 2 ____________________
2nd Skill Set Multiply by 2 ____________________
3rd Skill Set Multiply by 2 ____________________
Totals:
1st Set_____% 2nd Set_____% 3rd Set_____%

In this profile no one set of skills can have more that 64 %. Notice that the total percentage adds up to 96%, not 100%. You can add the remaining 4% to the set you think most appropriate after reading the following interpretation of the three different generic skill sets.

## Interpretation for Participants

Your self-assessment show that you have developed a certain ratio among three very generic, and very fundamental, skill sets. Most likely, you will score highest in one of the three skill areas. Let us look at what it means to score high in any one of these skill sets.

A high score in the first skill set means that your sensitivities and intelligence are strongest when paying attention to the qualities of things, qualities such as beauty or rust, the color purple or the mood that shows on someone's face. You like to initiate things and have a fresh imagination for inventing options. You can immerse yourself in the present like a child. You can enjoy art. You are creative and like to work with possibilities. You like spontaneity and freedom. It is relatively easy for you to be yourself and do your own thing without much regard for what others think.

A high score in the second skill set means that you are very capable of dealing with the actual world. You can command the facts, advance your own interests, and fight for what you want. You can tackle problems and get things done. Specific tasks are easy for you. You can be forceful and play the devil's advocate very well. You have a good memory and a sense of detail. The concrete world is your oyster.

A high score in the third skill set means that your mind does very well with figuring out patterns such as piecing together a plot or a trail of guilt. While you can learn from tradition, you can also organize yourself for the future and apply creative ideas. You can see the whole picture and are interested in patterns, laws, and habits. You like to pay attention to how people are interpreting what you say. You are a capable mediator and appreciate context. You are good at "if...then" thinking.

Rarely will people show a perfect balance of all three skills at 32% each. Our aptitudes and experience lead most of us to develop a strongest skill area, a next strongest and a weakest, appropriate to our lives. For example, someone may show 34% in the third set, 12% in the second set and 50% in the first skill set. This means that while that person has given 34%, about a third of his energy to successfully developing skills, such as if...then reasoning, in the third set, he is weak in dealing with the actual world, 12%, and strong in dealing with the intuitive realm of skills in the first set, 50%.

Take a minute and complete your profile by adding your remaining 4% to the skill set or sets you think appropriate.

Final Percentage

First Set ________%
Second Set ________%
Third Set ________%

# Appendix II

Each participant's Skills Profile will result in a percentage distribution of what are considered the three generic skill sets referencing Peirce. So a person may show 50% in the second skill set, 30% in the third skill set, and 20% in the first set. In the language of Myers-Briggs the 50% would be dominant, the 30% auxiliary, and the 20% would be tertiary. (This would be indicated by the appropriate sequence of numbers, 231, the person would be an ISTJ or an ESTP.) So mapping these generic skills onto Myers-Briggs (mindful of the theoretical problems cited above), we can "loosely" expect the following distribution in the Type Table. Please note that there is no difference between the I's and the E's in this array. (Set skills are given by number 1, 2 and 3. There is a duplication of the first skill set in the N and the F classification with N tending toward the third set and F tending toward the second set. In this chart this reduplication of the first skill set has been ignored. This is admittedly crude and can be refined in multiple ways such as by fuzzy set theory, given the time and resources.)

Basically this is a translation from the Myers-Briggs to the three sets of skills. Every Myers-Briggs type, given that their performance skills developed in accord with their preferences, would have performance skills in the three sets with the strongest on the left and the weakest on the right in the chart below.

| | | | |
|---|---|---|---|
| ISTJ<br>231 | ISFJ<br>213 | INFJ<br>132 | INTJ<br>132 |
| ISTP<br>321 | ISFP<br>123 | INFP<br>123 | INTP<br>312 |
| ESTP<br>231 | ESFP<br>213 | ENFP<br>132 | ENTP<br>132 |
| ESTJ<br>321 | ESFJ<br>123 | ENFJ<br>123 | ENTJ<br>312 |

# References


Apel, Karl-Otto. 1981. *Charles S. Peirce, from Pragmatism to Pragmaticism*, University of Massachusetts Press, Amherst.

Bateson, Gregory. 1972. *Steps to an Ecology of Mind,* Ballantine, New York.

Bridges, William. 1994. *Job Shift,* Addison Wesley, New York.

Carnevale, Anthony. 1990. *Workplace Basics,* Jossey Bass, San Francisco.

Lacan, Jacques. 1978. *The Four Fundamental Concepts of Psycho—Analysis,* W. W. Norton, New York.

McCulloch, Warren. 1965. *Embodiments of Mind,* M.I.T. Press, Cambridge.

McNeil, Daniel and Freidberger, Paul. 1993. *Fuzzy Logic*, Simon and Schuster, New York.

Murphey, Murray. 1961. *The Development of Peirce's Philosophy,* Harvard University Press, Cambridge.

Myers, I.B. and McCaulley, M. 1985; revised from 1962. *Manual: A Guide to the Development and Use of the Myers-Briggs Type Indicator,* Consulting Psychologists Press, Palo Alto.

Peirce, Charles S. 1931–35. Collected Papers. C. Harthshorne and P. Weiss (eds.) vols. I–VI. Harvard University Press, Cambridge.

Rifkin, Jeremy. 1995. *The End of Work*, G.P. Putnam's Sons, New York.

Rosenthal, Sandra . 1994. *Charles Peirce's Pragmatic Pluralism*, SUNY Press Albany.

Ryan, Paul. 1993. *Video Mind, Earth Mind,* Peter Lang, New York.

Sebeok, Thomas, A. 1981. *The Play of Musement*, Indiana University Press, Bloomington.

*Success Skills Manual*. 1995. ETI, Ringwood, New Jersey.

United States Department of Commerce. 1992. *Skills and Tasks for Jobs: a SCANS Report for America 2000*, NTIS PB92–181379, Washington D. C.

* Special thanks to the worker-participants and to my co-workers at ETI, particularly Rita Carey, Barbara Brandt, Hiram Quinones, and Mary Polo.

# Chapter Six
# An Aye for an I: the Semiotics of *Lex Talionis* in the Bible

**Bernard S. Jackson**

The word that I would use to describe Bobbie Kevelson — both her oeuvre and her personality — is "challenging," in the friendliest of senses. Her work is challenging, and she continually challenges her colleagues to transcend their own limitations. If it is not too heretical to say so, she has functioned, in contemporary legal semiotics, as an archetypal Sender, one who invests others with the Goals and Competences to tell their own stories.

Not long ago, Bobbie published an article on the *lex talionis*,[1] in which she generously referred to some work of mine in the 1970s. I would like here to repay the compliment: to indicate how my thinking on problems like the *lex talionis* has been affected by my subsequent foray into semiotics, and to use this example to indicate an area where Bobbie's legal semiotics and my own appear to intersect.

I came to semiotics neither from philosophy nor linguistics nor literature. I came to it from comparative ancient law. My doctoral training was in ancient Jewish law.[2] Frequently, one encountered problems of interpretation of biblical texts, where the Bible itself provided insufficient data to come to any strong conclusions. Since the discovery of the Laws of Hammurabi in 1902, and increasingly in the light of the subsequent uncovering of pre-Hammurabi Law Codes, scholars have often resorted to comparative evidence in order to fill gaps in our knowledge of particular systems of ancient law, and to solve problems of interpretation. Such comparisons have not been restricted to the geographical area of the ancient Near East; Roman and Greek laws were included in a conception which some have described as *Antike Rechtsgeschichte*. Sadly, the enhancement of our data did not coincide with the period of greatest interest in underlying comparative theory. The "comparative jurisprudence" of Sir Henry Maine was already regarded as dated. In short, a scholarly epoch where theory was not matched by available data was succeeded by one in which data was used with little concern for underlying theory. At best, the "control" over the use of comparative sources to fill gaps in our knowledge of particular problems of ancient law was conceived in terms of often vague comparison of surrounding social context.

It was dissatisfaction with this state of affairs — the perception, from a Sender whose identity remains obscure, of a "lack" — which prompted me to embark upon a personal intellectual quest. Some of the issues which arise from the statement of talion in *Exodus* 21:22–25 may be used by way of illustration. First, there was a problem of meaning: what did "an eye for an eye" really mean to the original users? Some ancient sources seemed to indicate that we should take the phrase "literally": the Roman Twelve Tables prescribed *talio* for maiming another's limb, while explicitly including the possibility of monetary composition.[3] The Laws of Hammurabi include the following:

| | |
|---|---|
| 196. | If a man has put out the eye of a free man, they shall put out his eye. |
| 197. | If he breaks the bone of a (free) man, they shall break his bone. |
| 198–99 | (provide for money payments where the victims are persons of lower status or slaves) |
| 200 | If the man knocks out the tooth of a (free) man equal (in rank) to him(self), they shall knock out his tooth ... |

By contrast, the Rabbis were unequivocal: "'An eye for an eye' — that means money." The problem was compounded by the fact that very few instances can be found in the Bible of the actual implementation of talionic punishment: the one clear example involved the mutilation of a foreign, captured king, who is made by the narrator to view his fate as an instance of *divine* justice![4]

In debating this issue, students of Biblical law tended to line up in fairly predictable secular v. religious teams (I was in the former). The secularists saw the monetary "explanation" as unduly influenced by later religious tradition, and as essentially "apologetic" (for reasons to be explained). The religious team viewed the secularists as equally motivated by an underlying ideology, that of denying any distinctiveness to the biblical tradition, and reducing it to the common fare of other ancient (and impliedly less ethically-sensitive) cultures. In short, the pragmatics of the issue appeared to dominate the semantics; in the absence of clear criteria favouring one side or the other, one decided in accordance with the team with which one wanted to be identified. Nor, or course, was the line-up limited to religious v. secular. The words which Matthew put into the mouth of Jesus in the Sermon on the Mount added further tensions (*Matthew* 5:38–39):

> You have heard that it was said, 'An eye for an eye and a tooth for a tooth.' But I say to you, Do not resist one who is evil. But if any one strikes you on the right cheek, turn to him the other also ...

Here, one ethic was being superseded, or at the very least supplemented, by a new, superior morality. "An eye for an eye" was thus presented as inferior, even crude or barbaric (at least, again, if viewed "literally"). The Jewish secularists at least took heart from the fact that biblical law was not alone in espousing such a view.

The discovery of pre-Hammurabi codes — where the sanctions for bodily injuries were "fixed fines" rather than physical retaliation — prompted explicit debate on the significance of talion in evolutionary terms. Talion had previously been regarded as "primitive," an aspect of the vengeance system — redeemable, at best, by the understanding that it served to impose a limit: a single eye, and nothing but an eye, for the loss of an eye. The fact that the pre-Hammurabi codes, both Sumerian (Ur-Nammu[5]) and Akkadian (Eshnunna[6]), indicated specific sums of money for bodily injuries was seized upon by A.S. Diamond as sufficient to reverse the previous understanding of the normal evolution of the law in such cases.[7] These "fixed fines" did not represent "real compensation" (as understood by later lawyers[8]), but rather were arbitrary "sums" representing rough-and-ready justice. It was only later, he suggested, that this was seen as inadequate, and was replaced by the (often religiously-inspired) penal provisions of talion (which later, in due course, gave way to real systems of compensation).[9]

What I found particularly unsatisfactory about this debate was the lack of any real criteria as to what might count as an evolutionary progression. In the absence of such criteria, latter-day diffusionists have rejected entirely the possibility of evolutionary schemes, and sought explanations in terms of direct historical influence, sometimes entirely eschewing controls in terms of comparable, or even compatible, social conditions.[10] In the present context, a diffusionist solution was certainly attractive. There are many different ways in which the principle of talion might be, and has been, expressed. The choice of an eye, and (especially) a tooth, is hardly inevitable, yet both are found not only in the biblical formulations (or at least two of the three of them) but also in the Laws of Hammurabi. More generally, we find evidence that biblical law represented, in some ways, the climax of a scribal tradition of written law.[11] But this in itself presented as much a puzzle as a solution: in terms of economy, material culture, and social stratification, the Babylonian society of the second millennium appeared far more "advanced" than that of the Israelite monarchy. Did that make no difference to the possibility of influence? And if it did, what might that difference be?

In the absence of any real debate within ancient law at that time on such underlying theoretical and methodological issues (each side did, of course, accuse the other of *a priori* reasoning), I decided to look around, and see what insight I could glean from other sources. I had not heard of semiotics at that time. The directions for my initial quest were prompted by three "big names": Lévi-Strauss, Chomsky, and Piaget. Of these, the first had written about the "primitive mind" in contexts quite close to the concerns of ancient law. He was associated with "structuralism", and the term "structural" was also used by and of both Chomsky in linguistics and Piaget in cognitive development. (Indeed, the last, as I soon discovered, had himself written a book under that title.) My interest — and even more, my resolve — was fortified by the Edinburgh Gifford Lectures of 1972–73, in which the "quartet" of Anthony Kenny, John Lucas, C.H. Waddington, and Christopher Longuet-Higgins debated the development of mind, paying particular attention to the models offered by Chomsky and Piaget.[12]

There existed, in Britain at that time, a funding agency called the "Social Science Research Council".[13] The S.S.R.C. gave me the wherewithal, in 1981, to take six months off from my normal (and then heavily administrative) duties, to pursue further the theoretical possibilities of "structuralism" for law. I was provided with some funds for travel, as well as staff replacement. Within six months I managed to meet Chomsky (who was very interested), Lévi-Strauss (who was not), and Greimas (who didn't have a clue what I was up to). Fortunately, when I presented myself, without an appointment (no Contract) in Greimas's seedy office, he was accompanied by Landowski, who served both as translator and protector. Landowski secured Greimas's escape, but he and I rapidly became firm friends.

What was it that took me to *Rue Monsieur du Prince*, and how could such an encounter further my perplexities about the methodology of comparative ancient law? Some years before, the Paris Chamber of Commerce had commissioned the Greimassian group to write an analysis of some new French Commercial Law legislation, that on *sociétés commerciales*. The commission, I have reason to believe, was undertaken with some sense of bemusement, as well as challenge, but the result was summarized in what has become a classic article.[14] It was this that had attracted my attention. Whether, without it, the particular development of structuralism offered by Paris Semiotics would have attracted my attention, may well be doubtful. On such things, do academic careers turn. If blame is to be attributed, the Paris Chamber of Commerce has much to answer for.

It may seem odd that anyone should pursue an interest in an apparently formalist and purely synchronic account of sense construction, when the object was to enrich the methodology of comparative ancient law. I was increasingly convinced, however, that any exercise in making sense of ancient legal texts, both individually and in their historical relationships, needed to be based upon some conception of making sense in general. At the same time, it was always my intention to try to form a view of the relationship between such synchronic studies and other disciplines which offered an account of (what might be called) diachronic semiotics: theories of the *development* of thought and language. From Piaget, I was led to Kohlberg and Bruner. Latterly, I have been able to offer my students a synopsis of these traditions,[15] one in which I claim that semiotics can provide a useful integrating framework for other, more particular, disciplines of sense construction (particularly, aspects of linguistics and psychology), but within which, no doubt, further synthesis of the synchronic and diachronic dimensions remains to be effected.

Along the way, I have succumbed to the temptation to apply aspects of both the synchronic and diachronic models to ancient law.[16] I have also hinted at the kind of redirection which Historical Jurisprudence may receive from these sources.[17] But I have not, as yet, attempted to re-address directly the kind of substantive problems of comparative legal history which prompted my search in the first place. I am now ready to begin such a review. I do so with the instance presented to us by Bobbie Kevelson: the *lex talionis*.

The earliest collection of biblical laws in which the *lex talionis* occurs is the "Covenant Code" of *Exodus* 21:1–23:19. It occurs in the following paragraph (*Exodus* 21:22–25):

> 22 When men strive together, and hurt a woman with child, and her children come out, and yet no harm follows, the one who hurt her shall be fined, according as the woman's husband shall lay upon him; and he shall pay as the judges determine.
> 23 If any harm follows, then you shall give life for life,
> 24 eye for eye, tooth for tooth, hand for hand, foot for foot,
> 25 burn for burn, wound for wound, stripe for stripe.

Though the laws of the Covenant Code individually, and even the compilation of the Code as a whole, are generally dated earlier than the other biblical law collections (certainly in their present forms), it does not necessarily follow that every element in the Covenant Code dates from this earliest stratum. The Code shows various signs of later editorial activity,[18] and the paragraph here quoted is one of the most problematic. I argued nearly 25 years ago that much of it, and certainly the talionic formula, represented such later editions, reflecting changing understandings of the precise situation regulated (particularly, whether the pregnant woman caught up in the brawl survived or died).[19] In syntactic terms, the formula of vv.24–25 is a gratuitous addition. We have been told that there shall be "life for life" if any "harm" (*aswn*) follows; "eye for eye ... stripe for stripe" must refer to a non-fatal incident, but if it does indeed function as the apodosis to a norm regulating non-fatal injuries,[20] we lack the protasis to which this applies. That would make vv.24–25 unique in the Covenant Code. However, one of the later biblical collections does supply a more complete version of this norm. In *Leviticus* 24:19–21, we find:

> 19 When a man causes a disfigurement in his neighbor, as he has done it shall be done to him,
>
> 20 fracture for fracture, eye for eye, tooth for tooth; as he has disfigured a man, he shall be disfigured.
>
> 21 He who kills a beast shall make it good; and he who kills a man shall be put to death.

Even here, the formula does not appear as a simple apodosis. We do have a protasis, "when a man causes a disfigurement in his neighbour", and indeed the context of the giving of this law is said to have been an incident involving a quarrel.[21] The formula here serves as a set of concrete examples of a general principle. Indeed, it stands at the centre, not only of this small "sandwich" or "envelope", but rather of an elaborate literary chiasm:

| | | |
|---|---|---|
| G | 13 | And the LORD said to Moses, |
| F | 14 | "Bring out of the camp him who cursed; and let all who heard him lay their hands upon his head, and let all the congregation stone him. |
| E | 15 | And say to the people of Israel, Whoever curses his God shall bear his sin. |
| | 16 | He who blasphemes the name of the LORD shall be put to death; all the congregation shall stone him; |
| D | | the sojourner as well as the native, when he blasphemes the Name, shall be put to death. |
| C | 17 | He who kills a man shall be put to death. |

| | | |
|---|---|---|
| B | 18 | He who kills a beast shall make it good, life for life. |
| A | 19 | When a man causes a disfigurement in his neighbor, as he has done it shall be done to him, |
| | 20 | fracture for fracture, eye for eye, tooth for tooth; as he has disfigured a man, he shall be disfigured. |
| B | 21 | He who kills a beast shall make it good; |
| C | | and he who kills a man shall be put to death. |
| D | 22 | You shall have one law for the sojourner and for the native; for I am the LORD your God." |
| E | 23 | So Moses spoke to the people of Israel; |
| F | | and they brought him who had cursed out of the camp, and stoned him with stones. |
| G | | Thus the people of Israel did as the LORD commanded Moses. |

A similar pattern occurs in the third biblical legal collection (*Deuteronomy* 19:16–21):

| | |
|---|---|
| 16 | If a malicious witness rises against any man to accuse him of wrongdoing, |
| 17 | then both parties to the dispute shall appear before the LORD, before the priests and the judges who are in office in those days; |
| 18 | the judges shall inquire diligently, and if the witness is a false witness and has accused his brother falsely, |
| 19 | then you shall do to him as he had meant to do to his brother; so you shall purge the evil from the midst of you. |
| 20 | And the rest shall hear, and fear, and shall never again commit any such evil among you. |
| 21 | Your eye shall not pity; it shall be life for life, eye for eye, tooth for tooth, hand for hand, foot for foot. |

The talionic *principle* is here stated as the apodosis of a norm concerning (what we might call) perjury: "You shall do to him (the perjurer) as he had meant to do to his brother" (v.19). Of course, what he had sought to do may not have involved a physical sanction. We are told that the malicious witness accuses the victim of "wrongdoing", and this might entail sanctions of a variety of kinds. Nevertheless, the passage concludes by reiterating the concrete formula, thus endowing the paragraph with further end-weight.

This rapid survey of the three principal passages leads to the following conclusion: in not one of them is the talionic formula stated as the straightforward apodosis of a casuistically expressed law. In the first, it completely lacks a protasis; in the second and third it is stated as a vivid exemplification of a more general principle. In both formal and substantive terms, both the law of physical injuries in *Leviticus* and that of perjury in *Deuteronomy* would be complete without the "eye for an eye" formula.

We must take these literary phenomena into account when coming to a conclusion regarding the meaning of the law. This much, I venture to suggest, requires little assistance from semiotics. When, however, we pose the question of meaning more directly, I believe that insights from semiotics can make a crucial contribution to our historical understanding.

The version of semiotics which I advocate is one which places considerable stress, in a variety of ways, on the concept of narrative. Increasingly, I have come to appreciate the difference between two different approaches to the meaning of language, one of which I term "narrative", the other "semantic". What we nowadays understand by the "literal" meaning of a sentence is a "semantic" form of meaning: we replace one set of linguistic signifiers with another set (a paraphrase), such that the scope of the latter is equivalent to the scope of the former. In a legal context, we say that the literal meaning of a clause of a statute is everything "covered" by the words of the statute. This is based upon a spatial analogy (consonant, perhaps, with the connotations of the term "literal" itself, its Latin etymology being associated with writing). Thus, everything which falls "under" the umbrella of the sentence, and its individual words, is so "covered"; everything which does not fall under it is excluded.

There is, however, a quite different approach to the meaning of language, one which identifies that meaning not with an equally broad (but no broader) linguistic paraphrase, but rather with the typical images evoked by the words of the sentence.[22] I am increasingly convinced that we ought to read the language of biblical law in this way.

Take, for example, the following text on the rights of an owner on encountering an intruder on his premises (*Exodus* 22:1–2):

| | |
|---|---|
| 1 | If a thief is found breaking in, and is struck so that he dies, there shall be no bloodguilt for him; |
| 2 | but if the sun has risen upon him, there shall be bloodguilt for him. |

If we take those two verses together, the first verse refers to a nocturnal intruder because the second verse says "but if the sun has risen upon him" (i.e. refers to a daytime incident). That, indeed, is the traditional understanding. But v.1 in fact says nothing about night. Accordingly, some biblical scholars have argued that we can trace an historical development in this area of the law. Originally, the householder was entitled to kill the intruding burglar both by day and night (there being no restriction in v.1); it was only later, when someone decided to add verse 2, that a distinction was made and the first verse was taken to be restricted to the nocturnal intruder.

On a purely literal (semantic) reading we would have to say that the words of v.1 do indeed cover both day and night; it is only when we add the second verse that a distinction between day and night is introduced, thus by implication restricting the first verse to night. However, if we adopt a narrative approach, viewing verse 1 as belonging to a discourse of restricted code rather than elaborated code, we may conclude that the stereotypical activity of the burglar indeed was nocturnal[23] and that this would be understood in the discourse community to which the text was addressed. Thus the narrative image evoked by this verse, as opposed to the full range of meaning of its words, indicates in itself that a nocturnal intrusion is contemplated.

A second example again derives from the "Covenant Code" (*Exodus* 21:35):

> When one man's ox hurts another's, so that it dies, then they shall sell the live ox and divide the price of it; and the dead beast also they shall divide.

The Rabbis later interpreted the remedy here as "half damages": the actual loss of the owner of the dead ox was calculated and the owner of the live ox had to pay half that amount in monetary damages.[24] But that is not what the Biblical text actually says. According to the literal meaning, the price of the living animal is to be divided (it is taken to the market and sold) and the carcass itself is also physically divided. If the two animals had originally been of equal value, then such division of both price and carcass will indeed produce half damages. But such an exactly equal division of the loss will be produced only if it so happens that the two animals were originally of identical value. The Rabbis noted the effects in cases where the two animals were not originally of identical value — in order to prove that literal division of price and carcass cannot have been intended; the text really meant calculation and payment of half damages.[25]

I believe that on a narrative reading of the original text the question which would have been asked was: "what is the *typical* case envisaged by this verse?" Typically oxen are — oxen. There may be some prize winners, but typically in this situation we may assume not that the animals were of *identical* value but that they were of more or less equivalent value. Thus division of price and carcass will not produce exactly equal division of loss but rather an arbitrary division which will equate to a rough-and-ready form of loss division — more or less equal, but not precisely so. The practical point of the rule is that the parties can operate the remedy themselves: they do not have to go to a court to assess the damages; they go to the market, they cut up the carcass, there is no need for any third party adjudication. But this reading is premised upon the social understanding that the oxen are indeed of *more or less equal* value.

But then the Rabbis ask this question: what if the victim ox were hugely valuable, so valuable indeed even that the carcass of the dead ox is worth more than the selling price of the live ox? In such a case, the net result of division of price and carcass is that the owner of the goring ox is actually going to be enriched: he is going to get half of the value of something which is worth more than the entire value of his original ox (as well as half the market price of that ox). The Rabbis used this case as a *reductio ad absurdum* of the "literal" application of the remedy.[26] But the *reductio ad absurdum* works only if we read the biblical verse semantically, i.e. only if we assume that because the biblical verse says nothing about the relative values of the oxen therefore the issue of relative value is irrelevant. If, however, we take a narrative (restricted code) approach to the text and ask what would have been its original social understanding, then we may import the assumption that the oxen were of more or less equal value and that it would have appeared absurd to apply the same procedure in the extraordinary case where the carcass was worth more than the value of the live ox.

Let us return now to talion. If we were to adopt a "semantic" interpretation of vv.24–25, then a maximal interpretation of the institution is likely to result: talionic punishment *must* be imposed, irrespective of the circumstances in which the eye, tooth, etc. has been lost (since no limiting circumstances are stated), and irrespective of the physical condition of the offender (who might have only one eye already). The mandatory status of the rule would be derived from the fact that no criteria are stated for the application of a discretion; the unlimited range of the rule is equally derived from the lack of stated limitations. But to read the rule in this way not only abstracts it from its textual context but also imposes conventions of (semantic) reading more appropriate to, and no doubt derived from, our greater familiarity with the reading of modern legislation. If, on the other hand, we ask the question: what are the typical cases evoked by this language, then (a) we must look elsewhere in the Bible for evidence of what were then regarded as typical cases, and (b) we must be prepared to say, as we were in the case of the goring ox, that some cases would not have been regarded as within the meaning of the formula, even though they are "covered" by the meanings of its words.[27]

Once we look for textual clues to the images evoked by the talionic formula, we can identify some unsurprising limitations. The most obvious context is that of *Leviticus* 24, which appears to refer to intentional (if not necessarily premeditated) disfigurement. We should not, therefore, infer that "an eye for an eye" would have been regarded as appropriate even in cases of accidental disfigurement, despite the fact that the language of the formula imports no such limitation.

What of the nature of the sanction itself? There is abundant evidence in the Bible of private settlement where the kin are entitled to exact vengeance. If that institution, technically called "ransom" (*kofer*), applied even to capital offences (both murder and adultery are mentioned in this context) — as it did, in my view, for much of the biblical period[28] — then surely it must have applied equally to sanctions for non-fatal injuries. In this respect, both later Jewish[29] and external sources[30] provide support.

I turn now to the developmental question. What criteria might be available by which to decide where to locate talion in evolutionary terms? I am attracted to the view that typical patterns of development can indeed be traced, using a combination of cognitive, linguistic and literary criteria. The model of which I shall here make the most direct use is that of Jerome Bruner,[31] and in particular his sequence of forms of representation as encountered in the development of the language of children. He distinguishes three stages: enactive, ikonic, symbolic. Bruner's work stands broadly within the Piagetian tradition, and it is not difficult to draw parallels between this sequence and the more general cognitive structures of Piaget (which, for Piaget, underlie the development of language). The model may be further enriched by consideration of the cognitive and communicational structures of literacy (as opposed to orality) — as discussed by scholars like Walter Ong and Basil Bernstein, and particularly the latter's use of the distinction between "restricted" and "elaborated" code.[32]

Such criteria certainly help us to assess the relationship between different (discursive) *expressions* of talion; I am less convinced that we have grounds for any evolutionary interpretation of either the *practice* of talion (if there were such) or the *idea* of talion in the abstract.[33]

Bruner's notion of "enactive" representation is, in a sense, pre-linguistic.[34] The infant senses a need and learns that certain actions regularly serve to fulfil that need. The actions may later be performed without either sensing or fulfilling the need, but will still evoke the experiences of such need or fulfilment. Piaget had observed the behaviour of a six month old girl, Lucienne, who several times pulled the folds of the material on the side of her cot towards her and then each time released it. She then moved her hand, closely closed, to her eyes, and cautiously opened it, looking attentively at her fingers. She repeated this more than ten times. Bruner observed: "Lucienne expects to see the fold of cloth in her hand, having clenched her hand "as if" the cloth were still in it."[35] This reflects the fact that "action and external experience are fused."[36] The child here perceives "an irreversible and fixed succession of static images, each connected with an action".[37] The enactive form of representation, Bruner stressed, is "motivated". Even "looking" commences as a form of "enactive representation": it is not an unmotivated observation of what is there, but a selective activity, seeking performance of a goal, being "geared to a visual or auditory pattern" through which the child has become sensitive to some class of external events.[38] Later, we encounter a second stage, that of "ikonic representation", characterized by the capacity "to represent the world to himself by an image or spatial schema that is relatively independent of action".[39] We are thus moving from actual fulfilment of narrative goals to virtual fulfilment.

Can this tell us anything about any of the modes of expression of talion? In one respect, it can. The formula in *Exodus* can be divided, for both formal and substantive reasons, into two: "a life for a life" on the one hand, "an eye for an eye ... etc." on the other. In fact, the translation "a life for a life" is an interpretation, the Hebrew (*nefesh tahat nefesh*) being translatable either as "a person for a person" or (making some anachronistic assumptions) "a soul for a soul". There is, I have argued, strong evidence from both other biblical sources and the ancient Near East that "a life for a life" in *Exodus* 22:23 in fact refers to substitution of persons. The law here was dealing originally not with death of the pregnant woman, but rather the loss of the foetus, and the offender who caused such loss was required to render a person (from his family) in substitution. The Middle Assyrian Laws provide as follows (§A50):[40]

1. [If a man] has struck a married [woman] and caused her to lose [the fruit of her womb, the wife of the man] who [caused] the (other) married woman [to lose] the fruit of [her womb] shall be treated as [he has] treated her; [for the fruit

of] her womb he pays (on the principle of) a life (for a life), *napsate umalla*.

2. But, if that woman dies, the man shall be put to death; for the fruit of her womb he pays (on the principle of) a life (for a life), *napsate umalla*.
3. Or, if that woman's husband has no son (and) his wife has been struck and has cast the fruit of her womb the striker shall be put to death. If the fruit of the womb is a girl, he none the less pays (on the principle of) a life (for a life), *napsate umalla*.

The same Semitic root (*napsate* = *nefesh*) is used in both the Assyrian text and the Hebrew Bible. Moreover *Leviticus* 24:18 uses the same biblical expression, *nefesh tahat nefesh*, to reiterate the principle of compensation in respect of animals: "He who kills a beast shall make it good, life for life." This clearly means that he substitutes a live animal for the one whose death he has caused, not that an animal of the offender is killed in exchange.

In general, the laws of the "Covenant Code" reflect a situation of weak institutionalisation. They appear to be addressed, in many cases, not to institutions of the State (police, courts) but rather to the parties involved in disputes, guiding them as to measures of self-help which they are entitled, even recommended, to take. This applies through much of biblical law — even to homicide, where "prosecution" is in the hands of the "redeemer of blood", a kinsman of the deceased.[41] Thus, in the context of *Exodus* 21:22–23 we may assume that any initiatives are taken by the victims themselves, not the State authorities. Perhaps the unusual second person expression in the apodosis of v.23, "and *you* shall give", reflects not so much "pathos",[42] but rather an understandable recommendation that the family of the offender should take the initiative in providing the substitute, and not wait for the distressed woman and her husband to have to come forward and make demands. At any rate, the form of representation could be described as "enactive": it is through the performance of the action of giving and taking a substitute that the lack is recognised and met. In due course, no doubt, the presence of the substitute in the household of the victim may be seen as an ikonic representation of the lost person; ultimately, the situation may be translated into forms of symbolic representation: loss, remedy, rights, compensation.

One of the later biblical texts stresses the iconic aspect of talion. We have seen that the law of the perjurer in Deuteronomy states first the talionic principle, but then reverts to the concrete formula. Notice, however, how it introduces that formula (*Deuteronomy* 19:21): "Your eye shall not pity; it shall be life for life, eye for eye, tooth for tooth, hand for hand, foot for foot." The offence of the perjurer must be *visually manifest* on his body. No doubt this serves as a punishment for the offender, but the stress is laid upon the effects on the observer. They will continually be reminded of the offence, both of its iniquity and of the consequences of performing it. It is the immediacy of the visual representation of talion which Bobbie powerfully expresses in her article:[43]

> In the ancient *lex talionis* that which was emphasized was not a compensatory remedy but a representational response to an intended injury, such that the offence in its vivid, imagistic actuality could not be euphemized and that the punishment — the apparent punishment conveyed by a deterrent law — could be seen in the mind's eye and so acutely apprehended that it was, virtually, significantly, experiential.[44]

Yet the Bible, as already observed, embeds two of the three uses of the talionic formula within a more abstract principle, one couched in the terms of symbolic representation. It was as if to say that neither form is sufficient in itself; we need both the emotive immediacy of vision and the rational symbolism of abstract principle. Yet it would be wrong, in my view, to impose a strictly "semantic" reading even upon the biblical formulations of general principle: "then you shall do to him as he had meant to do to his brother" (*Deuteronomy* 19:19); "as he has done it shall be done to him" (*Leviticus* 24:19). These should still be viewed as expressions of "restricted code", such that some cases would be regarded as more typical and appropriate for application of the formula than would others.

Perhaps it was the fragmentation of such social knowledge, in the wake of the loss of Jewish political and legal autonomy with the destruction of the second Temple in A.D. 70, which prompted the Rabbis to a more radical view. The classical text occurs in a running commentary on the laws of Exodus, written probably around the end of the second century A.D.[45]

> "An eye for an eye" — that means money. You say it means money, but perhaps you are wrong and it really does mean an eye? — Rabbi Ishmael said that the Torah compares damage caused by a man to damage caused by a beast, and damage caused by a beast to damage caused by a man. Just as in the case of damage caused by a beast there is a monetary payment, so in the case of damage caused by a man there is also monetary payment.

This has often been viewed as a conscious reform of the law, abolishing even the discretion of the kin to demand talion in cases of non-fatal injuries. Its rhetorical structure has also been noted. It starts with a categorical conclusion: "An eye for an eye (means) money." Only thereafter does it proceed to justify this conclusion — by comparison with the (substitutory) formula (*nefesh tahat nefesh*) used in *Leviticus* 24:18 in relation to the killing of a beast. Rabbi Ishmael's argument responds to another voice in the text, one which proposes (only to be thus rejected) a "literal" interpretation. What force should we attribute to these respective voices, in their original discourse? Should we attribute to the authors (our) understanding that retaliation in kind (or at least its possibility) was previously the dominant understanding, so that the text is here deliberately using the structure of categorical statement, dissentient view then overriding argument from a proof text, in order to effect what it realised was a change in the dominant opinion? Or is it possible that "an eye for an eye (means) money" had, by that time, become almost self-evident; that a (mere) residue of earlier understandings survived, but these were seen now to be erroneous in the light of argument based upon other biblical texts? It is by no means unlikely that even the idea of talion had become so inconceivable that the dynamics of the text were in accordance with this latter interpretation. If so, we might say that the symbolic representation of monetary exchange had by this stage become "naturalised", to the extent that its earlier, ikonic form had now begun to appear bizarre.

"An eye for an eye, a tooth for a tooth." Why the choice of eyes and teeth? And why do some texts add hand and foot, others not? We may recall that the Laws of Hammurabi deal successively with eyes, bones (which presumably could be either hand or foot or others), and teeth (in that order).[46] In all cases, however, the Babylonian law is expressed in normal casuistic sentences; there is no hint yet of a formula, much less a symbolic representation in terms of general principle. Nor do we find anything comparable to the ikonic stress of Deuteronomy. The scribal tradition of the ancient Near East may well have provided the biblical writers, at some stage, with their choice of examples. But the use of those examples in the Bible is a function of the discursive structures of the Bible itself. How the rules of Hammurabi were conceived, or used, is a separate question, into which I shall not enter on this occasion.

The biblical texts do not stand in relation to each other in a clear developmental sequence. In particular, one "stage" does not disappear to make way for the next. All that is here claimed is that there is a developmental sequence in their appearance. Iconic representation is not likely to appear before there has been a stage of enactive; symbolic is not likely to appear before there has been a stage of iconic. But earlier stages may leave traces (the 19th century anthropologists called them "survivals") in later stages.

All this assists to some degree in answering the historical problems posed by the text of the Covenant Code. The formula of vv.24–25 is placed there, as we have seen, quite out of context. At best, we might argue, it is attracted by the *tahat* formula at the end of v.23 (*nefesh tahat nefesh*). Its very decontextualisation is a form of abstraction, despite the concrete imagery in which it is expressed. The "eye" here functions neither as the eye which sees the talionic punishment (*Deuteronomy* 19:21), nor as the absent eye taken in retaliation. It now functions as part of a formula: whatever damage has been suffered, you are entitled to seek comparable damage in return. It presupposes the form of symbolic representation found in both *Deuteronomy* 19:19 and *Leviticus* 24:19.

Indeed, vv.24–25 may be taken, in another sense, to represent the culmination of the scribal tradition of talion. We find there not only the four parts of the body listed in *Deuteronomy* 19:24, but also that different form of representation found in *Leviticus* 24:20: "fracture for fracture" (*shever tahat shever*).[47] For here the emphasis shifts from a distinct part of the body to the form of injury suffered by a range of possible limbs. The term *shever* is not repeated in *Exodus*, but the form of representation is: burn, wound, stripe (or bruise). This represents not simply a change from the location of the injury (its material place, susceptible to indexical representation) to the diagnosis of a generic condition; we may well view the burn, wound or stripe as nominalisations, only barely suppressing the iconicity of the act of burning, the act of wounding, the act of bruising.

Not even the Rabbis could erase the biblical signifier: it was still "an eye for an eye" that meant "money". It was only when they left the midrashic form of discourse and entered the mishnaic — an autonomous form of discourse, rather than a running commentary on the biblical text — that they invented a new set of signs to give effect to their understanding that the remedy consisted in monetary compensation (*Mishnah Baba Kamma* 8:1):[48]

> If a man wounded his fellow he thereby becomes liable on five counts: for injury, for pain, for healing, for loss of time, and for indignity inflicted. 'For injury' — thus, if he blinded his fellow's eye, cut off his hand, or broke his foot, [his fellow] is looked upon as if he was a slave to be sold in the market: they assess how much he was worth and how much he is worth now. 'For pain'— thus, if he burnt his fellow with a spit or a nail, even though it was on his finger-nail where it leaves no wound, they estimate how much money such a man would be willing to take to suffer so. 'For healing'— thus, if he struck him he is liable to pay the cost of his healing; ... 'For loss of time' — thus, he is looked upon as a watchman of a cucumber-field, since he has already been paid the value of his hand or foot. 'For indignity inflicted'— all is in accordance with [the condition of life of] him that inflicts and him that suffers the indignity. If a man inflicted the indignity on a naked man, or a blind man, or a sleeping man, he is [still] liable; but if he that inflicted the indignity was asleep he is not liable. If a man fell from the roof and caused injury and inflicted indignity, he is liable for the injury but not for the indignity, for it is written, *And she putteth forth her hand and taketh him by the secrets*—a man is liable only when he acts with intention [of causing injury].

At the same time, this market methodology is presented in vivid, narrative terms, so that we can still imagine the calculation which the offender must make, as to how much money he would give in exchange for suffering the pain, losing the limb, etc. Thus, this is no *mere* market calculation (a Third?): in giving the compensation, the defendant must feel (a First?) that personal, physical loss which he would suffer, were he not permitted to restore in this manner.

# Notes

1. Roberta Kevelson, "*Lex Talionis*: Equivalence and Evolution in Legal Semiotics", *International Journal for the Semiotics of Law / Revue Internationale de Sémiotique Juridique* VII (1994), 155–170.

2. *Theft in Early Jewish Law* (Oxford: Clarendon Press, 1972).

3. XII T. VIII.2: *Si Membrum rupsit, ni cum eo pacit, talio esto* (If a person has maimed another's limb, let there be retaliation in kind, unless he makes agreement for composition with him.)

4. *Judges* 1:5–7: " ... They (the tribe of Judah) came upon Ado'ni-be'zek at Bezek, and fought against him, and defeated the Canaanites and the Per'izzites. Ado'ni-be'zek fled; but they pursued him, and caught him, and cut off his thumbs and his great toes. And Ado'ni-be'zek said, "Seventy kings with their thumbs and their great toes cut off used to pick up scraps under my table; as I have done, so God has requited me." And they brought him to Jerusalem, and he died there."

5. §§18–22, commencing: "If [a man] cuts off the foot of [another man with ...], he shall weigh and deliver 10 shekels of silver" (§18, Roth's translation; similar provisions follow in respect of the "bone" (§19), "nose" (§20), "??" (text damaged) (§21), and "tooth" (§22). See M.T. Roth, *Law Collections from Mesopotamia and Asia Minor* (Atlanta: Scholars Press, 1995), 19.

6. LE §42: "If a man bit and severed the nose of a man,— 1 mina of silver he shall weigh out. An eye — 1 mina; a tooth — 1/2 mina; an ear — 1/2 mina. A slap in the face — 10 shekels he shall weigh out" (Yaron's translation; cf. LE 43–46). See R. Yaron, *The Laws of Eshnunna* (Jerusalem: Magnes Press and Leiden: E.J Brill, 1988, 2nd ed.), 69.

7. A.S. Diamond, "An Eye for an Eye", *Iraq* 19 (1957), 151–155; *idem*, *Primitive Law, Past and Present* (London: Methuen, 1971), 98–101, 398f.

8. Diamond, we may note, was a Master of the Supreme Court.

9. Diamond was a proponent of Liberal Judaism; he did not feel bound by the Rabbinic interpretation of biblical texts. Yet with this data he was able to avoid the apparently "primitivising" approach of the secularists.

10. Notably, Alan Watson, in a series of books commencing with *Legal Transplants* (Edinburgh: Scottish Academic Press, 1974).

11. Compare, for example, the provisions on goring oxen in Laws of Eshnunna §§53–55, Laws of Hammurabi §§250–252 and *Exodus* 21:28–32, 35–36.

12. A .J. P. Kenny, J. R. Lucas, C.H. Waddington and H.C. Longuet-Higgins, *The Development of Mind* (Edinburgh: Edinburgh University Press, 1973).

13. Later to be replaced by the Economic and Social Research Council: the ideological shift might have been made even clearer by calling it the Economic Science and Social Policy Research Council.

14. A. J. Greimas and E. Landowski, "Analyse sémiotique d'un discours juridique", in A. J. Greimas, *Sémiotique et sciences sociales* (Paris: Editions du Seuil, 1976), 79–128, now translated in *The Social Sciences: A Semiotic View*, trld. P. J. Perron and F. H. Collins (Minneapolis: University of Minnesota Press, 1990), 102–138 (= *Narrative Semiotics and Cognitive Discourses*, London: Pinter Publishers, 1990).

15. *Making Sense in Law* (Liverpool: Deborah Charles Publications, 1995).

16. E.g.: "Historical Aspects of Legal Drafting in the Light of Modern Theories of Cognitive Development", *International Journal of Law and Psychiatry* 3 (1980), 349–369; "The Ceremonial and the Judicial: Biblical Law as Sign and Symbol", *Journal for the Study of the Old Testament* 30 (1984), 25–50; "Some Semiotic Questions for Biblical Law", *The Oxford Conference Volume,* ed. A.M. Fuss (Atlanta: Scholars Press, 1987), 1–25 (Jewish Law Association Studies III).

17. "Law and Language: A Metaphor for Maine, A Model for his Successors?", in *The Victorian Achievement of Sir Henry Maine*, ed. A. Diamond (Cambridge: Cambridge University Press, 1992), 256–293.

18. E.g. *Exodus* 21:13–14.

19. "The Problem of Exod. xxi.22–25 (Ius Talionis)", *Vetus Testamentum* 23 (1973), 273–304, reprinted in my *Essays in Jewish and Comparative Legal History* (Leiden, E. J Brill, 1975), 75–107.

20. Presumably, not that which commences in v.22, since the legal consequence there is different.

21. *Leviticus* 24:10, cf. the terminology of *Exodus* 21:22.

22. The argument has been advanced recently that Hart's approach to the "core of settled meaning" involves the identification of those particular examples conceived to be exemplary. B. Bix, *Law, Language and Legal Determinacy* (Oxford: Clarendon Press, 1995), 9, describes Hart as using a "mixture of a paradigmatic and a criteriological approach to meaning ... our first move in

defining a general term for the purpose of a rule is to invoke the image, example, or particular situation at which the rule was aimed."

23. As seen from *Proverbs* 24:13–16: "There are those who rebel against the light, who are not acquainted with its ways, and do not stay in its paths. The murderer rises in the dark, that he may kill the poor and needy; and in the night he is as a thief. The eye of the adulterer also waits for the twilight, saying, 'No eye will see me'; and he disguises his face. In the dark they dig through houses; by day they shut themselves up; they do not know the light."

24. *Mishnah Baba Kamma* 1:4, with an example in 4:1; *Mekhilta ad Ex.* 21:29 (J. Z. Lauterbach, ed., *Mekilta de-Rabbi Ishmael* (Philadelphia: The Jewish Publication Society of America, 1933–35, 3 vols.), iii.82–83).

25. *Mekhilta ad Ex.* 21:35 (Lauterbach ed., iii.95–96).

26. *Mekhilta ad Ex.* 21:35 (Lauterbach ed., iii.95): "You must reason thus: What is the rule for those who cause damage? Are they to gain or to lose? Of course you are to admit that they are to lose."

27. Such arguments are not entirely remote even from modern jurisprudence: see Bix, *supra* n.22, at 72f., on the different language games involved in determining the "literal meaning" of an expression in the abstract, and using that expression to determine a case in court. Thus, though "no vehicles in the park" might semantically cover an ambulance entering the park in order to give emergency treatment, no one would dream of applying the rule in that case; it is simply too far distant from the image of breach which the rule evokes.

28. Ultimately it was banned for murder (*Numbers* 35:31–32), but not for adultery (*Proverbs* 6:31–35). For the arguments, see my *Essays, supra* n.19, at 41–50.

29. Josephus *Ant.* IV.280: "He that maimeth a man shall undergo the like, being deprived of that limb whereof he deprived the other, unless indeed the maimed man be willing to accept money; for the law empowers the victim himself to assess the damage that has befallen him and makes this concession, unless he would show himself too severe."

30. The Roman Twelve Tables VIII:2, *supra* n.3.

31. J. Bruner, et al., *Studies in Cognitive Growth* (New York: John Wiley & Sons, 1966).

32. W. Ong, *Orality and Literacy* (London and New York: Methuen, 1982); B. Bernstein, *Class, Codes and Control* (London, Routledge and Kegan Paul, 1971), 3 vols. See further my *Making Sense in Law, supra* n.15, at 77–88, 93, 110.

33. This emphasis on discourse as against ideas abstracted from particular discourses represents, in my view, one significant difference in approach between my semiotics and that of Bobbie.

34. *Making Sense in Law, supra* n.15, at 254f.

35. *Supra* n.31, at 12f.

36. *Supra* n.31, at 16f.

37. *Supra* n.31, at 17.

38. *Supra* n.31, at 11.

39. *Supra* n.31, at 21.

40. Translation of G. R. Driver and J. C. Miles, *The Assyrian Laws* (Oxford: Clarendon Press, 1935), 419.

41. *Numbers* 35:16–34.

42. As has been suggested by S. E. Loewenstamm, "Exodus 21:22–25", *Vetus Testamentum* 27 (1977), reprinted in his *Comparative Studies in Biblical and Ancient Oriental Literatures* (Neukirchen-Vluyn: Neukirchener Verlag, 1980), 517–525, at 524.

43. *Supra* n.1, esp. at 156f.

44. *Supra* n.1, esp. at 170.

45. *Mekhilta* to *Exodus* 21:24, Lauterbach's translation.

46. The pre-Hammurabi codes both have provisions for feet and teeth; LE has a provision for hands; neither has any provision for eyes.

47. I leave aside any possible connection between this and the "bone" of LH 197–198.

48. On the loss of meaning which such reduction of compensation to market terms involves, see Kevelson, *supra* n.1, at 164f.

# Chapter Seven
# Justice: The Iconophobic Icon


**Rolando Gaete**


## Justice and the Return of the Classical

Books about the law are austere. After the invention of printing, when illustrated juridical manuscripts ceased to be produced, books about the law would have at most one page with images, the frontispiece (the page facing the title page). And the image would be, more often than not, that of a rather large woman, a blindfolded Roman matron in Grecian robes holding scales and a sword.

This image was usually accompanied by letters imitating the stone-grey sobriety and solidity of Roman characters that is found in monumental or funerary inscriptions in public places, perhaps because they are "eternal letters."[1] Even uneducated people would recognize in this image—also found in the top of public buildings and in courtrooms all throughout Europe—that of a goddess from antiquity. Its description in Baroque and Rococo Pictorial Imagery by C. Ripa, a work on iconography written in the sixteenth century, when this image began to reappear after centuries of absence, could have been written today.[2]

> A blindfolded woman robed in white....She supports a pair of scales... with one hand. Her other hand holds a bare upright sword....She is blindfolded, for nothing but pure reason, not the often misleading evidence of the senses, should be used in making judgements....The scales, used to measure quantities of material things, is a metaphor for justice, which sees that each man receives that which is due him, no more and no less. The sword represents the rigor of justice, which does not hesitate to punish.

But why this return to the Classical at the dawn of Modernity? As Lacoue-Labarthe writes: "Since the Renaissance, Europe as a whole has been prey to the Ancient and it is *imitatio* which governs the construction of the Modern."[3]

Even when in competition with the ancient, the modern emerged as mimesis of Antiquity. Antiquity was the model, the archetype to be followed or subverted. In Gadamer's words:

> The concept of classical antiquity.... had both a normative and a historical side. A particular stage in the historical development of man was thought to have produced a mature and perfect formation.... What we call 'classical' is something retrieved from the vicissitudes from changing time and its changing taste....— a kind of timeless present that is contemporaneous with every other age.[4]

It is as if Modernity could not admit to have been given birth by History and had to ground itself on a time beyond time. Thus the French Revolutionaries imitated the ancients in order to legitimize themselves in front of the imaginary tribunal of History. The return to the Classical tells a story: that nothing is new. This story is told by the images on the walls of Les Invalides in Paris, where Napoleon is buried. His tomb is surrounded by massive frescoes in which he appears half-naked, half-covered by a toga, sitting like a Roman Senator surrounded by images from Antiquity.

Antiquity provided a measure that could be presented as permanent, almost eternal (*Roma Aeterna*). For centuries Roman law was considered not only another historical form of law but Reason itself, *ratio scripta*, a law valid for all times and all cultures. If that is what achieving the status of Classical means, it should be said that human rights have achieved that status today, insofar as they are presented as a final, end-of-History juridical conception valid for all possible cultural forms that humanity may take, forgetting their emergence in the North Atlantic region in the seventeenth century.

Dike for the Greeks, Iustitia for the Romans—the icon is a goddess and dwells where the immortals dwell, in a world beyond time. This representation of Justice as a Justice that transcends time has a long history. Nietzsche called it Egyptianism: philosophers "think they are doing a thing honour when they dehistoricize it, *sub specie aeterni*—when they make a mummy of it" (*Twilight of the Idols*, "Reasoning Philosophy," section 1).[5] Seen with Nietzschean eyes, the sword would stand for the Spirit of Revenge against the passing of time, against the "false" world of mortals, where time and death prevail. Of course, the genealogy of the sword can be traced back to the ancient Greek system of blood-vengeance whose overcoming by legal formalism is narrated by the *Oresteia*. But it is not the sword in isolation which is significant but the image of a blindfolded woman holding it in the name of an external measure brought from a truer world.

Another woman, Antigone, famously questioned the laws of the State with these words: "not such are the laws set among men by Justice, who dwells with the gods below." For the life of these heavenly statutes "is not of today or yesterday, but from all time, and no man knows when they were first put forth." Justice dwells in another world and its laws have no origin because where there is no time and no mortals there is no origin.

Alternatively, the Classical acts as a *figura*, to use a term that Auerbach borrowed from the Middle Ages to describe the co-opting of Greek, Roman and Jewish images by Christianity.[6] Thus, figural interpretation established the connection between Old and New Testament by reading the events in the Old Testament as mimetic prophecies of events in the New Testament. God made Eve from Adam's rib while Adam was asleep. The soldier pierced Jesus' side when he was already dead. Adam's sleep signifies or is the *figura* of Christ's death-sleep. Eve comes from Adam's side and the Church comes from Jesus' side. This linkage is guaranteed by the Plan of the Divine Providence.[7]

The Classical grants a higher form of being, less exposed to caducity and almost reaching sublimity. And yet, despite the claims that the Classical makes on us or perhaps because of their extravagance (the image of Napoleon in Les Invalides, the image of the Roman goddess brandishing a sword and with a cloth around her eyes), the difference between the sublime and the ridiculous is hard to tell.

## A Blindfolded Virgin

The modern icon of Justice we see in public places is not a mere reactivation of the ancient image of a goddess, borrowed as it were from a pre-Christian, pagan era. A modern statue of Justice may be similar to an ancient statue of Iustitia (except for the blindfold, which is a modern addition), but what we see is not what the Greeks or the Roman saw (whether Greeks and Romans saw the same is also a question worth pondering). Inevitably, the image has been Christianised.

Of course, this image of a pagan goddess cannot be found in books on canon law, but the dominant Christian imagination would subject the pagan image of a woman to a Christian sexology, as developed by the priestly orders. In a speech to the parliament of Paris in 1590, Louis D'Orleans said what everybody knew: "Justice is a chaste and pudique virgin."[8]

Is the blindfold, the only ornament which is added to the image, what makes her a pudic woman? Is the blindfold, covering the piercing (male?) eyes of the pagan goddess equivalent to a veil? Women must wear a veil because, unlike men, they are not "the glory and image of God," in the words of Gratian.[9] Or is the blinding of this powerful woman a form of castration, a metaphor for what is called today genital mutilation, which is usually justified in the light of a religious sexology?

In the medieval Christian order, as Legendre describes it, "virginity and castration [occupied] the most central place. They were the fundamental indices of what can be called the aesthetical of Ecclesiastical Rule, affirming the beauty of sexual penury and disinterest, in harmony with participation in the absolute of heavenly kindness."[10] This desire for purity was a desire for oneness: "the theatrical distinction between the pure and the impure" poses "virginity as the one and non-virginity *under the sign of the double*, bad sign, sign of division and reprobation (*binarius numerus non bonam habet significationem, sed signum divisionis et reprobationis*)."[11]

The virginity of modern, Christian Iustitia, purifies the terrible moment of the passing of judgment. As Robert Jacobs comments on an illumination of a manuscript by Berlin de Philippe de Beaumanoir, representing judgment as if it was given in the heavens, judgment was a divinely inspired act, a sacred act of divine revelation: a *sacramentum*.[12] When read, it was delivered in the past tense, as what the Court *had* decided (at some point in the past).

But the moment of judgment loses its sacred character in modern jurisprudence. At the time when the goddess Iustitia becomes the dominant icon, Thomas Hobbes was writing *Leviathan*, dreaming of a science of law based on the purity and oneness of a single Sovereign, beyond Good and

Evil, giving the modern State its Platonic essence, "sovereignty." Although Hobbes does not deal with the image of Justice, his legal scientism gave it its contemporary meaning, emphasizing the blindfold as a kind of blinker that would keep judges blind to anything except the will of the Sovereign. Otherwise "there would be as much contradiction in the laws as there is in the Schools." Law needs a single foundation: this can no longer be the mystery of judgment, it must be political authority. The blindfold stands simply for a doublet of the balance,[13] a more or less redundant reference to impartiality and due process of law. For example, Robert Cove writes of the blindfold as "the lack of sight [which] renders favouritism impossible.... Seeing not, she fears not.... She is cognisant of the import of keeping out information....[In other words] Procedure is the blindfold of Justice."[14]

As translated by a modern mind, we have the scales of Justice meaning decision-making, the blindfold meaning correct procedure, and the sword standing for the enforcement of the legal decision by the Sovereign. From this interpretation to a reassuring but flat definition of Justice there is only one step: Justice is a method of decision-making backed up by the threat of force. This modern definition, with its appeal to methods and procedures and institutions, is no doubt suitable in an era when technical and utilitarian thinking prevails. It is a didactic image, a rhetorical message, an edifying text, erected on the tops of civic buildings and on courthouses' walls, celebrating a city where the law is equal for all, applied by following the correct method. In this view, the Classical statue celebrates the superiority of a Weberian procedural legal order as it emerged in the modern West: it celebrates the formalised technical application of procedures.

As early as the twelfth century, Maimonides called proper procedure "righteous judgement" while commenting on the phrase of the Leviticus, "In righteousness shalt thou judge they neighbor":

> What is meant by a righteous judgement? It is a judgement marked by perfect impartiality to both litigants...not to show courtesy to one, speaking softly to him, and frown upon the other, addressing him harshly....If one of the parties to a suit is well clad and the other ill clad, the judge should say to the former, "Either dress him like yourself before the trial is held, or dress like him, then the trial will take place."[15]

Procedural equality of arms, then? A reinforcement of the symmetry between the parties represented by the scales? The scales are a very old symbol, already found in Egyptian iconography, in the "Book of the Dead" (ca. 1400 B.C.), where the soul of a dead person is shown being weighed in a balance.[16] The balance is a mimetological law, standing for the mimetic figures of the Lex Talionis: retribution, restitution, repetition, proportional equivalence, punishment as the mirror of the crime.[17] But the blindfold is more complicated than this image of symmetry. It has something to do with jurisprudential vertigo.

## The Blindfold as Jurisprudential Vertigo

Jurisprudential angst appears when the jurist confronts the vertigo of judgement and he or she has a glimpse of the other of law. The other of the legal order is not the illegal, which is the *conditio sine qua non* of the law and sets the law in motion, but it is that particular mode of judgement out of control that the Greeks called vertigo (the Greek concept of play as fear and uncertainty).[18] Hobbes felt this vertigo, and jurisprudence since has been concerned not to develop a knowledge about the law as much as to identify non-law, the Other to be exorcised, whether it is called politics or compassion or discretion or play. It is what Blanchot calls disaster, something excessive, "that to which we are destined without being party to it. The disaster is...not our affair and has no regard for us; it is the heedless, unlimited; it cannot be measured as terms of failure or as pure and simple loss."[19]

Liberal Jurisprudence, from Hobbes to Dworkin, has been shaped by this anguished desire to find a quasi-theological One that will make sense of the whole as a higher law. Ironically, it was anti-liberal Plato who thought that judging requires philosophy, some kind of master theory, that would define the measure of judgement.

For Hobbes, who turned this search and this concern for unity and coherence into an obsession and dealt with it in terms of a science of optics,[20] the One was the Sovereign's will or intention. Other versions of the One have substituted for the Sovereign in the twentieth century: a primary rule, a theory of justice, a groundnorm, *intentio operis*, the systemic coherence provided by certain codes, etc.

Although Liberal Jurisprudence claims to have broken with the Classical assumption of a hierarchical ontology of beings, it relies heavily on a belief in that metaphysical prejudice. Its "essence" has been reduced to method. But: why has the myth of Justice as equivalent to a rational method not taken a modern form when presenting itself in works of art? Why should Weber—if Weber is the hero of technocratic Justice—be presented in an ancient toga and talking in Greek?

## The Blindfold as Loss of the World

In modern jurisprudence, *iustitia* becomes *iustificatio*. From Hobbes to Habermas, from the search for a single source of authority to the search for criteria of validity which are universal and not only context-immanent, jurisprudence is concerned with the question of legitimacy, the application of a measure to power and the taking of a measure that must be manufactured contractually.[21] The true becomes *rectum* , i.e. a matter of imperium, *regere*, a matter of judgement, a judicial matter. It is related to the birth of modern philosophy and modern science: "Modern Philosophy began with the loss of the world."[22]

Modern philosophy claims a vision based on selective blindness. It has given us a model of reality based on "the 'video,' the universal vision that objectifies the world (makes it into an 'object') and that, in fact, establishes it as *the* objective world"; "this is equivalent to instituting a disembodied 'pure mind' (*nous*). For this 'pure mind' all the world becomes *object* [of vision]."[23] The blindfold is a blindness to the world or to the idols of the world, as Bacon described all those worldly commitments that were in the way of the perfect objectivity of science. The blindfold is blindness to what is superfluous, "inessential." The blindfold refers to the distance that judgement must take in order to be knowledge of truth. The space of that distance is what makes judgement just. As Goodrich writes: "How better to represent inaugural and mathematically repeated justice than as blind to the world"?[24]

By deworlding, the law edits the world. Klinck gives one example.

> Take, for instance, the Supreme Court's 1980 decision in *Rummel v. Estelle*. The Court held that a Texas statute requiring life imprisonment upon a third felony

> conviction did not, as applied, violate the eighth amendment. One lawyer explaining the case to another would ... recite the issues, describe how the Court framed the questions before it, and analyze the Court's use of precedent. There would be little or no mention of Rummel, the prisoner who faced a life sentence for committing three thefts involving a total of less than $250. But a non lawyer would tell a different story in another language. The average reader or listener would want to know what Rummel did, what he thought about his sentence, and whether it was fair to sentence him to life imprisonment for stealing less than $250.[25]

This example shows the blindfold at work. Jurisprudence legislates on the limits. In a technological society, as Western societies became in the modern age, Justice is equivalent to a jurisprudence of limits that separates law from ethics. Like science, jurisprudence purges the truth from its illusions and conceptualises it in general theoretical propositions. The ideal judge, like the ideal scientist, "is a disinterested spectator oblivious, among other things, to the pain and suffering of the Other."[26] "The law must blind itself to proper names...."[27] The image of Justice, equipped by the blindfold, the scales, and the sword, represents the overcoming of compassion. Compassion tilts the scales improperly, takes place when the blindfold is taken off, when the judge is prey of the illusion of mortal things.

In conclusion, the longevity of the ancient icon of Justice is due mainly to the vertigo of an absence of limits and grounds, which is reflected in the embarrassment that thinkers have always felt in the past when talking of justice and ethics. This embarrassment is the result of treading into a territory which is still governed by jurisprudential angst and metaphysical assumptions.

## The Fool's Laughter

The blindfold was originally a joke. It seems to be a settled historical fact (a thesis held by Ernst von Moller early this century which has never been challenged) that it appeared for the first time in a satirical illustration by Albrecht Dürer of Sebastien of Brant's *Ship of Fools* in 1494 where the text deals with a Justice taken over by querulous people. The illustration is very fifteenth century: the decoration of the room, the architecture of the medieval town that can be glimpsed at through a window, the clothes of the characters, the style, not yet concerned with the real as we see it but with telling a story in the light of what we know.[28] And the story was that of Justice being a querulous lawyers' justice, a protest that has echoes today: "what do law courts do but invite the greedy to accuse the even more greedy of offences arising from greed and aggression"?[29]

This satire followed a long tradition. The blindfold had always been something ominous: "In the imaginary of the Middle Ages and the Renaissance, all other blindfolded allegories, Death, Ambition, Cupidity, Ignorance, Error, Wrath are ominous", even Cupid, whose covered eyes are "more a denunciation of love's dangers than a celebration of its charms."[30] Sinagogia was also blindfolded because it was ignorant of Christianity. But the satirical story told by the blindfold was quickly forgotten. Blindness became not an obstacle but the condition of possibility of vision.

But the blindfold may tell us more about the fool than about Justice. The fool is standing behind the sitting goddess, and is tying the blindfold. The fool is not laughing. It is the illustration as a whole which is funny. It invites laughter: the blindfold clearly makes the scales and the sword useless. The goddess is no longer a goddess.

"There is no better starting point for thought than laughter—wrote Brecht—speaking more precisely, spasms of the diaphragm generally offer better chances for thought than spasms of the soul."[31] Against the Aristotelian search for pathos and responsible involvement, Brecht looked for estrangement and a relaxed, irresponsible indifference because only indifference would understand play as play.

Of course, play seems to be the most unsuitable model for an analysis of justice. Play is not serious, it generates no obligations, it is irresponsible.[32] The experience of time in play seems to be peculiarly inadequate for a thinking on Justice. Serious activities are futuristic, full of the future. They are on the way to an end. "Justitia [is] blindfolded...to suggest the sightless vision of interiority, of foresight, and so of the future."[33] Play may mime serious activities but it is not itself serious; it has no end, implying a purely aesthetic attitude towards life. The being of play is unreal. And yet Justice, like play, is indeterminate. Because it is indeterminate, Unger can speak of a "sense of being surrounded by injustice without knowing where justice lies."[34]

As an aesthetic concept, the ludic is both rule-governed and rule-breaking—governed by a law which is always to come. It is that "which gives the rule to art" (in Kant's words), thus "producing that for which no definite rule can be given," and which "ought not to spring from imitation, but must serve as a standard or rule of judgement for others".[35] Justice precedes all standards because it "precedes all thinking and acting."[36] It is this rule-free character that makes of it a source of jurisprudential anxiety. And a source of ethical anxiety: perceiving the ludic dimension in the experience of ethical responsibility, seeing the irresponsibility lying at the bottom of responsibility.[37] Because "no one can predict how a game will be played, no one can predict what a play will mean."[38] The danger of unlimited semiosis is that nobody can put a stop to the game or control it. And it is the blindfold itself which is playful in this sense, which can be recovered by the populace, who may recover the original interpretation of it as satire and social criticism, the satire which either shows that the fool is the wise person and Justice is a fool or which makes of the fool a fool and of justice a fool too.

In 1907, the government of Prussia prohibited the representation of justice by the blindfolded image in all palaces to be built after that year.[39] What was the government afraid of? Perhaps it was afraid of what Peirce called unlimited semiosis, the unstoppable translatability of signs into other signs, and the fact that no government can exclude the possibility of a reactivation of the early meaning of the blindfold. Or perhaps the government was aware of the danger that a lasting sign like the blindfold may change meanings. In some historical periods like our own querulous age, people may begin to wonder whether the goddess is not so much hiding her eyes as hiding the fact that she has no eyes at all.

# Notes

1. Cf. Armando Petrucci, *Public Lettering: Script, Power and Culture* (Chicago and London: The University of Chicago Press, 1993), p. 53.

2. Quoted in Denis E. Curtis and Judith Resnik, "Images of Justice," *Yale Law Journal* 96:1727 (1987), p.1731.

3. Philippe Lacoue-Labarthe, *Heidegger, Art and Politics* (London: Basil Blackwell, 1990), p. 78.

4. Hans-Georg Gadamer, *Truth and Method* (London: Sheed and Ward, 1975), p. 255–6.

5. I deal with the Platonism of human rights in Rolando Gaete, *Human Rights and the Limits of Critical Reason* (London: Dartmouth, 1993).

6. Eric Auerbach, *Mimesis* (Princeton: Princeton University Press, 1991).

7. *Ibid.*, p. 73–4

8. Quoted by Robert Jacobs, *Images de la Justice* (Paris: The Leopard D'Or, 1994), p. 205. Jacobs' book is an excellent extended commentary on images of justice from the past of various European countries which were exhibited during the Conference on "Justices of Europe" in the Palais de Justice in Paris in November 1992.

9. Corpus iuris canonici, Decretum, cause 33, question 5, canon 20 as quoted by Pierre Legendre, *L'amour du censeur: essai sur l'ordre dogmatique* (Paris: Editions du Seuil, 1974), p. 138 (my translation).

10. *Ibid.*, p. 136.

11. *Ibid.*

12. *Ibid.*, pp. 145–8.

13. Jacobs (1994), p. 233.

14. From R. Cover in: R. Cover, O. Fiss and J. Resnik, *Procedure*, as quoted by Curtis and Resnick (1987), pp. 1727–8.

15. Code of Maimonides, as quoted in D. E. Curtis and J. Resnick (1987), p. 1758.

16. Curtis and Resnick (1987), p. 1747, n. 32.

17. William Schweiker, *Mimetic Reflections: a study in hermeneutics, theology and ethics* (New York: Fordham University Press, 1990), p. 211–2.

18. Cf. Spariosu, Literature, *Mimesis and Play* (Tubingen: Gunther Narr Verlag, 1982) p. 37.

19. Blanchot, *The Writing of Disaster,* as quoted by D. Cornell, *The Philosophy of the Limit* (New York and London: Routledge, 1992), p. 99.

20. On Hobbes' use of the science of optics for a metaphysics of productive judgment, see H. Caygill, *Art of Judgement* (London: Basil Blackwell, 1989), Part I,1.

21. Cf. John Sallis (ed.), *Reading Heidegger* (Bloomington: Indiana University Press, 1993), p. 88.

22. Seyla Benhabib, "Epistemologies of Postmodernism," *New German Critique,* 33:1984 (fall), p. 106.

23. Carlo Sini, *Images of Truth* (Atlantic Highlands, New Jersey: Humanities Press, 1985), p. 89.

24. Peter Goodrich, *Oedipus Lex: Psychoanalysis, History, Law* (Berkeley and Los Angeles: University of California Press, 1995), p. 158.

25. S. Stark, "Why lawyers can't write," *Harvard Law Review* 97:1839 (1984), p.1390, as cited in D. R. Klinck, *The word of the law: Approaches to legal discourse* (Ottawa, Canada: Carleton University Press, 1992), p. 27.

26. Edith Wyschogrod, *Saints and Postmodernism* (Chicago and London: The University of Chicago Press, 1990), p. xxvi.

27. John D. Caputo, *Demythologizing Heidegger* (Indianapolis: Indianapolis University Press, 1993), p. 205.

28. E. H. Gombrich, *Art and Illusion* (London: Phaidon, 1959).

29. Judith N. Shklar, *Faces of Injustice* (New Haven and London: Yale University Press, 1990), p. 21

30. Jacobs (1994), p. 233.

31. Terry Eagleton, *Walter Benjamin or Towards a Revolutionary Criticism* (London: Verso Editors, 1981), p. 157.

32. Eugen Fink, *Spiel Als Weltsymbol* (Stuttgart: Kohlhammer, 1960). My references are to the French translation: *Le jeu comme symbol du monde* (Paris: Les Editions de Minuit, 1966).

33. Goodrich (1995), p. 157.

34. R. Unger, *Law in Modern Society: Towards a Criticism of Social Theory* (London: 1976), p. 175.

35. Immanuel Kant, *Critique of Judgement* (London: MacMillan, 1951), section 46.

36. Quoted in Sallis (1993), p. 91.

37. Cf. Fink (1966), p. 229.

38. *Ibid.*, p. 107.

39. Instruction of 18 January 1907, mentioned by Jacobs (1994), p. 234.

# Chapter Eight
# Revolutionary Play: *Inlaws/Outlaws* Twenty Years Later


## William Pencak


In the mid-1970s, when I was a graduate student in the history department at Columbia University, I had little idea that about 150 miles to the northeast, another graduate student at Brown University not only had created her own Ph.D. program in semiotics, but was in the process of pioneering the new field of legal semiotics. Even after our paths crossed at Penn State's Berks Campus in 1983, I still had no idea that one day I would become a semiotician myself and edit a collection of essays to honor both her remarkable scholarly achievements and her creation of the most non-institutional academic institutions imaginable—The Round Table for Legal Semiotics and the International Association for the Semiotics of Law. Least of all, however, did I imagine that when it came time to write an article on the impact of Professor Kevelson's thought, I would discover that the second (!) book she published in 1977, while still in graduate school, *Inlaws/Outlaws: A Semiotics of Systemic Interaction*,[1] is filled with exciting implications for the study of the crowds, riots, and revolution I myself was investigating at that very moment, the fruits of which appeared in several articles and my own first two books.[2]

So here again, twenty years after we both did our graduate work, Professor Kevelson has provided me with the opportunity to review the American Revolution and my own scholarly work through fresh eyes. *Inlaws/Outlaws* argues that the most important force for change and freedom in human history is the interrelationship among play, artistic and intellectual creation arising from play, statutory law, and political protest. Kevelson proves her thesis by analyzing the Robin Hood ballads as the poetic form which perpetuated the tradition of outlawry which emerged from the "play space" of the English forest. This was a realm of freedom where "the emergent individual rebelled and asserted the prioritized order of personal right, communal bond, and the enormous stakes risked in the plea for justice." There the "anarchistic outlaw" defied statutory law and established "an effective *praxis* for social change," for his rebellion created "competing orders of society and conflicting systems of law." The "Outlaw Ballad" and "Statutory Law" are "symbolic signs," the aesthetic expressions of an "agon" between, respectively, the sacred world of outlaw play space and the secular realm of the king and his courts. The Outlaw Ballad stands up against the state for the sacred law of divine justice and a common law guaranteeing communal and individual rights as superior to profane law of the king. Out-law is egalitarian, anarchic, created through interactive communication among all those who claim the right to speak; in-law is statutory, hierarchical, and handed down by decree.[3]

Kevelson writes that Robin Hood is only one of many mythic heroes who have given humanity its freedom. "Robin Hood is metonymous with Butcher, Potter, Hereward, Eustace, Gamelyn, Billy the Kidd [sic but eminently forgivable if not intentionally encompassing Captain 'Billy' Kidd the pirate as well!], Ali-Baba, Sinbad the Sailor, Prometheus, and all the figures of legend, myth, and history who can be substituted for the protagonist in the inlaw/outlaw controversy, in all lands, among the folklore of all people." Kevelson's prose in passages like this perfectly symbolizes her thought: rhapsodic phrases, play spaces of stunning insight, outlaws to academic convention and specialization, are spectacularly interspersed among the inlaws, or regular scholarly citations and arguments, granting us grace to transport her playing fields to our own academic pastures to the extent that we, too, are willing to become outlaws.[4]

Kevelson then notes that this "play activity" of outlaws intensifies during "marked historical periods when society is obviously undergoing critical change." She has therefore juxtaposed, "in order to gain a clear picture of the total semiotic structure of a society in painful transition. . . the *apparently* [my emphasis] least consequential activity—communal 'romantic' folk song exchange"—and the most "real consequential act—the judgments of courts on matters of life, death, and property."[5] The analysis she performs for the age of Robin Hood can be applied to the

American Revolution as well, especially its preliminaries in Boston, with the rebels playing the roles of the famous outlaw and his band.

Popular protest in Boston utilized nine elements that might be considered play.

1. Revolutionaries encouraged the involvement of boys.
2. Patriots used play as an excuse to minimize the protests and argue that the authorities' response was all out of proportion to the offenses committed.
3. Disguises and pseudonyms, including the presentation of adult rioters as boys, were employed not only to mask identities but to symbolize the fact that people were stepping outside their normal routines and creating new identities and a new structure of authority.
4. Humor was used to mock-punish, mock-execute, and mock-bury supporters of Britain.
5. New holidays and processions replaced older official celebrations and those sanctioned by popular custom. Some of these commemorated events in which the Bostonians themselves had participated, thus giving them a sense of creating a heroic, memorable society whose deeds supplanted those they had previously celebrated.
6. Much protest literature took the form of playful sarcasm.
7. Crowd activity replaced traditional symbols of law and authority with another system located out-of-doors in play-space, or indoors as the crowd moved into enclosed public spaces. A tree was dubbed the Liberty Tree to replace the province and town house as the central location of symbolic authority and punishment.
8. Officials who refused to enter into dialogue with the crowd and recognize the legitimacy of its space became targets of protest which compelled them to enter public space. The crowd thereby recast itself as the ultimate legal and moral authority, both in and out-of-doors, since it claimed the right to locate the seat of societal judgment and call its putative betters to account there.

9. Revolutionary songs redefined America as a play-space, or realm of nature exempted from the stultifying constraints of the tyrannies which confined most of the world's population.

Let us see how these points help us reconsider the nature of the American Revolution.

1. Schoolboys appeared in Boston's very first revolutionary crowd actions which protested the Stamp Act in August, 1765. "You would have laughed to have seen two or three hundred little boys with a flag marching in a procession on which was King, [William] Pitt, & Liberty forever, it ought to have been Pitt, [John] Wilkes, & Liberty," reported "Loyal Nine" crowd organizer John Avery, Jr. of the August 14 protest against Stamp Master Andrew Oliver.[6] "Boys and Children" were ostensibly responsible for starting the fire that signaled the riots of August 26, although "whispers from a person unknown," reinforced by physical coercion, "insult and outrage," insured they were not dispersed. Later that night, when Lieutenant-Governor Thomas Hutchinson's house was destroyed, "a number of boys from fourteen to sixteen years of age, some mere children, did a great deal of damage."[7]

Crowds of lads roamed Boston in the late 1760s to enforce the non-importation agreements. On February, 22, 1770, between sixty and three hundred schoolboys, symbolically imitating the European custom of placing the severed heads of traitors on poles, placed such an effigy on a post in front of the house of Theophilus Lillie, who was openly violating the agreement. When Ebenezer Richardson, a customs' informer who lived next door, tried to knock down the post, the boys began to throw sticks and stones at him. When he retreated to his house, "the boys assembled and said they were going to have a frolick," one witness reported; another noted that some men looking on laughed as the boys "carried the pageantry." Unfortunately Richardson did not see any humor in the affair and fired on the crowd, killing one lad and wounding another. Boys aged fourteen to fifteen "swearing and cursing," then throwing snowballs, sticks, and pieces of ice, also initiated the "Boston Massacre" two weeks later.[8]

2. Boys served two useful purposes in the Boston crowd. First, riots in which hundreds of people threatened British officials could be dismissed

as hysterical overreactions to boys at play. The prosecution's case in the Boston Massacre, for instance, rested on the assertion that "this violent attack [on the soldiers] turns out to be nothing more, than a few snowballs, thrown by a parcel of boys, the most of them at a considerable distance, and as likely to hit the inhabitants as the soldiers. . . a common case in the streets of Boston at this [winter] season of the year."[9] Defending the soldiers who fired on the crowd, John Adams commented: "We have been entertained with a great variety of phrases to avoid calling this sort of people a mob. Some call them shavers, some call them geniuses. The plain English is, gentlemen, most probably a motley rabble of saucy boys, negroes and molattoes, Irish teagues, and outlandish [foreign] jack tars [sailors]. And why we should scruple to call such a set of people a mob, I can't conceive, unless the name is too respectable for them."[10] Similarly, the Boston *Gazette* played upon the theme of age vs. youth in lamenting the death of the boy killed by Richardson: "Inhumanly murdered, the young lad . . . last week fell a sacrifice to the rage and malice of an old offender and his abettors." John Adams commented that "the ardor of the people is not to be quelled by the slaughter of one child and the wounding of another."[11]

The Boston patriots themselves assumed the name "Sons of Liberty" or "Liberty Boys" to identify their most prominent organization. Cornet Joyce, Jr., not his father, both of whom were executioners of Charles I, was a prominent figure in both print and in the Pope's Day processions. In these, boys tormented effigies of the Pope and Catholic Pretender while wearing bishop's miters and pretending to be "imps of the Devil."[12] Scholars Michael Wallace, Edwin Burrows, Winthrop Jordan, and Jay Fliegelman have emphasized the patriarchal and matriarchal metaphors which were employed by both Americans and Britons to define the relationship of sons—not daughters—to a father or mother country.[13]

Rebels also called attention to their youth and that of their land in song. Dr. Joseph Warren, the lawyer who defended the British soldiers accused of the Boston Massacre and who died at Bunker Hill, wrote of "Free Amerikay," "this maiden climate" inhabited by "sons" who will some day assume the mantle of their fathers: "Some future day shall crown us the masters of the main." William Billings, Bostonian patriot and perhaps the most famous colonial American composer, wrote in "Chester" of how "Their veterans flee before our youth, /And gen'rals yield to beardless boys."[14]

3. Besides identifying their rebellion with youth, the patriots played other games and assumed other guises. At the Tea Party, they disguised themselves as "Mohawks"—perhaps serving notice that Indians from North America could triumph over the East India Company. The participants wore rough blankets, painting their faces, and speaking in mock-Indian jargon they invented for the occasion.[15] Other pseudonyms of Bostonian writers identified with the common people—"Humphrey Ploughjogger" (John Adams), "Populus" (Samuel Adams)—or community ("A Friend to the Community," "Americanus," John Adams as "Novanglus" or New England). Classical heroes such as "Mentor," "Junius Brutus," Caesar's assassin, "Callisthenes" (Josiah Quincy), or concepts, "Vindex," "Candidus," (Samuel Adams) were also popular. Biblical figures including "Joshua" and "Elisha" and heroes of seventeenth-century British freedom struggles such as "Hampden," "Sidney," and "O. C".—Oliver Cromwell, also a wordplay on the nameof the powerful loyalist family allied to the Hutchinsons—reappeared to aid their spiritual descendants. Samuel Adams resurrected Puritan minister "Cotton Mather" as well.[16]

Loyalists and patriots traded self-praise and insults through impersonation. One exasperated loyalist urged readers to spurn "yon patriot bellowing loud" and "pull off the mask" of liberty which hid the "private grudge or party rage that forms the scheme." A loyalist pamphleteer, John Mein, gave aliases such as Johnny Dupe to John Hancock and Muddlehead to Otis, calling attention to former's funding of much protest activity and the latter's increasing insanity.[17] Patriots responded in kind: Mercy Otis Warren's play "The Group" featured prominent loyalists in the guises of Hazlerod, Meagre, Hateall, Beau Trumps, Humbug, Spendall, Dupe, and Fribble.[18] The rebels symbolically took on the mantle of past greatness when James Otis appeared on the cover of Bickerstaff's *Almanac* for 1770, supported by Liberty and Hercules, treading a serpent under his feet. In 1774, however, Gleason's *Massachusetts Calendar* depicted Governor Thomas Hutchinson at the hour of his death with a copy of Machiavelli's works at his feet as a devil, skeleton, serpent, and alligator torment him.[19] Boston crowd leader Ebenezer Mackintosh named his son Pasquale Paoli Mackintosh, thereby identifying Boston's cause with the struggle for freedom then going on in Corsica under Paoli's direction; Hutchinson, however, compared Mackintosh to Massianello, the Sicilian revolutionary he considered a destructive bandit.[20] Disguises and play became vehicles through which revolutionaries could identify with cosmic struggles from the Bible, antiquity, British history, and even the eternal struggle of God against the Devil.

4. Elements of humor abounded in the protests against Britain beginning with the Stamp Act riots. Stamp Master Andrew Oliver's effigy was hung from the large elm that would become the Liberty Tree. A poem was attached to it: "Fair freedom's glorious cause I've meanly quitted/For the sake of pelf;/ But ah! The Devil has me outwitted,/ And instead of *stamping* others, I've *hang'd* myself." A devil's imp in obvious imitation of the annual Pope's Day festivities pointed a pitchfork at the effigy, while the Devil peeped out of a boot, a pun on the name of former British Prime Minister Lord Bute who was widely if erroneously believed to be responsible for the Act. The boot had a "Green vile" sole symbolizing Britain's current head of government, George Grenville. A crowd in a "joyous" mood gathered at the site and insisted on mock-stamping all the goods being brought into town, for the Tree was on the only road into Boston over the narrow neck that connected it to the mainland. The stamps were playfully considered "the mark of the Beast," foretold in the Book of Revelations. The effigies were then paraded around town, beheaded, and burned in the manner of Pope's Day figures.[21]

Similarly, when Thomas Hutchinson's house was destroyed on August 26, the crowd went out of its way to stamp upon furniture, books, and other items before destroying them: the footprints on Hutchinson's manuscript collection and draft of his *History ... of Massachusetts-Bay* may be viewed in the Massachusetts Archives via microfilm. The obnoxious loyalist printer John Mein (pronounced Mean) was especially vulnerable to puns on his name, as when he stood in for the Pope and was burned in effigy in 1769: "*M*ean is the man, M—n is his name,/ *E*nough he's spread his hellish fame; /*I*nfernal furies hurl his soul,/ *N*ine Million times from Pole to Pole."[22] These four verses also formed an acrostic with his name. Loyalist Justice of the Peace John Murray suffered humorous abuse twice. In 1769, when he attempted to release a man on bail who was implicated as an accessory in the beating of James Otis by a customs officer, a crowd refused to let him take depositions in the case, pulled off his wig, and carried it behind him on a pole as he was escorted out of Fanueil Hall at the head of a raucous procession. When he arrived on the scene of the Boston Massacre the following March, his authority was greeted with sneers and snowballs: "Here comes old Murray with the riot act," signifying that the crowd would not even consider dispersing were he foolish enough to try to re-establish order. "Hillsborough treats," named for the newly-appointed British Secretary of State for the Colonies, or feces, were smeared on the houses and in one instance the person of merchants who refused to sign non-importation agreements, symbolically indicating what the populace thought of them and the British goods they attempted to sell. The *Boston Gazette* was especially pleased when Thomas Hutchinson's two sons, "the TWO CHILDREN," finally signed the agreement after their shop had been repeatedly targeted.[23] In an interesting role reversal, the revolutionaries' adolescent behavior in intimidating the importers was projected onto two adult merchants whose sole claim to importance was their powerful father. And British soldiers were taunted with cries of "lobsters" or "bloody backs" to rub symbolic salt in the wounds of the brutal floggings they received.[24]

The ultimate instance of brutal yet playful revolutionary humor was tarring and feathering, which made a human being resemble a chicken. The pseudonymous Joyce, Jr. was captain of the "Committee for Tarring and Feathering" established in 1774 by Boston's leaders to limit the number of such incidents to where they were considered absolutely necessary. "Modern dress," "the American Mode," a "New England jacket," and, especially, "a new method of macaroni making as practiced at Boston," were euphemisms for the punishment.[25] Macaronis (from the Italian "ma carone"—my dearest one—Italian clothes, art, and opera were cultural affectations of the contemporary British aristocracy) were dandies, London's eighteenth-century Eurotrash; tarring and feathering mocked aristocratic pretensions just as the original British words to "Yankee Doodle," who "stuck a feather in his cap and called it macaroni," made fun of Americans' efforts to imitate their "betters." Americans, of course, reversed the reversal and adopted the song as their own.[26]

5. Bostonians also redefined themselves by creating new public festivals. Pope's Day itself was transformed and then went into eclipse. No longer did the North and South End mobs battle for possession of their respective effigies: on November 5, 1765, the crowds, united behind a smartly-uniformed Ebenezer Mackintosh, marched together through the streets. In a mock-coronation ceremony, Mackintosh had been inaugurated as "First Captain-General of the Liberty Tree" on November 1, appropriately All Souls Day. Accompanying Mackintosh was General William Brattle, a future loyalist, but at the time a staunch patriot and commander of the province's armed forces. By placing Mackintosh at the head of the column, the mob and the militia were equated—indeed, the membership overlapped considerably—as defenders of communal liberty, and Mackintosh granted equal symbolic generalship with Brattle. No longer did a mob dressed as shabbily as they could, with blackened faces (although the Tea Party seems to have borrowed these customs) enter the houses of the well-to-do, practice "anticks," "demean themselves with great insolence," and break windows if their hosts refused to reward their efforts with small sums of money. Beginning in 1765, this more raucous forerunner of Halloween was institutionalized as play merged into politics and respectable inhabitants joined in the procession. Largesse was now administered through distribution of refreshments paid for by prominent Whigs such as John Hancock. Henceforth, the Pope and Pretender were either supplanted or supplemented by images of Governor Francis Bernard and his successor Thomas Hutchinson and other villains from both sides of the Atlantic. The newly-appointed Customs Commissioners had the misfortune to arrive in Boston on Pope's Day 1767, to be met by a large crowd parading the usual devils, Popes, and Pretenders with signs on their breasts: "Liberty & Property & No Commissioners."[27] Threats of murder conveyed through symbolic execution could thus be simultaneously interpreted as no more than playful public ritual.

Boston patriots annually celebrated events such as the August 14 riots and the repeal of the Stamp Act, but no commemoration was more striking than the annual remembrance of the Boston Massacre of March 5, 1770. Each year, elaborate tableaux and symbolic re-enactments of the event preceded the Massacre Oration, where the people were exhorted not to betray the honored dead by failing to defend their liberties. Joseph Warren's speech in 1775, some six weeks before the battles at Lexington and Concord, predicted the impending war and rhapsodized that by preparing to sacrifice themselves in the manner of Crispus Attucks and his fellow heroes, they would earn eternal salvation in establishing a country where virtue and happiness could coincide—a play-ground, in other words.[28]

> Having redeemed your country, and secured the blessing to future generations, *who*, fired by your example, shall emulate your virtues, and learn from *you* the heavenly art of making millions happy; with heart-felt joy—with transports all your own, YOU CRY, THE GLORIOUS WORK IS DONE. Then drop the mantel to some young ELISHA, and take your seats with kindred spirits in your native skies.

Work will be finished, millions will be happy, people will go into transports of ecstasies, and there will be no more need for Elijahs to battle tyranny. Little transition will be required from the "heavenly art" practiced in America to the heavenly joys of the afterlife. Warren has placed his cause and his countrymen's deeds in a long chain of heroism dating back to the Bible and extending indefinitely into the future. Ironically, he himself would prove one of the necessary sacrifices when he died at Bunker Hill that June. In the 1776 Massacre oration, minister Peter Thatcher took language straight out of Thomas Paine's pamphlet *Common Sense,* published that January, to reinforce the idea of America as a sacred space in which freedom, compared to a beautiful woman, can receive the erotic love denied her elsewhere:[29]

> Freedom is offered to us, she invites us to accept her blessings; driven from the other regions of the globe, she wishes to find an asylum in the wilds of America; with open arms let us receive the persecuted fair. . . and when the earthly scene

> shall be closing with us, let us expire with this prayer upon our quivering lips, O GOD LET AMERICA BE FREE.

The "wilds" of America, out-law space, has become an "asylum": a Sherwood Forest, a place that is both safe and wild, a play-space, in other words. The outlaws have taken over, and the rest of the world has been revalorized as outside true law and God's will.

6. In the years preceding the revolution, America was being redefined as a space not only of freedom, but a land of play and humor, in songs and literature as well protest and ritual. Logical argument may have been the tool of the pamphlets and speeches addressed to royal governors and Parliament, but sarcasm which often turned vicious dominated the cartoons, broadsides, almanacs, and popular literature which conveyed the revolutionary message to the general public. Take, for instance, a poem which appeared in the *Boston Gazette* on December 2, 1765:

> Spurn the Relation—She's no more a Mother,
> Than Lewis to George, a Most Christian Brother,
> In French Wars and Scotch, grown generous and rich
> She gives her dear children pox, slavery, and itch.

Humor can barely hide the fact that even at this early stage in the colonial protests, America's relationship with Britain is placed on a level of Britain's to France, two nations which had been at war for most of the eighteenth century. All the colonies get from what is no longer a mother—the "monster" of Paine's *Common Sense* has already appeared to devour her young—is slavery and venereal disease with its intimations of whoring and illegitimacy. In the Massachusetts legislature, James Otis not only denied Parliament the right to legislate for the colonies on constitutional grounds, but morally condemned the M. P.s who had voted to tax America. All they learned at Oxford and Cambridge was "smoking, whoring, and drinking." "Button-makers, pin-makers [industrialists], horse-jockeys [nobles], courtiers, pensioners, pimps, and whoremasters" dominated the House of Commons. They not only wished to violate America, treat her as a pimp would use a whore, they had abused and destroyed their own play-space and were now seeking to do the same elsewhere. The persecuted fair maid of freedom could only retain her virginity apart from such perversions.[30]

Historians have not paid sufficient attention to the force of the identification of loyalists and the British with excrement and disgusting forms of sexual intercourse. The force of these statements can best be realized if we remember the introduction of similar forms of protest and language into political discourse during the 1960s by student protesters. Further, tarring and feathering involved stripping the victim naked, turning him into a chicken, and placing him on a rail in a manner which caused pain to his genitals—symbolically speaking, robbing him of his masculinity and humanity and identifying him with a female bird known for its cowardice.

7. Massachusetts protesters signified their own play-space, a miniature Sherwood Forest, in the form of the Liberty Tree. The focus of public authority shifted as of August 14, 1765, from the official government buildings to the outdoors, from no longer legitimate authorities to a people who symbolically entered the state of nature every time they met to discuss their rights and protest violations against them. The tree was an old elm in a grove of trees on the sole road out of Boston over the narrow "neck" which separated it from the rest of Massachusetts. It linked town and country. Here enemies of the people were executed in effigy or made to acknowledge the people's supremacy, rather than in the courts or at the usual sites of government The crowd insisted that Stamp Master Andrew Oliver resign there when his commission arrived. Despite the fact that he had written to Britain and asked leave to resign, promised not to execute the act in the meantime, refused the customs' commissioners requests to issue stamps, and even published a notice in the *Boston Gazette* that "he had taken no measures to qualify himself for the office, nor had he any thoughts of doing so," the Sons of Liberty deemed his reply unsatisfactory. They demanded a public resignation: "N.B. Provided you comply with the above, you shall be treated with the greatest politeness and humanity. If not . . . . !" Oliver had no objection to resigning, but aware of the symbolic importance of the place where he did so, "he sent to T. Dawes [a leading patriot whose nephew William was the other rider with Paul Revere] to desire him to interpose and at least procure leave for him to

resign at the town house but after two or three consultations nothing more could be obtained than a promise of having no affront offered and a proposal to invite the principal persons of the town to accompany him." Crowd leader Mackintosh escorted him in the pouring rain to the Liberty Tree where he resigned again. Significantly, the principal damage inflicted on Oliver's house during the August 14 riot was to tear down his garden fences, break his windows, and batter down his door. The barriers he erected between himself and the crowd, symbolically between two types of law, came down. Mackintosh and the mob also threatened to kill him if they could find him—a powerful threat against an official which drove home the crowd's insistence that Oliver's authority merited a swift end if he would not submit to the people.[31]

Twelve days later, the first demand the mob made when it surrounded Hutchinson's house was that he come out, speak with them, and deny he had anything to do with writing or enforcing the Stamp Act. Like Oliver, realizing that by entering the out-law space of the crowd he would symbolically acknowledge its superior authority, Hutchinson termed this "an indignity to which he would not submit," just as he had refused repeated requests from both newspapers and private parties to proclaim his innocence of supporting the Stamp Act to the world. All he needed to have done was to have published some private correspondence unearthed by Edmund S. Morgan in which he opposed it every bit as eloquently as his political opponents.[32]

8. Hutchinson and Oliver refused to speak to the people assembled outside of regular governmental institutions, acknowledge the populace's authority, and accept their own accountability to them. At issue was who were the people and in what capacity could they be represented. In 1747, justifying the mob that resisted a massive naval impressment, a group including the young Samuel Adams argued in their protest newspaper, *The Independent Advertiser*, that it was "notorious, the sober sort, who dared to express due sense of their injuries, were invidiously represented as a rude, low-lived mob."[33] Similarly in 1765, John Adams could only deduce that Oliver and Hutchinson were in fact secret abettors of the Stamp Act—itself evidence of a scheme "to reduce the body of the people to ignorance, poverty, dependence"—because by refusing to vindicate

themselves before the crowd, they showed " a contempt of that equality in knowledge, wealth, and power, which has prevailed in this country."[34]

Hutchinson's and Oliver's refusal at the time of the Stamp Act to put themselves on a plane of equality with a group they considered "rabble" in fact symbolized the manner in which a Massachusetts administrative elite—negatively signified as "pensioners" or recipients of unearned income in the form of government salaries—had been distancing itself from the people of Boston for a quarter-century. Beginning around 1740, they began to live as much as possible in suburban country houses constructed in imitation of the British gentry. Many, although not Hutchinson and Oliver, joined the Anglican church their countrymen spurned as a mask for Popery. (They did, however, betray a suspicious cosmopolitanism by attending Anglican services from time to time.) And the elite intermarried and socialized among themselves, turning itself more and more into a group that believed itself entitled to rule and receive deference.[35] The people symbolically tried to break down these barriers by tearing down Hutchinson's and Oliver's fences and entering their houses in violation of the privacy they had so carefully cultivated. They not only insisted that Oliver resign, but that he do so in a humiliating manner at a site where his authority counted for nothing vis-a-vis the Sons of Liberty.

Hutchinson, by refusing to speak to the crowd, was obliged to flee from it or suffer death. He in fact appeared willing to die. He only left his house when his elder daughter refused to go without him. His unwillingness to communicate with the crowd except in his official role, combined with the remarks he made from the bench of the Superior Court over which he presided as chief justice the next day, explains why Hutchinson was detested. First, he stated that the distress of his family was "infinitely more insupportable than what I feel for myself." Hutchinson had antagonized the people precisely by being overly solicitous of his family in obtaining government positions for his relatives and socializing primarily with an extended kinship network. He had adopted a privatized personal life he refused to view as incompatible with his official responsibilities Then he apologized for the fact that he had to wear old, borrowed clothes instead of his usual judicial robes, which had been destroyed. He objected to being placed on a level with the crowd, in other words. He also expressed indifference to his life, for he did not clear his name "through timidity.... They can only take away my life, which is of but little value to me when deprived of all its comforts, all that is dear to me, and nothing surrounding me but the most piercing distress."[36] Apart from his possessions and official symbols of office, Hutchinson was saying, life was not worth living. These remarks must only have added to the hostility of a town which had suffered from protracted poverty and depression and where men were claiming it as a badge of honor to die in defense of their liberties.

Hutchinson only then revealed his true stance on the Stamp Act, in the official venue of the superior court, not before what he had already deemed a new "model of government" where "the authority is in the populace."[37] In a scene which moved even his opponents, he called "GOD to witness (and I would not for a thousand worlds call my *Maker* to witness to a falsehood) . . . that I never, in New England or Old, in Great Britain or America, neither directly nor indirectly, was aiding, assisting, or supporting, or in the least promoting or encouraging what is commonly called the STAMP ACT, but on the contrary, did all in my power, and strove as much as in me lay, to prevent it." Hutchinson's lobbying occurred in private letters to influential people rather than in published or public statements, yet another sign of his estrangement from the evolving popular political culture. While his conduct and writings show him to be as aware as contemporary theorist Jürgen Habermas that people from a previously apolitical "private sphere" were demanding political authority, he refused to grant them any legitimacy.[38]

The out-law crowd not only insisted the government acknowledge the superiority of its space, or law, but it encroached on in-law space as well. The people entered the legislative chamber in Massachusetts for the first time in 1766, when a gallery was built to accommodate them. No longer were debates kept secret so representatives could speak their own minds without fear of reprisal.[39] And during the trial of Ebenezer Richardson, they encroached on the precincts of justice. When Chief Justice Peter Oliver charged the jury to find a verdict of justifiable homicide, his life was threatened: " 'D—n that judge, if I was nigh him, I would give it to him,' [someone shouted]; but this was not a time, to attempt to preserve decorum; preservation of life was as much as a judge dared to aim at." The mob shouted out to the jury "'Blood requires blood'" and hissed the judges as they left the court.[40]

While compelling native sons like Hutchinson and Oliver to come down to their level, the Bostonians insisted that customs commissioners and British soldiers had no right to share their space at all. The customs commissioners were "warned out" of town in effigy the day of their arrival—a practice New Englanders reserved for newcomers which informed them they would not be supported by the community if they became indigent. They were then actually chased out the next year by being subjected to rituals in which the crowds searched and seized *their* premises and possessions. In yet another instance of the crowd assuming the powers of government it assembled at the Liberty Tree, condemned, and then burned a boat belonging to customs commissioner Harrison in June, 1768, following a mock vice-admiralty court proceeding. In July, customs commissioner Robinson had his house thoroughly searched in the hopes of finding him. In imitation of the searches undertaken by the customs service for contraband, it was conducted " not by virtue of any writ of assistance, but by candle light." "Out-houses [note the first place mentioned, where one finds excrement], bales, barrels, meal tubs, trunks, boxes, packs, and packages, packed and unpacked, and in short, of every hole and corner sufficient to conceal a ram cat, or a commissioner, they could find neither." The commissioners got the message and fled to the protection of the British fleet.[41]

When the soldiers came to Boston in 1768, even the provincial council tried to deny them barracks in the town, which caused their commander to quarter his troops on the Boston Common, land collectively possessed and used by the inhabitants of the town. Since soldiers deserted with the connivance of the people—some seventy men within two weeks of their arrival—sentries were ordered to be especially careful. Bostonians balked at responding "Friend" to the usual challenge of "Friend or Foe" and hauled soldiers into sympathetic local courts for assault if they attempted to stop them. Given the cheapness of rum and the fact that soldiers had almost nothing to do, fights broke out, intensified by the fact that men receiving military pay would perform unskilled labor in their spare time more cheaply than those who depended on it for their entire livelihood. The fatal violent clash materialized after a year and a half; the outcome of the "Massacre" of seven Bostonians led to fierce threats that the inhabitants of the province would join the townsfolk in massacring the twelve hundred troops, which induced Governor Hutchinson to exile them to barracks on Castle William, an island in Boston Harbor.[42]

9. Two lyrics written in response to the Boston Massacre illustrate the redefinition of America in the song literature of the revolution as approximating a felicitous—rather than the chaotic Hobbesian or Lockean — state of nature, a land of play, an out-law space different from the rest of the world.[43] One tune, "Unhappy Boston," straightforwardly condemned the soldiers as "fierce barbarians grinning over their prey," which accompanied the famous and false Paul Revere engraving showing soldiers firing in unison at Captain Preston's command on helpless civilians. The poet appealed to God, "a judge who can never be bribed," who "strips the murderer of his soul," if somehow the loyalists on Massachusetts's "venal courts, the scandal of the land," connived to free the accused troops, which they ultimately did on obvious grounds of self-defense. The courts, or the official law, have become the scandal of "the land" or the natural society. The song opens with a lament: "Unhappy Boston, see thy sons deplore,/Thy hallowed walks besmear'd with guiltless gore." Boston is a sacred space invaded violated by "savage bands." Britain and its soldiers are placed outside true law as barbarians who enjoy slaughter. Defining Boston as inhabited by guiltless sons, the identification of America with childhood and innocence is confirmed; its law is one with the divine, and hence true law, rather than the non-law of the legal authorities.

The other Massacre song, "You Simple Bostonians," sarcastically yet playfully assumes the voice of British troops. The patriots falsely claimed that this tune was "much in vogue among the friends to arbitrary power," but they published it to arouse the populace against the arrogance of an army which, although stranded on an island in the harbor after the Massacre, supposedly cherished thoughts of murderous revenge. The Bostonians are signified as "simple" to call attention to the fact that the British did not think much of their pride in their literacy and knowledge of their rights. The colonists' identification with a more natural society than Europe is also mocked when they are called "pumpkins." "Of your

Liberty Tree, I'd have you take care," is the first threat the pretended soldier-songwriter makes, but destruction of the symbol is only a prelude to the total destruction of American society: "For if that we chance to return to the town,/ Your houses and stores will come tumbling down." In short, if the Americans thought having a few British soldiers in Boston was a violation of their liberty, they only had to wait for a larger fleet and army: "And to a bleak island, you shall not us drive,/ In every house, you shall have three or four,/And if that will not please you, you shall have half a score." In other words, there are many more European than American Britons, and they were determined to keep coming until the Liberty Tree and all it signified came down. (In fact, after Britain sent a large army to enforce the Coercive Acts, the Liberty Tree was chopped down.)

As with many revolutionary songs, "You Simple Bostonians" sets new words to an English tune, in this case the popular "Derry down," which is the chorus to each of four verses. It is most instructive to see what lyrics are being replaced. The English "Derry down" began as a patriotic war-time song about a "Liberty Hall" written by George Alexander Stevens in 1757. It begins with the dismissal of "Old Homer. . . Grecians or Trojans" as "heathenish" heroes who need to be replaced by "hearts of oak"—or heroic, contemporary Britons, especially sailors. In the American version, it is the British who have become tyrants rather than heroes, and the in-law, in-door liberty "hall" of justice and government has been replaced by the out-law, out-door liberty tree, a confined space by an open one. The juxtaposition is especially telling because the only liberty hall the British soldiers in Boston possess is the "bleak" forticiation in the middle of a New England harbor. The use of "simple" Bostonians is also telling since the Bostonians had not been dismissing their classical heroes, but rather holding up a virtuous antiquity as a model to a corrupted Britain as their pseudonyms, that is play personae, suggested. Unlike the British "Liberty Hall," the Bostonians dismiss the "hearts of oak" rather than the classics.

But in Britain itself, a comic parody of "Derry Down" had quickly supplanted the original version. "Liberty Hall" was symbolically transformed from a symbol of British justice and civilization into George Colman's song "Lodgings for Single Gentlemen," which bemoaned that in

"London, that overgrown place" there were plenty of bad, expensive lodgings, and "Will Waddle, whose temper was studious and lonely,/Hir'd lodgings that took Single Gentlemen only;/But Will was so fat, he appear'd like a ton,—/Or like two single gentlemen roll'd into one." If "You Simple Bostonians" is mocking the parody instead of, or in addition to, the original "Derry Down," "Single Gentlemen" refers to the exile of the British troops to the harbor island, to the problem of finding space for them in a land of liberty. The soldiers are thus identified with the comic, ineffectual "Will Waddle." "Waddle," of course, is the way a duck moves on the water, but in a person it implies the pathetic efforts of someone who is overweight to move from place to place. The soldiers, shifted from location to location in the course of their stay in Boston until they were exiled, were waddling indeed. The threat that they might return in greater numbers is dismissed by association of more soldiers with the overcrowding of London apartments by comic figures in the play *My Night Gown and Slippers* in which the "Derry Down" parody was sung.[44]

The greatest of the song adaptations made by the Bostonians rewrote the English patriotic tune "Heart of Oak" itself—still sufficiently famous that a British colleague could instantly recall its tune and words in 1996! Written by the great actor and playwright David Garrick in 1759 at the height of British triumphs in the Seven Years' War, it was performed in a play *Harlequin's Invasion* which revealed the utter contempt in which the British held—or pretended to hold—the possibility of a cross-channel invasion. The song reeks of the arrogance and jingoism which maintained its momentum after the war and led to the crackdown on colonial autonomy:[45]

> Come, cheer up, my lads, 'tis to glory we steer,
> To add something more to this wonderful year;
> To honor we call you, as free men, not slaves,
> For who are as free as the sons of the waves?
> Heart of oak are our ships,
> Heart of oak are our men:
> We are always ready
> Steady, boys, steady,
> We'll fight and we'll conquer again and again.

Further stanzas bemoan the fact that Britain's enemies are so afraid of her that they are always running away, and she must pursue them even to get them to stand and fight. The song concludes with welcome anticipation of an invasion which will permit the British "to drub 'em on shore as we drubb'd 'em at sea."

There is much to unpack here. First, American colonials had a rather different experience of the connection of the British navy to freedom: they universally detested and resisted naval impressment and frequently helped the suffering sailors to desert.[46] Second, in "Heart of Oak" Britons define themselves in the same terms American patriots use later. They too are sons of liberty who possess a unique space for freedom, although in this case "the waves" of which Britain was the world's undisputed master. A drinking song sung in the play spaces of theaters and taverns, "Heart of Oak" urged men to fight, be cheerful, and praise "our soldiers, our sailors, our statesmen," all perceived as vehicles of liberty.

The American version of "Heart of Oak," the "Liberty Song," was written by Philadelphia lawyer John Dickinson.[47] Ironically, in light of the fact that Dickinson would oppose signing the Declaration of Independence, he mailed a copy of the song to Boston's James Otis on July 4, 1768. The lyrics and tune achieved great popularity there, manifested by two parodies which soon appeared as well. Dickinson's freemen do not define liberty through conquest, which is the only activity they undertake in Garrick's version. They answer the call not of Britain but of a "fair LIBERTY" (again, a beautiful woman) as "AMERICANS," symbolizing the intercolonial unity for which Dickinson and Otis were hoping. The Americans' heroes are not the European British, but "our worthy *Forefathers*" who receive the "Cheers" Garrick gives to the contemporary British soldiers, sailors, and statesmen of whom the Americans had different opinions. "To climates unknown [they] did courageously steer," Dickinson notes, indicating the waves are not the true home of freedom, but in fact an obstacle that have to be overcome to obtain it: "Thro' oceans to deserts for freedom they came,/ And dying bequeathed us their freedom and fame." Deserts, however, become revalorized as spaces where "the TREE their own hands had to LIBERTY rear'd." "Growing strong and revered," they "Cry'd" out in "transport[s]" of joy that "Our children shall gather the fruits of our pain." America is a land where men are born to freedom, as the new refrain emphasizes; "In FREEDOM we're BORN, and in FREEDOM we'll LIVE,/Our purses are ready,/Steady, friends, Steady,/ Not as SLAVES but as FREEMEN our Money we'll give." America is a land where people no longer suffer, but enjoy: the Liberty Tree not only symbolizes the contemporary struggle, but now retrospectively signifies the American experience from the beginning. The ocean, the site of British freedom, has always been an ordeal for those immigrating to America—imagine being "Steady, friends, steady" on waves! The colonists needed to establish their own playground of liberty. And a playground it is, for as a verse Dickinson sent in later as an addendum rhapsodizes: "How sweet are the labors that Freemen endure,/That they shall enjoy all the Profit, secure —/No more such sweet labors AMERICANS know,/If Britons shall reap what Americans sow." In America, labor is made sweet and transformed from endurance to enjoyment, and will remain so as long as Britons, who are now defined as a separate group from Americans, do not steal the harvest, or tread on American space.

However, Dickinson predicts a dire future if Americans are not "Steady" in temporarily forsaking the joys of their land to sternly defend their right to maintain sole possession. "Swarms of PLACEMEN and PENSIONERS soon will appear," he foretells, "Like locusts deforming the charms of the year." An enchanted land will be devoured by "swarms" of insects—a nice touch which refers both to the author's opinion of the moral stature of British office-holders and to the Biblical plagues which were but temporary obstacles to a chosen people bound for a land flowing with milk and honey. The next stanza urges unity: "By *uniting* we stand, by *dividing* we fall"—Franklin should not be given credit for everything memorable said in the eighteenth century! After assuring his readers that Heaven has blessed "each generous deed" they will commit in sacrificing for freedom, Dickinson offers them a destiny preferable to being mere heirs to glorious forefathers who dropped freedom in their laps. Dickinson's generation, too, can emulate the deeds of a glorious past rather than sycophantically enjoy their playground as children of heroic forefathers: "All ages shall speak with *Amaze* and *Applause*, /Of the *Courage we'll shew* IN

SUPPORT OF OUR LAWS." British North America, some two million people (one-fifth slaves plus a sizable contingent of white bound indentured servants) will be the wonder of the ages. Dickinson has predicted a forthcoming war in which not British law, but OUR LAWS will be defended—that is, the out-laws of the playground. "To DIE we can bear,—but, to SERVE we disdain,/For SHAME is to Freemen more dreadful than PAIN." Reputation and avoidance of unjust laws which reduce men to slaves can be achieved in opposition to the Britain which claimed to stand for "freemen not slaves" in "Heart of Oak." You are slaves, Dickinson is telling the British as he appropriates the song and its symbols.

Dickinson's final verse represents something of a backtracking, as this is only 1768, from the logical consequences of an argument Thomas Hutchinson saw so clearly three years earlier. The first eight verses of the song find nothing positive in Britain, extol formation of a separate identity, and define America as a space of freedom as opposed to the slavery imposed by a British law now defined as alien rather than the source of liberty—like the waves, it must be crossed, transgressed, to find real or out-law liberty. But suddenly Dickinson sings: "This bumper I crown for our SOVEREIGN'S health,/And this for BRITANNIA'S glory and wealth;/That wealth and that glory immortal may be,/If She is but *just*—and *We* are but *Free.*"

The last two lines reverse the apparent reversal of the first two: loyalty to Britain is conditional on Britain leaving the colonies alone. What makes Britain glorious is redefined from the conquest bragged about in Garrick's "Heart of Oak" to an imperial power that refuses to impose her laws on the unwilling. Britain, in other words, should adopt a defensive posture to secure liberty, like America, rather than that urged in Garrick's song. But just as Garrick dares his nation's foes to try to invade Britain, Dickinson has no problem should England decide to suppress America. She has the enviable choice of remaining a playground of freedom or becoming the wonder of the world in defending it.

"The Parody" of Dickinson's song appeared in *The Boston Gazette* a little over a month after Dickinson's original was published. Since *The Gazette* was Boston's leading patriot paper, the fact that the parody was supposedly written by a tory from Castle William—that is, one of the customs commissioners who had been obliged to flee earlier that year—indicates the patriot leadership knew taunting only enflamed their constituents with a zeal for liberty. "Come shake your dull noddles, ye pumpkins, and bawl/And own that you're mad at fair Liberty's call," the song begins, insulting the Americans' intelligence, pride in their agrarianism, manhood (children bawl) and sanity in their refusal to submit to the Townshend Acts, all in two lines. "Old Satan" rather than heroic planters of the Liberty Tree is now the rebels' ancestor, and the only tree they should enjoy is Tyburn, the gallows of London. American abundance is denied as the patriots are termed "brats and bunters"—children, that is, but obnoxious ones—who far from living in a land of plenty hope to "feather their nests" by "reaping what other men sow." America, as the British maintain, is exploiting the mother country rather than the reverse. Now the patriots become insects who will "melt like the locusts when winter is near" when "red coats appear." Future ages will remember the rebels as "numskulls. . . rascals, fools, whoresons. . . the vilest banditti that swarmed." Real freedom is protection from "mobs, knaves, and villains." Here the patriots are having fun, joyously assuming in a drinking song the very criticisms loyalists made of them. They deal with contempt through parody and play.

"The Parody Parodied" of Dickinson's song appeared in the almanac published by the patriot printers Edes and Gill for 1770. It is rather more serious than the first parody, in that while condemning "Ye insolent tyrants! who wish to enthrall/Ye minions, ye placemen, pimps, pensioners, all," the king appears in the seventh of eleven verses and is the recipient of much good will in the hope that he can guarantee American liberty. The writer is certain that although "oppress'd and reproach'd, our king we implore,/Still firmly persuaded our rights he'll restore." But what if he does not? "When our hearts beat to arms, to defend a just right, /Our monarch rules there, and forbids us to fight." War in defense of liberty is already being contemplated; only the belief that a just monarch will realize his true greatness lies in defending American rights restrains hearts that already wish to take up arms against his evil advisors. For the next stanza assures the latter that no threats "could make us submit to their chains for a day." Only lingering "affection" for Britain "prevent[s] the fierce conflict which threatens *your* [my emphasis] fall!" Americans have been sufficiently goaded into an armed struggle which they are confident they will not only win, but sure that their victory will bring about Britain's demise, not theirs. America's glory, of which "all ages shall speak, with amaze and applause," will be "Of the prudence we show in support of our cause." The refrain defines Americans as the "sons of Freedom" who will "never surrender,/But swear to defend her,/And scorn to survive, if unable to save."

Thomas Paine's 1776 pamphlet *Common Sense*, indispendable in provoking the final break with Britain, made Americans realize the logic of their actions over the past decade. Paine also declared America a natural, sacred play-space—"the palaces of kings are built upon the ruins of the bowers of paradise" —and an "asylum" for a "Liberty" harried round the globe. He too wrote a song, "Liberty Tree," which put *Common Sense*'s ideas into verse.[48] The original tune of the song was "The Gods of Greece," suggesting America had supplanted an idealized Greece and Olympus in which its gods dwelled as the best society possible. Instead of Apollo bringing light to the world, the song begins: "In a chariot of light from the regions of day,/The goddess of Liberty came./Ten thousand celestials directed the way,/ And hither conducted the dame." In her hand she bore "a fair budding branch from the gardens above. . . as a pledge of her love,/And the plant she named 'Liberty Tree'." The tree served as the aegis for an enchanted playground which also resembled the idyllic image of another ancient society beloved by Americans—the Biblical Hebrews. "Beneath this fair tree, like the patriarchs of old,/Their bread in contentment they ate./Unvex'd with the troubles of silver and gold,/The cares of the grand and the great." A prosperous society without class distinctions—a basically egalitarian people—dwelled in the "bowers of paradise" that had yet to bear the weight of king's palaces. Paine's description of pre-revolutionary America is remarkably similar to the primitive society he describes at the beginning of *Common Sense:* "Let us suppose a small number of persons settled in some sequestered part of the earth, unconnected with the rest. . . . Some convenient tree [in the song as in the protest movement, the "Liberty Tree"] will afford them a State

House, under the branches of which, the whole colony may assemble to deliberate on public matters." Americans have redefined the state of nature, feared by British philosophers Thomas Hobbes and John Locke as anarchy which required government as a cure, as a state of free, limited government.

Paine, in his song and great pamphlet, has codified revolutionary play activity as equivalent to the great act of founding government. It serves as the basis of a just civil society to replace the rest of the world's corruption. America is a "continent"—a vast, open space—England a "small island," "and it is very absurd in supposing a continent to be perpetually governed by an island." Instead, in America "THE LAW IS KING" and should symbolically be crowned as such in a play coronation ceremony: "but lest ill use should afterwards arise, let the crown at the conclusion of the ceremony, be demolished, and scattered among the people whose right it is." Out-law in the American play-ground emerges as the only human law worthy of the name.

In the middle of the "Liberty Tree's" second stanza, Paine signifies old England as the helpless dependent of its American colonies: "With timber and tar they old England supplied and supported her pow'r on sea." American wood and its products, the fruits of trees and liberty, are responsible for England's navy. Furthermore, Americans fought "her"—Britain's—battles "without gaining a groat". Nevertheless, America's wealth and character remained natural and unspoiled. Her only problems arose from her connection with the mother country, which had been the beneficiary of the colonists' freedom and largesse, not the other way round. However, "King, Commons, and Lords," grouped together as "tyrannical powers," were uniting "to cut down [the Liberty Tree] this guardian of ours"—much as the British soldiers had literally done in Boston. The remedy is for "the far and the near... [to] unite with a cheer,/In defense of our Liberty Tree." The colonists' true mother is the goddess of Liberty, symbolically represented by "The Pine Tree Flag," a precursor of the stars and stripes, and by the green boughs patriots lacking uniforms placed in their hats. These identified them as adherents of natural law embodied in a natural America against loyalists, who usually sported pieces of paper signifying statute law.[49]

When the colonists finally secured independence at Yorktown in 1781, British and American use of two songs suggest both sides understood the power of music and the symbolism of ballads to make the meaning of the triumph clear. As angry British soldiers hurled their weapons to the ground at the surrender, their band began to play "The World Turned Upside Down":[50]

> If buttercups buzzed after the bee,
> If boats were on land, churches on sea,
> If ponies rode men, and if grass ate cows,
> If cats should be chased into holes by the mouse,
> If the mammas sold their babies to gypsies for half a crown,
> If summer were spring, and the other way round,
> Then all the world would be upside down.

Sung in most settings, this would be a silly, playful song, but in the sorrowful context in which the British fife-and-drum corps performed it, it even loses its playfulness. The natural unspoiled world has triumphed over the world of toil and long-established society. The industrious bee has yielded to a beautiful flower, nature (the pony) has triumphed over men, the meek (undomesticated) mouse has put the malicious (domesticated) cat to flight, and a mother (country) is divesting herself of her children as Britain symbolically loses half her crown. Bereft of America, the joy, the play, has gone out of a Britain ready to turn from Merry Olde England into the land of Blake's dark Satanic mills.

The other song associated with Yorktown, "The Cornwallis Country Dance," was set to the tune of the immortal "Yankee Doodle."[51] "Yankee Doodle" originated as a British song in the French and Indian War to make fun of the inept (doodle means dolt) Americans, but was adopted as a badge of honor in yet another example of revolutionary play by the rebels. The most famous verses were written in 1775 by Edward Bangs, a Harvard sophomore, who mocked the "tarnal pride" of General Washington, the gaudy dress of his entourage, and a "thousand men,/As rich as Squire David." The most interesting stanza suggests Washington and the non-New Englanders in the army were so foppish that they would not only make terrible soldiers, but were not even real men: "The flaming ribbons in his hat,/They looked so taring fine, ah,/I wanted pockily to get,/To give to my Jemimah." But the joke is on "Yankee Doodle" himself, who some trench diggers threatened to bury in their work: "It scared me so I hooked it off,/Nor stopped as I remember,/Nor turned about till I got home,/Locked up in mother's chamber." Making fun of the expected cowardice of an inexperienced militia, but at the same time suggesting to them that the alternative is to run back to mother, Barnes is trying to shame the troops who would jocularly sing this song into defending their masculinity as an essential element of their liberty. Otherwise, they must abandon the out-of-door play space of the camp for mother's chamber—an enclosed space of not-play, symbolically the security and protection offered by a mother country at the price of freedom.

"Yankee Doodle" became the tune of the Revolution, the only one to survive in the popular imagination into the twentieth century: "For every loyalist stanza there were a hundred improvised by Yankee bards."[52] One verse even became, if I can get playful, a meta-narrative in which patriots confident of victory conflate fighting, feasting, and having fun in America and in the army: "Yankee Doodle is the tune,/That we all delight in;/It suits for feasts, it suits for fun,/And just as well for fightin'." "The Cornwallis Country Dance" not only told the British authors of the original "Yankee Doodle" that the Doodles were having the last laugh on them, but it plays with the idea of play itself. So pathetic had been Cornwallis's efforts to capture Nathanael Greene's army in the southern theater of war in 1780 and 1781 that they resembled a dance more than a campaign to be taken seriously. Cornwallis engaged in "much retrograde and much advance and all with General Greene, sir." He then "jigged" with Lafayette before he was, literally, played out: as his voice in the song states: "My guards are weary grown with footing country dances,/They never at St. James's shone at capers, kicks, and prances." In other words, formal European warfare poorly equipped his troops to handle Greene's mobile tactics.

The song then contrasts unfavorably the courage and masculinity of British soldiers with American: "Men so gallant ne'er were seen while sauntering on parade, sir,/Or wriggling oe'r the Park's smooth green or at a masquerade, sir." British troops saunter arrogantly, but only excel in drill, not in battle. The stultifying society in which they are forced to live poorly prepares them for real warfare: their movements are compared to "wriggling" as do insects or people trying to squirm out of something, to escape from a tough situation, a very undesirable quality in soldiers. A masquerade is a formal, aristocratic European ball with dancing, but one where people are disguised—men cannot realize their true potential in old-world societies and armies. The British are revalorized as mock or play soldiers, as the following lines suggest: "Yet are red heels and long-laced skirts for stumps and briars meet, sir,/Or stand they chance with hunting shirts or hardy veteran feet, sir." The British soldiers appear to be men dressed up as women: their red coats might as well be red heels (worn by high-class ladies or, alternatively, prostitutes) and the Scottish kilts "long-laced skirts." The real "veterans" are the frontiersmen who by the end of the war had become some of the best soldiers in the world, who hunt in forests rather than parade in parks or at masked balls. They roam wide and free in loose-fitting clothing, rather than the confining garb which symbolize the social and military discipline Europe required.

In fact, the British can't even win on their own terms. When cooped up at Yorktown, Cornwallis challenged all to "minuets" and "lessons for a courtly ball his soldiers studied nightly." At the conventional warfare these dances symbolizes, however, De Grasse and Rochambeau, the French commanders, proved better formal dancers. Washington was no slouch, either:

> And Washington, Columbia's son, whom easy nature taught, sir,
> That grace which can't by pains be won, nor monarch's gold be bought, sir,
> Now hand in hand they circle round, this ever-dancing peer, sir,
> Their gentle movements soon confound the Earl, as they draw near, sir.

By Yorktown, the Americans could match the British at their own maneuvers. Washington possessed a "grace" obtained through living in a new land, acquired from an "easy nature." That land was dubbed Columbia, a name considered for the United States that emphasized its natural condition at the time of discovery. Americans did not require harsh discipline nor payment to be good soldiers. The war's hardships melted in the heady days after the surrender; the triumph of "nature" over tyranny was defined as "easy."

Washington, in short, beat Cornwallis because Americans knew how to play and the British, who once did, had forgotten:

> His music he forgets to play, his feet can move no more, sir,
> And all his soldiers curse the day they jiggled to our shore, sir,
> Now Tories all, what will you say? Come, is this not a griper?
> That while your hopes are danced away, 'tis you must pay the piper.

Cornwallis was ultimately immobilized until he not only could not play, he could not move at all. His army was cooped up as his foes gleefully danced round and round. Out-law space has basically become the whole continent except for a tiny bit of the Yorktown peninsula, and Cornwallis must even surrender that. Furthermore, it is the losing loyalists and Indians who must pay up—in the form of confiscation of their lands as their opponents enjoy themselves. A piping musician is the recipient of the territory as Americans acquire even more outlaw space.

What can we learn from examining the American Revolution from the perspectives of play and song by analogy with Roberta Kevelson's treatment of Robin Hood and the outlaw ballads? People do not move easily to reject a system of government and make a revolution. A decade before the Declaration of Independence, people in Boston were already playing at murdering their rulers and symbolically setting up a new government after placing themselves in a state of nature. Much like the warfare of primitive people like the Yanomano of the Amazon or Maring of New Guinea, where chest-slapping and arrow-dodging respectively prefigure and try to avert deadly conflict, the revolution's history, to reverse Karl Marx's dictum, appeared first as farce, then as tragedy (or triumph).[53] Americans in their streets and songs played out ideas they only put into formal writing and revolutionary praxis in 1775 and 1776. They were psychologically preparing for independence, they were symbolically, playfully declaring it beginning in the mid-1760s. Or, to put it in old-fashioned Puritan terms the New Englanders would have understood, play was preparation for salvation.

What happened in the Revolution, in the critical decade 1765–1775 in Boston especially, was the spontaneous, eclectic creation of new ideas, under the pressure of unprecedented critical events, to justify an emerging new form of political society. Historians, enamored of influences and borrowings which, after all, stress the relevance of their professional bailiwick, have missed the boat in two ways. It is relatively easy, and safe, and boring, to show correspondence between New Whig, Old Whig, Florentine republican, Roman classical, Puritan/Biblical, or English constitutional/common law ideas and those set forth in the erudite pamphlets elite revolutionaries wrote to persuade themselves, each other, and their supporters in Britain that they were justified in taking the momentous step of rebellion. (In lieu of a footnote, round up the usual suspects.) It is much more difficult, and dangerous, and exciting to argue that revolutionary ideology, like the polity it supported, and what it claimed to be, was something new under the sun. For in the songs of the streets we do not hear the language of Locke, Hobbes, Machiavelli, Trenchard and Gordon, Moses, Winthrop, Cicero, Coke, or the stern virtue of a Christian Sparta. We hear praise for an America where, and where alone, the chaotic state of nature is subtly transformed into the good natural society—the space of leisure, happiness, and ordered liberty. We also sense the exuberance of youth—the enthusiasm of relatively young men for their young land. The irrepressible and protean Benjamin Franklin was the exception who proved the rule: nearly every other prominent man his age was a loyalist.

Also, the American Revolution only could have occurred if the gap between elites and masses was bridged. For it does not advance our understanding to delineate class antagonisms, which always exist and always take some form or other, when what must be explained is how a political elite joined with a largely apolitical populace to make a revolution. To assign primary agency to leaders *or* followers is also to miss the boat; it makes as much sense to argue whether sodium *or* chloride is the essential ingredient in table salt. The essence of the situation was creative interaction. What was remarkable was General William Brattle and Shoemaker Ebenezer Mackintosh leading a parade together, or Philadelphia lawyer Jonathan Dickinson writing the "Liberty Song" sung by artisans in the streets of Boston, or ne'er-do-well Tom Paine spurring on Congress to realize that independence was the logical consequence of their action. Until things became deadly serious after Lexington and Concord, humor, play, and song were vital in permitting boundaries to be stretched and new rituals, political entities, and ideas to be tested. Tension and conflict could be mediated, underplayed if not shrugged off, in an atmosphere of genial male camaraderie, in a fluid environment with no predictable outcome.

The interpretation of the Revolution advanced here corresponds to the "network analysis" of social protest advanced by late twentieth century sociologists, an interpretation remarkably consonant with Peirce's and Kevelson's notion of a universe evolving to unpredictable ends through creative interaction.[54] Protest cannot be explained by fixed interests or statically-defined social or economic groups, but only by the dynamic interaction of diverse elements in associations, informal, or formal yet fluid, which bring them together. Agendas for change are not inflexible reflections of particular positions, but emerge from a common position of hostility diverse groups share toward an unresponsive elite and, by extension, those pro-elite groups to whom that elite is indeed responsive. Now that sympathetic theorists of revolution, people of the Left, are free of the need to justify or even consider the static and sterile self-representations advanced by twentieth-century faux-Marxist regimes in support of their statist tyrannies, America's revolution no longer appears anomalous. As Timothy Wickham-Crowley has pointed out in his study of Latin American revolutions, the cooperation of intellectuals—like the young lawyers and pamphleteers in Boston and other port cities in the 1760s—and people of all classes have been required to topple successfully what he has termed "mafiacracies" or "patrimonial praetorian regimes." Here a small number of families dominate leading government positions and are sustained by military force or some equivalent, a fair representation of the Hutchinson-Oliver group in Massachusetts.[55] Jack Goldstone's postulation of a state fiscal crisis, elite alienation, and multi-class mobilization as the sources of revolution also fits the American scene—as indeed it does the classic French and Russian Revolutions—in which a government became increasingly estranged from its subjects.[56] Conflict among revolutionary groups usually becomes prominent or dominant only when the old regime has been toppled.

Speaking in the House of Lords in January, 1775, urging his fellow M. P's not to send more troops to America and provoke a separation, William Pitt told this story. A person of "respect and authenticity" had stated:[57]

> That these were the prevalent and steady principles of America—That you might destroy their towns, and cut them off from the superfluities, perhaps the conveniences of life; but that they were prepared to despise your power, and would not lament their loss, whilst they have— what my Lords?—their *woods* and their *liberty*.

The question before us today is whether we can possess liberty with woods that have been turned into paper. America's revolutionary outlaw ballads do not linger in our heritage, except for "Yankee Doodle." They do not evoke nostalgic and romantic memories, as the English legend of Robin Hood does for an industrial power which mourns the vanished forest. For not only did Robin's American counterparts survive, they went beyond being pardoned by good King Richard. The revolutionaries supplanted the king himself and, as Paine suggested, made outlaw law the king. It is as though the Merry Men of Sherwood Forest had taken over England's government instead of the hearts of its people. As such, our government is now theoretically hemmed in by paper guarantees of liberty, by the Declaration of Independence's injunction that it exists only to further our "life, liberty, and pursuit of happiness," and by the Constitution's the Ninth and Tenth Amendments, which stipulate that the states and the people retain all powers not specifically delegated to the government.

But can an institutionalized play space be a play space at all? Once America is defined as the land of freedom, does standing against a government that in theory only exists to support freedom become logically impossible? Samuel Adams thought so: he was the most vociferous opponent of Shays's Rebellion in Massachusetts in 1786 and 1787: "In monarchies the crime of treason and rebellion may admit to being pardoned or lightly punished, but the man who dares rebel against the laws of a republic ought to suffer death."[58] Whether freedom, and what sort, can survive in a government based on revolution that outlaws revolution is an interesting question: for starters, the Confederacy posed it as the War for Southern Independence. I shall not attempt to answer it here.

# Notes

1. Published by the Research Center for Lanugage and Semiotic Studies (Bloomington: Indiana University) with The Peter de Ridder Press (Lisse, The Netherlands). Her first book, The Inverted Pyramid: An Introduction to the Semiotics of Media Language, had been published by the same institution and press earlier that year.

2. See, for example, *War, Politics, and Revolution in Provincial Massachusetts* (Boston: Northeastern University Press, 1981); *America's Burke: The Mind of Thomas Hutchinson* (Lanham, Md.: University Press of America, 1982); with John Lax, "The Knowles Riot and the Crisis of the 1740s in Massachusetts," *Perpsectives in American History*, 10 (1976):163–214; "The Social Structure of Revolutionary Boston: The Evidence from the Great Fire of 1760 Manuscripts," *Journal of Interdisciplinary History*, 10 (1979): 267–278; with Ralph Crandall, "Metropolitan Boston Before the American Revolution," *Proceedings of the Bostonian Society* (1985): 55–77.

3. Kevelson, *Inlaws/Outlaws*, 12–13, 66.

4. *Ibid.*, 78.

5. *Ibid.*, 88.

6. John Avery, Jr. to John Collins, Aug. 19, 1765, in Ezra Stiles, *Extracts from Itineraries and Other Miscellanies of Ezra Stiles* (New Haven: Yale University Press, 1916): 435–437.

7. *Boston Post-Boy,* Sept. 2, 1765; *Boston Newsletter*, Sept. 5, 1765; Peter Shaw, *American Patriots and the Rituals of Revolution* (Cambridge: Harvard University Press, 1981): 191–193, 265–266, notes 35–36.

8. John Adams, *Legal Papers*, L. Kinvin Wroth and Hiller B. Zobel, eds., 3 vols. (Cambridge: Harvard University Press, 1965): 2: 396–399, 420.

9. *Ibid.*, 3: 108; 114–115; 92.

10. *Ibid.*, 3: 266.

11. *Boston Gazette*, Feb. 26, 1770; Adams, *Legal Papers,* 2: 400.

12. Shaw, *American Patriots,* 190; Alfred F. Young, "Pope's Day, Tar and Feathers and Cornet Joyce, Jr.: From Ritual to Rebellion in Boston, 1745–1775," unpublished paper, Anglo-American Historians' Conference, Rutgers University,

1973; Albert Matthews, "Joyce, Jun." *Colonial Society of Massachusetts Pulibcations* , 8 (1903):89–104, and "Joyce, Jun., Once More," *ibid.,* 9 (1904): 280–294.

13. Edwin G. Burrows and Michael Wallace, "The American Revolution: The Ideology and Psychology of National Liberation," *Perspectives in American History*, 6 (1972): 167–306; Winthrop D. Jordan, "Familial Politics: Thomas Paine and the Killing of the King," *Journal of American History*, 60 (1973): 294–308; Jay Fliegelman, *Prodigals and Patriots: The American Revolution Against Patriarchal Authority, 1750–1800* (New York: Cambridge University Press, 1982).

14. Oscard Brand, *Songs of '76: A Folksinger's History of the Revolution* (New York: M. Evans, 1972): 43, 147.

15. Benjamin W. Labaree, *The Boston Tea Party* (New York: Oxford University Press, 1964): ch. 7; Dirk Hoerder, *Crowd Action in Revolutionary Massachusetts* (New York: Academic Press, 1977): 257–264; Alfred F. Young, "George Robert Twelves Hewes (1742–1840): A Boston Shoemaker and the Memory of the American Revolution," reprinted in *In Search of America: The William and Mary Quarterly, 1943–1993* (Williamsburg: The Institute for Early American History and Culture, 1993): 258–260.

16. I have culled these names at random by leafing through Arthur M. Schlesinger, *Prelude to Independence: The Newspaper War Against Britain, 1764–1776* (New York: Knopf, 1956) and Philip Davidson, *Propaganda and the American Revolution* (Chapel Hill: University of North Carolina Press, 1941).

17. Schlesinger, *Prelude to Independence*, 142, 106.

18. John Adams, *Works,* ed. Charles Francis Adams, 10 vols. (Boston: Little, Brown, 1850–1856): 10: 99.

19. The image of Hutchinson is reprinted in my *War, Politics, and Revolution,* 195.

20. George P. Anderson, "Ebenezer Mackintosh: Stamp Act Rioter and Patriot," and "A Note on Ebenezer Mackintosh," *Colonial Society of Massachusetts Publications* 26 (1927): 15–64, 348–361; Thomas Hutchinson to Thomas Pownall, Mar. 8, 1766, reprinted in Edmund S. Morgan, *Prologue to Revolution: The Stamp Act Crisis* (Chapel Hill: University of North Carolina Press, 1959): 125.

21. Davidson, *Propaganda,* 175–177; Shaw, *American Patriots,* 8–13.

22. Shaw, *American Patriots,* 17; Hoerder, *Crowd Action*, 207–208, 227.

23. Hoerder, *Crowd Action*, 207–208, 227.

24. Adams, *Legal Papers*, 3: 86.

25. Alfred F. Young, "English Plebeian Culture and Eighteenth-Century Radicalism," in Margaret Jacob and James Jacob, eds., *The Origins of Anglo-American Radicalism* (London: George Allen and Unwin, 1984): 185–212.

26. For a thorough discussion of the origin and transformation of "Yankee Doodle," see Irwin Silber, ed., *Songs of Independence* (Harrisburg; Stackpole Books, 1973): 69–80.

27. Shaw, *American Patriots,* 16, 188; Hoerder, *Crowd Action,* 117–118.

28. Hoerder,*Crowd Action*, 185; Robert Middlekauff, *The Glorious Cause: The American Revolution, 1763–1789*, New York: (Oxford University Press, 1982): 157; Shaw, *American Patriots,* 17.

29. Davidson, *Propaganda*, 197–198.

30. New England Papers, vol. 2: 91, 96–98, Sparks Ms. vol. 43, Houghton Library, Harvard University.

31. Edmund S. Morgan and Helen M. Morgan, *The Stamp Act Crisis: Prologue to Revoluition* (Chapel Hill: University of North Carolina Press, 1953): 163–172, 179–180, 368–369.

32. Josiah Quincy, ed., *Reports of Cases Argued and Adjudged in the Superior Court of Judicature of the Province of Massachusetts Bay Between 1761 and 1772* (Boston: Little, Brown, 1865), 173; Hutchinson, *History of. . . Massachusetts*, 3: 88; *Boston Evening Post,* Aug. 19, 1765; *Boston Gazette*, Aug. 26, 1765; Morgan, ed., *Prologue to Revolution* , 122, 126; Edmund S. Morgan, "Thomas Hutchinson and the Stamp Act," *New England Quarterly*, 21 (1948): 461–492.

33. *Independent Advertiser,* Feb. 8, 1748; Dec. 5, 1749.

34. Adams, *Works*, 2: 167.

35. John M. Murrin, "Anglicizing an American Colony: The Transformation of Provincial Massachusetts" (Yale University, Ph.D. thesis, 1966); Rowland Berthoff and John M. Murrin, "Feudalism, Communalism, and the Yeoman Freeholder: The American Revolution Considered as a Social Accident," in James Hutson and Stephen Kurtz, eds., *Essays on the American Revolution* (Chapel Hill: University of North Carolina Press, 1973): 256–288; Pencak and Crandall, "Metropolitan Boston."

36. Quincy, ed., *Reports of Cases, 170–173.*

37. Morgan, ed., *Prologue to Revolution*, 124.

38. Jürgen Habermas, *The Structural Transformation of the Public Sphere* (Cambridge: MIT Press, 1989).

39. Samuel Alleyne Otis to ?, June 17, 1766, Otis Papers, vol. 2, Butler Library, Columbia University.

40. Adams, *Legal Papers*, 2: 405.

41. Young, "George Robert Twelves Hewes," 256; Shaw, *American Patriots,* 188.

42. John Shy, *Toward Lexington: The Role of the British Army in the Coming of the American Revolution* (Princeton: Princeton University Press, 1965), ch. 7; Hiller B. Zobel, *The Boston Massacre* (New York: Norton, 1970), esp. chs. 12, 16; pp. 206–211 (for threats to massacre soldiers).

43. Brand, *Songs of '76*, 20–22.

44. W. Chappell, *The Ballad Literature and Popular Music of Olden Time* (London: Chappell and Company, 1855): 677.

45. *Ibid.*, 715–717. Noted on these pages. Boswell, Johnson's biographer, when visiting Corsica, remarked that the inhabitants asked him to sing an English song and he sang "Hearts of Oak." Never did I see men so delighted with a song as the Corsicans were with "Hearts of Oak. 'Cuore di querco,' cried they, 'Bravo Inglese.' It was quite a joyous riot. I fancied myself to be a recuriting sea-officer—I fancied all my chorus of Corsicans aboard the British fleet." Croker's edition of *The Life of Samuel Johnson*, vol. x: 233.

46. See Lax and Pencak, "The Knowles Riot:" and Pencak, *America's Burke*, ch. 2, for even Thomas Hutchinson's life-long, principled opposition.

47. John Dickinson, *Political Writings, 1764–1774*, ed. Paul Leicester Ford (Philadelphia: The Historical Society of Pennsylvania): 421–432, has the text of his song and both parodies.

48. Brand, *Songs of '76*, 58–61; quotations from *Common Sense* accessible in many versions: see extended selections in Richard D. Brown, ed., *Major Problems in the Era of the American Revoluiton, 1760–1791* (Lexinton, Mass., D. C. Heath, 1992): 149–151, 159–162, for excerpts which follow.

49. Charles Royster, *A Revolutionary People at War: The Continental Army and the American Character, 1775–1783* (Chapel Hill: University of North Carolina Press, 1979): 237; William Pencak, "'The Fine Theoretic Government of

Massachusetts is Prostrated to the Earth': The Response to Shays's Rebellion Reconsidered," in Robert A. Gross, ed., *In Debt to Shays: The Bicentennial of an Agrarian Rebellion* (Charlottesville: University Press of Virginia, 1993): 128.

50. Brand, *Songs of '76*, 159–160.

51. *Ibid.*, 156–158.

52. Silber, ed., *Songs of Independence*, 80.

53. John Keegan, *A History of Warfare* (New York: Knopf, 1993): 94–102.

54. Mustafa Emirbayer and Jeff Goodwin, "Network Analysis, Culture, and the Problem of Agency," *American Journal of Sociology*, 99 (1994): 1411–1454, has an excellent summary of this literature. I thank my friend Kurt Seidel, currently a graduate student in the Department of Sociology at New York University, for acquainting me with this important body of work which dovetails so well with the analysis I present.

55. See especially Roger Gould, "Multiple Networks and Mobilization in the Paris Commune, 1871," *American Sociological Review,* 56 (1991): 716–729, and "Trade Cohesion, Class Unity, and Urban Insurrection: Artisanal Activism in the Paris Commune, 1871," *American Journal of Sociology,* 98 (1992): 721–754.

56. Timothy P. Wickham-Crowley, *Guerrillas and Revolution in Latin America: A Comparative Analysis of Insurgents and Regimes since 1956* (Princeton: Princeton University Press, 1992); Jack A. Goldstone, Ted Robert Gurr, and Farrokh Moshirir, eds., *Revolutions of the Late Twentieth Century* (Boulder: Westview Press, 1991). For a good discussion of such approaches to revolution see Jeff Goodwin, "Toward a New Sociology of Revolutions," *Theory and Society*, 23 (1994): 731–766.

57. William Pitt [Earl of Chatham], speech in House of Lords, Jan. 20, 1775, reprinted in Max Beloff, ed. *The Debate on the American Revolution,* 3d. ed. (Dobbs Ferry: Sheridan House, 1989): 191–192.

58. William V. Wells, *The Life and Public Service of Samuel Adams*, 3 vols. (1865; reprinted Freeport: Books for Libraries Press, 1969): 3: 246.

# Chapter Nine
# Recovering Meaning from Chaos?: Word Play and the Challenge of Sense

**W. T. Scott and H. O'Donnell**

## Theoretical Preliminaries

### Clues

There is surely no concept more basic to both semiotics and forensic legal studies than that of the clue, "the small facts upon which large inferences may depend," as Sherlock Holmes puts it in discussing his method. This remark comes in a chapter of *The Sign of Four* entitled "The Science of Deduction," ably discussed in Eco and Sebeok (1983: 20ff). This excellent collection of essays systematically examines the fascinating parallels between Peirce and Holmes with regard to their views on finding out the non-obvious from the obvious, but perhaps overlooked, or puzzling surface detail.

This is, of course, the basic semiotic move, the shift from the evident signifier to the non-evident signified. However we construe these difficult terms, and however elaborate and contentious our classification of the varieties of semiosis becomes, it seems unexceptionable that the move just described—through something perceptually present to something else not otherwise available for consideration—is basic, not only in detective work of various sorts, but in survival for this and other species experiencing a world of change and uncertainty. To live at all is to signify, giving out and drawing in interpretable phenomena. In this ubiquitous and unending process, all signifiers are essentially clues.

Semioticans trace the roots of their attempts to generalize about signification to ancient medicine and its symptomatologies. However, more basic and perennial still are the clue-using techniques of the diviner, the hunter (and the hunted), the pathfinder, the herdsman, farmer and, indeed, the lover. More sophisticated examples would include all the investigative empirical sciences, especially those that decode information-based structures, such as the various branches of biology. These, and most of the humanities/social sciences disciplines, are metaforensic in that they seek to make sense of data which is already and primarily semiotically constructed. In legal context, for example, data such as confessions and contracts are meant to be meaningful, but the point, familiar to semioticians, holds in most domains where phenomena are analyzed and interpreted.

## Solutions

At this more abstract level, it is clear that the higher forms of problem-solving, particularly of scientific reasoning leading to valid and reliable explanatory knowledge of all sorts, not merely the triumphant demonstrations of what must be so that we find in Holmes' exploits, are dependent on chains of the basic interpretive move from given to not-given. A valid generalization stands in a particular semiotic relationship to the domain it covers, as Peirce showed in the third and least discussed of his three triads.

Peirce, of course, devoted many years of his working life as both a scientist and a philosopher to examining the relationships among deduction, induction, and what he calls abduction, more commonly nowadays the hypothetico-deductive method. The typical starting-point, for Holmes at least, is some neglected trifle, which might just be made sense of in such a way as to help make sense of other, less peripheral, pieces of evidence, and so warrant the construction of an internally coherent account of all the relevant facts. Good interpretations or explanations have other qualities, of course, among them Popperian falsifiability, economy, and the monopoly, *pro tem* at least, of plausibility. However, the Holmesian method of assembling mutually supportive interpretations of seemingly unimportant details, so as to warrant a hypothesis which then gathers in the obviously relevant facts, leading to incontestable, but otherwise concealed, final facts—the culprit, the method—has rightly been seen as a paradigm for all the routes to knowledge that entail decoding in the face of "evidence" characterized by complexity, opacity, incompleteness, and deceitfulness, whether accidental or deliberate.

## Semiotic Solutions

For legal forensics, as already noted, the interpretive process is frequently carried out upon texts of various sorts, usually displaying, and being accorded, the three features of having been deliberately *designed*, designed as *texts*, and as texts of a *particular sort*. They thus exemplify advanced cases of Peirce's symbolic mode of signifying, wherein the signifier-signified relationship is arbitrary, and conventional-intentional: they have been made to mean and the reader must re-make that meaning by recognizing, in several senses, the authority of the text in which the need for interpretive guesswork has been minimized, and potential perversity in interpretation made difficult to sustain. The fact that there appear to be no perfect instances—a single-form text that can only allow of one interpretation, always, everywhere (with the possible exception of some mathematical proofs)—does not preclude the theoretical possibility of texts that approximate to such an exalted state of semiotic potency. Many scientists, for example, would consider that they work with representational systems that approximate that state very well indeed, capturing the final and complete truth transparently.

Numerous clues exist as to the need for human beings of all sorts to make proper sense, by forensic scrutiny, of the verbal and other texts that cultures force upon us. There is world-wide demand for horoscopy, and astrological prediction generally, to take an example akin to the method of patching together disregarded trifles in such a way as to form a plausible and reassuring pattern. More seriously, all cultures expect their language users to master a wide range of nuanced and oblique word/meaning relationships, such as we find in tact, euphemism, sarcasm, irony, mimicry, teasing, and other forms of humor, wordplay, joke- and story-telling of all sorts, politeness/deference devices, and many others.

These few examples are mentioned here in illustration of the highly-skilled, conscious, and typically effective uses of, in particular, language that everyday life-experience demands of us, and in anticipation of the standard objections to all that has been said so far about our human capacities for making sense of and in the world.

## Semiotic Failure

Such objections nowadays amount to a near-orthodoxy across the human sciences, appearing under the banners of Critical Theory, Discourse Theory, or the all-encompassing Postmodernism. It would be tedious to reiterate here the well-known denunciations of the meaning making, and sharing, powers of human communities deploying semiotic resources such as language or mathematics, that have appeared (see Scott 1996: 240ff). For present purposes, we need only note that the positive and universalist, or least generalist, aspirations of the discussion above would separately and jointly be anathema within the deeply relativist and oppositionalist postures that unite contributors to these writings. The twin ideas that a text could, or should, have a reasonably clear unitary meaning and that such meaning could be encoded in a transparent but robust semiotic form so that all but the incapable and the perverse in its target interpretive community would be very likely to recover just that meaning, should they give it their attention, are particularly obnoxious and heretical in these distempered times. (An embedded heresy is that of the speech or interpretive community, redolent as that concept is of relative normativity and homogeneity, when deviance and conflictual heterogeneity are taken to be, or are propagandized as, the real state of social being under capitalism/patriarchy.

However. it is precisely this possibility that the present paper seeks to defend, not least (and as ever) by offering itself as a text to an audience some of whom will wish to deny its claims about shared understanding (having first, and necessarily, understood these claims). It will do so by focusing, in the Holmesian manner, on a disregarded piece of evidence for the power of language to achieve highly specific yet deliberately obscure signification, the crossword.

## Making Relative Sense

In the brief list above of ways in which ordinary language use routinely demonstrates the semiotic effectiveness of words, and the interpretive powers of the linguistically competent majority of our fellow citizens, wordplay was mentioned. Crosswords are, obviously, one sort of wordplay, directly descended from the riddles, acrostics, playfully ambiguous proverbs, sayings, and entire stories such as fables, allegories, and so on, which all cultures, especially in their pre-literate phases, generate. The functions of these are various, among them entertainment and teaching/learning of key values and life experience. The main point here is that they all require a strongly interpretive, indeed, forensic, relationship between utterers and hearers and the deliberately challenging text, a relationship which is qualitatively different from that which we adopt for face value, presumedly literal, texts.

Anyone who chooses to become involved with the sort of semiotic experience that the crossword offers does so in the knowledge that the writer of the clues has a definite meaning in mind, that sufficient of the evidence needed to unearth it is there in the cryptic texts called clues, but that the evidence may be barely sufficient to inform even a guess at the shape of the signifier. In addition, many clues in the more difficult crosswords require possession of particular categories of cultural capital: for example, the *Times* newspaper in the UK once offered Latin and Greek crosswords, and until recently Classical mythology, the works of Shakespeare and the Bible were regular sources for compilers. Another example is the tendency, in the UK at least, for compilers to assume certain pronunciation habits, typically those of the prestige form of British English. Many educated and intelligent persons nowadays lack knowledge of these, let alone the good grasp of spelling which is a very useful asset to bring to the crossword problem. However, as we will see, the compiler of cyrptic crosswords prides him/herself on giving enough information in the clue to make such cultural capital unnecessary (although it does, of course, help in guessing solution, the logic for which can then be worked out retrospectively).

This returns us to the metatheoretical issues introduced in earlier paragraphs, especially to the issue of relativism/relativity with regard to the commonality of our cultural inheritance, hence the intelligibility of allusions to specific elements of that inheritance. The debate has special resonances in the United States, where the desire to pursue and promote a common culture is part of the national mythology, although heavily questioned by multi-culturalists and other enemies of normativity, such as those whose views were briefly alluded to above. In principle, however, *any* modern culture, perhaps even that anthropologist's lodestone, the undisturbed culture, faces the same paradoxical problem of reconciling differences and samenesses within and without, at and over time, indeed of how to conceptualize and label the boundaries/frontiers that separate "ours" and "theirs."

In conditions of postmodernity these problems are acute. However, one need not leap either to despair or elation at rediscovering that the melting pot is both global in scope and infinitely fissile in content. Multi-dimensional plurality, continuous discontinuity are constants in life and culture and constitute the *rasion d'être* for all the effort that we invest in developing and compulsively exploring our semiotic resources, from talking to oneself through to "participation" in global, or near-global mediated events. These resources for meaning exist because we need them to transcend the differences between self and other, and work because we make them work. This fact is so routine that we generally do not notice it (from the first principle of communication theory) and find it difficult to believe, even if we are not already disinclined to believe it, as so many sceptics, relativists, and others discussed above, persist in declaring themselves to be. What follows in this paper is an attempt to justify the power of everyday, and *a fortiori,* careful language use to achieve semiotic goals in considering some essential features of crosswords. These are seen as texts designed to make the decoding process very difficult but, equally, to enable just those answers that are obviously and indubitably correct, if the forensic effort is sufficient. With its reliance upon cleverness rather than knowledge the cryptic clue helps to create a particular "imaged community" (Anderson, 1983) united by that alone. (Note that this imagined community exists within the broader imagined community of, with regard to crosswords, newspaper readers, an archetypal imagined community in Anderson's original discussion of the concept.)

Conversely, the fact that crosswords and the clues they offer vary across cultures will prompt discussion of how these differences may themselves be read as clues—indexical signs—of significant cultural differences.

## The fundamental principles

All crosswords currently being produced in Europe—both in the UK and beyond—are based on two fundamental principles. These are *synonymity* and *reference*. While synonymity involves the solution being a word or phrase which means the same as the clue, reference involves identifying a person, place etc. referred to in some way in the clue. A few examples taken from a simple crossword will make the operation of these principles clear:

*Synonymity* :

Organ of smell (NOSE);
Spoil utterly (RUIN)

*Reference*:

Island of E. Canada (NEWFOUNDLAND);
Captain Nemo's vessel (NAUTILUS)

No matter how "advanced" or cryptic a crossword might be, one (or both) of these principles will be found in operation at one level or another in the clue. The concept of synonymy is, of course, logically dependent upon the concept of reference, in that it postulates the possibility of two identically referring signifiers. In both traditional philosophical discussion, and in the critical theory literature, the more basic concept has been shown to be problematic (see Lyons 1977, volume 1, chapters 7–9, for a classic survey of the issues and approaches). Certainly, the claim made above that the good clue refers, by various devices to be discussed below, to a single definite "object," the answer, raises the more general questions about the varieties of reference.

Singular definite reference, for example, where just one signifier takes us unerringly to just one signified is difficult to exemplify, even at word or phrase level. Very closely defined and discursively restricted technical terms for highly stable physical phenomena, such as rare metals, might approximate to this state of one-to-oneness between signifier and signified. Many traditional literary theorists would argue that such a state of semiotic being is only achieved by the fully-formed literary text in which all aspects of the signifying plane are mobilized so as to contribute to the therefore holistic signified. However, students of other sorts of texts, such as constitutions and the amendments, or divine revelations, would deny that any singular meaning ever existed: even if it did, it is unrecoverable, or at least must be contested and made to compete with rival readings, in forever differing circumstances. Similarly, the well-known complications caused by the denotation-connotation/reference-sense discriminations suggest caution with regard to strong and absolute claims about one-to-oneness in semantics/semiotics.

That these have been referred to as discriminations rather than distinctions suggests a way forward, one which avoids full-blooded absolutist claims in favor of moderately relativist claims. In this spirit, we suggest the general rule that X usually means Y, in the main and in most co-text and context settings, for most members of a shifting interpretive community C. Subsidiary meanings, including connotations/special senses, deviant meanings, wordplay, nonce-usages, etc., form a semantic penumbra around that main meaning, and are often parasitic upon it.

This, on inspection, typically turns out to be anything but monolithic 'in itself': even the most concrete and primitive components of componential semantics are capable of further analysis. However, to acknowledge complexity and diversity in the semantic scope of a given signifier is not to concede either that there is no coherent center, or that the clusters surrounding any such core are infinite and chaotic. For practical purposes, we can get by in linguistic life knowing that TO MURDER embodies at least two concepts: causality and death. The exhaustive analysis of either, and others that are bundled in, could occupy us indefinitely, and so on *ceteris paribus* for most of our lexical knowledge. An approximate but sufficient grasp of the main elements of the main meaning(s) denoted and connoted is all the language-user needs, and all that we need to capture in a descriptive or even an explanatory account of reference.

With regard to synonymy, the conclusion we have just reached concerning the plurality of the signified—one signifier referring to a range of more rather than less related signifieds—extends to the level of the signifer. In synonymy, a range of signifiers refers to the same signified.

Once again, there is no need to escalate the terms of the discussion by demanding an account justifying the extreme case, where two or more signifiers refer with exact equivalence, in all co-texts and contexts, to exactly the same unitary signified. An approximation to that semantic relationship is, we argue, rightly taken for granted by all language users, who routinely use definition, paraphrase, circumlocution, euphemism, sarcasm, ambiguity, hints, and so on to negotiate their business by exploiting the flexibility of the signifier-signified relationship at word level.

To summarize, we can and do say the same thing in different ways, different things in the same way, and assume the fact that signifier and signified are arbitrarily related. Were this not so, those who deny or denounce the efficacy of language and other semiotic resources would have no effective resources for either complaint or remedy.

## Continental European crosswords

### Simple Crosswords

The crossword puzzle began life in the United States in the 1920s and quickly made its way to Great Britain. In its original form—the one which still predominates in the United States—it used very simple forms of clues, of the kind exemplified earlier. In Britain, however, the crossword quickly developed into something much more demanding. Initially this more demanding approach took the form of calls on specialized knowledge of various kinds—mostly literary and/or historical references and a familiarity with rather more esoteric vocabulary, and an extensive use of puns. Sometime during this period the crossword migrated to Continental Europe, where these are still the dominant features. Towards the end of the thirties and in the forties, however, the truly cryptic crossword developed in Britain (its main features are discussed below). Although traces of the cryptic crossword can be found in some European countries, it is nowhere developed to anything like the extent it has now reached in the UK (for more information on the history of the crossword see Arnott, 1981).

Although crosswords are fairly popular in Continental Europe, many European newspapers do not carry a daily crossword at all: so far as we are able to ascertain, none of the German or Italian quality daily newspaper feature such a daily puzzle, though some—for example the *Frankfurter Allgemeine Zeitung*—do include one in their weekend magazine. Continental European crosswords also fall broadly into the "simple" and "advanced" groups, though it is not the case that both groups are represented in all countries, since many countries—particularly in southern Europe—feature only the simple category.

## The Clues

Many European crosswords offer a more complicated and/or indirect relationship between clue and solution. Since such clues usually manipulate their language to some degree, they are often untranslatable. We have chosen as examples those which can be translated to some extent successfully, even if explanatory notes are required to make their operation clear (solutions reproduced in the original language are given below in italics).

**Austria**

***Der Standard* (quality daily) 2 February 1996**

He saw the little Rose standing, back to front you put your money in it (*KNAB*) ["Knab" is an old-fashioned poetic term for "boy", and the reference is to the German poem "Sah ein Knab ein Röselein stehen" ("A boy saw a little Rose standing"). "Knab" in reverse gives "bank".]

This piece of news is generally seen by salesgirls as a buyer (*KUNDE*) [This terms means both "news" and "customer".]

An unusual feature of *Der Standard*'s puzzles is clues which are based on rhymes, these often being literary in origin. Such clues often featured in British cryptic crosswords of the 1930s (Arnot, 1981: 65), but would certainly not be accepted by a British crossword editor today.

***Falter* (high-brow weekly newspaper) 36**

It is poetry when this writer is addressed formally (*POESIE*) [Add

"Sie"—the formal pronoun in German—to "Poe" to get "Poesie", a German word for "poetry". The term "Sie" is provided in the clue.]

A *foursome* in a muddle: do the Romans have fountains there? (TREVI)
[The German for "*foursome*" in a muddle' is "verwirrt zu *viert*" (original italics). The word in italics is an anagram of "Trevi". The part of a clue to be anagrammatized would never be indicated physically in this way in a British cryptic crossword, though anagrams are also highlighted in this fashion in *Der Standard*.]

This is the only Continental European crossword we have found which features cross-referential clues, i.e: clues which contain as part of their definition a reference to the solution of other clues:

After 15 across it causes a temporary reclamation of land (EBB TIDE)
[The answer to 15 across was (FLOOD).]

As we shall also see in the case of German advanced crosswords, German-language puzzles are those which come closest to the British model with their aggregative clues, their anagrams and their puns. By and large, however, these are all relatively modest by British standards.

As well as these fairly advanced puzzles, the Austrian popular daily newspaper *Kurier* provides in its weekend "Leisure" supplement what might be termed a middle-brow crossword.

Several features of these puzzles are worth noting. One is a considerable number of clues which involve either completing a quotation from a literary (or occasionally a political) source, or identifying its author:

A comedy which ends with a wedding is the beginning of a ... G. B. Shaw (TRAGEDY)

It has been said that it is the worst form of government, with the exception of all others. Sir Winston on democracy, 1947 (CHURCHILL)

This kind of clue is considered distinctly "unmodern" in the British cryptic crossword (Manley, 1986: 18), as will be discussed further below. A further feature which cannot be adequately illustrated here is the occasional appearance of clues written in Austrian dialect.

**France**

***L'Express* (quality weekly magazine) 25 May 1995**

It is particularly dear to us (COSTLY)
X or Y (SO AND SO)
Removed from the balcony to the flowerbed (DEFENESTRATED)

A common feature of *L'Express*'s crosswords are words whose meaning changes if a single letter is changed. The solution requires two letters to be written in the same box:

Shown to advantage, or not shown to advantage, according to the fourth (ENC$^{H}$/$_{R}$ASSEES) ["enchâssées" means "set" as of a jewel, "encrassées" means "soiled"]

This puzzle also contains an anagram which makes no sense in its new form, something which could not possibly happen in a British cryptic crossword:

A completely disorientated caïd (*ADCI*).

**_France Dimanche_ (popular weekly magazine) 20 January 1996**

A period during which they took off a lot (TERROR) [The verb "to take off"—"décoller"—provides an indirect reference to "col", or "neck".]
Nicer in the mouth than in the face (TART) [The French word "tarte" means both a "tart" and a "slap".]

Even more than the other French puzzles studied this one offers a mixture of quite teasing and very straightforward clues. Other examples from this same crossword include "Denied" (REFUSED), and "Skiable area" (PISTE).

**_France-Soir_ (popular daily) 20 January 1996**

This newspaper offers its readers four levels of crossword puzzle. Every day there is a "mots fléchés", as well as a "two-speed" blocked puzzle with two sets of clues, "normal" and "difficult". On Saturdays there is a more demanding puzzle entitled "les mots croisés souriants" ("the smiling crossword"). It is a mixture of fairly straightforward and rather more teasing clues:

Roman trio (III)
When lost, they wander around (SOULS)

***Le Figaro magazine*** **(quality Sunday magazine) 27 July 1995**
They have a future in the popular press (HOROSCOPES)
Bad humor (PUS)
It was given a mise-en-Seine by Renoir [ROUEN]
This crosswords also features a literary clue:
Le Jourdain (two words) (BOURGEOIS GENTILHOMME) [The clue is the name of this character in the Molière play.]

***Le Nouvel Observateur*** **(quality weekly magazine) 25 May 1995**
Has the last word (RIP)
He will never be the hero of the day (SLEEP WALKER)

As can be seen, the main features found in more advanced French puzzles are puns together with unexpected or even humorous definitions, as well as the occasional literary clue.

**Germany**
***Frankfurter Allgemeine Zeitung*** **(quality daily) 7 April 1995**
This priest is really well turned out (*PATER*) ["Pater" is a "priest". The phrase for "well turned out" is "in einem schönen Aufzug", which means literally "in a nice lift". A type of open lift in Germany is called a "pater noster"]
He made a fool of the fat one (first name) (STAN) [The German clue is "Der hat einen Dicken für Doof gekauft (vorn)." Laurel and Hardy were known in Germany as Dick and Doof. The adjective "dick" means "fat", while "doof" means stupid. The phrase "jemanden für doof verkaufen" means "to make a fool of someone"—a compact and ingenious but still relatively transparent clue.]

Like the *Kurier* crossword mentioned above, this crossword also contains a "quotation clue" (i.e: one whose solution is the missing word from a literary quotation) whose answer is "Rumpelstiltskin".
***Stern*** **(weekly magazine) 16 February 1996**
Who knows? It lives extravagantly on the roof of the world (YETI) [The phrase for extravagantly—"auf großem Fuß"—means literally "on a large foot".]

Britons who won't budge one centimetre from a centimetre stick with it (INCH)

Powerful symbol in workers' fist (CARNATION) [This clue involves a pun on the word "Arbeiterfaustdick", where the term "faustdick" means "powerful" and "Arbetierfaust" means "workers' fist"]

**_Die Zeit_ (highbrow weekly newspaper) 2 February 1996**

This particular puzzle is entitled "Um die Ecke gedacht" —"Thought round the corner".

Modest daily work of creator of aphorisms: the more daring the claim, the more predictable the ... (*EINSPRUCH*) [a pun on "Einspruch", which means both "objection" and, as two words, "ein Spruch", an "aphorism"]

Star in the heart of a Babylonian patron of parks (MIRA) ["Mira"—the name of a star—appears in the name of the Babylonian queen "Semiramis", credited with the creation of the famous hanging gardens]

The clues in *Die Zeit* are sometimes written in regional dialect to indicate that the solution is a regional term either within Germany, or within the broader German-speaking area.

As can be seen, the typical German "advanced" clue is fairly lengthy, uses a rather literary style (not necessarily obvious in these translations) and is based most often on puns.

**Holland**

***NRC Handelsblad (quality daily) 13 January 1993***

This puzzle is presented as a "Cryptogram", and is the only one we have encountered which copies the British feature of indicating the number of letters in the solution at the end of the clue.

The weather for (not) watching TV (SNOW)

It couldn't be faster (ASAP)

Dutch advanced clues combine punning with teasing definitions.

**Spain**

Advanced crosswords are relatively unusual in Spain. We have found only two, as indicated below.

***El Temps* (Catalan-language weekly magazine) 25 July 1994**

The magazine from which the crossword clues given below were taken is available only in the Catalan-speaking part of Spain. This crossword was described as being based on the *Times* and in fact had two sets of clues, these being described as "tortuous":

Don't mention it! (TABOO)

Don't do this by a thread or you'll be in danger (HANG)

The water sport practiced by Romulus's brother (*REM*) ["Rem" means both "Remus" and "rowing" in Catalan]

Some of these are very close to certain kinds of British cryptic clue as detailed below. Others, however, despite similarities, remain on a much simpler level:

The poor saint has got into a muddle (*ANTS*) [This is an anagram of "sant" meaning "saint", but has no meaning in itself, an unthinkable solution for a British clue.]

Understood with the head and even with the heart (*CAPIT*) [The Catalan for "head" is "cap" and the word for "breast" it "pit" - together they give (at least phonetically) "capit" meaning "understood". However, both the words "cap" and "pit" actually appear in the clue, something which would never happen in a British cryptic crossword, where at least one of them would have to be rendered cryptically. Also, in a British crossword some method would have to be found to indicate the reduction of the double consonant resulting from the juxtaposition of "cap" and "pit".]

Such crosswords appear on a very irregular basis in *El Temps*.

***La Vanguardia***

These examples were taken from *La Vanguardia*'s interactive Castilian crossword on the Internet (see Note 1). They were taken on February 8 March 1996.

It mixes its ink with water (SQUID)

By and large *La Vanguardia* —in both its Castilian and Catalan crosswords—relies mainly on unusual definitions. However, it also offers one of the anagrams to come closest to the British style of anagram:

Terrible laments which make you lose your cool (*MOLESTAN*) [The answer is an anagram of "lamentos", the Spanish for "laments", and is part of the verb "to bother".]

**Sweden**

***Svenska Dagbladet*** (quality daily) 28 June 1992

Is often left by a grubby little hand (FINGERPRINT)

Has meddled in someone else's life (BIOGRAPHER)

The main technique used here is that of unorthodox definition.

## The complex European Crossword Summarized

As can be seen, the more complex crossword is essentially a northern European phenomenon, with very scant representation in the Mediterranean countries. It is, therefore, a characteristic of societies with long-standing educated and literate working classes, where the ability to read on its own is not a sufficient condition for social distinction. As the examples given above show, the range of techniques used for complicating the relationship between clue and solution in these crosswords is fairly clear. By far the most common is indirect or unorthodox definition, where the association between clue and solution is rendered opaque in some way, without being actually coded. Puns are used and less occasionally words can be joined together or one word can be hidden inside another. The essential point however, when we come to compare such clues to the British cryptic clue, is that there is always a literal relationship between solution and clue. Language continues to function normally—if rather stretched at points—in the Continental crossword. At no time does it become the kind of anti-language typical of the British cryptic puzzle.

In all the crosswords studied, these more complex clues are accompanied by much more straightforward ones of the type typical of the simple crossword, a mix of styles which the British cryptic crossword does not allow for.

## The British cryptic crossword

The daily crossword is a fundamental element of the British press, and operates on a vast scale. All UK-national and all Scottish morning and evening newspapers carry at least one, as do all regional and most local newspapers, and most weekly magazines, in particular the television magazines. While the tabloids in general carry only a "quick" crossword, the broadsheets will carry a quick crossword and a more demanding, cryptic crossword, most often a 15x15 grid (though the leading Scottish tabloid, the *Daily Record* also features an entirely respectable 13x13 cryptic daily crossword entitled "The Wee Thinker"). Most Sunday newspapers usually feature a prize crossword (sometimes two), as do most of the dailies in their Sunday editions Some newspapers will also regularly feature a particularly difficult crossword, of which the Glasgow-based *Herald'* s "Wee Stinker"—appearing every Monday— is a good example.

The English-language cryptic crossword is quite unique in Europe, occurring only in the UK and (probably for reasons of long-standing cultural hegemony, or at the very least for reasons of cultural similarity) in the Republic of Ireland. Its uniqueness springs clearly to view when it is compared with its Continental European counterparts. In this paper we will analyze the main distinguishing features of the British cryptic crossword in contradistinction to European puzzles, and attempt to situate this unique phenomenon within the broader framework of British culture and society as a whole.

## The Clues

The British crossword—both simple and cryptic—is formally much more highly organized than anything found in Continental Europe. Its pattern of empty and black squares is always symmetrical about at least one axis, and is most often symmetrical about two. There are also strict conventions regarding the relationship between black squares and squares into which letters are to be written (known technically as "lights"), and after how many "unches" (non-intersecting lights) an intersection should take place. The examples given below are taken mostly from issues of the *Herald* from early 1996 but are typical of UK and Irish broadsheet crossword clues in general, as selected clues from other newspapers will show:

All clues in a British cryptic crossword provide some kind of definition of the solution. They fall into four broad groups as regards how this definition is organized:

1. Those in which there is a "lateral" transfer of meaning from the clue as a whole to the solution. In other words, the entire clue is a single, if indirect, definition.
2. Those which offer two relatively straightforward alternative definitions.
3. Those which offer a straightforward definition (synonym or referent) and a second definition which is coded.
4. Those which combine features of the first and the third group: they are both encrypted and operate as a total definition.

How these four groups operate is explained below.

## Encoding Techniques

### Single Definition

Clues in this first group are common to both British and Continental European advanced crosswords. However, while they are the mainstay of the Continental version, they never dominate in the British puzzle. Of the twenty-eight or thirty-two clues in a British cryptic crossword, clues belonging to this first group will seldom account for more than half, and their number may be as low as three or four.

*1. Associative*: These clues offer indirect or unorthodox definitions of the solutions:

What some brides put behind them (TRAINS)

An example from the *Telegraph*:

It records only the shining hours (SUNDIAL)

*2. Complementary/collocative*: The solution consists in finding the other half of a standard pair, or similar.

Ivy's associate (HOLLY) [From the Christmas carol "The holly and the ivy."]

It's proverbially blissful (IGNORANCE) [From the proverb "Ignorance is bliss".]

This is a reasonably productive kind of clue and is obviously dependent on knowledge of the culture's sayings, stories, songs, etc.

3. *Puns*: Puns are, of course, a kind of associative clue, but always contain a much more studied play on the double meaning of a word or phrase in the clue. They are often the most entertaining clues:

He has found a job at last (SHOEMAKER)
Presumably one doesn't run after it (LAST TRAIN)

Many crosswords puns have been around for a long time, and continue to appear from time to time in contemporary puzzles, much to the entertainment of seasoned solvers (here we have a very particular example of subcultural relativity). Some have acquired almost legendary status. Classic examples include (Manley, 1986: 26):

A wicked thing (CANDLE) [A candle has a "wick" and is, therefore, "wicked".]
He was rushed from the start (MOSES) [Moses was abandoned in a basket of "rushes" as an infant.]

These and other puns push the meaning of words almost to the limits
Grubby residence (COCOON) [The residence of a grub.]
Willing rider (CODICIL) [A rider in a will.]

A variation on this kind of clue often involves references to literary works:

More work (UTOPIA)
Hardy heroine (TESS)

**Double Definition**

Clues in this group could be described as triangulative, since the solution is a third term which is synonymous with two terms given in the clue.

Emphatically not at home (OUT AND OUT)
It isn't corruption. It is corruption. (TAINT)

Although the commonest arrangement is two definitions, occasionally clues can contain more. A particularly famous clue of this kind is the following:

Left harbor gate bearing wine (PORT)

Where every single word of the clue is a synonym of the solution, and a recent "Wee Thinker" clue featured three synonyms and one referent:

Notice beak charges man! (BILL) ["Beak" is an old-fashioned upper-class term for "headmaster".]

Triangulative clues are fairly common. They can often be the starkest kind of clues, with little or nothing to suggest what is required.

**Single Definition Plus Encrypted Definition**

This third group is by and large unique to the British cryptic crossword. Clues of this type occurring in Continental Europe—mostly in German language puzzles, though one or two also appear in the Catalan puzzle given earlier—make very modest demands on their readers by comparison. While clues of this group are in the minority in European puzzles, they are by far the biggest group of clues in the British cryptic crossword. The definition is always either the first or the last element in the clue. Some of the techniques explained below are almost never found on their own:

1. *Abbreviative*: Cryptic crosswords abound with abbreviations of all kinds. Common examples include "Dr", "MD" (Medical Doctor) or "MO" (Medical Officer) for "doctor", "AB" (able-bodied) for "sailor", "RI" (Rex et Imperator) for "state", "RE" (Royal Engineer) or "GI" for soldier, "CH" ("Companion of Honor") for "companion", "SS" (Sailing Ship) for "ship" and so on. Crossword dictionaries—see, for example, Howard-Williams (1986)—contain extensive lists of such abbreviations for solvers:

Doctor should prescribe no water (DROUGHT) ["Dr" + "ought", a synonym of "should".]

Points of the compass are routinely used to provide the letters "n", "s", "e" and "w", or occasionally an entire solution:

All points broadcast (NEWS)

Chemical symbols feature widely, as do international car registration symbols and abbreviations from chess or music: “p” (“piano”) for “soft”, “f” (“forte”) for “loud”. Numbers are often replaced by Roman numerals: “L” for fifty, “C” for one hundred, and so on:

No townsperson has beer after 6.50 (VILLAGER) [“VI” + “L” + “lager”.]

While abbreviations often appear in isolation in simple crosswords throughout Europe, abbreviative clues in British cryptic crosswords are almost always combined with other encryption techniques.

2. *Acrostic*: The solution is made up of the first letters of some of the words in the clue, and is sometimes also indicated by the remainder of the clue. In the following examples the appropriate letters are underlined.

It’s <u>d</u>aft, <u>i</u>t’s <u>o</u>bvious <u>t</u>hat <u>i</u>t’s <u>c</u>razy, initially (IDIOTIC)

A variant on this type of clue is when the solution is made up of the last letters of some of the words of the clue, or occasionally from both first and last letters, giving a double acrostic:

Globes <u>or</u> <u>b</u>ulb<u>s</u> at each end (ORBS)

Revel <u>or</u> <u>g</u>aiet<u>y</u> ends (ORGY)

Such clues invariably contain adverbs such as “initially” or “finally”, or other related ways of indicating which letters are to be used in the acronym. Occasionally the element indicating the presence of an acrostic can be transferred to the solution:

Eh? They’re extreme (ENDS OF THE EARTH) [The letters “e” and “h” of “Eh” are the “ends” , i. e.: the first and last letters of the word “earth”.]

3. *Aggregative*: The solution is achieved by adding together different words or part of words. These words will appear either as synonyms or references in the clue, or may be standard abbreviations, or may be indicated in other ways.

Threatening ring with MI intelligence (OMINOUS) [The letter “o” is often referred to as “ring” or “circle” or even “love” from the zero score in a tennis match. “Nous” is a synonym of “intelligence”.]

There is a vast array of indicators to show that this type of clue is involved. Verbs such as “goes to”, “gets”, even “marries” indicate parts to be joined. Although occasionally one of the elements to be aggregated can be physically present in the clue, they cannot all be expressly named as in the Catalan case mentioned earlier. In fact it is much more common for all of them to be rendered cryptically. The aggregative clue is a very productive kind of clue.

4. *Anagrammatic*: Part of the clue is an anagram of the solution, which is indicated by the remainder of the clue. In the following examples the word(s) anagrammatized appear in italics (though they do not in fact appear like this in the actual crossword). This is a very common kind of clue

*Point* out a device for climbers (PITON)
*Miners get* formed into military groups (REGIMENTS)

Normally, all the letters of the anagram will be present in the clue. In more advanced crosswords, however, part of the anagram itself may be rendered cryptically:

Show lac's not torn up (DEMONSTRATION) [The solution is an anagram of "s" + "not" + " torn" + "amide": the substance "lac" is an example of an amide.]

The presence of an anagram can be indicated in a great many different ways. Past participles such as "scattered", "formed", "ordered", "involved", "broadcast", adverbs such as "out", "maybe", "possibly", nouns such as "row", "confusion", "chaos", present participles such as "wriggling", "distributing", or even just the preposition "from" - all these are capable of indicating that there is an anagram in the clue.

A variation on the anagrammatic clue identified by Howard-Williams (1986: 15-16) is where the term indicating the presence of the anagram is transferred to the solution, as in the case of the acrostic clue given above. His example is:

Cat ham (ACT BADLY) ["Act" is an anagram - "badly" - of "cat". To "ham" is to "act badly".]

A more recent example from the *Herald* is the following:

Rat gone? It's only moderate (NO GREAT SHAKES) ["No great" is an anagram - "shakes"- of "rat gone".]

5. *Apocopative:* The solution is found by removing part of a word either given in or referred to in some way by the clue.

An example from the *Telegraph*:

Nothing's lacking from court brief (CURT) ["Court" minus "o" (nothing) gives "curt", a synonym of "brief".]

Apocopative clues are usually indicated by items such as "takes off", "loses", "drops" and so on, or simply by the indications " without" or "not". Alternatively, parts of words can be indicated by adjectives such as "endless" or "first" or nouns such as "start" or "half", or even individual letters can be identified by specific references to their location in a word: "mid-January" for U, "fourth July" for Y, and so on, though this is more common in combined clues, as explained below.

6. *Cross-referential*: A clue which uses the solution to another clue as part of its own answer.

Passionate about M88 (STORMY) [The solution to clue 88 was "story" - when placed around "m" this gives "stormy".]

7. *Deletive*: The solution is found by removing part of a longish phrase alluded to in some way by the clue.

Cody. Heartless male (BULL) [Sheriff Bill Cody was given the nickname "Buffalo Bill". Removing the "heart" ("heartless") of this nickname - "ffalo Bi" - leaves 'bu-ll', or "bull", also meaning "a heartless male".]

This is similar to the apocopative clue, but stretches over a number of words.

8. *Heteroglossic*: This kind of clue makes use of words from other languages. Thus syllables such as "le", "la" or "les" can be indicated by "the French", "der", "das" or "die" by "the German", "el" by "the Spanish", and so on."Un" or "une" can be rendered by "a French" or even "one in Paris", "one in Marseilles", and so forth. "To the French" can be "au" or "a la".

Graduate gives the French some hay (BALE) ["BA" - "Bachelor of Arts" - and "le".]

Forbid the Spanish to mention Christmas (NOEL) ["No" + "el".]

Such clues are almost always used in connection with other encryption techniques, seldom appearing on their own as in the clue from *Aftonbladet* given in Appendix I. Their linguistic demands are usually very simple, but occasionally something a little bit more demanding does occur, particularly in relation to French:

An English remark, but how French! (COMMENT)

In more advanced crosswords, however, quite devious foreign-language clues can sometimes appear, as in the following offering from the "Wee Stinker":

Treffen incubus (NIGHTMARE) [The solution is not only a synonym of "incubus", it is also an anagram of "German hit". One of the English translations of the German verb "treffen" is "hit". This is a very obscure clue.]

9. *Inclusive*: One or more words are included inside another to provide the solution.

Volcano captured by force in South-East Asia (VIETNAM) ["Etna" inside "vim".]

This is a very common kind of clue. It will often be indicated by terms such as "included", "imported", "swallows", "round", "about", "inside", "outside" and so on. Like the aggregative clue it is very productive.

10. *Orthographic*: In this type of clue, the unusual spelling of one (or more) of the words - which will usually involve the duplication or omission of a consonant, or occasionally the replacement of one consonant by another - will give some hint as to the solution.

Does a transplant job on the 'ead and behaves affectedly (PUTS ON AIRS) [The dropping of "h" from "head" points to the dropping of "h" from "hairs", making the link with the "transplant job on the 'ead".]

See seaweed and s-steal a shrub (ALGARROBA) [The duplicated "s" of "steal" points to the double "r" of "r-rob".]

11. *Phonetic*: The solution is a word which sounds like another word referred to in some way by the clue.

Is paid pots, say (URNS) [The phonetic similarity is between "urns" and "earns".]

Heard team sounded unhappy (SIGHED) [Homophony between "sighed" and "side".]

An example from the *Scotsman*:

Reported how patients wait for the doctor (INTERN) [Homophony between "intern" and "in turn".]

Phonetic clues are frequently indicated by terms such as "say", or "they say", "sounds" or "sounded", by phrases such as "we hear", or by even less obvious hints such as "according to reports". The phonetic system on which phonetic clues is based is that of Received Pronunciation. Symptomatically, this is always the case even in a Scottish newspaper such as the *Herald*, even where this does not provide complete homophony for Scottish speakers ("urns" and "earns" are in no sense pronounced identically in Scotland, nor are "turn" and "tern" nor "sighed" and "side").

12. *Reverse*: The solution is a word (or occasionally part of word) referred to in the clue, but spelled backwards. This is usually suggested in the British cryptic crossword by terms such as "return", "reverse" or "back", or, in the case of vertical clues, "up" or "rising".

An example from the *Telegraph*:

Backroom boy from North Africa (MOOR)

A variation on the reverse clue is the palindrome, which is the same in both directions:

It's a matter of principle, whichever way you look at it (TENET)

Some Continental European crosswords—in particular those with dense interlocking patterns—also regularly feature entire words written backwards (or upside down) as their "solutions", something which cannot happen in the British puzzle where anything written backwards must either be a word in its own right, or be subsumed into a larger unit which is written the right way. The technique for indicating the presence of a word spelled backwards is also quite different from the one described here. In the Continental European cases the existence of a word in reverse is always explicitly signposted by the indication "al revés" (or the abbreviation "rev") in Spanish, "à l'envers" in French, by the abbreviation "antis" in Greek and so on (all of these meaning literally "backwards"). There is no need to decode the existence of a reverse word from the clue itself.

13. *Sociolectal*: The sociolectal clue will make reference to some form of non-standard English to achieve a fit between clue and solution. It differs from the orthographic in that the non-standard form is

referred to rather than represented graphically. The following example is from the *Guardian*:

Rustic one, tense by the sound of it, uneducated (UNTAUGHT) ["Un" is a rural English pronunciation of "one".]

Occasionally it is old-fashioned forms which are used:

American citizen Kane traveling in the old surroundings (YANKEE) [The first and last letter of this solution form "ye", a pseudo-old-English form of "the".]

Although individual dialect terms can appear in the sociolectal clue, the clues themselves are never actually written in dialect, as was the case with the clues from *Die Zeit* mentioned earlier. The British cryptic crossword is the unassailable preserve of Standard English, as we already noted in connection with the phonetic clue.

Sociolectal clues are almost always combined with other techniques: in the examples above they are combined with a phonetic clue and an anagram

*14. Substitutive*: One or more of the letters in a word is replaced by another to provide the solution.

An example from the *Guardian*:

Chap with hose - nothing for one to be a supervisor (FOREMAN) [A "chap with a hose" is a "fireman". If we substitute "o" (nothing") for "i" (one) we have "foreman", a synonym of "supervisor".]

*15. Transverbal*: The solution appears quite literally within the clue, but covers a number of different words. In the following examples the transverbal element is given in italics.

Partly desir*ed if ice*d cake factory (EDIFICE)

In Ferrar*a violi*nists consume Italian fare (RAVIOLI)

This type of clue is most commonly indicated simply by the preposition "in", though "some" is also a fairly common indicator.

**The "& Lit" Clue**

There is a certain category of cryptic British clue which also claims to have a "literal" relationship with its solution. This is the so-called "& lit" clue which is simultaneously cryptic and in itself a reasonable "definition" of its own solution (Manley, 1986: 54-56). A recent example from the *Herald*:

Get a tube-shaped loaf (BAGUETTE) [An anagram of "get a tube".]

Another from the *Times*:

Lots of temporary accommodations round university here (CAMPUS) [This rather nice definition of a "campus" is also an inclusive clue: "camps" ("temporary accommodation") around "u" (a standard abbreviation for "university").]

Such "& lit" clues are much prized by both setters and solvers though, despite their claims to being "literal" definitions, a certain amount of indulgence is sometimes required by both parties.

**Increasing the Level of Difficulty**

Virtually any of the above techniques can be compounded with others to provided more complicated clues. Many clues combine two techniques:

1. *Abbreviative-anagrammatic.*

50X50 is roughly infinite (LIMITLESS) [An anagram of "L times L is".]

2. *Acrostic-aggregative.*

Last in pub always gets older drinks (BEVERAGES) ["B" + "ever" ("always") + "gets older" ("ages").]

3. *Acrostic-phonetic.*

An example from the "Wee Thinker":

Extremely keen you are not, we hear (KNUR) ["K" and "n" are the "extremes" of "keen". "You are" is a phonetic rendering of "ur". A "knur" is a "knot", which sounds like "not".]

4. *Aggregative-anagrammatic.*

*Pearl* queasy, goes to doctor in Sicilian capital (PALERMO)

5. *Aggregative-apocopative.*

Article endless river excites (THRILL) ["Th" + "rill".]

6. *Aggregative-inclusive.*

Orator expected to hold 'em in eager excitement (DEMAGOGUE) ["due"- "em" - "agog"]

Assume mail delayed about mid-January (POSTULATE) ["U" is the middle letter of "January".]

7. *Aggregative-phonetic*.

One imitating policeman said why to spiteful woman (COPYCAT) [Homophony - again imperfect in Scotland - between "y" and "why".]

8. *Anagrammatic-apocopative*.

S. Americans, perhaps 50% of them (INCAS) [An anagram of "icans", which is half (50%) of "S. Americans".]

9. *Anagrammatic-complementary*.

Sanctimonious name for Simon's contact (PIEMAN) [The answer comes from the nursery rhyme "Simple Simon met a pieman going to the fair". "Pieman" is an anagram of "pi" (sanctimonious) and "name".]

*10. Anagrammatic-deletive*.

A spiral canal without air: plan replacement for it (SCALA) [If the letters of "air plan" are removed - "without" - from "a spiral canal" we are left with "scaal", an anagram - "replacement" - of "scala".]

11. *Anagrammatic-substitutive*.

An example from the "Wee Stinker."

Adam, confused, learned Greek for Latin. Right? (GARDENER) ["L" is a standard abbreviation for "Latin", as is "G" for "Greek". If we replace the "l" of "learned" with "g", we get "gearned:". Add "r" ("right"), and we have an anagram - "confused" - of "gardener", a fairly standard crossword synonym for "Adam".]

12. *Complementary-triangulative*.

An example from the *Guardian*:

Silk's associate held a watching brief (SATIN) [Ie: "sat in". There is a further pun here on the meaning of "silk" as "advocate".]

*13. Punning-triangulative*.

Relieved by the bosses (STUDDED)

14. *Reverse-transverbal*.

Poet's cave, retreat of some hermi*t or g*remlin (GROT)

Some clues combine three techniques:

*1. Acrostic-anagrammatic-deletive*.

Originally importer into Barcelona, with no need for coal (IBERIAN) [If the letters of "coal" are removed from "Barcelona" we are left with "brena". Add "ii" - the first letters of "importer into" - and we have an anagram of "Iberian".]

2. *Acrostic-anagrammatic-inclusive*.

Each one *drove by* between the end of June and the end of July (EVERYBODY)

## Complicating Techniques Summarized

The number of possible permutations is very large. In fact, most clues in a standard cryptic crossword will combine at least two techniques, and some may combine three or at times even four. Seasoned crossword solvers will not only expect, but will actually look forward to combinations of this kind as an essential part of any reasonably challenging crossword puzzle.

Beyond these combinatorial clues, the level of difficulty can, of course, also be increased by targeting abstruse or esoteric terms. This occurs both at the level of the clue and the solution. The use of obsolete or obsolescent synonyms for the individual elements of aggregative or inclusive clues is quite common: "tar" or "jack" or "salt" for "sailor", "con" for "study", "main" for "sea", but some of these—"pi" for "good", "or" for "before"—can be frankly esoteric. At the level of the solution, anyone tackling an advanced cryptic crossword can expect to meet such curios of the English language as "rorqual", "aliquot", "praetor" or even "deipnosophist".

## The Disarticulation of Language in the British Cryptic Crossword

As this taxonomy of clue types should make clear, the British cryptic crossword puzzle subjects language to a triple disarticulation:

1. language is disarticulated semantically at the level of the clue.
2. language is disarticulated syntactically at the level of the solution.
3. language is disarticulated socially at the level of the crossword puzzle as a whole.

### Semantic Disarticulation

Words in cryptic clues are treated as mere accumulations of letters to be bent, fashioned, machined, trimmed, inverted, substituted and so on, absolutely as required by the needs of the clue. In aggregative and inclusive clues, as well as anagrams and acrostics, the usefulness of the meaning of the "absorbed" words is exhausted as soon as the synonym or referent is found: the function of the resulting term is merely to provide a set of letters which can be moved around like the pieces of a jigsaw puzzle. Adverbs can refer not to their related adjectives, but, in breach of the rules of English word-formation, to homographic nouns, as when "mainly" means "by the main" (i. e.: "by the sea"): "When the beach is mainly covered" (HIGH TIDE) (we might usefully contrast this clue with the EBB TIDE clue in the Austrian weekly *Falter* given above). Words originally identified on the basis of their pronunciation can find that same pronunciation ignored in the solution, as in the *Guardian* clue "Reportedly stood in line encircling the ship, being obstinate" (CUSSED), where the letters "cued" are first identified by their homophony with "queued", but lose that pronunciation entirely in their final combination.

For all their remarkable ingenuity and creativity, these encryption techniques can be seen to effect an evacuation of meaning from language. In his *Crossword Manual* renowned setter Don Manley (known to solvers as Duck) repeatedly urges his readers to ignore the meaning of the clue and "Concentrate on the words, please!" (1986, 40), by which he clearly means how they are *spelled*. Language thus becomes a store of individual letters or groups of letters which happen to be related to or enclosed in other words.

**Syntactic Disarticulation**

When the various elements derived from the decoding of the clue are re-articulated into the solution, it is not only the integrity of the words but often the actual syntax of the clue which is overruled. Punctuation of all kind is disregarded, as in the anagram of "Crest, it" (TRISECT) given earlier, or as in "Shot drug-crazed man" (CRACKPOT), where the actual breakdown of the clue is "shot" + "drug" on the one hand (the cryptic part), and "crazed man" (the definition) on the other. Text given inside quotation marks is almost never an actual quotation, capital letters hardly ever indicate a proper noun. Divisions between words are shifted, as in the *Guardian* clue "Spoil cat climbing up on me", where the letters of the solution—resulting from "me" + "ssup" ("puss" backwards, ie "climbing up")—are realigned to read (MESS UP), or in the "Wee Thinker" clue "Go harum-scarum for sport and religion" where the resulting "ru" ("rugby union") and "shinto" ("religion") are reassembled as (RUSH INTO). Or divisions are created where none existed, as in the *Telegraph* clue "Let, but not a single tenant paid the rent?", where the synonym of "let"—"allowed"—is refigured as (ALL OWED).

Words appearing after others turn out to have the meaning they would have if they were in front, as, for example, when "man almost" actually means "almost 'man'" (i.e: most of the letters of the word 'man'). In fact, it is impossible to tell from a typical cryptic clue whether a word such as "before" is a preposition governing the following word, or an adverb indicating that the preceding word belongs logically earlier in the sentence, as in "Slowly move straw before songbird" (CHAFFINCH) [ie: "chaff" ("straw") before "inch" ("slowly move"). As Araucaria, veteran setter for the *Guardian,* points out (1994: 5): "crossword clues are collections of disjointed fragments, and even the best of these seldom linger in the mind".

**Social Disarticulation**

The internal disarticulation of language is, however, merely a step towards a much more radical disarticulation of language from social meaning. This disarticulation is quite clear if the cryptic crossword is compared either with the standard European crossword, or with the "quick" crossword of the British popular press, or even with the more complicated European puzzle.

On the one hand, these non-cryptic crosswords are located within what can still be identified as a basically educational discourse of broadening general knowledge. The *Sunday Express*'s crossword is actually known as "The General Knowledge Crossword". In fact, some publications print the solutions on the same page as the puzzle, so that there is not even the need to wait for the following issue to see what the answers were. European puzzles abound with references to aspects of their own country's history, geography, mythology and so on: mountains, rivers, place names, ancient gods, authors are all standard fare, as are, on a slightly different level,

Biblical characters and figures from world culture (cinema, music, literature etc). On the other hand, in the non-cryptic British crossword and even in the case of the more advanced European crosswords the relationship between clue and solution remains meaningful. Clues such as "A drink before retiring" (NIGHTCAP) are entirely acceptable "explanations" of their solutions, even if the meaning of terms such as "retiring" here may not necessarily be the one that first springs to mind. The lengthy French and German clues illustrated earlier may be convoluted, but they are syntactically correct and constitute acceptable explanations or references to the solution which are understandable on their own terms.

However, as the taxonomy of encrypting techniques given earlier will have made obvious, the bulk of clues in a British cryptic crossword have no global relationship with their solution. This is not to say that the clues make no sense. On the contrary, a great deal of ingenuity is invested into producing clues which do make sense and which actually follow their own sets of rules. But their total textual meaning bears little relationship with the solution. A statement such as "Being denied support of masses in Mexico I can mount revolution" sustains a coherent narrative, but has no immediate connection with its solution (EXCOMMUNICATION) [an anagram - "revolution" - of "Mexico I can mount" combined with a pun on the meaning of "masses"]. The link between "Man deceived, perhaps, when Managing Director is fired" and (ISLE) ["misled" without "MD"] is even more tenuous (the ultimate reference is to the Isle of Man).

The contrived nature of the cryptic clues in fact subtends the contrived nature of the cryptic crossword in itself. It has no educational function, no matter how vague: as Arnot puts it (1981: 85) "Inherent cleverness overrules general knowledge". None of the terms which eventually go into the crossword grid have any function other than to fill in the spaces available. No cryptic crossword solver expects to learn anything by such a process. Or rather, anything learned is simply information which might help to solve a future puzzle. In other words, usefulness is defined within the framework of crossword puzzle solving, and bears no relationship whatsoever with the outside world. Meaning may be re-articulated into the solution after the disarticulation inherent in the clue, but it is re-articulated into social meaninglessness. While codes were initially intended to protect information which was so valuable that no-one else was to be allowed access to it, cryptic crosswords obfuscate - but never entirely obscure - information which is in entirely worthless in itself. The value of the cryptic crossword derives from a quite different source.

## The Recovery of Meaning as Pleasure and Power

The sheer scale and enduring ubiquity of British cryptic crosswords attests eloquently to the pleasure afforded to solvers by an activity in which absolutely no newspaper reader is under any compulsion to participate. These pleasures are not difficult to identify:

1. There is the intellectual pleasure of solving the puzzle, of meeting the challenge set by the complier. The aim of the compiler is not to produce a crossword which no one can complete—such crosswords have occurred, but are usually considered to be poor form—but to be original enough to make the solver work at the code. This kind of pleasure is similar to that involved in completing a jigsaw puzzle or finishing a particularly complex computer game.
2. There is the pleasure derived from enjoying the sheer ingenuity of the clues, particularly those of the first group. It is virtually impossible not to smile at a clue such as "Grubby residence" (COCOON) or "He finds work at last" (SHOEMAKER). Many solvers come to recognize and admire the work of individual compilers in this way. Legendary clues include one which consisted of no words at all, the solution being (MISSING), or "O" for (CIRCULAR LETTER) (Augarde, 1984, 61). Another is "Neither A to G nor P to Z" (WATER) [the missing letters of the alphabet are "H to O", pronounced identically to $H_2O$, the chemical symbol for water] (Paterson, 1996). A clue in the *Herald* in 1995 was "XX", the solution being (NECKERS) [two people kissing]. As Howard-Williams puts it (1986: 10): "in the final analysis the solver should be able to tip his hat and say 'Oh, I see; well done',

even if, once the answer is known, he or she adds 'What a nerve!'".

3. For seasoned solvers, there is the pleasure of recognizing "classic" clues reappearing from time to time, bringing an increased sense of being "in the know". In the words of Araucaria (1994: 5), "we get our laughs by reminding you of old jokes unexpectedly—by recycling chestnuts". As anyone who does puzzles from more than one newspaper will know, there is something of a "common market" in crossword clues.
4. Beyond the pleasures inherent in the puzzle, there is often the social pleasure involved in doing the puzzle on a co-operative basis. Many crosswords are done by several members of a family or a group of friends, or by colleagues in the staff room or in the factory canteen. Some newspapers even organize crossword dinners where solvers can get to know each other socially.

The ludic elements of crossword puzzles are undeniable. But there is more to them than that. The meaning of the British cryptic crossword is not contained in the crossword—on the contrary, meaning in the normal sense is destroyed in the crossword—but emanates from the place of such crosswords in British society as a whole. When cryptic crosswords first appeared in the late 1920s and 1930s they were, as originally developed by leading compiler Torquemada (translator and literary critic Edward Powis Mather) a fairly patrician affair with their rhyming clues, their many literary references and their obscure vocabulary (some early puzzles in the *Times* even appeared in Latin and Greek). In the late 1930s and above all the 1940s, however, the cryptic crossword was reformulated by the now legendary compilers Afrit (A. F. Ritchie) and Ximenes (Derrick Macnutt) into the form it has today in the newspapers of the aspiring British middle class—or more precisely of the aspiring English middle class: its English origins still being visible in the assumption of Received Pronunciation in phonetic clues in Scotland and Ireland. This new form was based on the so called "square dealer" principle (Arnot, 1981: 73), according to which clues were to be solvable on their own terms without reference to specialized knowledge.

For all its apparent obscurity, therefore, the contemporary British cryptic crossword is in fact more democratic than its Continental European advanced counterparts. It addresses (to use a somewhat old-fashioned terminology) a primarily petit-bourgeois rather than a bourgeois readership. Once the encrypted part of the clue has been decoded, the relationship between the defining element of the clue and the solution is often quite simple (e.g., from the examples given earlier: "film"—"western"; "military group"—"regiment"; "uneducated"— "untaught"). Since the codes listed above are all entirely "learnable", in principle *anyone*, irrespective of wealth, social position, occupation (and even, to a lesser extent, education) can solve the puzzles. This point is made by Paterson (1996): "fanatics range from Dartmoor inmates to eminent doctors; captains to cabin-boys". In fact, the simplest method available to a setter to make a puzzle more demanding is to increase the proportion of lateral clues and reduce that of cryptic ones. In principle all cryptic clues are solvable, a claim which cannot necessarily be made for lateral clues.

The full emergence of the British cryptic crossword in its contemporary form in fact coincided with a period in British history in which notions of modernism and democracy were very much to the fore—not least in the post-war "land fit for heroes"—but when the political and social realities of the British state lagged in many respects far behind the official statements of public political discourse. Britain was then—and continues to be now—the western country in which vested hereditary interests are most deeply entrenched, and in which political and economic power is most anonymous, most secretive and most hierarchical. It is a society which has failed to modernize fully in many important respects (Anderson: 1992). In the absence of a genuine modern meritocracy, the cryptic crossword has come to operate as a surrogate meritocracy in which those with genuine talent can claim their legitimate prize.

It is no coincidence that literary and "quotation" type clues have died out. As veteran setter Barbara Hall puts it: "The old-fashioned use of quotations, where the answer is the source of the quotation, is not a cryptic clue ... because you either know it or you don't. A good clue should give you two chances" (in Paterson 1996). In fact, those few British cryptic crosswords which do want to be elitist in some way—the *Sunday Times* crosswords, for example—do so not so much by using more difficult coding techniques, but by making the clues refer to esoteric words or knowledge taken from literature or other elite domains, in very much the same way as the Continental advanced crosswords.

The cryptic crossword in the UK enjoys a level of social prestige comparable to other informal meritocracies such as being a member of the high-IQ club MENSA or appearing on the BBC's highbrow question and answer program *Mastermind.* The prestige attaching to success in the *Times* crossword championships is almost legendary. This holds good even in Scotland with its tradition of greater public democracy: the prize for completing the "Wee Stinker" may only be a T-shirt—a typically complex Scottish statement: simultaneously distancing and celebratory—but these are much sought-after items among the crossword-solving fraternity.

The uniqueness of the British cryptic-crossword-puzzle meritocracy is that it is fundamentally based on meaninglessness. It is, therefore, beyond the undoubted pleasures which it affords, both a self-perpetuating symbol and a recognition of the meaninglessness of meritocracy in Britain. It embodies a fourfold dislocation. The semantic, syntactic and social disarticulation of language inherent in the puzzle provide a permanent vehicle for the on-going political disarticulation of intellectual effort on an industrial but entirely non-threatening scale. As Paterson again puts it (1996): "crosswords are an extremely safe occupation".

Despite this, however, it remains a fact that success rates among crossword solvers remain remarkably high. Experienced solvers will have consistent success rates in excess of 95%, while even more casual solvers will usually complete over half the puzzle. Clues, no matter how abstruse, will eventually yield, provided that the rules agreed by the crossword community are observed.

As with crosswords, so in life.

# References


Anderson, B. 1983. *Imagined Communities*, Verso, London.

Anderson, P. 1992. *English Questions*, Verso, London.

Araucaria [John Graham]. 1994. "Foreword", in John Perkin (ed.) *The New Penguin Book of the Guardian Crosswords 3*, Penguin, London.

Arnot, M. 1981. *A History of the Crossword Puzzle*, Papermac, London.

Augarde, T. 1984. *The Oxford Guide to Word Games*, Guild Publishing, London (see in particular Chapter 6, "Crosswords").

Eco, U. and T. A. Sebeok. 1983. *The Sign of Three,* Indiana University Press, Bloomington.

Howard-Williams, J. 1986 . *The Complete Crossword Companion*, Wordsworth Editions, Hertfordshire.

Lyons, J. 1977. Semantics, 2 vols. Cambridge University Press, Cambridge.

Manley, D. 1986. *Chambers Crossword Manual*, Chambers, Edinburgh.

Paterson, R. 1996. "Boxed in around and down in a cryptic questionnaire", in *Scotland on Sunday*, 28 January 1996.

Scott, W. T. 1996. "The Emprie of Signs and the Information Revolution," in *Spaces and Significations*, Peter Lang, New York.

# Chapter Ten

# Conceptual Iconicity and Grammatical Rules: Towards a "Reflexive Grammar"

**Marcel Danesi**

This work is dedicated to Professor Roberta Kevelson, a scholar who has played a major role in shaping my own thoughts about, and approach to, the study of signs. As one of the world's leading Peircean theorists, her accumulated work constitutes a far-reaching disquisition on the nature of meaning and culture. Kevelson has taught a whole generation of semioticians that human meaning-making is the essence of freedom, hardly ever fixed or absolute, but constantly assuming manifold expressive forms.

## Introduction

Despite considerable research on the nature of grammatical rules since the publication of Chomsky's *Syntactic Structures* in 1957, and despite the theoretical work on the nature of grammatical systems that the Chomskyan paradigm has made possible, growing numbers of linguists are becoming increasingly skeptical that such an approach can ever adequately explain the conceptual richness of even a single sentence. The purpose of this essay is to suggest that the notion of grammatical rule as it now stands is probably too narrow and too removed from the conceptual properties of discourse.

Since the early seventies there have, of course, been attempts to make grammar more sensitive to communication (e.g. Hymes 1971, Halliday 1975, 1985). But little work has been done on how rules might reflect concepts outside of the research of Langacker (1987, 1990) and his followers. What is least understood in my view is the connection between "conceptual iconicity" and grammatical rules. Considering the sentence as itself a kind of complex signifier made up of simpler signs (the words in it), then the hypothesis to be put forward here is that its connection to the signifed (what the sentence means) is motivated in those sentences where the referential domain is metaphorical. The basis for making this hypothesis is the research on metaphor that has been inspired by Lakoff and Johnson's pivotal 1980 analysis of this intriguing phenomenon. This line of inquiry has provided valuable data and insights into how it may be possible to relate the conceptual iconicity of sentence meanings to specific grammatical categories.

## The Arbitrariness of Grammatical Rules?

Language literally comes *natural* to humans. It is acquired without effort or training during infancy. Indeed, the only requirement for learning any language is adequate exposure to samples of it from birth to about age two. So natural is speech to humans, in fact, that one hardly ever considers what it is that one does while speaking. This is perhaps why Chomsky (1986) has even gone so far as to view language as a physical organ that he claims is as innate as, say, the ability to use the eyes and the nose for seeing and smelling. For Chomsky, the speech faculty is determined by a set of "universal principles" present in the brain at birth that are subjected to culturally-specific "parameters" during infancy. But Chomsky maintains that these are subsidiary and not crucial to the emergence of language and, thus, that the role of the linguist is to search out the universal principles which make up the speech faculty. These are set into motion by what he calls a LAD, a "language acquisition device" that each child has at birth for the automatic processing of language input according to the properties of the universal grammar. Whether or not such an "organ" exists, the thrust of the Chomskyan paradigm has been the entrenchment of the view that the properties of grammars are arbitrary, with no simulative or replicational features to the domain of meanings they capture (Skousen 1989). However, this view has been coming under attack more and more, supported by the findings emanating from the work on so-called iconic or "cognitive" grammar in the last decade and a half (see, for instance, Craig 1986, Simone 1995). The view adopted here is, in fact, that in their origin grammatical rules—i.e. rules of how sentences generate meaning—are hardly arbitrary; rather, they are tied to more rudimentary (non-arbitrary) forms of semiosis.

The view that grammatical rules are arbitrary has, actually, a long history behind it. The British philosopher John Stuart Mill, writing as late as 1867, believed rules of grammar to correspond to universal thought forms. The rules of the grammar that such universalist paradigms allow are derived from the abstract, logical properties of the rule systems themselves; they are not viewed as having any iconic connection to their referential domains, or "thought forms" as Mill called them (Larson 1990, Higginbotham 1992). In such approaches, meaning is held to be objectively determinable in the syntactic structure of language, i.e. it is seen as being intertwined in large part with the abstract syntactic properties of sentences.

## The Iconicity-Hypothesis

As is well known, for Saussure (1916) the relation between the signifier (the physical part of the sign) and its signified (the mental concept to which it refers) was a matter of convention. Only in a few exceptions did Saussure concede that the form of the signifier was motivated iconically or indexically by some characteristic of the referent. Saussure claimed, in essence, that the process of signification—the relation that is established between signifier and signified—unfolded in conventionally-determined ways, independent of the sign-user's viewpoint or modeling propensities. The arbitrariness of signification was extended by Chomskyan linguists to encompass sentences—i.e. sentences, like individual signs, are considered to have an arbitrary connection to their referents.

Although this view has been disputed by various schools of linguistics and semiotics, particularly those of a Peircean orientation, Saussure's "arbitrariness theory" of signification remains, by and large, the mainstream one, especially in linguistics. The main counter-argument to Saussurean theory inheres in the etymological observation that, *in their origin*, verbal signifiers constantly reveal an attempt to model or indicate some salient feature of their referents; i.e. verbal signifiers are forged, wittingly or not, as iconically-motivated models, or as indexical markers, of some aspect of their referents. It is only after the signs have become conventionalized through frequent usage and routinization in a cultural context that they take on progressively abstract qualities, so that their original iconic or indexical relation to the referent is attenuated or lost to awareness. This view of signification can be called the 'iconicity/indexicality hypothesis' (henceforward I-Hypothesis); it constitutes the counterclaim to Saussurean and Chomskyan arbitrariness theory, since it maintains that there is a tendency to connect the forms of language, *in their genesis*, to some perceived aspect of their referents.

The I-Hypothesis does not imply that all signs or sentences are created iconically or indexically, but that the *tendency* to do so is paramount in human semiosis. The purpose of the present study is to explore ways of showing how the perceived metaphorical characteristics of some sentence referents influence grammatical categories in non-arbitrary ways

In *Syntactic Structures* Chomsky (1957: 48) compared the goal of linguistics to that of chemistry. A good linguistic theory should be able to generate "all grammatically possible utterances," in the same way that a good chemical theory "might be said to generate all physically possible compounds." A decade later, he went on to define verbal creativity as "the speaker's ability to produce new sentences that are immediately understood by other speakers" (Chomsky 1966: 10). But what does this mean? For Chomskyan linguists, it would seem that verbal creativity unfolds within a system of arbitrary rules and logical principles that allow for the generation of an infinite class of sentences and their formal semantic properties. It is hardly the kind of creativity that one would associate with poetry or common discourse, for that matter.

The research on metaphor in linguistics, psychology, and semiotics over the last three or four decades has come forward to provide evidence to suggest reasons why this view is not tenable in its entirety. If the Chomskyan notion of linguistic theory were correct, then the main kinds of sentences that humans would produce consistently would be literal; all others would be occasional deviations or stylistic options. But nothing could be further from the truth. As Howard Pollio and his associates showed in 1977, the average speaker of English invents approximately 3000 novel metaphors per week (Pollio, Barlow, Fine, and Pollio 1977). Their work clearly demonstrated, in other words, that metaphor is hardly a discourse aberration or option; rather, it constitutes a fundamental aspect of language. As Winner (1982: 253) has aptly remarked, the experimental literature has made it conspicuously obvious that if "people were limited to strictly literal language, communication would be severely curtailed, if not terminated." Now, the question that the research on metaphor raises is: Do the rules of grammar reflect the metaphorical properties of discourse (i.e. its conceptual iconicity)? And if so, how can these be worked into the formulation of grammatical rules? Certainly, to continue ignoring the role of metaphor in language, and to keep it separate from the rules of grammar, is now an indefensible stance.

## Concepts and Grammatical Rules

In the same way that a formal study of the melodies and harmonies of music in themselves does not quite seem to reveal the true nature of music, so too the study of grammatical systems in isolation does not reveal the true nature of language. The kind of rule system that Chomskyan grammarians attempt to set up is based on observing logical relations among the units in the sentences of languages, in the same way that musical theorists attempt to establish the rules of melody and harmony by examining how notes in actual pieces of music are put together. This approach, however, has no way of accounting for how the choice and deployment of the rules is tied to the thoughts and feelings that people have when they talk or respond to a piece of music. It simply shows what constraints or limits govern sentence formation. These rules are, therefore, comparable to the kinds of artificial rules used by foreign-language students and computers when attempting to produce sentences in the language they are studying or programmed to generate. Discourse texts produced by computers and foreign-language learners alike (at the beginning of their study of a new language) will manifest a high degree of grammatical accuracy, but they will invariably lack the conceptual appropriateness that characterizes the corresponding discourse texts of native speakers. To put it another way, students and machines "speak" artificially with the formal structures of the language as they have been taught them or programmed to do respectively, but they are unable to "think" in terms of the conceptual system that underlies the structures: i.e. students typically make up target language sentences as artificial "carriers" of their own native language concepts through the rules they have been taught; machines generate them in response to the rules programmed into them. When these coincide with the ways in which concepts are relayed by native speakers *naturally*, then the student and machine texts coincide serendipitously with culturally-appropriate discourse texts; when they do not, they manifest an asymmetry between sentence form and conceptual content. What student and machine discourse typically lacks, in other words, is what can be called *conceptual fluency*.

My claim is that to be conceptually fluent in a language is to know, in large part, how that language "reflects" or encodes concepts on the basis of metaphorical reasoning. And my proposal is that the linguist can show how this is carried out by examining the ways in which the vehicles of metaphors produce meaning. This kind of knowledge is by and large unconscious in native speakers. If I were to speak about "ideas" in English, my mind would automatically scan conceptual domains that typically reveal an A (topic) is B (vehicle) structuring. So, if I were to say something like "I don't get the point of your idea," or "I don't quite see how your idea is parallel to mine," the conceptual domain enlisted by my mind has the form *ideas are geometrical objects*. Of course, my mind can search out other appropriate domains—e.g. "Your ideas are coming to fruition," or "Your ideas are growing on me" (conceptual domain = *ideas are plants*); "Your ideas are well constructed," or "Your ideas are grounded on a solid foundation" (conceptual domain = *ideas are buildings*); etc.—or combine them in various ways. The grammatical categories that are used in actual discourse are consistently linked formally to such conceptual domains. The task of linguistics should be, in my view, to develop an appropriate apparatus for showing how grammatical rules and conceptual knowledge of this kind are interrelated.

The notion of conceptual iconicity is not new. It has been implicit in the work of certain linguists and philosophers for quite some time. It simply has never been identified as such. The philosopher Herder (1744–1803), for instance, saw an intimate connection between language and what he called "ethnic character." Subsequently, Wilhelm von Humboldt (1767–1835) gave this hypothesis a more testable formulation when he portrayed the structure of a particular language as interdependent with the thought and behavior of the people using it for communication. Needless to say, von Humboldt's perspective went contrary to the views of the Port Royale grammarians who saw language as the product of the universal logical laws of the human mind. It was shortly after von Humboldt's alluring pronouncements that the study of "language and mind" was given its first scientific research forum with the establishment of the journal *Zeitschrift für Völkerpsychologie und Sprachwissenschaft* (1860–1890) by Moritz Lazarus and Heymann Steinthal. In this century, work on language and thought has been pursued by both those espousing a Humboldtian perspective—e.g. Sapir (1921), Whorf (1956), and others (e.g. Lucy 1992)—and those advocating a universalist Port Royale perspective—e.g. Chomsky and his followers (e.g. Pinker 1994, Jackendoff 1994).

The paths of psychology and linguistics crossed permanently after the demise of the *Zeitschrift für Völkerpsychologie und Sprachwissenschaft* at the turn of the present century. That was the point in time when psychologists became keenly interested in researching the interconnection between language and mental processes in an empirical manner (e.g. Wundt 1901, Mead 1904, Ginniken 1909), thus establishing psycholinguistics *ipso facto* as a subfield of both linguistics and psychology. However, to the best of my knowledge, the term *psycholinguistics* was not coined until 1946 by the psychologist Proncko in the *Psychological Bulletin*. Then, in 1951, George Miller gave this emerging new interdisciplinary field of inquiry a clear focus and scope by outlining the points of contact between the mental capacity for language and its modalities of use in actual communication. With the publication of the proceedings of the Indiana University conference on psycholinguistics a few years later in 1953 (Osgood and Sebeok 1954), this fledgling new scientific enterprise came forward to establish itself as an autonomous branch of both linguistics and psychology, becoming today one of the more productive and fascinating branches of the study of language (see Glucksberg and Danks 1975, Titone and Danesi 1985, Garnham 1985, McNeill 1987, Levelt 1989, Taylor 1990, Caron 1992 for diverse but complementary overviews and discussions of the disciplinary scope of psycholinguistics).

Most of the work in psycholinguistics on metaphor since the late seventies suggests that a rethinking of language in terms of conceptual, rather than strictly grammatical, terms will require a new and major focus in the study of how sentences are formed. Actually, this was the goal of Sapir and Whorf—a goal that has never been truly entertained by mainstream linguistics until very recently. The North American version of linguistic science took its characteristic shape and methodological orientation from Leonard Bloomfield's 1933 textbook entitled simply *Language*. In the same way that Euclid's *Elements* bestowed systematicity and unity upon the study and practice of geometry through its coherent synthesis of geometrical concepts and techniques, so too did *Language* provide the fledgling science of linguistics in the thirties, forties and fifties with an organized repertory of notions and procedures for carrying out detailed investigations and analytical characterizations of specific languages. This is the main reason why, in my view, Bloomfield's *Language*, and not the work bearing the same title and published more than a decade earlier by Edward Sapir (1921) came to be accepted by the majority of linguists as the point of reference for conducting empirical research and for developing models of language design.

While Bloomfield's work constituted the first true "textbook" in the history of North American linguistic science, Sapir's book was the first real attempt to provide a framework for studying the relation of language to cognition and culture. And whereas for most of this century linguists have diligently pursued the investigation of language systems *per se*, along the lines laid down first by Bloomfield and later by Chomsky, they have recently started to move more and more toward the adoption of Sapir's original paradigm.

The question that Sapir sought to answer throughout his life is probably as old as civilization itself: How is thought related to language? He was intrigued, in other words, by the possibility that human ideas, concepts, feelings and characteristic social behaviors might be mirrored by the verbal categories that specific cultures employ to codify them. Sapir suspected that the most direct route to the mind was through language. Due to his tragically early death, Sapir was never able to design and carry out a research program aimed at examining his idea rigorously and systematically. As is well known, it fell on the shoulders of Sapir's brilliant student Bejamin Lee Whorf (1956) to elaborate substantively upon his mentor's views and to give them a more empirically-testable articulation. Whorf posited, in essence, that the categories of one's particular language are much more than simple mediators of thought. He saw them as being the "shapers" of the very thought patterns they embody: "The world is presented in a kaleidoscopic flux of impressions which has to be organized by our minds—and this means largely by the linguistic systems in our minds" (Whorf 1956: 153). But Whorf's experimental program for studying the language-thought nexus could not have been devised without his teacher's profound insights. Sapir saw language as being much more than a communication system. He considered it to be a kind of cognitive filter through which humans come to perceive and understand the world around them. To quote from *Language* (1921: 75):

> Human beings do not live in the object world alone, nor alone in the world of social activity as ordinarily understood, but are very much at the mercy of the particular language system which has become the medium of expression for their society. It is quite an illusion to imagine that one adjusts to reality essentially without the use of language and that language is merely an incidental means of solving specific problems of communication or reflection. The fact of the matter is that the "real world" is to a large extent unconsciously built up on the language habits of the group.

Despite the intrinsic appeal of this view, no one, including Whorf, has really ever come forward to confirm or disconfirm it. The alternative view—that those distinctions which are important to a culture will ultimately be differentiated and codified verbally—has just as much intellectual appeal. But on its own it does not invalidate Sapir's intriguing hypothesis. In actual fact, Sapir did not see thought as *determined* by linguistic categories, as is often believed; he merely assumed a correlation between thought and verbal expression with a series of important points of contact between them.

The work in psycholinguistics on prototypical, or basic-level, categories is in many ways complementary to, or even locatable within, the Sapirean paradigm. In Roger Brown's classic 1958 paper "How Shall a Thing Be Called?," the concept of prototypicality can be seen to have crystallized in his observation that children do not learn the names of objects at the most general or at the most specific levels. Rather, as Brown suggested, children seem to acquire first those categories characterized by the most typical name for them. Brown observed that a *dime,* for instance, can be called *money* ( general term) or a 1972 *dime* (specific term). But we somehow feel that the word *dime* is its "real" name. This word, therefore, defines a "prototypical" concept, whereas *money* involves a movement conceptually upward toward a superordinate category, and *1972 dime* a movement downward toward a subordinate category. The fact that children's concepts seem to develop primarily in the way that Brown described, has forced many psychologists to rethink long-held notions on how the mind processes and categorizes information. If nothing else, the theory of prototypicality has, as Paivio and Begg (1981: 159) have aptly quipped, purged us "of the notion that the relation between the world and our view of it is totally arbitrary."

## The I-Hypothesis

The I-Hypothesis has been the target of a number of intriguing and suggestive studies over the past sixty years. For example, the work on so-called sound symbolism in linguistics can be considered to fall under the rubric of this hypothesis. In one study, Roger Brown (1970: 258–273) asked native speakers of English to listen to pairs of antonyms from a language unrelated to English and then to try to guess, given the English equivalents, which foreign word translated which English word. The subjects were asked to guess the meaning of the foreign words by attending to their sounds. When he asked them, for example, to match the words *ch'ing* and *chung* to the English equivalents *light* and *heavy*, not necessarily in that order, Brown found that about 90% of English speakers correctly matched *ch'ing* to *light* and *chung* to *heavy*. He concluded that the degree of translation accuracy could only be explained "as indicative of a primitive phonetic symbolism deriving from the origin of speech in some kind of imitative or physiognomic linkage of sounds and meanings" (Brown 1970: 272).

Sound symbolism theory in linguistics was pioneered by Morris Swadesh throughout his professional career (see Swadesh 1971 for his last published statement on this topic). Swadesh drew attention to such suggestive features as the fact that many of the world's languages used [i]-

type vowels to express such indexical parameters as "nearness," in contrast to [a]- and [u]-type vowels to express the opposite notion of "distance." Such coincidences suggested to him that the notion of nearness is represented unconsciously by the relative nearness of the lips in the articulation of [i]; while the complementary notion of distance is represented by the relative openness of the lips in the pronunciation of the [a] and [u] sounds.

It is beyond the purpose of the present study to discuss the research on sound symbolism (see Hinton, Nichols, and Ohala 1994 for recent views). But the presence of iconicity in language is not limited to phonology. The I-Hypothesis simply extends the findings related to sound symbolism to grammar, suggesting, in other words, that iconicity is operative at all levels of language.

## Some Specific Proposals

It is perhaps the research of Lakoff and Johnson in linguistics over the past two decades (e.g., Lakoff and Johnson 1980, Lakoff 1987, Johnson 1987) that is the most Sapirean in orientation and thus the most germane to developing an apparatus for studying how the I-Hyptothesis works at the level of grammar; i.e. how grammar rules reflect the elements of human conceptual systems. The essential claim made by these two scholars is that our most common concepts are forged via metaphor. Consider, for example, the following common metaphorical portrayals of health (Lakoff and Johnson 1980: 15 and 50):

1. You're at the peak of your health.
2. My health is down.
3. You're in top shape.
4. My body is in perfect working order.
5. My body is breaking down.
6. My health is going down the drain.
7. His pain went away.
8. I'm going to flush out my cold.

The first three sentences represent health in terms of an orientation analogy: i.e. the state of being healthy is conceptualized as being oriented in an upwards direction, while the opposite state is conceptualized as being oriented in a downwards direction. This is probably because in our culture, as Lakoff and Johnson (1980: 15) point out, serious "illness forces us to lie down physically." Sentences (4) and (5) compare health, and its converse, to a machine. And in the last three sentences health and its converse are envisaged as being entities within a person. This is why they can go away, why they can be flushed out, and so on. Such examples reveal that "health" is an abstract metaphorical topic and that its various conceptualizations (as orientation, as an entity, as a machine, etc.) are its vehicles. The end result is a way of thinking and talking about health in English that takes place unconsciously in the domain of metaphor—*healthiness is up/unhealthiness is down, healthiness is a well-functioning machine/unhealthiness is a malfunctioning machine,* etc. The work of Pollio et al. (1977) and the many surveys of the use of metaphor in everyday communicative behavior (e.g., Dundes 1972, Beck 1982, Kövecses 1986, 1988, 1990) have made it obvious that this kind of know-how, which can be called "metaphorical competence," is an intrinsic feature of discourse. The implications are quite clear: metaphorical competence can be examined in ways that are parallel to the ways in which other competencies (linguistic and communicative) have been investigated by linguists.

The gist of the work on metaphor has shown, as Lakoff and Johnson (1980: 5) remark, that we experience and understand "one kind of thing in terms of another." As an example of how it might work in actual discourse programming consider the following hypothetical situation. Let us say that I am practicing the piano (Danesi 1995: 99). It is a rainy day and I am playing a sad piece of music. Someone walks into the room where I am playing and asks me how I feel. The sad music and the rain outside have put me in a frame of mind that leads me to make a commentary on my mood. Seeing raindrops on a nearby window, I might answer my interlocutor with "I'm feeling drippy." In the context of the experiential domain in which the utterance was uttered it makes perfect sense. The reason why it makes sense to my interlocutor is because it "reflects" an underlying metaphorical concept—*mood is an environmental state* ("I'm feeling under the weather," "I'm in a stormy mood today," etc.). This example shows how experience of the world (seeing a drip and associating it with feeling sad) is first conceptualized metaphorically (*mood is an environmental state*), and then verbalized in the form of a contextually-appropriate discourse text.

Research on so-called anomalous strings (e.g., "Colorless green ideas sleep furiously") has shown, moreover, that metaphorical competence has a powerful influence over sentence processing, forcing people to extract meaning from virtually any well-formed combination of words (e.g., Pollio and Burns 1977, Pollio and Smith 1979). If people are required to interpret such strings, then they will do so, no matter how contrived the interpretation might appear. This suggests that metaphorical thinking is a dominant form of sentence processing, and that literal thinking might actually constitute a special, limited case of communicative behavior. In the absence of contextual information for an utterance such as "The murderer is an animal," we are immediately inclined to apply the metaphorical mode in processing what it means. It is only if we are told that the murder was committed by a biological animal that a literal interpretation becomes possible.

Now, the work on metaphor suggests that many sentences are metaphorical and therefore conceptually iconic. Does this iconicity finds its way into the grammar? If it does, then the next step is to show how the concept is transferred to the grammatical system and categorized as a rule.

As a concrete example of how this might be done, consider the use of the prepositions *since* and *for* in sentences such as the following (Danesi 1995: 81–82):

9. I have been living here *since* 1980.
10. I have known Lucy *since* November.
11. I have not been able to sleep *since* Monday.
12. I have been living here *for* fifteen years.
13. I have known Lucy *for* nine months.
14. I have not been able to sleep *for* five days.

An analysis of the complements that follow *since* or *for* reveals that those that follow the former are "points in time," i.e. they are complements that reflect a conception of time as a "point" on a "timeline" which shows specific years, months, etc.: "1980," "November," "Monday," etc. Complements that follow *for*, on the other hand, reflect a conception of time as a "quantity:" "fifteen years," "nine months," "five days," etc. These two conceptual domains—*time is a point* and *time is a quantity*—are the image-schemata that Lakoff (1987) and Johnson (1987) so ably talk about. They are, clearly, conceptual domains that result from metaphor, reflecting our propensity to imagine an abstract notion like "time" in terms of something concrete. Now, these can then be seen to have a specific effect at the level of language by producing a grammatical dichotomy—complements introduced by *since* are reflexes of the conceptual domain *time is a point*; those introduced by *for* are reflexes of the conceptual domain *time is a (measurable) quantity*. This is the rule of grammar that we have been searching for—it now relates how two specific domains of conceptualization have worked their way into the grammar. In a word, this rule stipulates how a grammatical dichotomy *reflects* a conceptual dichotomy.

This conceptualization of time is also present in such other logical systems as algebra. The only way to solve a problem such as the following is if the solver has access to the above domains:

> John is five years older than Mary. In four years from now, he will be twice her age. What is the present age of each?

This problem can be solved algebraically by setting up a linear equation as follows: The letter symbol x can be used to represent Mary's present age. Therefore, John's present age can be represented by $x + 5$. The reason for this is because we have access to the conceptual domain *time is a point*. John's age-point is "5 points" away from Mary's age-point, which can be considered the origin or "point 0" on a timeline.

Identical reasoning can now be applied to represent John's and Mary's ages in four years time. We simply move their age-points "up by four" on the timeline. This translates into $x + 4$ for Mary and $x + 5 + 4$ ($= x + 9$) for John. Now we shift to the conceptual domain time is a quantity to relate their ages further. John's age is quantifiable as twice that of Mary's age. This is, of course, a relation that can be expressed by multiplying Mary's age by two: $x + 9$ [John's age] = $2(x + 4)$ [twice Mary's age]. Solving this equation reveals that Mary is at present one year old and John six.

Take, as one other example, the ways in which different languages treat weather verbs (e.g., Ruwet 1991). In a Romance language like Italian, for example, the verb *fare* "to make" is used to convey a weather condition—*fa caldo* (literally) "it makes hot," *fa freddo* (literally) "it makes cold." The condition of "hotness" and "coldness" is conveyed instead by the verb *essere* "to be" when referring to objects—*è caldo* "it is hot," *è freddo* "it is cold"—and by *avere* "to have" when referring to people—*ha caldo* "he/she is hot," *ha freddo* " he/she is cold." The use of one verb or the other—*fare, essere, or avere*—is motivated by an underlying image schema of bodies and the environment as containers. So, the "containment context" in which the quality of "coldness" or "hotness" is located determines the verbal category to be employed. If it is in the environment, it is "made" by Nature (*fa freddo*); if it is in a human being, then the body "has" it *(ha freddo*); and if it is in an object, then the object "is" its container (*è freddo*).

To summarize, the point to be made here is that our unconsciously embedded concept of *time* as a "point on a line" and as a "quantity," or of "hotness" and "coldness" as being contained in Nature, people, or things, constitute conceptual domains that have reflexes or "markings" in the grammars of specific languages. Knowledge of such differentiated reflexive properties is what guides competent translators implicitly when they convert one language text into another successfully. As Bressan (1987: 69) has put it, the translator interprets diverse "markings" in the source language on the conceptual-semantic level, and then compares them to their closest equivalents in the target language: i.e. for Bressan the task of the translator is to "determine [conceptually-appropriate] devices for more accurate translation." *Grammar* in this framework is definable, therefore, as a system that formalizes conceptual iconicity, i.e. it produces a stable *conceptual* system.

As a final consideration, any refinement or elaboration of the notion of "reflexive grammatical rule" will have to take into account the presence of different "orders" of metaphor. Take, for instance, the following two North American conceptual models of thinking: *thoughts are movable objects* and *thinking is visual scanning*. These models are instantiated frequently in common discourse by utterances such as the following (from Danesi and Santeramo 1995):

### Thoughts are movable objects

15. Work it over in your mind.
16. Turn that thought over in your mind.
17. You should rearrange your thoughts carefully.
18. You should put your previous thoughts in order before going forward with your plans

### Thinking is visual scanning

19. You must look over what you've written.
20. I must look into what you've told me a bit further.
21. She saw right through what you told her.
22. I'm going to see this thing completely out.

These sentences suggest that we conceptualize thought processes as extensions or analogues of physical objects and events. Thoughts, like objects, can be moved, arranged, located, etc. They can also be seen, looked into, etc. Often, this involves pre-established conceptual domains, such as, for instance, those based on Euclidean geometry:

### Thoughts are geometrical figures

23. I don't see the point of your argument.
24. Their ideas are diametrically opposite.
25. Their ideas are parallel.
26. That's an example of circular reasoning.
27. His thinking is rather square, isn't it?

These examples show that there are different degrees or "orders" of concepts. The *thinking is visual scanning* model, for example, is a first-order concept because it connects a perceptual *Gestalt—seeing*—to an abstraction—*thinking*—directly. But first-order concepts can become themselves the vehicles of higher-order concepts. So, the *thoughts are geometrical figures* model reveals a second-order conceptualization, since geometrical figures and notions are themselves concepts.

## General Implications

As Henry Schogt perceptively remarks (1988: 38), one can no longer ignore the growing body of evidence that shows how all languages "have meaningful units that articulate human experience into discrete elements." The discussion in this paper has attempted to demonstrate how the discrete elements of sentences reflect conceptual iconicity. The idea would be at first to identify and catalogue the vehicles that underlie specific topics, and then match them to the grammatical categories that reflect them. So, for instance, when analyzing sentences that allude to the weather in Italian (the topic), it will be necessary to keep in mind how the conceptualization of hotness/coldness as substances that are contained in specific contexts (the vehicles) is codified into a selection rule involving the verbs *fare, avere*, and *essere* (including relevant morphological information). It is interesting to note that in Italian "being right," "being sleepy," etc. are also conceptualized as "contained" substances. This is why to say "I am right," "I am sleepy," etc. in Italian one must say *ho ragione* ("I have reason"), *ho sonno* ("I have sleepiness), etc.

Actually, the idea of making conceptual iconicity the basis for the description of language has been attempted by Langacker (e.g. 1987, 1990) and some of his followers. In my view, they are on the right track, especially in showing how grammatical rules are iconically-motivated, i.e. how they reflect our direct perception of things in the world as they stand in relation to one another. For instance, the following is a highly reduced paraphrase of how they explain the conceptual difference between an active and passive sentence such as *Sally ate the apple* vs. *The apple was eaten by Sally*. In traditional theories of syntax, the passive is considered to be a derivative of the active: i.e. through some abstract mental rule anchored in a general principle of grammatical design, passives can always be reconstructed as actives. This means that active sentences are cognitively more salient than passives. Apart from the fact that it really does seem unlikely to think of active sentences as abstract forms "waiting" to be passivized by the demands of grammar or conversational style, there are sentences which are, seemingly, conceivable only as passive: e.g. *The Bible was written at the dawn of time*. When viewed from the vantage point of an iconic theory of grammar, on the other hand, the sentences *Sally ate the apple* and *The apple was eaten by Sally* reveal a different conceptual organization. In active sentences the subject is in the *foreground* of the mind's eye, while the object is in its *background*. The *action* implied by the verb is the link between the two. The overall mental view that such sentences evoke is that of the subject as an agent, a "perpetrator" or "executor" of the action. A change from passive to active changes the position of the foreground and the background in the mental view. The cognitive effect is to give more salience to the object as "receiver" of the action. In other words, the passive form literally gives the mind a different "angle" from which to see the world. Syntax, or the putting together of separate words to create a whole new perspective, view, idea, etc. is a remarkable feat of human mentality. It adds perspective to representation in the same way that the juxtaposition of color, line, depth, etc. adds perspective to painting.

## Questions for Future Research

The notions of conceptual iconicity and "reflexive grammar" raise some specific questions for future research. First, are all concepts iconic? And, if not, to what extent is the conceptual system based on metaphorical reasoning? As Way (1991: 18) judiciously suggests, before "Lakoff and Johnson's claim that all language is metaphorical can be properly evaluated, we must come up with a more careful analysis of how we ordinarily use the concept of 'literal'." Second, if reflexive grammar is a plausible construct, then a portion of future work on language will have to document how grammatical and semantic categories reflect conceptual structures or domains. The guiding question then becomes: What are the verbal cues that reveal conceptual domains? In this paper, for instance, the structures *since* and *for* were related to the conceptual domain as reflexes of differentiated metaphorical vehicles: *time is a point* and *time is a quantity*. The work on cognitive grammar by Langacker (e.g. 1987, 1990), as mentioned, is also leading the way in showing us how analyses of this type might be envisioned. A third question is to determine to what extent and in what ways conceptual iconicity relates to, or is embedded in, world knowledge. Is world knowledge built up from metaphor as some would claim? And if so, how is this incorporateable into an extensive analysis of language? Some possibilities have been explored in the past (e.g. Pike 1967), and I believe that this kind of exploration is the wave of the future in linguistics. I would also add another caveat: metaphorically-shaped knowledge is perhaps just one possible form in which knowledge of the world is coded by humans. As Levin (1988: 10) has aptly remarked, there appear to be many modes of knowledge: "innate knowledge, personal knowledge, tacit knowledge, spiritual knowledge, declarative and procedural knowledge, knowing that and knowing how, certitude (as well as certainty), and many other varieties." The more appropriate goal for linguistics should be, therefore, to determine to what extent language reflects metaphorical knowledge and to what extent it reflects other forms of knowledge. Finally, future work should attempt to determine to what extent the phonological, grammatical, and semantic systems are reflexive, to what extent they are interactive reflexively, as well as which specific reflexive properties apply to each system.

In sum, the bulk of the work on grammatical systems in linguistics has traditionally excluded the I-Hypothesis. The present study has aimed to show, however, that sentence form is probably shaped by iconic factors in the referential domain much more than traditional grammatical analysis would admit. The effect of conceptual iconicity on category assignment in grammar has been taken up somewhat in the linguistic literature, but it has produced opposing views. Needless to say, there is always bound to be controversy over innovations in theories and practices in linguistics. But, in my opinion, such controversy can only generate even more interesting and comprehensive research frameworks within which to address issues of general importance to linguistics and semiotics. This is, after all, the nature of true scientific inquiry.

One thing is certain: to ignore metaphor in a theory of grammar is to ignore a large segment of the native speaker's competence. As Mitchell (1993: 3) so aptly remarks, the conceptual system "encompasses recognition, categorization, and analogy-making, and its central feature is the fluid application of one's existing concepts to new situations."

Grammatical properties cannot be studied in isolation. Saussure's contention that the relation between signifier and signified is largely a matter of convention, and Chomsky's parallel contention that the relation between sentence form and the referential domain to which is alludes is arbitrary and determined by fixed rules of an abstract grammar, simply do not take into account the ever-present tendency in the human species to metaphorize.

# References

Beck, B. 1982. "Root Metaphor Patterns," 2 *Semiotic Inquiry* 86–97.

Bloomfield, L. 1933. *Language,* Holt, Rinehart and Winston, New York.

Bressan, D. 1987. "Enigmatic Devices in English-Italian Translation," *6 Multilingua* 69–75.

Brown, R. 1958. "How Shall a Thing Be Called?," 65 *Psychological Review* 14–21.

Brown, R. W. 1970. *Psycholinguistics*, The Free Press, New York.

Caron, J. 1992. *An Introduction to Psycholinguistics,* University of Toronto Press, Toronto.

Chomsky, N. 1957. *Syntactic Structures,* Mouton, The Hague.

___. 1966. Topics in *The Theory of Grammar*, Mouton, The Hague.

___. 1976. O*n the Nature of Language. In: Origins and Evolution of Language and Speech*, H. B. Steklis, S. R. Harnad, and J. Lancaster (eds.), New York Academy of Sciences , New York, pp. 46–57.

___. 1986. *Knowledge of Language: Its Nature, Origin, and Use*, Praeger., New York.

Craig, C. 1986. (ed.). *Noun Classes and Categorization,* John Benjamins., Amsterdam.

Danesi, M. 1995. *Giambattista Vico and the Cognitive Science Enterprise*, Peter Lang , New York.

___. and Santeramo, D. 1995. *Deictic Verbal Constructions*, Urbino: Centro Internazionale di Semiotica e di Linguistica.

Dundes, A. 1972. "Seeing is Believing," 81 *Natural History* 9–12.

Garnham, A. 1985. *Psycholinguistics: Central Topics,* Methuen, London.

Ginniken, J. van. 1909. *Principes de psychologie linguistique*, Paris: Alcan.

Glucksberg, S. and Danks, J. H. 1975. *Experimental Psycholinguistics: An Introduction,* John Wiley & Sons , New York.

Halliday, M. A. K. 1975. *Learning How to Mean: Explorations in the Development of Language,* Arnold, London.

___. 1985. *Introduction to Functional Grammar*, Arnold, London.

Higginbotham, J. 1992. "Semantics in Linguistics: An Outline for an Introduction," 2 *Golem* 7–10.

Hinton, L., Nichols, J., and Ohala, J. J. (eds.). 1994. *Sound Symbolism*, Cambridge University Press, Cambridge.

Hymes, D. 1971. *On Communicative Competence,* University of Pennsylvania Press, Philadelphia.

Jackendoff, R. 1994. *Patterns in the Mind: Language and Human Nature*, Basic Books, New York.

Johnson, M. 1987. *The Body in the Mind: The Bodily Basis of Meaning, Imagination and Reason,* University of Chicago Press, Chicago.

Kövecses, Z. 1986. *Metaphors of Anger, Pride, and Love: A Lexical Approach to the Structure of Concepts,* John Benjamins, Amsterdam.

___. 1988. *The Language of Love: The Semantics of Passion in Conversational English,* Associated University Presses, London.

___. 1990. Emotion Concepts, Springer, New York.

Lakoff, G. 1987. *Women, Fire, and Dangerous Things: What Categories Reveal about the Mind,* University of Chicago Press, Chicago.

___. and Johnson, L. 1980. *Metaphors We Live By,* Chicago University Press, Chicago.

Langacker, R. W. 1987. *Foundations of Cognitive Grammar*, Stanford University Press, Stanford.

___. 1990. *Concept, Image, and Symbol: The Cognitive Basis of Grammar*, Mouton de Gruyter, Berlin.

Larson, R. K. 1990. "Semantics," in *Language: An Invitation to Cognitive Science*, D. N. Osherson and H. Lasnik (eds.), MIT Press, Cambridge, pp. 23–42.

Levelt, W. J. M. 1989. *Speaking: From Intention to Articulation,* MIT Press, Cambridge.

Levin, S. R. 1988. *Metaphoric Worlds,* Yale University Press, New Haven.

Lucy, J. A. 1992. *Language Diversity and Thought: A Reformulation of the Linguistic Relativity Hypothesis,* Cambridge University Press, Cambridge.

MacLellan, C. G. H. 1994. "Metaphors and Prototypes in the Teaching and Learning of Grammar and Vocabulary," 32 *International Review of Applied Linguistics* 97–110.

McNeill, D. 1987. *Psycholinguistics: A New Approach,* Harper & Row, pp. 23–42.

Mead, G. H. 1904. "The Relation of Psychology and Philology," 1 *Psychological Bulletin* 375–391.

Miller, G. 1951. *Language and Communication*, New York: McGraw-Hill.

Mitchell, M. 1993. *Analogy-Making as Perception: A Computer Model*. MIT Press, Cambridge.

Osgood, C. E. and Sebeok, T. A. (eds.) 1954. *Psycholinguistics: A Survey of Theory and Research Problems*, Indiana University Press.

Paivio, A. and Begg, I. 1981. *Psychology of Language,* Prentice Hall, Englewood Cliffs.

Pike, K. 1967. *Language in Relation to a Unified Theory of the Structure of Human Behavior,* Mouton, The Hague.

Pinker, S. 1994. *The Language Instinct: How the Mind Creates Language*, William Morrow, New York.

Pollio, H. and Burns, B. 1977. "The Anomaly of Anomaly," 6 *Journal of Psycholinguistic Research* 247–260.

___. and Smith, M. 1979. "Sense and Nonsense in Thinking about Anomaly and Metaphor," 13 *Bulletin of the Psychonomic Society* 323–326.

___. Barlow, J., Fine, H., and Pollio, M. 1977. *The Poetics of Growth: Figurative Language in Psychology, Psychotherapy, and Education,* Lawrence Erlbaum Associates, Hillside, N. J.

Proncko, N. H. 1946. "Language and Psycholinguistics," 43 *Psychological Bulletin* 189–239.

Ruwet, N. 1991. *Syntax and Human Experience,* University of Chicago Press, Chicago.

Sapir, E. 1921. *Language,* Harcourt, Brace, and World, New York.

Saussure, Ferdinand de. 1916/1966. *Course in General Linguistics,* Payot, Paris.

Schogt, H. 1988. *Linguistics, Literary Analysis, and Literary Translation*, University of Toronto Press, Toronto.

Simone, R. (ed.) 1995. *Iconicity in Language,* John Benjamins, Amsterdam.

Skousen, R. 1989. *Analogical Modeling of Language,* Kluwer, Dordrecht.

Swadesh, Morris. 1971. *The Origins and Diversification of Language*, Aldine-Atherton, Chicago.

Taylor, I. 1990. *Psycholinguistics: Learning and Using Language*, Prentice-Hall, Englewood Cliffs.

Titone, R. and Danesi, M. 1985. *Applied Psycholinguistics: An Introduction to the Psychology of Language Teaching and Learning,* University of Toronto Press, Toronto.

Way, E. C. 1991. *Knowledge Representation and Metaphor,* Kluwer, Dordrecht.

Whorf, B. L. 1956. *Language, Thought, and Reality*, J. B. Carroll (ed.). MIT Press, Cambridge.

Winner, E. 1982. *Invented Worlds: The Psychology of the Arts,* Harvard University Press, Cambridge.

Wundt, W. 1901. *Sprachgeschichte und Sprachpsychologie,* Eugelmann, Leipzig.

# Chapter Eleven

# Great Webs and Tapestries and Fabrications: A Tribute to Roberta Kevelson

**Willem J. Witteveen**

> The great webs and tapestries and fabrications of the law are like artworks which hide once-powerful symbols in the borders of the woven fabric.
>
> Roberta Kevelson

## Great Webs

In Kenneth Burke's famous definition, man is characterized as "the symbol-using (symbol-making, symbol-misusing) animal" (Burke 1968, p. 3). Various other traits are added to this definition of man, not the least of which is the idea that man is the "inventor of the negative (or moralized by the negative)", a phrase which introduces moral and legal discourse. But the making, using, and misusing of symbols is surely central to any semiotic understanding of human communication; its primacy in the definition is entirely justified when semiosis is taken to be, as Umberto Eco states, "the process by which empirical subjects communicate" (Eco 1976, p. 316). Eco also adds something of importance, to wit that communication is made possible by "the organization of signification systems". So starting out with man as maker and user of symbols, attention shifts quickly to the availability of such "signification systems" which are the necessary condition of symbol using.

Imagining signification systems is not quite like making or (mis)using other symbols. It is an activity that takes place at a different level. Creating maps or models of what goes on in the making, using, and misusing of symbols is a task which requires reflexivity. It proceeds from an awareness of semiotic processes. It is like asking someone who knows his way around a forest to make a drawing of this forest as seen from the top of a distant mountain. Paths that are familiar from daily experience are from this elevated vantage point shown to have unsuspected connections with other paths and to be part of a vast network —while the pattern as a whole, the weblike structure, is invisible from the ground.

Yet, recognizing the difference between making symbols for practical use and imagining "systems of signification", both are similarly efforts in symbolizing activity. We can perhaps see this most clearly when we see that in both instances semiosis does not encounter inherent or natural limits. Semiosis is unlimited, in the famous Peircean phrase. This is true on the level of practical symbol-making, symbol-using, and symbol-misusing, and it is equally true on the level of the design of maps or models of processes of communication. Different inhabitants of the forest will produce different mental maps of the terrain, reading their experiences differently. But also the mapmaker on the top of the mountain cannot reach definitive results, cannot exhaust meanings. As soon as a different elevated vantage point is taken, the map changes, sometimes drastically (compare a view of the forest from one mountain with that from another mountain and both of these with the view obtained from a passing airplane).

How do man and "signification system" relate to one another? Everywhere we turn, thinking about semiosis, we can find signs that potentially have meaning, once we allow them to enter our minds as signs. We are going to be in for surprises. Peirce, the father of semiotics, writes:

> Since man can think only by means of words or other external symbols, these might turn round and say: "You mean nothing which we have not taught you, and then only so far as you address some word as the interpretant of your thought". In fact, therefore, men and words reciprocally educate each other; each increase of a man's information involves, and is involved by, a corresponding increase of a word's information.... It is that the word or sign which a man uses IS the man itself (Peirce 1958, 5.313–5.314).

The symbols we think by turn round and interrogate us. The signs we use, use us and become part of us: "my language is the sum total of myself" (Peirce, continuing). This view of the importance of signification is not only liberatory, suggesting a mutual increase in knowledge ("reciprocal education"), but also threatening, reducing man to "an external sign" (still Peirce's words).

It is easy to see that jurists are symbol-using animals. As legislators, advocates, and judges they do their part in "moralizing by the negative", that is to say in making, upholding, challenging, and interpreting the rules. The law is a language both empowering its speakers (by speaking law a human being becomes a jurist), and limiting, constraining, defining them as "external signs" in a particular system of legal signification. No legal speech act can be committed in total innocence of these basic facts. Anyone trained in the law, anyone capable of seeing the world through the lenses of legal categories, is at least dimly aware of being a symbol-using animal. But reflexivity can be prevented. Basic facts of legal communication can often safely be ignored. Too much awareness of legal semiotic processes can even hinder effective performance. The liberating and threatening relation to the systems that generate legal meaning and make the jurist into the person she is, need not be openly confronted.

Those who do reflect on their condition as symbol-using animals, surprisingly often come to see the "systems of signification" in terms of the metaphor of *the great web*. When Ronald Dworkin introduces his ideal judge, Hercules, he is concerned to show with what attitude and what art of reasoning this perfect judge approaches legal problems. In interpreting statutes or in reasoning on the basis of precedent, Hercules must suppose that it is understood in his community "that judicial decisions must be taken to be justified by arguments of principle rather than arguments of policy" (Dworkin 1977 , p. 115). When Hercules interprets law, he must take a principled decision and justify his arguments accordingly. In this way the systematic nature of law is highlighted as well as its further evolution through principled judicial decision-making. Judges as interpreters of the law aim to achieve "right answers", which represent the only correct solutions to the interpretive problem. In order to be able to postulate this "right answer thesis", it is necessary to have a picture of law as a "seamless web" (Dworkin, 1977, p. 115). In later work, Dworkin stresses the dynamics of legal change through constructive interpretation. The system of law is seen to be gradually turning into the best it can potentially be. The web of legal significance is in this theory of law both outside of the Herculean judge—the true form of the legal universe—and it is shaped and perfected through interpretive activities in the hard cases of real life.

> The judge must choose between eligible interpretations by asking which shows the community's structure of institutions and decisions—its public standards as a whole—in a better light from the standpoint of political morality (Dworkin 1986, p. 256).

The metaphor of the great web of legal significance need not take this constructivist format, however. Robert Benson's depiction of the semiotic web of legal interpretation stresses the openness of interpretation to a welter of influences and the arbitrary nature of closure:

> The metaphor (of the semiotic web) sees the individual surrounded by a cultural web of signs. (...) A reader looking at a sign explains it in terms of another sign in the web, and that sign in terms of another, and so on in what Charles Peirce called a process of "unlimited semiosis", a process which ends only when the reader loses interest after registering the last sign within the mind, or acting in a certain way (Benson 1989, p. 260).

Circling through the semiotic web, Benson's reader engages texts, sources of texts, and other readers, while being influenced by her own particular values, psychological characteristics, and historical, cultural and social circumstances. When the circling stops, after traversing only parts of the available web structures, "meaning" has been arrived at. Symbols are ready for use.

Here we see two very different conceptions of the "system of significations" shaped by the metaphor of the web of law. Dworkin's idealized judge resembles the walker in the forest who miraculously achieves the perfect vantage point from which to see the whole forest in its true light, unfolding its potential through time. Benson's pragmatist reader is like the pilot of a helicopter circling above the woodland, now zooming in on a group of trees, now taking a higher altitude to see a pattern of roads, circulating until the helicopter is landed at some place, knowing there is always more to see but for the moment satisfied with all the reasoning traversed.

## Great Webs and Tapestries

In talking about tapestries of law, the metaphor used to imagine the abstract idea of a "system of signification" undergoes a subtle change. Tapestries are webs that are woven, systems made out of materials according to a *design*. The woven web is not part of the natural and social world surrounding a weaver, but a "system of signification" all one's own, an addition to what is there rather than a selection from an overcrowded environment of signs. The attraction of a tapestry of law is that this both involves a creative act and a protective act. The tapestry is a model of law charting its possibilities and potentialities but of such simplicity, harmony, and stability that this model effectively obscures from view the threatening reality of being part of a system of external signs, which is forever in motion. The tapestry of law allows certain properties of the legal system to be marked, while relegating equally important aspects or properties to the background. Law is turned into order. The tapestry is the knotted view of the forest, seen from one point of view, happily excluding other organizations of experience.

From the history of law we can learn that three tapestries representing different theoretical understandings of the nature of law are woven again and again. From the materials of these three types of tapestry later jurists weave their new creative and protective textures. (Historically, this does not exclude quite different models of law but these rarely achieve social dominance.) What these tapestries have in common is that they have a vantage point that organizes all of law's phenomena into a certain fixed pattern. They provide answers to many questions at once. They can be used for practical purposes, as well as offering some theoretical guidance. Typically, these three tapestries frame perception and by framing perception organize legal experience.

The first view of the nature of law opens up from the familiar hills of *positivism*: law consists of the collection or system of rules that have been called into being by competent lawmaking authorities. Quite complex theories of positivism have been articulated, but what matters most for this perspective on law is captured in this simple formula. The central idea of positivism comes easy to anyone contemplating the nature of law. This tapestry of law is a textual one indeed: law is seen to be contained in texts, in constitutions, statutes, judicial opinions, contracts; in short, in documents that are binding on some audience they rightfully address. The authority of law is given with the existence of texts that bind and that have been created by the proper authorities in the right manner. This view of law immediately clarifies the work of jurists as well: they are the competent readers and writers of the texts of law. At the same time, positivism does not imply a statical view of law. The system of rules can and will change, but all of its changes find expression in texts of law that in the end are binding upon the members of the community. The dynamics of the legal system are textually documented.

The advantages and disadvantages of the positivist frame for legal experience are not hard to imagine. Positivism is conducive to the development of legal methods that are text-based and can be used to solve problems in the practical working of the legal system. It leads to a clear division of labour between jurists and non-jurists (the jurists being experts in the service of their communities). Positivism contains the promise of complete knowledge of all valid law. This supposedly furthers the ideals of legal transparency and legal certainty. Under democratic conditions, the positivist frame will set up the representatives of the people as the makers of new law-texts (positivism as the legal ideology of representative democracy). In this connection, positivism promises to be an instrumentalism, allowing political and social choices to be transformed into valid and binding legal rules. These benefits show corresponding disadvantages, however. Textual legal methods are no guarantee for solutions that will work well in the practice of law; indeed, the vast terrain of activities undertaken to implement law, to live by its rules in social life, is completely invisible from the positivist vantage point. The expertise of jurists often means power for people of law, at the expense of the knowledge and power of ordinary citizens (and, it must be said, often also at the expense of their political representatives who formally are empowered to make laws but in fact are dependent on legal expertise). The complexity of any system of rules that purports to cover all relevant topics diminishes rather than enhances legal certainty. The promise of instrumentalism is often a false promise, in which case social choices cannot be effectuated at all or with counterproductive and unintended effects.

The biggest problem often associated with positivism concerns the exclusion of content from law. Positivism is a formalism. Law is reduced to a set of validated rules. But what about the quality of these rules, individually and taken together, what about their justice? This question leads jurists towards the elevated observation post of *natural law*. The variety of natural law theories is immense, but the central point about the nature of law is usually this: the rules of law are imperfectly realized interpretations of the ideals of justice. Rational human beings can in principle discover the demands of justice, especially by confronting injustice. Over and above the collection of rules that positivism declares to be all the law there is, in natural law one postulates a system of ideal law, which allows for critical comparisons. This view of law is broader than the textual view of law. The ideal rules are not always enacted in binding legal documents but are unwritten ("written in the hearts of men", writes Cicero). The force of natural law precepts does not derive from their recognition by competent authorities at all but from their value and validity for all human beings that live together under law.

Again, there is a balance of advantages and disadvantages. An important point in favour of natural law is its critical potential. By thinking about principles of law as critical standards a given system of positive laws has to meet, natural law gives a strong impetus for improvements of the law as textual system. Where positivist interpretations of democracy are formalist too, referring the problem of the quality of law to the people's representatives, the natural law interpretation of the ideal of democracy, while not necessarily rejecting representative government, recognizes the relevance of the moral convictions of the ordinary citizens. But alongside these strong points, there are weaknesses in the natural law position. It is hard to ascertain the content of the principles that ideally should guide law. A debate about the justice of rules soon leads to the discovery that there are various abstract principles that oppose one another or that afford very different interpretations. When these claims about the content of justice have to be compared with one another, the natural law perspective does not tell us which principle to prefer. Similarly, the thesis that moral convictions of the ordinary citizens should be relevant in law-making does not provide an uncontroversial answer to the question whether the moral convictions of the representatives should be made less relevant. From the perspective of positivism, the history of natural law thinking shows that reasonable human beings that are each supposed to know the principles of justice have never in fact achieved consensus about the meaning or practical application of these universal principles.

Positivism and natural law tell opposing stories. The third view of law does not occupy the middle ground but it articulates an entirely different conception of what characterizes the enterprise of law. The focus of this third approach is on the interactions between people involving rules of law. For *interactionism*, law is a human activity. Law is always constructed, effectuated, and disbanded by the actions of people in social settings. Law is a particular way of organizing human groups. Understanding the social aspect of law makes interactionism resemble a helicopter surveying the landscape, sometimes coming close in order to study the exact doings of people, sometimes gaining height to generalize about the vicissitudes of human communication. The rules of law are in this view certainly important, as are principles of justice. Their importance derives from human activities, from what people do to each other. Not the law in books, but the law in action is what counts here.

The main attraction of interactionism is perhaps its bringing together of very different aspects of law: the interactionist lawyer must study the rules, but also reckon with the actual working of legal institutions; she must take seriously the values and principles contained in legal notions but she must also scrutinize the concrete expectations and aspirations of people in an actual legal conflict. The interactionist frame encompasses all of these different dimensions of the law. A good lawyer cannot only go by the book but must be responsive to real life situations. Yet, from the standpoints of both positivism and natural law, the difficulties with this sweeping view of law can quickly be detected. For positivism, there is great value in demarcating valid from invalid law, rules of law from ethical imperatives, legal commands from political desiderata. Interactionism, showing the incompatible positions of the participants in discussions about law, does not allow for these desirable demarcations. The natural law proponents are disappointed at the inability of interactionist approaches to articulate clear and universal norms and principles. To them, interactionism easily slides into an empty relativism, in which all claims find recognition, only to lead to the painful discovery that the lawyer cannot provide rationally founded solutions to legal problems.

The debates between adherents of these three positions are interminable. No one side can offer arguments that are compelling when they are interpreted from within the perspective of its opponents. When debates like these in fact take place—something which does not demand great theoretical sophistication but can occur during the course of moderately hard law cases—important topics of the legal culture are recirculated. In the process, considerable refinement of the theories is a possibility but, interestingly, this sophistication does not do away with the simple versions. Of course, the way the three tapestries have been described is a crude caricature in comparison to legal theories worthy of the name. The positivism of Austin or Hart is more subtle than the positivism sketched here; Grotius' or Dworkin's natural law theories show only a superficial resemblance to the account of natural law on offer; interactionist theories by Fuller or some legal realists can conceivably produce answers to the charges leveled at them. But the point of seeing the three tapestries—views of the law as system of signification—as being woven again and again, is another one: it is precisely the crude, caricatured views that are most easy to find, that show their practical usefulness in legal reasoning. A history of legal semiosis should take them seriously.

In her legal semiotic writings, Roberta Kevelson repeatedly enters into the question of legal systems of signification. She sees pragmatic approaches in law, not only those of Holmes and the legal realists, but also those of continental writers like Gény, as theories that have been influenced by or can be reconstructed as exercises in Peircean semiotics. Peirce is, in her words, the *catalyst* of modern legal science, the influence that had revolutionary consequences for legal thought, even if this influence more often than not (Holmes and Gény being the exceptions) went unnoticed (Kevelson 1987, p. 69–82). My comment on this is that not only can all pragmatic forces in modern legal thinking plausibly be classed with Peirce, but the dynamics of legal debate alternating between the three positions sketched above in such crude outline, can also be understood semiotically and on Peircean lines. The interminable debate is an exercise in unlimited semiosis. Engaging each another, the three positions clash, never being able to once and for all win the debate. Positivism is not the definitive winner, natural law does not forever reign supreme, interactionism is rarely acknowledged for longer than a fleeting moment. As the debate continues, new arguments do not neatly fall into one of the three caricatured positions but make their own combination of elements. Much human rights ideology these days for instance, combines a natural law like belief in universal human rights with strict attention to the ways in which systems of positive law have incorporated these laws and at least some awareness of the practical difficulties in making real life problems square with abstractly recognized rights.

So, in the course of time, something carries over from older debates, from incompatible views, into current theories. Kevelson gives us the perfect metaphor for understanding this complicated process of recirculating meanings. It extends from the view of systems of legal signification as tapestries. They are "like artworks which hide once-powerful symbols in the borders of the woven fabric". When in early modern history absolute kings acquire central power (like Louis XIV in France), they relegate oppositional symbols to the margins of the tapestries that give symbolic expression to their power.

> The griphon, once the full antagonist of the lion in the conquest of the patriarchical and ideological realms of the Western world, becomes further and further altered in public representation, so that what was once a primeval dragon is now merely a stylized claw of that great emerged lion-force. The griphon is now merely the *fleur de lis* adorning the talisman of the lion who is the signifying king of the courts (Kevelson 1993, p. 67).

A historical semiotics of legal signification systems must paradoxically be forward-looking. The interest of uncovering debates between "tapestries" of law that were designed to create greater coherence than is warranted by the basic facts of legal signification, is not that of a historical reconstruction, still less that of a "wish to return to a more simple age". This forward-looking interest is Peircean in its embrace of the nonpredictable, in its acceptance of the consequences of words that can be revolutionary and unforeseen. As Kevelson says it so well:

> The utopic wish for the return of an old idealized order is always the urge to self-destruct, to let the feared "inevitable" happen. The creative mode, by contrast, is to let the *nonpredictable* happen and grow and become more complex, more self-designing, more chaotic and more possible "in the long run"; it is spontaneous (Kevelson 1993, p. 68).

## Great Webs and Tapestries and Fabrications

In speaking of webs *and* tapestries *and* fabrications, Kevelson makes use of the ancient rhetorical figure of the *trikolon*, or list of three. This rhetorical device is highly suitable for purposes of narration, since it creates the impression of completion, of having stated all that needs to be said (Atkinson 1984). But is this list of three not at the same time the figure of repetition? Are "webs", "tapestries", and "fabrications" different signs for the same thing? Let us go back to Kenneth Burke's definition of man as the "symbol-using animal". Webs, tapestries and fabrications are different kinds of symbol-using. Through the metaphor of the semiotic web, the jurist pictures herself as surrounded by a vast cultural network of signs, glimpses of which can be seen, but which in its entirety is beyond understanding. Through the man-made model of the tapestry—the self-constructed simplified view of the legal universe—the jurist makes sense of many complicated facts at one stroke and reaches a vantage-point from which answers can be given to recurring puzzles about the nature and validity of law. Fabrications are stories about law. They are openly fictive and do not purport to reflect reality or be part of it. They are ways of moralizing about law and life, in a context of critical distance to the practices of law. They are perhaps not true, but one can learn something through telling stories.

Italo Calvino's *Invisible Cities* is a book about story-telling, a fabrication of fabrications. "Kublai Khan does not necessarily believe everything Marco Polo says when he describes the cities visited on his expeditions." (Calvino 1979, p. 10) But the great emperor listens more attentively to the tale of the traveler than to other messages about the actual situation in his realm. "Only in Marco Polo's accounts was Kublai Khan able to discern, through the walls and towers destined to crumble, the tracery of a pattern so subtle it could escape the termites' gnawing." (Calvino 1979, p. 10) The story Marco Polo tells about the city of Eudoxia is a story about the semiotic web, imagined as a tapestry. Eudoxia is a chaotic city, apparently without structure or design. In it, a carpet is kept, "laid out in symmetrical motives", which shows the city's true form. It can be used as a map; all of its signs correspond to places in the city and "all the things contained in the city are included in the design".

> All of Eudoxia's confusion, the mules' braying, the lampblack stains, the fish smell is what is evident in the incomplete perspective you grasp; but the carpet proves that there is a point from which the city shows its true proportions, the geometrical scheme implicit in its every, tiniest detail (Calvino 1979, p. 76).

The inhabitants of Eudoxia use the carpet as a symbolical organization of the city, and through contemplating it "each can find, concealed among the arabesques, an answer, the story of his life, the twists of fate." When an oracle is asked how two dissimilar objects, a carpet and a city, can have such a mysterious bond, the oracle replies that one of the objects "has the form the gods gave the starry sky and the orbits in which the worlds revolve" while the other object is "approximate reflection, like every human creation". The interpreters of the oracle conclude that the carpet's harmonious pattern must be of divine origin.

Jurists contemplate the tapestries of law that as models of the legal universe show everything in its place. The design is surely wonderful. But when they are about to forget that semiosis is unlimited and that spontaneous order is not fixed, but creative, Calvino concludes his fabrication in these words:

> You could, similarly, come to the opposite conclusion: that the true map of the universe is the city of Eudoxia, just as it is, a stain that spreads out shapelessly, with crooked streets, houses that crumble one upon the other amid clouds of dust, fires, screams in the darkness (Calvino 1979, p. 77).

# References


Atkinson, Max. 1984. *Our Masters' Voices. The Language and Body Language of Politics,* Methuen, London.

Benson, Robert. 1989."The Semiotics of International Law: Interpretation of the ABM Treaty", *International Journal for the Semiotics of Law,* vol. 2, #6.

Burke, Kenneth. 1968. *Language as Symbolic Action*, University of California Press, Berkeley.

Calvino, Italo. 1979. *Invisible Cities,* translation William Weaver, Pan Books, London.

Dworkin, Ronald. 1977. *Taking Rights Seriously,* Harvard University Press, Cambridge.

___. 1986. *Law's Empire,* Cambridge ,The Belknap Press of Harvard University Press, Cambridge.

Eco, Umberto. 1976. *A Theory of Semiotics,* Indiana University Press, Bloomington.

Kevelson, Roberta. 1987. *Charles S. Peirce's Method of Methods*, John Benjamins, 1987, Amsterdam.

___. 1993. *Peirce's Esthetics of Freedom*, Peter Lang, New York.

Peirce, Charles Sanders. 1931–1958. *Collected Papers*, 8 vols. Harvard University Press, Cambridge.

# Chapter Twelve
# A Précis of the Intersemiosis of Perception and Understanding

John Deely

## Framing the discussion

One of the oldest philosophical discussions of which we have record concerns the relation of human intelligence to the intelligence exhibited by other biological forms, especially, of course, animal forms high on the scale of life as judged by similarity to ourselves—what Powell used to term "the humanesque analogy".[1] The bottom line in this discussion always comes down to the question of whether there is a qualitative difference in kind separating human understanding from the "understanding" or intelligence of other animal species, or merely a quantitative difference of complexity and degree? The situation is like pregnancy: either the woman is pregnant or she is not, regardless of how far along the pregnancy may be. So, similarly, either anthropos has an understanding species-specifically distinct in kind, or it is simply the manifestation in varying degrees of modalities of apprehension that are also to be found elsewhere in the animal world.

Of course, discussion of the issue has normally been muddied by the fact that few of the participants actually cared a whit about the communication systems of the non-human animals. Their concern was most often to assert "the uniqueness of man", often with a view to further conclusions about personal immortality, at least since the medieval rise of Christianity as a major influence on philosophical speculation.

Older than Aristotle, nonetheless, the question before us has always found proponents on either side of the binary issue. The issue was rendered more acute, of course, after the work of Darwin, which made the adoption of an evolutionary model for nature and mind all but unavoidable. Darwin conceived of all evolution as a matter of degrees of difference, and so, down to the present, have many others.

With the emergence of semiotics, I think it becomes possible to put this discussion on a whole new footing, to formulate the matter in terms of unprecedented clarity, and to resolve the issue without any reference to religious concerns or belief in some supposed "after-life".

## Requirements of the Discussion

First of all, it is no longer possible to participate intelligently in this discussion without taking account of the fact that there are qualitative differences in the communication systems of all biological species or forms. Not only the human species, but, it would seem, every species exhibits species-specific modalities of apprehension and consequent communication.[2] So the question of whether human understanding differs qualitatively or only quantitatively from the cognition of other animals becomes to a large extent moot. Every cognitive organism belongs to one or another species, and every cognitive species is distinguished by apprehensive modalities peculiar to itself. This point is quite independent of the question of whether underlying such differences is not simply a difference in arrangement of basic material particles.

Of continuing relevance here is the Aristotelian idea of substance as the formal unity to which different material arrangements (of genes, in current parlance) give rise and which in turn makes that arrangement cohere as a unity so long as the individual exists with a distinguishable identity—Aristotle's famous answer to the ancient question of "whether the world is one or many".[3] Later modifications of Aristotle's original conception of substance transformed it from a notion having positional as well as self-referential or "absolute" value into the notion of something wholly self-contained, as we find in the work of Kant and, typically, throughout the rationalist works of the classical moderns (a transformation which led to the rejection of the notion of substance among the empiricists). But this perverse development can hardly gainsay the value of the original notion of substance as something self-identified within a network of external contingencies without which the individual would have neither existence nor place. This individuality, being relative from the outset and throughout, therefore, can be more or less pronounced; and it is empirically the more pronounced as we ascend in observation the scale of being from those material particles and interactions for which we have no empirical grounds for abducing the presence of life to those forms where life becomes more and more clearly evident as a warranted abduction, ending in ourselves where our very existence as thinking beings is its own warrant—this I think is the enduring value of the Cartesian formula, *Cogito ergo sum*. For while it is equally true of any action—drinking, running, breathing—that the action implies existence (*agere sequitur esse* was the way the medievals epitomized the general situation), yet the action of thinking as involving a self-awareness, a reflective activity which has itself for its own object, is the only action where an existing subject grasps itself, i.e., makes of its own physical reality an object. In this case physical existence not only intrudes itself as such as part of the objective realm (the order of whatever exists as known[4]), but to be a thing partly objectified is also to be oneself.

Yet the experience of the self by the self in reflective thought is far from the only instance where the physical as such is transformed, by the simple addition of a cognitive relation to a cognitive organism, into something objective.[5] The *Cogito* is simply the fixed point where such a coincidence of the two orders is always inescapable—a situation quite different from that which Descartes tortured the data to construe.[6] Thus we may exist without thinking; we may become, as they say, vegetables through some disaster or misfortune. That we exist while thinking is all that thinking can assure. This is one of the points at which semiotic thought departs definitively from the epistemology of classical modernity. To say that all thought is in signs is to say that all thought is of objects signified, that all ideas give rise to relations at whose suprasubjective term are the objects—whether mere objects or objects which are also things—which the ideas are not.[7] For nothing prevents an object signified from having and revealing itself (or at least appearing) to have, precisely within the signification—that is to say, as part and parcel with the significate—an existence which does not reduce to the signification. This is what the formula *cogito ergo sum* actually gets at when read semiotically: the self given in thinking is given as other than the thinking, even though accessed only through the thinking.[8] The complement of Descartes' maxim would appear to be Aristotle's maxim about perception: that when its objects are not present in sensation it is a mystery whether they continue physically to exist.[9]

I cannot think without existing, and I cannot exist without an environment. Whenever I think, both my physical existence and something of my physical surroundings enter into my awareness. In both cases, what is objectified—myself along with whatever part of the environment—is something that exists physically, now made also to be objectively. But this is the statement of a discovery, not the assertion of a dogma. How the discovery comes about, it seems to me, is the key to the difference between perception and understanding. To see how this is so it is necessary to approach the matter from a semiotic point of view.[10]

If we may credit the testimony of the first thinker to systematize the requirements of a semiotic a point of view, the first requirement is to adopt a standpoint which transcends the difference between objects which have also a physical existence and objects which have only an objective existence, for the sign, as giving to experience whatever structure it has beyond the sheerly biologically determined, is our avenue equally to both sorts of object. [11]

I proceed here under the idea that Poinsot's testimony on this point is valid. I begin with Poinsot's *primum semeioticum*, however, as taken heuristically rather than for granted, so that the course of the discussion should make this *primum* self-refuting or critically validated. As to which of the two, the final decision falls to you.

## Tentatives of Terminology and A Semiotic Point of View

Let us call the species-specifically distinct dimension or form of awareness proper to humans "understanding", let us call the dimension of awareness generically common to human beings and other animals "perception", and let us call the dimension of awareness out of which perception arises in the brute interactions between organisms and the physical environment "sensation". These designations are posited not to beg any question, but simply to provide markers under which our steps toward an answer to our specific question can be identified.

We need to consider the function of a semiotic point of view. Any point of view, after all, is simply a unified way of looking at things. It constitutes formally the unity of what it objectifies. To "adopt a point of view" is to do nothing more than to thematically objectify in a definite way. A point of view, however, may either find unity or create unity in what it objectifies. What about the semiotic point of view? Fundamentally, does it find unity or make unity across its objective field?

The question is hardly empty. As old as Augustine, the question is also as recent as Scruton, who pointedly, as some of you may remember, reviewing Eco's work for a New York publication around 1982, inquired how could there be a science of structures as diverse as buttons and clouds? Augustine, to be sure, lacked Scruton's semiotic callowness; yet he does not seem fully to have realized either the novelty of his proposal that there can be a unified notion of *signum* applying to natural and cultural phenomena alike, or the necessity of justifying his proposal in terms of any structure of reality independent of the mind. For the mind indeed is the principal beneficiary and consumer of signs. Might it not also be the omnipotent sign maker? If the entrails of an animal can foretell the outcome of battle and the coincidence of stellar order at birth can foretell fate and character, surely anything can be made a sign. There is hardly need to root the structure of signification in anything other than mind!

That, however, is not the question. The question is not whether the mind can make a sign out of anything, but how a sign is in the first place possible? When the mind makes a sign, what is it that it does? Or when the mind finds a sign, what it is that the mind reveals? More generally, when semiotics arises as the knowledge derived from the study of the action of signs, what is it that semiotics expresses?

Poinsot was the first thinker successfully to answer precisely the question of *how* there can be something in common between inferences from natural phenomena and inferences from cultural phenomena. In so doing, he marked the trail that leads from the origin of semiosis in nature to the culmination of semiosis in thought.[12] Poinsot saw that the proper contrast to consider in our experience of the environment is not that between subjective and objective, such as the moderns misconceived, but that between existing subjects and the networks of relations between them.

The two-way dependencies which contrast with the situation of subjective existence (and, at the same time, sustain its possibility) and presuppose (either as maintaining or being maintained by) it have no such being in themselves. Their "constitution", if we may so speak in the case, is wholly external to the beings maintained and maintaining. If we are to say that the being maintained, the substance, has a subjective existence, then we must say by contrast that the maintained and maintaining "beings" are entirely *intersubjective*, having whatever further "nature" they have but indirectly, through the respective properties (or "accidents") of substances which they maintain or by which they are maintained.[13]

Notice that there is not yet an explicit question of semiosis or cognition. We are talking so far about the intersubjective components of the environmental situation called by the Latins *pure relations*, but more specifically *physical relations*,[14] within and upon which the subjective centers of being and action depend.[15] To distinguish within the pervasive relational networks the case of substances that are clearly living, the Latins introduced the term *soul* (or *anima*). Along with soul enters the possibility of mind, "mind" being nothing more than an expression to designate those souls capable of cognition—"animals" in contrast with "plants".

When mind enters in, what does it do? Initially, it simply relates the cognitive organism apprehensively to various aspects of the physical surroundings that are other than the organism itself but upon which the organism vitally depends,[16] adding to those aspects but relation to the organism as cognizing. Mind first of all *objectifies something of the prejacent physical*. Since the organism, being a substance (an individual formally unified from within), is from the first enmeshed in a whole intersubjective complex of physical relationships,[17] the first thing that "mind" does is simply allow the organism to be aware particularly of the termini of those relations which constitute food or, in the case of motile organisms, danger. "Mind" begins by providing the organism with a partial map to facilitate its survival in the physical world. This is the rudimentary sense of the semiotic term *Innenwelt*.

But mind soon does more than passively register some part of the organism's surroundings. There is more to mind than pure or simple *sensation* (defined by the Latins as the *actio sensibilis in sensu*). Mind takes an interest in what is there according to the preferences of the substance to which it belongs. These preferences are initially determined by the organism's biological heritage or nature. It is enough to realize that the sensations an organism experiences at the core of perceptions exist *in between* the individual constitution of the organism knowing and the material constitution of the environmental aspects of which the organism becomes aware to see that the question of whether the sense qualities belong to mind or object is nugatory. They belong to the interaction of organism and physical environment insofar as that interaction provides a purchase for organisms to survive.[18] This fundamental point about the sensory core of perception could hardly better be made than in the following quotation from a work of the French geneticist, François Jacob (1982: 56):

> No matter how an organism investigates its environment, the perception it gets must necessarily reflect so-called "reality" and, more specifically, those aspects of reality which are directly related to its own behavior. If the image that a bird gets of the insects it needs to feed its progeny does not reflect at least some aspects of reality, there are no more progeny. If the representation that a monkey builds of the branch it wants to leap to has nothing to do with reality, then there is no more monkey. And if this did not apply to ourselves, we would not be here to discuss this point.

Since we are here to discuss the point, let us move on to the further point that the making present in cognition of one object or objective aspect of the environment by another fulfills the minimal sign function, all right, but it does not yet reveal what is distinctive about semiosis. All that we have seen so far is that there are sign relations which are not the creations of mind upon which relations the mind, as organ of apprehension partially depends in perception. But to see what is unique about the action of signs we have to move beyond the environment as prejacent physical, which is exactly what perception, in transcending its sensory core, achieves. The physical world, already objectified in sensation, in perception is given an organization proper to itself[19] as a result of the nature of the perceiving organism. It is not yet a question of "Clever Hans", but of the requisites for survival; it is a question of the world of experience which is proper to every organism in a species-specific way.[20]

## From Sensation to Umwelt as Species-Specific Objective World

What an organism needs in order to survive and thrive is a matter of supreme indifference to the physical environment. It is up to the organism not only to achieve a selective awareness of its environment in sensation, but to realign those elements and to add to them as necessary to compel the environment, against its prejacent indifference, to support the organism.[21] We enter into the domain of perception, thus, in its contrast with simple sensation, as soon as begins the twofold and correlative process (at once psychological in the Innenwelt and objective in the Umwelt) of *combining* environmental elements differently in cognition than they are combined in physical being independently of the organism and *adding* through cognition yet new relationships specifically based on the organism's needs and desires.[22]

Note that the self-interest already present in sensation is magnified in perception. Thus, with perception deceit and cunning enter into the objective world, as well as territoriality and care for offspring and all the rest of the distinguishing behaviors of a species. Perception adds to sensation's web that flurry of further apprehensive strands that go well beyond the immediate proportions of physical interaction verified in sensation to construct in its totality an objective world suited to the specific needs and interests of the perceiving lifeform.[23] Here the distinctiveness of the action of signs begins to reveal itself: what is, is put at the service of what is not yet. The "ideal element", the "interpretant", regulative of action toward the future—whether virtually in a stone or actually in a mind—which is to be different from what simply is, enters into semiosis and is the reason for its triadicity.

## How Is the Distinctiveness of Semiosis in General Possible?

Now how is this distinctive action of signs possible? Poinsot's answer is that the whole process of sign action is rooted in the feature which distinguishes pure relations as such, whether physical or objective, from all that distinguishes the individual according to its intrinsic constitution.

Relation is able to be physical in either case, i.e., the case when it is and the case when it is not objective, depending only on the circumstance external to the relation itself of whether the terminus of the relation has a material correlate in the environment formally corresponding with the fundament of the relation.[24]

What Poinsot is calling our attention to at this point is that even those relations involved in perception which do not bear on anything here and now physically existing are no different as relations from those that do so bear. For every relation as such refers its subject to that which the subject itself is not, and this is no less true when the term of an apprehensive relation terminates at an object or aspect of an object lacking physical instantiation than when it terminates at an object or aspect thereof existing physically as well as objectively.[25] Objective relations, when they terminate at what is not physically real, either through a strategy to bring about a state of affairs not yet existent or through an error of judgment, are nonetheless relations.

Transcending subjectivity and connecting one subject with something that that subject itself is not is what reveals the true essence of the purely relative. What is decisive is not that it be intersubjective but that it be *transsubjective* or *suprasubjective*, that is, always conveying the individual subject beyond itself and connecting it with some object other than itself, indifferently to the subjective dimensions and status of that object. The action of signs in constructing an Umwelt is thus revealed as possible in the first place because relations are not tied to a subjective ground which is necessarily physical. Relations, considered according to this proper being as suprasubjective, may just as well terminate in a pure object which has no status here and now other than that of a being cognized or known.

But the condition is transitive. A relation which terminates one time at an object which is also physically real may terminate at another time at an object no longer physically real; and a relation which terminates at a physically nonexistent object may terminate at another time at an object become physically real. The notion of reality needs to accommodate this actual situation of human experience. The previous notion of reality, a heritage of Greek thought to the Latins, but certainly a heritage of Latin to modern thought, both scientific and philosophical,[26] will no longer do. We need a specifically semiotic notion of reality wherein the line between what is real and unreal is a shifting one. In semiosis the possible indifference of relation to the physical status of its term is realized; and this is both why the sign relation as such must be triadic and why a physical relation, as such dyadic, may yet become *also* an arm within a sign relation.[27] What distinguishes the two cases of a relation existing now apart from and now as incorporated within a semeiosy is the same thing that distinguishes physical interaction from semiosis.[28] The distinctiveness of semiosis is verified even when all three of the terms joined by semeiosy have a physical existence.[29] The case of the nonexistent object signified provides but the sharp exacerbation to the point of disclosure of what is true of all semiosis as such.

## Semiosis beyond Perception

There is semiosis in nature as well as in cognition;[30] but the semiosis peculiar to human understanding finds its operational existence initially in terms of the intersemiosis which perception makes possible as developing around a sensory core.[31] Understanding, arising within perception, goes beyond it to make accessible to human perception objective structures which, as such, are entirely hidden to all other biological species on this planet. The origin of species-specifically human language has its roots in this divide that understanding opens between perception and its initially sensory core. Perceptual semiosis both reveals and constructs objects strictly in terms of the self-interests of the organisms involved. The human animal goes beyond this determinate correlation by sometimes asking what are those objects, quite apart from any biological interest which we find in them, insofar as they exhibit an independence of relations to us.

Questioning in this mode is possible—here we come to the most theoretically difficult point—only for a mind that is able to grasp relations as such in their difference from the terms related, because only such a cognitive capacity is able to grasp the difference within experience, otherwise hidden,[32] between objects which as such wholly reduce to our experience of them and objects which as such give evidence of a hold on existence to which our experience has no choice but to accommodate itself in a more than social way. The problem of the difference between perception as such and perception suffused with understanding goes to the fact that relations as such are not sense-perceptible.[33] The apprehension of animals other than the human is exhausted in the experience, manipulation, and control of objects in their sensory aspects. What never enters into the objectification proper to sense perception is an awareness that what is experienced depends in its structure on a series of relations transparent to sensation but which give to perception at once its connections with the environment and its arrangement of those connections to suit the organism's individual tastes and species-specific needs.[34] Then, since signs as such consist in relations, the consequence is that, as Maritain put it, such animals use signs without knowing that there are signs. They have no means of separating the sign relations which yild the objects of experience from the objects yielded. The apparently unified way in which objects are given in sense perception conceals the profound differences between things in their own right which have been in part objectified and those other aspects of the perceived object which have been introduced entirely on the basis of the organism's own needs and desires.[35] The animal lacks the means to distinguish the relations given with and by object experienced from their terms by seeing the difference between mind-dependent and mind-independent elements in the structure of the Umwelt.[36]

## The Dependency of Understanding on Perceptual Semiosis

Yet here is the crucial point. If sense perception had not *already provided* understanding with that whole series of cognition-dependent relations which, in interweave with the physical relations of sensations as such (i.e., prescissively considered) and behavioral interactions, constitute the Umwelt as an objective world in contrast with and partially transcendent of the physical environment, understanding would have no material with which to begin its proper work of discriminating between "appearance" and "reality" in any of the manifold forms and variety of contexts to which this contrast pertains.

The partial coincidence and partial divergence of objective structures with structures of physical being within sensation and perception is thus the zoösemiotic basis and ground from which anthroposemiosis takes rise, not by transcending but by transforming from within the originally biological Umwelt.[37] The notion of primary modeling system introduced into contemporary semiotics by Soviet thinkers ought properly to be identified, exactly as Sebeok first suggested,[38] with the notion of Umwelt rather than with the notion of language. The primary modeling system is the Umwelt, different for each species and constructed through the action of signs in ways determined first of all by a species' biological constitution as this channels what and in what ways physical interactions within the transspecific physical environment become objectified, and to what degree. Language, the aspect of modeling unique to the human species, is a subordinate or "secondary" modeling system within this more primary whole. It is the instrument whereby, through verbal markers specifically, is transcended the functional cycle through which all other biological forms relate to the physical world by the movement to extinguish the physical stimulus in its objective protrusion into the Umwelt (by fleeing a hostile factor or devouring a sought one).

In this way language makes possible the consideration of alternatives divorced from the immediate needs of biological interaction, and opens the way to possible worlds different from the actual one of the Umwelt here and now.[39] Such alternatives underlie the retention within human perception of, in J. von Uexküll's phrase (1940: 27ff.) "neutral objects". Yet just these environmental factors, ignored by all the other animals, become capable of being, as T. von Uexküll notes (1987: 163), sign vehicles for anthroposemiotic enterprises of natural science.

Thus we find in previous philosophical tradition, especially in the semiotic of John Poinsot, prior to the moderns (who, despite themselves, for want of an adequate distinction between the sign as a suprasubjective means of communion and its subjective foundation in representation, were forced to despair of a passage beyond the mind's own creations), a little-realized way of grounding the putative distinction between understanding and perception ("intellect" and "sense") precisely in terms of relation: perception reveals objects as they are only relative to the dispositions, needs, and desires of the organism perceiving, whereas understanding reveals in these same objects the further dimension of existence in their own right independent of relations to the knower. Not until the semiotic of Charles Peirce do we encounter again a serious attempt to follow this Ariadne's thread. But the thread appears now clearly to lead to the center of semiotic consciousness. Here Guagliardo's remarks (1995: 4) a few months before his death bear citing:

> The "father" of semiotics is frequently held to be the American philosopher Charles S. Peirce, who himself studied the Scholastics. But [in that case account needs to be taken of] the *Treatise on Signs* written by John Poinsot, a contemporary of Descartes: drawing upon the thought of Aquinas on signs, Poinsot had already developed a new discipline within philosophy (a need also seen but not addressed by John Locke), laying the groundwork for an entire field of study which has come into its own only in recent years. ... [Those concerned with the grounding of our knowledge of the physical world] and postmoderns alike, in their reaction against the moderns from Descartes to our own century, can find a common resource in Poinsot's work on signs. Of special importance is Poinsot's view of the foundational nature of the sign, indifferent in its being to the order of mind-independent or mind-dependent being, and so prior to the distinction between "real" and "unreal", providing the passage between both. Poinsot's semiotics can thus move our thinking beyond the time-worn, polemical conflicts of [the] moderns, offering in their place a new basis from which ... postmoderns can view and pursue common concerns of our day.

## The Semiotic Animal

Crucial to understanding the intersemioticity of Poinsot's early modern and postmodern contemporary semiotic formulations are Sebeok's distinction between language and communication, and the notion of human language used for communication as an exaptation rather than an adaptation of any pre-existing zoösemiotic system as such (Sebeok 1986a; Deely 1994). But central to both these formulations is the point that this paper has been concerned to establish, namely, that anthroposemiosis consists specifically in an intersemiosis of perception and understanding whereby the intrinsic indifference of the action of signs to the signification of what is or is not at any given moment is brought to its highest point of explicit realization, the point at which it can be itself thematized and explored on its own terms. These terms turn out to be the very terms of semiosis itself. If, therefore, semiotics is that knowledge that arises from observation and reflection upon the action of signs (as biology is that knowledge that arises from observation and reflection upon the activity of organisms), and semiotics has as its principal upshot the realization that all of human knowledge in whatever field, together with the experiences upon which human knowledge depends, develops through this action which semiotics thematizes, then we can see the definition of human nature that semiotics calls for in terms of genus and difference: the human being is the *semiotic animal*, the only animal that knows that there are signs.

This definition will serve to mark for future generations the transition from modern to postmodern thought, even as Descartes' definition of the human as a *res cogitans* served to mark the transition from ancient and medieval thought[40] to rationalistic and empiricist modern thought. For in this new definition are symbolized both the *recovery* of that possibility of an understanding of physical and natural being which the Greeks and the Latins prized but which their epistemological paradigm had led the moderns to rule out, and the *realization* constitutive of semiotic consciousness, namely, that the action of signs as resulting or this planet in anthroposemiosis provides the sole means whereby the mind has that possibility of "becoming all things"—*anima est quodammodo omnia*—in that convertibility of being with truth that is the elusive, asymptotic goal of the community of inquirers needed to support intelligence in its scientific and literary aspects, which are found as expressions only of the human species.

In saying that the human being is the semiotic animal we give voice to the realization that, like nature itself apart from anthropos, all other animals use signs without knowing that there are signs. In such knowledge the human being realizes the source of its difference from the other life forms, the *humanitas* of the human animal, as well as the universality of the process on which all the life forms depend. Indeed, it would now appear, this process is perhaps the ultimate source of that general progress in physical nature from simple to complex forms that we have heretofore called "evolution".

# References


Aristotle. c. 348-330 B.C. *Metaphysics.*

Bacon, Roger. c.1267. "De Signis," text ed. Fredborg, Nielsen, and Pinborg in 34 *Traditio* 81–136.

Beuchot, Mauricio, and John Deely. 1995. "Common Sources for the Semiotic of Charles Peirce and John Poinsot", 48 *Review of Metaphysics* 539–566.

Dalcourt, Gerard J. 1994. "Poinsot and the Mental Imagery Debate", 72 *The Modern Schoolman* 1–12.

Deely, John. 1965. "Evolution: Concept and Content; Part I", 0 *Listening* 27-50.

___. 1969. "The Philosophical Dimensions of the Origin of Species," 33 *The Thomist.* Part I, 75–149, Part II, 251–342.

___. 1975. "Reference to the Non-Existent", 34 *The Thomist* 253–308.

___. 1982. *Introducing Semiotic: Its History and Doctrine,* Indiana University Press, Bloomington.

___. 1984. "Semiotic as Framework and Direction", in Deely, Williams and Kruse 1986, 264–271.

___. 1985. "Editorial Afterword" and critical apparatus to *Tractatus de Signis: The Semiotic of John Poinsot.* Berkeley, CA: University of California Press, 391–514.

___. 1987. "John Locke's Place in the History of Semiotic Inquiry", in *Semiotics 1986*, Jonathan Evans and John Deely (eds.) Lanham, MD: University Press of America, 406–418.

___. 1986a. "Semiotic in the Thought of Jacques Maritain", 6 *Recherche Sémiotique/Semiotic Inquiry* 1–30.

___. 1988. "The Semiotic of John Poinsot: Yesterday and Tomorrow", 69 *Semiotica* 31–127.

___. 1990. *Basics of Semiotics,* Indiana University Press, Bloomington.

___. 1994. *The Human Use of Signs; or Elements of Anthroposemiosis.* Rowman & Littlefield, Lanham, MD.

___. 1994a. *New Beginnings. Early Modern Philosophy and Postmodern Thought,* University of Toronto Press, Toronto.

___. 1994b. "What Happened to Philosophy between Aquinas and Descartes?" 58 *The Thomist* 543–568.

___. 1995. "A Prospect of Postmodernity," 30 *Listening* 7–14 (in press).

Deely, John, Guest-editor. 1994. John Poinsot Special Issue, 68 *American Catholic Philosophical Quarterly*.

Deely, John N., Brooke Williams, and Felicia E. Kruse, (eds.) 1986. *Frontiers in Semiotics,* Indiana University Press, Bloomington.

Furton, Edward James. 1995. *A Medieval Semiotic,* Peter Lang, New York.

Greimas, Algirdas Julien, and Jacques Fontanille. 1991. *Sémiotique des passions*. Paris: Les Editions du Seuil. English translation by Paul Perron and Frank Collins under the title: *The Semiotics of Passions. From States of Affairs to States of Feeling* , University of Minnesota Press, Minneapolis.

Guagliardo, Vincent. 1992. "Hermeneutics: Deconstruction or Semiotics?", in *Symposium on Hermeneutics*, Eugene F. Bales (ed.) Privately circulated. Conception, MO: Conception Seminary College, 63–74.

___. 1993. "Being and Anthroposemiotics", in *Semiotics 1993*, Robert Corrington and John Deely (eds.), University Press of America, Lanham, MD.

___. 1994. "Being-as-First-Known in Poinsot: A-Priori or Aporia?", in Deely 1994: 375-404.

___. 1995. "Introduction" 30 *Listening* 3–6.

Haldane, John. 1996. "Intentionality and One-Sided Relations", 9 *Ratio* New Series, 95-114.

Herculano De Carvalho, José g. 1967. *Teoria da linguagem. Natureza do fenómeno linguístico e a análise das línguas.* Coimbra: Atlântida.

___. 1969. "Segno e significazione in João de São Tomás," 2 *Estudos Linguísticos*, 129-153.

___. 1970. *Teoria da linguagem. Natureza do fenómeno linguístico e a análise das línguas,* Atlântida, Coimbra.

Jacob, François. 1982. *The Possible and the Actual*, University of Washington Press, Seattle.

Krampen, Martin.1981. "Phytosemiotics", 36 *Semiotica* 187–209.

Kronin, John D. 1994. "The Substantial Unity of Material Substances according to John Poinsot," 58 *The Thomist* 599–615.

Maroosis, James. 1981. *Further Consequences of Human Embodiment: A Description of Time and Being as Disclosed at the Origin of Peirce's Philosophy of Community.* Doctoral dissertation. University of Toronto, Department of Philosophy.

___. 1993. "Peirce and the Manifestation of Self-Transcendence", in *Semiotics 1993*, Robert Corrington and John Deely (eds.), University Press of America, Lanham, MD.

Murphy, James Bernard. 1990. "Nature, Custom, and Stipulation in Law and Jurisprudence," 43 *The Review of Metaphysics* 753–8790.

___. 1991. "Nature, Custom, and Stipulation in the Semiotic of John Poinsot," 83 *Semiotica* 33–68.

___. 1994. "Language, Communication, and Representation in the Semiotic of John Poinsot," 59 *The Thomist* 569–598.

Peirce, Charles Sanders. 1931–35. *The Collected Papers of Charles Sanders Peirce.* 8 vols., Harvard University Press, Cambridge. (Cited here as CP)

___. c. 1890. "A Guess at the Riddle", CP 1.354–368, 1:373–375, 1:379–416.

Perron, Paul, and Paolo Fabbri. 1993. "Foreword" to English trans. of Greimas and Fontanille 1991 ,7–16.

Poinsot, John. 1632. *[1985] Tractatus de Signis*: *The Semiotic of John Poinsot* . University of California Press, Berkeley.

___. 1635. *Naturalis Philosophiae Quarta Pars: De Ente Mobili Animato*, in B. Reiser 1937: 1–425.

Ponzio, Augusto. 1990. *Man as a Sign. Essays on the Philosophy of Language*, Susan Petrilli trans., Mouton de Gruyter, Berlin.

Powell, Ralph A. 1983. *Freely Chosen Reality,* University Press of America, Washington, D. C.

___. 1986. "From Semiotic of Scientific Mechanism to Semiotic of Teleology in Nature", in *Semiotics 1986*, John Deely and Jonathan Evans (eds.), University Press of America, Lanham, MD, 296–305.

Ransdell, Joseph. 1986. "Semiotic Objectivity", in Deely, Williams, and Kruse 1986: 236–254.

Reiser, B. (ed.) 1930, 1933, 1937. The *Cursus Philosophicus Thomisticus* of Joannes a Sancto Thoma [John Poinsot]. 3 vols., Marietti, Turin.

Sebeok, Thomas A. 1978. "'Talking' with Animals: Zoosemiotics Explained," in Deely, Williams and Kruse 1986: 76–82.

___. 1986. "The Doctrine of Signs" in Deely, Williams, and Kruse 1986, 35–42.

___. 1986a. "The Problem of the Origin of Language in an Evolutionary Frame," 8 *Language Sciences* 169–176.

___. 1987. "Language: How Primary a Modeling System", in *Semiotics 1987*, John Deely (ed.), University Press of America, Lanham, MD., 15–27.

___. 1988. "The Notion 'Semiotic Self' Revisited", in *Semiotics 1988*, Terry Prewitt, John Deely, and Karen Haworth (eds.), University Press of America, Lanham, MD, 189–195.

___. 1989. "Ernst Cassirer, Jacques Maritain, and Susanne Langer", in *Semiotics 1989*, John Deely, Karen Haworth, and Terry Prewitt (eds.), University Press of America, Lanham, MD, 389–397.

Sebeok, Thomas A., (ed). 1977. *How Animals Communicate* . Indiana University Press, Bloomington.

Sebeok, Thomas A., and Donna Jean Umiker-Sebeok,(eds.) 1979–. *Studies in Animal Communication,* Indiana University Press, Bloomington.

Tachau, Katherine H. 1988. *Vision and Certitude in the Age of Ockham. Optics, Epistemology and the Foundation of Semantics 1250–1345.* E. J. Brill, 1988, Leiden.

von Uexküll, Jakob. 1934. *Streifzuge durch die Umwelten von Tieren und Menschen.* Berlin, trans. by Claire H. Schiller as 'A Stroll through the Worlds of Animals and Men' in *Instinctive Behavior: The Development of a Modern Concept,* Claire H. Schiller (ed.), International Universities Press, Inc., New York, 5–80.

___. 1940. "Bedeutungslehre", *Bios* 10. Leipzig , trans. by Barry Stone and Herbert Weiner as "The Theory of Meaning" in 42 *Semiotica* 25-82.

von Uexküll, Thure. 1987. "The Sign Theory of Jakob von Uexküll", in *Classics of Semiotics,* Martin Krampen, Klaus Oehler, Roland Posner, Thomas A. Sebeok, and Thure von Uexküll (eds.), Plenum Press, , New York, 147-179.

# Notes

1. The phrase "humanesque analogy" is discussed in Deely 1965.

2. For details, see Sebeok Ed. 1977, Sebeok 1978, and Sebeok and Umiker-Sebeok series 1979–.

3. For a detailed spelling out from a standpoint of Latin Scholastic natural philosophy, see Deely 1969. Very late in the Latin development some thinkers came to call substance a *transcendental relation* or *transcendental relative being*. The qualification "transcendental" in the expressions is intended to make the point that a substance rises above the internal and external networks of relations upon which it at every moment depends insofar as it forms a unified center of action and being in its own right. The qualification "relation" or "relative being" is intended to make the point that the dominance of a substance over the external and internal sustaining network is never strictly absolute (never permanently secure) but always in the nature of a balancing act (cf. Poinsot 1632: 89/41–47, and 90/2–5, 13–20, 22–26) with no possibility of a safety net, so that one misstep or one fatal intrusion into the balanced systems—sooner or later inevitable—always proves fatal.

4. There was among the Latins a fragmentary and only implicitly systematic use of the term "objective" which was consistent with their original use of the notion of sign as applicable to natural and cultural phenomena alike, but which, in modern philosophy, came to be quite reversed. This reversed use, thoroughly established by our own time, nonetheless proves incompatible with the general doctrine of signs and is, I would go so far as to say, ultimately incoherent. This incoherence, I suggest, is what we see at play in the interminable struggle within modern philosophy between "realisms" and "idealisms", a struggle which continues to confuse and delay semiotic developments. Semiotics in effect compels us to go back to the medieval notion of objective as whatever exists as known, but now to thematize and systematize that usage in light of the discovery that the sign is what every object presupposes. This was part of the essential project of *The Human Use of Signs* (Deely 1994), and I continue it here.

5. See the arcane early semiotic discussions (Poinsot 1632: Book III, Questions 1 and 2) of the difference between, on the one hand, the experience of objects which have as such a physical dimension within their very objectification here and now and, on the other hand, objects cognized without an accompanying verification here and now of any such dimensions. This difference was clumsily labeled "intuitive versus abstractive cognition" under the historical determinism of the transitional influence of Duns Scotus who, toward the opening of the 14th century, turns Latin epistemological and ontological discussions in the semiotic direction that would culminate in the *Tractatus de Signis* of Poinsot (see Tachau 1988; Beuchot and Deely 1995; Deely 1994a) at the very moment that Descartes turned what was to become the classical modern development toward the dead-end of an idealism (classical modern idealism, common to Rationalism and Empiricism in their fatal shared assumption reducing signification to

representation in the idea of ideas of human understanding) confining the mind to its own workings.

6. This was most effectively demonstrated, perhaps, in the phenomen-ological work of Merleau-Ponty; but one of the best attacks upon the problem from within semiotics has been that of Greimas and Fontanille 1991. See the "Foreword" to the English trans. of this work by Perron and Fabbri 1993.

7. This was the essential insight of the late Latin Hispanic thinkers (beginning at least as early as Soto, who may have taken the idea from his Paris professors) who founded their semiotic epistemology by sharply distinguishing representation as such from signification, and pointed out that, in the sign, the representative element as such does not constitute the sign but merely provides the foundation or basis upon which the pure relation in its proper character as suprasubjective constitutes the sign as terminating at a significate which is irreducibly other than the representation which founds its objectivity. These considerations are summarized by Poinsot at the very outset of his *Tractatus de Signis* (see esp. the 2nd Preliminary Chapter, 25/11–27/6; and Book I, Question 1, 116/14–117/17, 121/19–123/25, etc.).

8. The disappearance of the self in a stream and flow of detached associations, images, and ideas, as portrayed by Hume among others, we may say, is a direct consequence of the classical modern failure to distinguish between representation as such and signification which we noted above (note 7) as one of the cornerstones of semiotic thinking.

9. Aristotle, c.348–330BC: Met. VI, 1799: "of things capable of being otherwise we do not know, when they have passed outside our observation, whether they exist or not."
Similarly Met. VII, 1635: "when we come to the concrete thing ... whether sensible or intelligible ... of these there is no definition, but they are known by the aid of thought or perception; and when they go out of our actual consciousness it is not clear whether they exist or not ...."

10. See "Semiotics: Method or Point of View?" in Deely 1990: 9–21.

11. It is only through the use of signs that we come to realize any such distinction between the physical, the objectified physical, and the merely objective. Poinsot makes this point the departure for his *Treatise on Signs* (1632: Book I, Question 1, 117/28–118/18).

12. The first glimpse of Poinsot's semiotic outside his Latin context came with the work of Jacques Maritain in the 1930s (see Deely 1986; Sebeok 1989). This work was followed up first by Herculano de Carvalho (1967, 1969, 1970), then by me (see the discussion of reviews in Deely 1988), and more recently by a growing list of scholars. In 1994–1995, there were no less than three Special Issues of journals dedicated to or containing articles on the work of Poinsot: the John Poinsot Special Issue of the *American Catholic Philosophical Quarterly* LXVIII (Summer

1994), with articles by Beuchot, Cahalan, Coombs, Doyle, Guagliardo, Raposa, Rasmussen, and Wells (see Deely Ed. 1994); the *John Poinsot Issue* of *The Thomist* 58.4 (October 1994), with articles by Deely, Murphy, and Kronen; with further articles by Deely 1995 and Dalcourt 1994.

A 1995 monograph by Furton continues the expansion of the literature; but, on close examination, the title of this work, *A Medieval Semiotic*, proves more accurate than its subtitle, *Reference and Representaton in John of St. Thomas' Theory of Signs*. Wherever Poinsot's doctrine of signs exceeds the requirements of Furton's preoccupation with "realism" in the sense of the 19th century Thomistic revival—e.g., in Poinsot's opening move to establish the sign in its proper being as indifferent to the physical status of its constitutive relation, or in his decisive establishment that the sign consists not in two relations but one relation which is irreducibly triadic—Furton forces the text back to a presemiotic standpoint. The medieval semiotic Furton presents is closer to the views of Roger Bacon (cf. Bacon c.1267), despite his use rather of the text of John Poinsot. Nevertheless, if the reader keeps in mind that he is reading a "semiotic" reduced to the perspective of an Aristotelian physics, this study is not without merit in presemiotic terms.

Finally, mention should be made also of the work of Maroosis treating Poinsot in an explicitly Peircean context (Maroosis 1981, 1993); other work of Murphy (1990, 1991, 1994); and, sadly, of the exceptionally promising work of Vincent Guagliardo (1992, 1993, 1994, 1995), whose premature death on August 13,1995 was a great loss to the developing understanding of the doctrine of signs.

13. Poinsot 1632, 99/22–42: "Quod vero relatio praedicamentalis dicitur esse in subiecto, non tollit, quin totum suum esse sit ad aliud, totum, inquam, id est proprium et peculiare ipsius esse, in quo differt ab aliis generibus absolutis; supponendo tamen rationem communem accidentis, scilicet esse in aliquo, ratione cuius non habet esse ad aliud, sed nec id excludit."
"... transcendentalis relatio non est primo et per se ad aliud, ut dictum est, sed ab alio vel circa aliud, ut dependentia vel causalitas aut aliquid simile; quod aliquando salvari potest non per id, quod de facto est sed per id, quod convenire potest, vel postulat, ut conveniat. Relatio autem praedicamentalis, quia totum suum esse habet ad aliud, non consurgit
nisi ex positione extremorum. Unde altero illorum deficiente deficit.".
See also Powell 1983, 1986.

14. As part of the constitution of the world of nature prejacent to human existence and experience alike.

15. Later, by a series of unfortunate translations which continue to haunt and bedevil philosophical discussion today, the Latins came to speak of this physical order of being as the "real world" or "reality", *ens reale*; but this expression in reality gave voice to a cultural preoccupation, not to an exclusive notion but to an oppositional one (see the discussion of the point in Deely 1985: 465–467, esp. 466n107), for in their reflective and critical moments the Latins, at least the better among their philosophers, well recognized that the world of culture even taken *as such* is no less "real" than the world of nature of which culture is both complement and part.

But this is another story, the beginning of which can be found in the diagram "Divisions of being in the structure of experience" in Deely 1982: 26.

16. Poinsot 1632, 99/6–21: "relatio transcendentalis ... tota earum species et essentia sumatur ab alio vel dependeat ab alio, ... sicut ... dependet ... actus ab obiecto sicut a causis, a quibus habent esse et specificationem. ... Et ideo dicitur, quod respicit terminum ... ut ab alio vel circa aliud vel quocumque alio causalitatis modo ...". The reader is well invited to ponder *in situ* this tortured ellipsis.

17. We might well picture this complex as a web and the organism as the spider which spun the web and waits at its center for what the web will catch. This indeed was one of Jakob von Uexküll's core metaphors (1934: 14) in his development of the idea of Umwelt: "As the spider spins its threads, every subject spins his relations to certain characters of the things around him, and weaves them into a firm web which carries his existence".

18. This holds also, as we shall shortly see, for organisms such as our own to develop investigations in either direction—the direction of mind with its underlying nature, or the direction of physical environment in *its* underlying nature or natures.

19. Poinsot, echoing Cajetan from a hundred years before, says laconically: "differences among physical things as such are one thing, differences among objects as such are quite another"—see Poinsot 1632: *passim*.

20. This is the rationale for the semiotic notion of Umwelt as *a species-specific objective world*, a notion that so scandalized Roland Posner when I proposed it in these terms at the "Semiotics: Field or Discipline?" State-of-the-Art Conference organized by Michael Herzfeld at Indiana University's Bloomington campus in 1984 (see "Semiotic as Framework and Direction" in Deely 1984). Posner—in this hardly alone (cfr. Deely 1994: Gloss 2 on ¶9. p. 136)—failed to understand the specifically semiotic notion of objectivity that the sign, as that which every object presupposes, implies in order for semiosis to be possible in the first place in its distinctive role of mediating the physical and the objective in the achievement of thirdness.

21. "We suppose that there are iconic specifications, or ideas, at work in perception, just as there is cognition there. For if perceptions are higher in the knowing process than are sensations, they also require higher forms of specification, or at least ones ordered in a higher way, in order to bring forth a higher level of awareness. But specifiers of a more perfect and elevated type are seen to be necessary particularly when the objects represented are of a more abstract character [i.e., more removed from the here-and-now immediacy of sensation], as is the case with such perceptible but unsensed characteristics as hatred, hostility, offspring, parents, and so forth. For these formalities are not represented in the external senses, and yet they are known in perception; therefore there exists some principle representative of them, which must not be so material and imperfect as to obtain at the level of the sensed objects as such, at which level the cognitions

of external sense are constrained. Therefore it must be a form of specification more perfect than a specification of external sense, which represents only sensed [as contrasted to perceived] things" (from Poinsot 1635: 259b9–32, included in the 1985 Deely edition as note 8 to Book II, Question 2, at 243/22. See also note 27 to Book II, Question 2, at 249/20).

22. Poinsot 1632, 50/29–32 (repeated at 72/5–8: "tunc efficitur ens rationis, quando intellectus nititur apprehendere, quod non est, et ideo fingit illud ac si esset ens"—"mind-dependent being is produced whenever the understanding attempts to apprehend that which does not exist, and therefore construes that which is not as if it were a being." How these remarks, here framed explicitly in terms of understanding, apply also to perception in its proper mode and dimension of apprehension, Poinsot elsewhere makes explicit (68/17–31): "But that sense is able to know fictive being materially ... is proved by this fact, that internal sense synthesizes many things which outside itself in no way are or can be. Sense therefore knows something which is in itself a constructed or fictive being, although the fiction itself sense does not apprehend, but only that which, in the fictive being, offers itself as sensible." See note 33 below for the conclusion to which this phenomenological appeal is added.

23. Continuing Jacob (1982: 56): "The external world, the 'reality' of which we all have intuitive knowledge, thus appears as a creation of the nervous system. It is, in a way, a possible world, a model allowing the organism to handle the bulk of incoming information and make it useful for its everyday life. One is thus led to define some kind of 'biological reality' as the particular representation of the external world that the brain of a given species is able to build. The quality of such biological reality evolves with the nervous system in general and brain in particular."
Note that in this text cited from Jacob there lurks a cultural interpretant or bias in favor of the inadequate medieval and renaissance notion of "reality" described in note 15 above. The "model world" in question is much more than a mere "creation of the nervous system" inasmuch as it necessarily includes, on Jacob's own accounting, necessary elements representing—"transcendentally representing" in the late Latin terminology discussed above—the physical environment on which the species is dependent for survival and hence giving rise to those intersubjective connections which, as we have seen, give physical reality to the suprasubjective being in which relations as such minimally and always consist. By emphasizing one-sidedly the role of the brain Jacob gives vent to that same modern reductionism which so consistently mars the otherwise semiotically superb work of Paul Bouissac (and sometimes Sebeok). The notion of model and modeling system is highly useful and, indeed, indispensable to understanding the semiotic Innenwelt but, at the same time, it cannot be used as fully equivalent to the notion itself of Umwelt, for the reasons I detailed in *The Human Use of Signs* (Deely 1994: ¶s 123, 127–128).

24. In the case where an "idea" is involved, this requires no more than a structure physically objective (physical in its objectivity, "intuitively grasped", in the terminology of the Latin epistemological discussion—see note 5 above) correlated with the iconic representation in which the idea psychologically considered exists

as but the fundament for the (suprasubjective and at least prospectively intersubjective) relation in which the idea semiotically considered consists and which terminates at the physically objective structure or feature in question. See especially the materials on relation added to the electronic edition of Poisnot 1632: Σ21. Article 5. "Whether Relation is Formally Terminated at Something Absolute or at Something Relative" (Reiser 1933: 595b25-600b23).

25. I first discussed this point in 1975 ("Reference to the Non-Existent"); but the first to take up the discussion in the currently dominant circles of English-speaking philosophy has and John Haldane, whose forthcoming article on "One-Sided Relations" has just been accepted by a major analytic journal; I do not yet have full details.

26. "...one thing that did not change in the 17th century as scientific understanding came to displace philosophy from the central role in the academies and culture of Western civilization was an uncompromising sense of 'reality' as a natural world prejacent to and independent of the human mind, a world governed by laws which form the proper object of human understanding, ... the object and goal of ... [physics]. ... What changed was only the methodological convictions about how this world of nature could best be penetrated by human understanding", even though "the modern philosophers both in England and on the Continent found themselves absolutely baffled when it came to explaining how the realist pretensions of the new sciences might be justified at the level of the theory of knowledge. Thus rose with Berkeley idealism in the distinctively modern sense of that term, and with Hume skepticism also in the modern sense. Kant, the master of all the moderns in philosophy and the systematizer of an idealism so ruthless as to strangle even the hope of a knowledge of whatever of nature be in any sense prejacent to and independent of human thinking, nonetheless took it for a scandal in philosophy that no proof of the existence of a mind-independent natural world had so far been given ... To all this semiotic provides a welcome and long-overdue alternative, an idea whose time has come ... absolutely revolutionary respecting the past of philosophy and science alike" (Deely 1984: 265–266). See "The Semiotic Definition of Reality" (Deely 1986a: Section 3); and cf. Ransdell 1986.

27. From Poinsot 1632: 137 note 4 (editorially appended from the 1663 Lyons text): "Similarly, those relations by which a sign can be proportioned to a signified are formally other than the sign-relation itself, e.g., the relation of effect to cause, of similitude or image, etc., even though some recent authors confound the sign-relation with these relations, but unwarrantably: because to signify or to be caused or to be similar are diverse exercises in a sign. For in signifying, a substitution for the principal significate is exercised, that that principal may be manifested to a power, but in the rationale of a cause or an effect is included nothing of an order to a cognitive power; wherefore they are distinct fundaments, and so postulate distinct relations. These relations, moreover, can be separated from the sign-relation, just as a son is similar to the father and his effect and image, but not a sign. The sign-relation therefore adds to these relations, which it supposes or prerequires in order to be habilitated and proportioned to this significate rather than to that one." See further Book I, Question 3, 160/10-21, and the discussion in note 13 of that same Question, pp. 163-164.

28. Indeed, even in the purely physical order, relations as such anticipate the indirectness of semiosis' thirdness (Poinsot 1632: 88/17–28: "Et licet ad omnem entitatem et formam requiratur causa, specialiter tamen ad relationem dicitur requiri fundamentum, quia aliae formae solum requirunt causam, ut producantur in esse et existant, relatio autem propter suam minimam entitatem et quia ex proprio conceptu est ad aliud, requirit fundamentum non solum ut existat, sed etiam ut sit capax existendi, id est ut sit entitas realis."

29. For detailed discussion of this crucial point, see Deely 1990: 23ff., 1994 throughout, and "Mediation of the objective" in 1994a: 223–226.

30. See Krampen 1981 for the original extension of semiosis to the plant world in a programmatic statement; for extension beyond this to physical nature in its full extent see: "The Doctrine of Signs" (Sebeok 1986); "The Grand Vision" (Deely 1989 as published in Deely 1994a: 183–200); and "Physiosemiosis and Phytosemiosis" (Deely 1990: Chapter 6).

31. Poinsot 1635: 263b41–264a11, included in the 1985 Deely edition of Poinsot 1632 as note 3 at 67/3: "It is not necessary that everything known in the understanding or cognized by internal sense should be apprehended by the external senses. It is enough if all those things are virtually contained in the formal specification that is emitted by the object and then by sense, and can be unfolded in the higher power. Thus St. Thomas says in the Summa theologica, I, q. 78, art. 4, reply to objection 4, that, although the operation of the understanding arises out of sense, the understanding yet cognizes many facets of the thing apprehended through sense that sense cannot perceive, and the same holds for the estimative power 'although to a lesser extent.' It can well be, therefore, that something can be known through internal sense that is not known directly and formally by external sense, but is some modality or respect founded on those sensibles and virtually contained in them". Thus, besides the relations perception introduces to form sensations into objects perceived and the relations understanding introduces into the objects of perception, there are also relations understanding generates on the basis of its proper activity as distinct from what is proper to perceptual activity, principal among them being, I would argue, the self-relation of objects which gives rise to intelligibility in the first place: see *The Human Use of Signs* (Deely 1994), esp. ¶s295–296; and cf. Peirce c.1890: CP 1.357.

32. Poinsot 1632: 74/37–48: "The basic awareness of human understanding does not compare one thing to another by affirming or denying, but it does indeed compare by differentiating one thing from another and by attaining the order of one thing to another .... Simple apprehension, therefore, has enough comparison for forming a mind-dependent being. Moreover, we do not deny to sense perception the formation of a mind-dependent being on the grounds of the absence of comparison [since there are indeed perceptual comparisons as well as intellectual ones: see note 33 below], but on the grounds of the absence of a knowing of universality, because sense does not cognize the more universal rationales by discriminating between true being and constructed or fictive being, which is something that simple apprehension does do; for simple apprehension

discriminates between categorial things and those things that are not in a category of mind-independent being."

33. Poinsot 1632, 67/1–68/31: "We say that the internal senses [i.e., in our terms, perceptions prescissively taken as such] 'formally speaking' do not form mind-dependent beings, that is, they do not form them by discriminating between mind-dependent being and physical being, and by conceiving that which is not a being after the pattern of physical being. Materially, however, to cognize a mind-dependent being is to attain the very appearance of a being physically real, but not to discriminate between that which is of the mind and that which is of the physical world. For example, the imaginative power can form a gold mountain, and similarly it can construct an animal composed of a she-goat, a lion, and a serpent, which is the Chimera [of Greek mythology]. But in these constructions the imagination itself attains only that which is sensible or representable to sense. Yet internal sense does not attain the fact that objects so known have a condition relative to non-being, and from this relative condition are said to be constructed, fictive, mind-dependent, or mental–which is formally to discriminate between being and non-being.
"The reason seems clear: internal sense cannot refer to anything except under a sensible rationale; but the fact that that which is represented to it as sensible happens to be opposed to physical being, does not pertain to internal sense to judge, because internal sense does not conceive of being under the rationale of being. The fact, however, of anything's being regarded as a constructed or fictive being formally consists in this, that it is known to have nothing of entitative reality in the physical world, and yet is attained or grasped on the pattern of a physical entity; otherwise, no discrimination is made between mind-independent being and constructed or fictive being, but only that is attained on whose pattern a mind-dependent being is formed. When this object is something sensible, there is no reason why it cannot be known by sense. But sense attains only that which is sensible in an object, whereas the condition relative to the non-being in whose place the object is surrogated and whence it fictively has being, does not pertain to sense. For this reason, sense does not differentiate a constructed being, under the formal rationale of being a construct, from a true being."
"But that sense is able to know fictive being materially is manifestly the case. Not, indeed, from the fact that even external sense can, for example, cognize a fictive color or appearance, because this color, even though it is the color [of a given object] only apparently, is nevertheless not a fictive being, but one true and physical, that is to say, it is something resulting from light. But that sense grasps mind-dependent beings is proved by this fact, that internal sense synthesizes many things which outside itself in no way are or can be. Sense therefore knows something which is in itself a constructed or fictive being, although the fiction itself sense does not apprehend, but only that which, in the fictive being, offers itself as sensible."

34. From Poinsot 1635: 263b13–41, included in the 1985 Deely edition as note 17 to First Preamble, Article 3, at 73/22: "Relations are not known in perception under the modality proper to relation, that is to say, with a comparison to a term or by discourse, nor are they known in general, but as they obtain on the side of the fundament or as they are exercised therein, not as relation can be apprehended as an actual significate and according to its own being. But the foundation of the

relations knowable in sense perception [e.g., 263a38-39, 265b21: aversion, friendliness, offspring, hostility, parents, etc.] is the sensible thing itself according as it founds harmony [utility] or disharmony [harmfulness]. But the sensible thing is not sensed in this way by external sense, because that founding of harmony or discord is not color or sound or smell or anything that is perceived by external sense, yet the relation itself as contrasted to [counterdistinguished from] the fundament and as understood comparatively to the terminus is not attained in perceptual evaluation without collation [i.e., the sort of comparison that is possible only consequent on the capacity for understanding the related things as existing independently of the interests of the perceiving organism]. And when it is said that relations of the sorts in question are not in any way sensible directly or indirectly, the answer is that directly they are not anything thus sensible nor are they formally sensible, but they are indeed sensible fundamentally, insofar as they are founded in those sensible individuals, as, for example, inimicality-to-a-sheep is founded in the nature and qualities of a wolf."

35. See note 33 above.

36. Poinsot 1632, 73/16–74/9: "internal sense so compares or relates one thing to another by forming a proposition and discourse, that the sense does not formally cognize the very ordination of predicate and of subject and of antecedent to consequent by distinguishing a fictive from a physical relation. And similarly, sense cognizes a gold mountain as regards that which is sensible in those represented parts of gold and a mountain, not as regards the rationale of the construction or fiction as distinguished from a mind-independent reality. To cognize in this regard is to cognize not formally that which is constructed in the rationale of a being, but materially that on whose pattern is constructed that which in itself is not. But the extrinsic denomination that follows on the cognition of sense, insofar as an extrinsic denomination is not a mind-dependent relation formally but fundamentally, is then a mind-dependent relation formally when it is cognized on the pattern of a [mind-independent] relation."

37. In the end, this transformation is so radical that a new term is called for to label it. I have suggested, without any particular commitment to the suggestion except for its reason, the use of the term *Lebenswelt* for the species-specifically human Umwelt. I chose "Lebenswelt" partly out of deference to Husserl's original conception of the "lifeworld" as that out of which science and philosophy alike arise and to which they must constantly recur (even though this conception remains presemiotic in Husserl's own work and formulations), and partly out of consideration for the syntactical symmetry this term allows with the originally German term Umwelt as it has come to contemporary semiotics from the work of Jakob von Uexküll through the mediation principally of Thomas Sebeok. Especially through the linguistic framing of this base, the human Umwelt becomes a uniquely malleable one, a Lebenswelt, open to reconstitution along alternative lines of objectification in ways no other Umwelt on this planet is open.

38. See, e.g., Sebeok 1987: 24.

39. It is in this way, I suggest, that is best met the “need to explain in what way alterity is able to infiltrate the very sphere of the symbolic” (Ponzio 1990: 197).

40. —which concurred in defining the human being as the *animal rationale*—

# Chapter Thirteen
# The Cognitive Self and the Virtual Self[1]

**Thomas A. Sebeok**

When a man, such as me, reaches his 76th year, he has earned the right to glance at himself or—as in the case at hand—his "self." It was a little over twenty years ago, in fact, when I became attentive to, as so many have before me, the notion of identity or, to be more precise, interested in the problem of what I had dubbed the "semiotic self" (Sebeok 1979, 1989, 1992). That the "self" is a sign—or, rather, an amalgamated projection of composite nonverbal sign-assemblies called *Supersigns*—is hardly in doubt (cf. Sebeok 1994:18; Krampen 1994). Of course, in man, verbal signs contribute, though optionally so, as well. By the latter I refer to certain idiosyncratic habits of any speaker, which are constant markers, plus certain variable factors which the linguist and semiotician John Lotz classified together as "pragmatic features" of the sound wave (1954:378–380). These may include exhibitions of the emotional attitude that the message source maintains while speaking (anger, conviction, irony, or the like). Although such studies, building upon classical rhetorical texts, recommenced in the early 1950's (Moses 1954; see also Stankiewicz 1972), acoustic features of this kind, or kindred ones, have never been satisfactorily explored, let alone systematized. *Mutatis mutandis*, verbal expressions realized in other media, or channels, as, notably so, calligraphy, can be analyzed for "self revelations" in comparable ways.[2] Even the manner in which a Morse code operator taps out the code as a linear series of dots and dashes betrays his identity to an experienced listener or seasoned "watcher" of a distant instrument that faithfully reproduces the encoded pulses at their genesis.

Peirce's scattered views on the human self, along with George Herbert Mead's and Royce's, were effectively reexamined, following Colapietro's accomplished integrative effort (1989; see also Short's far-reaching 1992 review article), in a recent book by the Berkeley sociologist Wiley

(1994:30–32, 171, and passim). While I acknowledge the heritage and the scholarly merits of these and other recent works that deal with semiotic antecedents, I do not pursue them here, although there is one fascinating paradox I would like to return to in the future. This aporia (to apply a fashionable term), which was studied separately by Mary Haight (1980) and Karen Hanson (1986), refers to the literally impossible (ibid. 105), or, at best, oddly incoherent conceit of "self-deception." I believe that questions of the sort both of these authors raise could further be elucidated by semiotics and immunology, especially in the light of such molecular deceptive phenomena as camouflage, mimicry, perversive morphology, and the like. A strategy of defensive evasive structure, a concealment of lethal binding sites, has been hypothesized, among others, for the HIV virus. But I have not tried to provide here even a minimal survey of other considerations of the "self," for plenty of those already exist. I prefer instead to explore some novel aspects of the broader biosemiotic perspectives introduced in my previous papers on this topic, as well as to consider some implications of the pair of complementary titular attributes, cognitive and virtual, may pose in this context.

Biosemiotics, firmly rooted in classical and modern Medical Semiotics, is a contemporary offshoot of General Semiotics on the one hand, yet, on the other, it became viable as a new "Paradigm of Biology." Two German scientists—Eder and Rembold of the Max Planck Institute for Biochemistry (Martinsried)—elected (1992), at the 22nd International Ethological Conference held in Kyoto, to so style converging developments they perceived in this respect. Energetic inquiries are crowding in from both sides of an often erroneously grasped divide: mistakenly so, because, on deeper analysis, the general sign science turns out to embed the life science together to constitute a comprehensive conjoined science—a "natural semiotics," in the words of sophisticated observers as the late Italian oncologist and prolific writer on semiotic themes, Giorgio Prodi (in Sercarz 1988:55–56; also Eder 1992:61–63).[3]

From the semiotics verge, I attempted to summon into presence the state of the art in several books and two consecutive conference reports (see Sebeok 1991a: 100–113, 1992, and 1996a,b). The far more diversified biomedical side, in its burgeoning incarnations, harks back preeminently to the pioneering labors of Jakob von Uexküll in theoretical biology (e.g., 1928), to those of his son, Thure von Uexküll, chiefly in the medical applications of the doctrine of signs (e.g., 1988:123–150), and to the equally seminal ones of Heini Hediger, in animal psychology (e.g., 1980).

This century's pertinently proliferating developments can be emblematized, inter alia, by the following series of declarations:

Peirce's well-known axiom, "that all this universe is perfused with signs, if it is not composed exclusively of signs" (5:448 [1905]);

Mead's view, that "through the medium of communication with a self...the biologic individual becomes essentially interrelated with the self" (1934:372);

Thure's remark about his father, Jakob: "Of particular interest to Uexküll was the fact that signs are of prime importance in all aspects of life processes" (1987:147);

Jacob's statement, that "The genetic system and the immune system...function as memories of the past of the species and of the individual respectively" (1982:54);

Edelman's observation, that "By selfhood I mean not just the individuality that emerges from genetics and immunology, but the personal individuality that emerges from developmental and social interactions" (1992:167); and

Gergely's characterization of the human immune system as "the most perfect semiotic system in the Universe" (1995).[4]

Of the dozen or so branches of biosemiotics, only the last mentioned was called upon in my 1977 paper. This hybrid has since been dubbed both "semioimmunology" and, better, "immunosemiotics" (Sebeok 1991a: 108). The latter term is associated with Tomio Tada, a renowned immunologist of the Faculty of Medicine at the University of Tokyo. Tada had "framed the definition of this science as the study of the general principles underlying the structure of sign systems perceived by different cells of the immune machinery." Thus, in all mammals, "restrictions in partner cell interactions must exist as part of an intracellular semiotic system" (Sercarz 1988: v, vii; see also P.A. Bretscher, ibid., 293–303).

The reason for having invoked immunosemiotics as aforementioned should become evident from the ensuing summary of the main propositions advanced in my first paper on the self (1979), where I argued approximately as follows:

1. There are two ill-defined (see ii, below) comprehensions of the animal "self":

The Cognitive Self and the Virtual Self

a. *immunologic,* or biochemical, with semiotic overtones; and

b. *semiotic*, or social, with biological anchoring.

*Gloss* to 1. These coupled, complementary perspectives (a-b) appear to be in good conformity with the passage from Edelman quoted above, but only as a first approximation to a very intricate matter. As F. Jacquemart and A. Coutinho, of the Pasteur Institute, pointed out, "The notion of the self is perhaps one of the oldest in human history. This is precisely what makes it difficult to analyse" (in Sercarz 1988:173).

2. The arena of the immune reaction (Ir) is contained within the skin. The arena in which the semiotic self officiates—and which contains the former—is between an ill-defined region of the body beneath the skin of an organism and the outer perimeter of what I have labeled the "Hediger bubble," discussed, and provisionally redefined, thus: "a variably shaped impalpable sphere of personal space that admits no trespass by strangers and is defended when penetrated without permission" (Sebeok 1977:1063).

*Glosses* to 2.

i. The late Heini Hediger, successively the Director of the Bern, Basel, and Zürich Zoos, was the most remarkable animal psychologist of our times. He wrote an impressive dissertation in 1935 on (among a host of other topics) the specificity of animal flight-reaction, the measurability of flight-distances, and space-time systems in animal social behavior. In the course of a highly productive scientific career, Hediger came to hone and reshape the discipline that he founded and christened zoo-biology ever closer in accordance with semiotic principles (1990:415–439). He came to write: "I believe that eventually the explanation for the extremely complex and, so far, underresearched problem of the relationship between man and animals will be obtained by means of signal study or semiotics" (1985:177).

Although adherents of the Umweltlehre seem unaware of the personal connection between the two men, von Uexküll *pére* in fact received the younger scholar in Hamburg in 1934 with utmost cordiality. Many years afterwards, Hediger came to acknowledge that he was "extremely impressed by von Uexküll's Umwelt-Lehre" (ibid. 149). His own extensive researches on animal "biological distance," "individual distance," or minimum remove within which one may approach another, and "social distance," or maximum separation between the members of any animal group—plainly semiotic concepts, all three—were in a fertile sense logical extensions of the Umweltlehre.[5]

ii. By "ill-defined," I mean that the immune code, along with the genetic code and the neural code (brain/mind), is only one of three or four powerful intercommunicating mammalian pattern-recognition systems, each with capabilities of learning and memory housed within our bodies (Sebeok 1991b: 85–86, 88–89). In addition, the bloodstream carries around within the organism, reliably if relatively slowly, valuable packages of information. The properties of these systems are, however, as yet far from our capacity to comprehend or precisely represent. As Edelman has emphasized (1987), the three are architectonically much the same, differing mainly as to the time scale on which they respectively function. "The evolutionary system works on a time scale of hundreds of thousands of years, the immune system in a matter of days, and the brain in milliseconds" (Pagels 1988:135). Furthermore, the mammalian body's three information systems—biosemiotic systems *par excellence*—two evolved from the same bacterial ancestry and all three are governed by a language-like generative syntactic device

(Chomsky 1980:136–139, Jerne 1985, Sebeok forthcoming).

I now provisionally proffer to combine under a single designation the meshwork of this triad of selves: the Supersign *cognitive self*. The much abused adjective "cognitive" is meant here to suggest unlimited semiosis, in Peirce's sense, with respect to a potentially infinite string or cluster of interpretants. Too, metaphorically, I intend "cognitive self" to be roughly equivalent to Jacob's master image for his own fascicle of inner selves, *la statue intérieur* (1987). The expression further implies a competence on the part of the central nervous system, or "brain," to discriminate the organism, or "self" within which it is lodged, from its Umwelt, or, broadly, from "the rest of the world." This disciminative capability evolved from the *primal ontogenetic* as well as *phylogenetic sign relation*, namely, the opposition between "ego" and "alter" (Sebeok 1991a: 103), realized chemically in the earliest free-living cells.

3. Invasion of (1a) is signified by the immune reaction —recognition followed by a triggered response; of (1b) by anxiety (as used in Sebeok 1979; see also below), with the latter serving as an early warning system for the former.

*Gloss*. Anxiety, defined by Freud in explicitly semiotic terms, "as a signal indicating the presence of a danger-situation" (Sebeok, ibid. 263), is indeed an indexical sign (id. 1995).[6] Anxiety is activated when the self is at peril from an event assigned sufficient, marked weight by the endangered organism. The triggering index may take a quasi-biological, non-verbal shape, such as an olfactory trace of a leopard predator for a baboon prey, or be of a semantic character, such as some verbal assault whereby a stranger intrudes upon the territorial preserves of the self (in the sense of Goffman 1971:28–61).

4. Transmission errors may occur in both processes, with potentially devastating effects on the self. The capacity of an HIV virus to impede or destroy the immune self through docking to the self-recognition receptor CD4 may be the most notorious contemporary example among many other autoimmune diseases.

In 1989, several opportunities encouraged me to reconsider and add to what I had written a decade before. My interest now re-focused more narrowly: "The body has—or rather consists of—a veritable armamentarium of more or less palpable indexical markers of unique selfhood" (Sebeok 1989: viii). The ones I came to discuss now included phenotypic fingerprints and, on the genotypic plane, DNA "fingerprinting." Species odors and group odors—metonyms for distinctive functions in humans and other animals, and singular personal scents of particular individuals—are in part biological, in part cultural (e.g., diet-derived) tokens of selfhood. Le Guérer reminds us that "Humans produce a characteristic odor in the air around them that reflects [read: indexes] their diet and/or health, their age, their sex, occupation, race... the most direct and profound impression we can have of another person is his (or her) smell" (1992:23). Napoleon, for one, allegedly became so enamored of eau de cologne (originally a plague prophylactic) that he splashed a vial of it over his head every morning (Classen 1994:73).

I have also raised the empirically testable question whether speechless creatures are capable of internal self-representation. Is this or that animal aware of its appendages, its shadow upon the ground, its body-size? Such items can be semiotically charged features in a bundle of deconstructable idiosyncratic features of the self. The same is true of proper names, which, in humans, take a predominantly verbal form but in the rest of the animal kingdom are indexed by a wide variety of nonverbal means (Sebeok 1986:82–96).

In my 1992 paper, I examined the establishment and maintenance of self-images in terms of symptoms and the coherent sets of indexical signs called, at least since Galen, syndromes. I also raised this question: where, with respect to the body's *milieu exterieur*, is the "semiotic self" located? I also claimed that the semiotic self is engaged in continual scanning, or monitoring, or a process of meta-interpretation of its modeling system: "Any self can and must interpret the observed behavior of another organism solely as a response to its interpretations of its universe, 'behavior' meaning the propensity that capacitates it to link up its *Umwelt* with those of other living systems within its niche" (id. 1992:339–340).

A book edited by Alfred I. Tauber, on the *Organism and the Origins of Self*, containing several important articles by various authors on "The Immune/Cognitive Self," appeared too late for me to take into account when my paper mentioned above went to press (1991). This collection has since been superseded by Tauber's own reflective book, *The Immune Self: Theory or Metaphor*, which does take account of the Sercarz conference report in a brief discussion of how "semiotics...might be applicable to immunology with respect to the kind of phenomena both study" (1994:169). Unfortunately, however, evidently under the impression that Saussure "has had a decisive influence in semiotics" (ibid.), Tauber's analysis is flawed by his blurring of the crucial differentiation between linguistics, a model which pertains only to humans, and semiotics, which bears upon the immune systems of other species as well.

In the meantime, there appeared a rich and stimulating book by Synott—but the author of which, alas, seems to be unaware of the complementary undertakings of either Sercarz or his colleagues or of Tauber and his—on "the meaning of the body." Synott argues (1993:1 and passim) that it and the senses, like the organs and "parts" of the body, are socially constructed, and that the body is also, and primarily, as Sartre among others (1966) had held as well, "the self."

Lastly, I want to consider what significations, if any, such expressions "Virtual Self" or "Virtual Subject" may have. In the most straightforward, uncomplicated way, I take the phrase "Virtual Reality" (VR) to refer to the 3-D representation of "*object worlds*."[7] Although René Descartes deemed "object worlds" questionable, he never did doubt his own "subjective" thinking substance, his mind; hence the dictum: *Cogito ergo sum* (*Discourse*, 1637, Part IV). VR upgrades, as it were, Pseudo-Reality (e.g., achieved by TV, with such now standard extensions as cable networks, satellite dishes, and videocassette recorders). So drug induced states, whether by use of stimulants such as cocain or depressants such as alcohol, bring mankind a step closer to controlled escape from reality, and hallucinogens, such as certain types of mushrooms containing *psilocybin*, fly-agaric, cannabis, LSD, etc., promote the fabrication of VRs (cf. O'Flaherty 1984; Wright 1987).

Gödel's Incompleteness Theorem fuses subject with object. It entangles the observer with the observed (cf. Hofstadter 1979: 699). By doing so, it demonstrates how self-reference can produce either paradox or indecision or both. The lingering dilemma has always troubled semioticians: this is the distinction, or duality, between the *private character of signs* (notably, of symptoms, like the Freudian feeling of anxiety; see above) versus the *public character of their signified objects*. It implies limits to which the human self has the plasticity to become "disembodied" (beyond a paranoid- schizoid mode), or externalized, that is, "objectified" in any meaningful way, so as, for instance, to enable one to modify the style, color, material, sex of her/his own body—morphing by cosmetic surgery, maybe like Michael Jackson, or turning into a "borg," a hybrid entity combining life forms (like the nerve cell of a leech) and machine elements (a silicon chip) (cf. Sebeok 1991b: 98–99; and as also thoughtfully envisaged in Dery 1996).

The clandestine interpreter of symptoms is, by definition,
the semiotic self. This interpreter corresponds, on the cellular lever, to what Jakob non Uexküll identified as the *Ich-Ton*, usually rendered into English as "ego-quality." As he wrote: "The ego-qualities of the cells that are concentrated in our sense-organs...are perceived as signs.... All these signs consist exclusively of ego-qualities" (1982:34, 84). The notion of *Ich-Ton* corresponds in all particulars to the word I now italicize in Peirce's classic definition of a sign: "A sign...is something which stands to *somebody* for something in some respect or capacity" (2.228). That "somebody" is of course the semiotic self. (See note 4, below).

Whereas one can quite as comfortably contemplate an infinite number of *object* worlds in VR as a limitless number of "possible worlds" (à la Leibniz) that are made feasible by information-driven and rich syntax-endowed combinatorial systems like the genetic code, the immune code, the neural code (Black 1991: 161–162), the verbal code, and comparable natural and cultural devices of copying of information from one site to another, the postulation of multiple *subject* worlds would seem to lead back to the blind alley mentioned at the outset—the apparently insoluble paradox inherent in the notion of "self-deception."

# References


Black, Ira B. 1991. *Information in the Brain: A Molecular Perspective,* MIT Press, Cambridge.

Chomsky, Noam. 1980. *Rules and Representations,* Columbia University Press, New York.

Classen, Constance, et al. 1994. *Aroma: The Cultural History of Smell.* Routledge, London.

Colapietro, Vincent M. 1989. *Peirce's Approach to the Self,* SUNY Press, Albany.

Edelman, Gerald M. 1987. *Neural Darwinism.* New York: Basic Books.

___. 1992. *Bright Air, Brilliant Fire: On the Matter of the Mind,*Basic Books, New York.

Damasio, Antonio R. 1995. *Descartes' Error: Emotion, Reason, and the Human Brain,* Picador, London.

Dery, Mark. 1996. *Escape Velocity: Cyberculture at the End of the Century,* Grove Press, New York.

Eder, J. and H. Rembold. 1992. "Biosemiotics—a paradigm of biology: biological signalling on the verge of deterministic chaos". 79 *Naturwissenschaften* 60–67.

Furnham, Adrian. 1988. "Write and wrong: the validity of graphological analysis". *13 Skeptical Inquirer* 64–69.

Goffman, Erving. 1971. *Relations in Public: Microstudies of the Public Order,* Basic Books, New York.

Gray, Chris Hables (ed.) 1995. *The Cyborg Handbook,* Routledge, New York.

Haight, M. R. 1980. *A Study of Self-Deception,* Harvester, Brighton.

Hanson, Karen. 1986. *The Self Imagined: Philosophical Reflections on the Social Character of Psyche,* Routledge & Kegan Paul, New York.

Hediger, Heini. 1980. *Tiere verstehen: Erkentnisse eines Tierpsychologen.* Kindler, Munich.

___. 1985). "A lifelong attempt to understand animals," in *Leaders in the Study of Animal Behavior: Autobiographical Perspectives*,Bucknell University Press, Lewisburg, 144–181.

___. 1990. *Ein Leben mit Tieren im Zoo und in aller Welt,* Werd Verlag, Zürich.

Hofstadter, Douglas R. 1979. *Gödel, Escher, Bach: an Eternal Golden Braid,* Basic Books, New York.

Ingold, Tim, (ed.) 1988. *What Is An Animal?* Unwin Hyman, London.

Jacob, Francois. 1982. *The Possible and the Actual,*University of Washington Press, Seattle.

___. 1987. *La statue intérieure,* Odile Jacob, Paris.

Jerne, Niels Kaj. 1985. "The generative grammar of the immune system,"229 *Science* 1057–1059.

Krampen, Martin. 1994. "Supersign".In *Encyclopedic Dictionary of Semiotics,* Thomas A. Sebeok (ed.). Berlin: Mouton de Gruyter. 2:1025–1026.

Le Guérer, Annick. 1992. *Scent: The Mysterious and Essentials Powers of Smell,* Turtle Bay Books, New York.

Lotz, John. 1954. "The structure of human speech". 16 *Transactions of the New York Academy of Sciences*, Ser. II, 373–384.

Markley, Robert. (ed.) 1996. *Virtual Realities and Their Discontents,* Johns Hopkins University Press, Baltimore.

Mead, George Herbert. 1934. *Mind, Self, and Society: From the Standpoint of a Social Behaviorist*, University of Chicago Press, Chicago.

Moses, Paul J. 1954. *The Voice of Neurosis,* Grune & Stratton, New York.

O'Flaherty, Wendy. 1984. *Dreams, Illusion, and Other Realities,* University of Chicago Press, Chicago.

Pagels, Heinz R. 1988. *The Dreams of Reason: The Computer and the Rise of the Sciences of Complexity,* Simon and Schuster, New York.

Peirce, Charles Sanders. 1931–1958. *Collected Papers,* Harvard University Press, Cambridge.

Sartre, Jean-Paul. 1966 [1943]. Being and Nothingness, Washington Square Press, New York.

Sebeok, Thomas A. 1977. "Zoosemiotic components of human

communication," in *How Animals Communicate*, Thomas A. Sebeok (ed.), Indiana University Press , Bloomington, 1055–1077.

___. 1979. "The semiotic self," *The Sign & Its Masters*, University of Texas Press, Austin, 263–267.

___. 1986. *I Think I Am a Verb: More Contributions to the Doctrine of Signs*, Plenum Press, New York.

___. 1989. "The semiotic self revisited". Foreword to: *Sign, Self, Society,* Benjamin Lee and Greg Urban (eds.), Mouton de Gruyter, Berlin, v-xiv.

___. 1991a. *Semiotics in the United States,* Indiana University Press, Bloomington.

___. 1991b. *A Sign Is Just A Sign,* Indiana University Press, Bloomington.

___. 1992. "'Tell me, where is fancy bred?': the biosemiotic self"., in Sebeok and Umiker-Sebeok 1992: 333–343.

___. 1994. "What do we know about signifying behavior in the domestic cat *Felis catus*)?," 1 *Signifying Behavior* 3–31.

___. 1995. "Indexicality". in: *Peirce and Contemporary Thought: Philosophical Inquiries,* Kenneth Laine Ketner (ed.),Fordham University Press , New York, 222–242.

___. 1996. "Global Semiotics," in: *Proceeedings of the Vth International Congress of the International Association for Semiotic Studies,* Irmengard Rauch and Gerald Carr, (eds.), Mouton de Gruyter, Berlin.

___. Forthcoming. "Semiotics and the biological sciences: initial conditions," in: *Semiotics as a Bridge Between the Humanities and the Sciences: Proceedings of the First University of Toronto Semiotics Research Unit Annual Conference*, Marcel Danesi (ed.),Mouton de Gruyter, Berlin.

___ and Jean Umiker-Sebeok (eds.) 1992. *Biosemiotics: The Semiotic Web* 1991, Mouton de Gruyter, Berlin.

Sercarz, Eli E., et al. (eds.) 1988. *The Semiotics of Cellular Communication in the Immune System*. Berlin: Springer Verlag.

Short, T. L. 1992. "Peirce's semiotic theory of the self," 91 *Semiotica* 109–131.

Singer, Milton. 1984. *Man's Glassy Essence: Explorations in Semiotic Anthropology*. Bloomington: Indiana University Press.

Stankiewicz, Edward. 1972. "Problems of emotive language," in: *Approaches to Semiotics*, Thomas A. Sebeok, et al. (eds.) The Hague: Mouton , 239–276.

Synott, Anthony. 1993. *The Body Social: Symbolism, Self and Society*. Routledge, London.

Tauber, Alfred I,( ed.) 1991. *Organism and the Origin of Self,* Kluwer, Dordrecht.

___. 1994. *The Immune Self: Theory or Metaphor?* Cambridge University Press, Cambridge.

Thom, René. 1983. *Mathematical Models of Morphogenesis,* Ellis Horwood, Chichester.

Uexküll, Jakob von. 1928. *Theoretische Biologie*. Berlin: Julius Springer.

___. 1982 [1940]. "The Theory of Meaning," 42 *Semiotica* 1–87.

Uexküll, Thure von. 1987. "The sign theory of Jakob von Uexküll," in: Martin Krampen, et al., *Classics of Semiotics*, Plenum, , New York, 147–179.

___. and Wolfgang Wesiack. 1988. Theorie der Humanmedizin: Grundlagen artzlichen Denkens und Handelns, Urban & Schwarzenberg, Munich.

Watson, O. Michel. 1974. "Proxemics," in: 12 *Current Trends in Linguistics*, 311–344.

Wiley, Norbert. 1994. The Semiotic Self., University of Chicago Press, Chicago.

Wright, Robert. 1987. "Virtual Reality," 67 *The Sciences* 8–10.

# Notes

1. I. My earliest paper on facets of the multiple "self" was prepared for presentation and discussion at a Conference on Anxiety (December 1977), convened in Bad Homburg, Germany, under the sponsorship by the Werner-Reimers-Stiftung. This version first appeared as Sebeok 1979.
   II. Different parts of the next paper were also presented in Germany, in two juxtaposed meetings in June 1990: a Colloquium on Psycho-Neuro-Immunology, held in Tutzing, and a Colloquium on Models and Methods in Biosemiotics, held in Glotterbad. Already in press at the time, this paper was preprinted as Sebeok 1989. The two aforementioned pieces were later republished together as revised companion chapters in a book of mine, Sebeok 1991b: 36–48.
   I subsequently elaborated several dimensions of my topic as follows —
   III. In Sebeok 1992; and thereafter in a sequence of lectures:
   IV. At the University of Liverpool conference on "Linguistic Representations of the Subject" (July 1994), under the title "The Semiotic Subject and Self";
   V. At the National Institutes of Health, in Bethesda, MD, for the Washington School of Psychiatry, as the Annual Edith Weigert Lecture, titled "The Self: A Biosemiotic Conspectus" (November 1994). A transcript of my tape recorded lecture will appear in a book of *Proceedings*, co-edited by John Mueller and Joseph Brent.
   VI. At the University of Porto, Portugal, conference on "Perception and Self-Consciousness in the Arts and Sciences," delivered in September 1995, under the above title, "The Cognitive Self and the Virtual Self," being published (in the English version) in a volume celebrating Roberta Kevelson.
   Lectures IV–VI are currently also being assembled for separate publication, expected to appear, combined with I–III, as a sequence of revised and integrated chapters within a small book (planned for 1997).

2. The foregoing is not to imply the scientific adequacy of graphology, which, "from an objective and dispassionate evaluation," according to Furnham's critical conclusion, "is quite simply invalid" (1988:69).

3. The phrase "nature semiotics" is used by Kergosien (in Sebeok and Umiker-Sebeok 1992:145–170) in a similar, but not identical, sense to Prodi's "natural semiotics."
   The book edited by Sercarz et al. (1988) contains the contributions from an unprecedented workshop on the semiotics of cellular communication in the immune system. This meeting took place in September 1986, near Lucca, Italy. Professor Sercarz, of UCLA, was kind enough to invite me to be among the semioticians from Italy (Eco, Prodi, Violi) and Germany (Thure von Uexküll) who did participate. I keenly regret my inability to have joined them, owing to a prior commitment to the World Archaeological Congress being held in Southampton that same week (see Ingold 1988: 63–76).

4. Personal reflection and comment by the Hungarian Academician Janos Gergely (March 30, 1955).

5. The term *Umwelt*, which I prefer to render in English as "model," corresponds, in the human context, to Shakespeare's celebrated locution, (man's) *glassy essence* ("Measure for Measure," II, 2). The tag was garnered and fascinatingly applied to man's nature by Peirce—for instance, in his Lowell Lecture of 1866—and then was featured in the title of Singer's astute book-length meditations on this theme (1984). However, Singer did not make the connection with the concept of a subjective *Umwelt*, or semiotic "bubble," for he knew of its Uexküll-Hedigerian bio-psychological roots only from our discussions, viz., by hearsay.
   In other directions, Hediger's ideas about various types of "distance" in the world of animals, came, after the mid–1960's, to provide a rationale for a semio-anthropological inquiry known as Proxemics, launched by Edward T. Hall (e.g., Watson, in Sebeok 1974:317, 340). They also strongly influenced, although this is seldom properly credited, zoosemiotic investigations everywhere.

6. The indexical character of this sort of relationship is interestingly analysed by Thom (1983:267–269), showing that even a false index can have semiotic value for an organism, as in Pavlov's well-known conditioning experiments.

7. Both the "real" and fictive literature of VR and related subjects has become very large and sprawling. For two recent anthologies of the "real" kind, see Gray 1995 and Markley 1966. I found the measured contribution of Katherine Hayles, on "Boundary Disputes: Homeostasis, Reflexivity, and the Foundations of Cybernetics," on pp. 11–37 in the latter collection, typically useful, although several other pivotal sources should be added to her account; I mentioned several of them in my own survey (1991a: 68ff.)

# Chapter Fourteen
# Leeward Bound

**Roberta Kevelson**

A bill of lading passes from the hand of the tattooed seaman who makes the weekly run between Hong Kong and Formosa to the dealer of oriental art. The latter holds the paper fast against the breeze with the tweed sleeve of his western-cut coat, checks off the number on the sheet against the actual merchandise unpacked: rice-patterned porcelain teacups, ginger jars, teak folding screens inlaid with lotus of ivory, jade, and jasper, nods assent, transfers the information to his sales book: *Export U.S.A.* They are waiting for him outside. The parade beings; he is to ride with the menagerie—the paper-costumed, larger-than-life animal symbols of the Zodiac. He is the rear quarters of the Rat. He pulls the zippered costume about his person; the four-legged creature takes its place. Unnoticed in the clamor and the colored fireballs he slips out from under and is last seen pushing through the crowd. It is a while before they realize that the haunches of the rodent have gone slack.

In a supermarket a woman in her thirties, with pink hair rollers poking through her sequined square of nylon kerchief, inches impatiently forward in the check-out line. Her turn is next. Suddenly she raises her head, listens to the loudspeaker announcing "specials" of the hour, leaves her double-tiered wire cart laden with groceries where it is, causing a traffic jam, and purposefully strides through the parking lot. The next day the local paper runs a feature article; she is among the missing.

There is nothing unusual when from time to time—every day in fact—individuals throughout the world decide to turn their backs on assignments, commitments, goals, and resolutely head in an altogether different direction. Who knows why. Daily, rivers are dredged, search parties are under way, bloodhound instincts of a million hearts sniff in vain. Logic leads nowhere. But when the sheer number of those among the missing mount, a universal vibration occurs. Not once upon a time, but so recently as last week, an editor of a leading newspaper prophesied in terms as vague and picturesque as "plague" or "swarms of locusts"—and so brought to print euphemisms for unnamed fears and hand-in-hand, fear's cousin, dreamt desires.

Organizations spontaneously decided to hold conventions. Family circles communicated, decided suddenly they should, and about time, meet. This summer a record for precipitation was set. Streams long dry filled and overflowed. Never, at least for a hundred years, had tides risen quite so high. Beaches were desolate, except for isolated areas here and there along the entire shore of the Atlantic Ocean where strangers huddled, waiting for the rain to stop. Conversation was sparse. No one spoke about the weather. It was there. It would be obvious to anyone that these beach squatters had little in common. They were impelled to the ocean, had dropped all other plans; they shared a change of heart.

Each of these persons undoubtedly had a story to tell. And then what? To record them all would necessitate compiling innumerable volumes of case histories. Eulogies are out of order; they are not dead, and simply summarizing with praise for "all famous men" would be beside the point. What concerns us, in this mass migration toward the edge of the earth, is not a question of life or death, but curiosity. Why, then, do truisms come true, events recur, and why are they unswervingly followed through?

Consider, for example, the common phrase: the game is not worth the candle. For those who have turned about the light is out. The situation becomes more clear. On a universal scale, through webs of paths and streams and fields the periphery is reached, and by infinite persons suddenly blinded, persistently pushing forth.

It was fortunate, then, that at least one small town, surrounded by rivers and forests, could still consider itself off the beaten track, as they say, and thus still continue to celebrate the first Sunday in August, which had always been festival day. Each year the picnic grounds were prepared, relay races run, trees felled in seconds flat, preserves brought forth and tasted, and custard frozen, twisted into gravity–defying peaks. At sunset the fuse of the oldest cannon was lighted. They say it used to fairly leap from its crouched iron joints, lift off the ground, following for a moment its roar. Later as a grand finale fireworks were set off. The thing was done. . . all's right with the world. Even the weather failed to dampen spirits. Mid-summer, and the blackest of nights. Dense fog draped the platform. An unveiling? A revelation? Only the committee knew, for they alone had selected the theme.

A theatre-in-the-round had been improvised around the bandstand where the fife and drum corps, after parading through town, had concluded their concert with a martial interpretation of the Salvation Army's theme song: "When the Sheaves Come Marching Home." The cannon had been fired, and tactful, no one remarked that its roar had diminished and was really not much more than an explosive sneeze followed by an admittedly vigorous honking of its nose.

Blindly groping over legs, indiscriminately those of people and rented chairs from the funeral parlor, the audience assembled. It stared at the platform until the curtain parted to reveal a mammoth goldfish bowl. The depths of the sea glowed with phosphorescent light. Mermen and their maids acted out in scaly modesty aquatic vignettes of "life," as it might conceivably be lived on the sandy resorts of a lost Atlantis. The show was cleverly contrived. The fishbowl was really an above-ground swimming pool (the distributor's name was conspicuously printed on the side, between the frame and the tank's molded Plexiglas sides.) Like a collapsed suspension bridge the diving board extended from a weather-eaten, wave-lashed pinnacle of featherstone—improvisation for Gibraltar Rock. The artists who performed in this water-ballet, who the town was frightfully fortunate to have found on an off-tour day, really made the occasion. Ever so much more.

They enacted immaterial and utopian scenes of suggestive intimacy, evasive familiarity, as they appeared to simultaneously touch and elude one another; they swelled and shrank as they flipped gracefully in and out the water weeds. The played as nymphs would play at being people, and the people watching held their collective breath in direct proportion to each performer's significant submersion. The background music was a medley of Handel, and enhanced atmosphere that was at once playful, religious, otherworldly—and yet as marvelously novel as television would be in four dimensions.

Except for the illumination within the water the park lights were dimmed, and any shuffling of feet by those who might have craved more action was muffled by the thick turf and the constant rippling of water down gullies of the artificial rock.

Now suddenly, as each pair of water people entwined tails as to execute an everlasting embrace, the fuses blew; the mountain toppled tip first into the fish bowl. Water splashed and soaked the people in the privileged first few rows quite thoroughly. Mermen and maids alike, humanly fearful of strange electric currents in the water, leapt from the water to the nearest and the safest laps, thus destroying the illusion of their art but at the same time reviving those latent dreams which the audience shared as a body for union with the enchanting elements of the sea. Professionals to the core, the show went on.

The water people shed their forked flippers, and after a few moments in the shrouded night it was impossible to distinguish player from played upon. The event turned into a general free-for-all. Discs were quickly switched; bands played dance music in the dark and in the dark partners exchanged the old for new, or who knows if it wasn't the other way around? All kicked off their shoes, made much of misfortune, and the midsummer's frolic would have so concluded if some witless technician had not conscientiously remedied the situation, expertly spliced wires, and lit the platform up. However, the floodlights were reversed. All was not total ruin. Quickly the curtain was drawn. Audience and actor were one. But on stage a new act had begun.

It was not planned that way: congratulations upon denials. On stage Mickey and Minnie Mouse joined hands, but were completely ignored as they bowed, first to the overturned chairs of the theatre-in-the-round, then as protocol demands, to the backs of the people fox-trotting on the dampened ground, and then to the band which from its box still played on. Bowing to each other they knocked heads and frowned. Some few deviates in the crowd, not yet fully in the swing of swinging around, announced to the deep green walls of the night that a Punch and Judy show was next.

But Punch or Mickey or whoever holding center stage was not behaving according to form. He was not beating Judy or Minnie down with a stick, but was crawling on all fours. They both scurried around, searching, sniffing, groping on the darkened platform for something lost. A stick-pin? A ring? For the strings which should rightly have been tied to limbs and necks, which weren't wooden. The rodents crept toward each other. No one watched. No one cared. No one listened to them squeak, or raise themselves and hold each other semi-erect with foremost paws. No one noticed they rubbed noses or heard them whisper that the time was now, as once again.

From the shadows in the park creatures small and furry, like a knubby blanket, slipped slowly surely, relentlessly beyond the limits of the park, clawed over the fence. Main Street was rolling along.

But the festival was more than a success. Everyone was right at home. Here, from the homely celebrations throughout the world, as from puddles, brooks, streams, rivers, across plains and over hills, waters of a universe converged and through them swam the lemmings toward a certain shore that warmly bathed in a current circling and flowing west, between the Straits of Gibraltar, and still further and further west.

Finally, in full dress like penguins in tails and white breasts, animated cartoon creatures assembled, counted, and rubbed noses. Just as they had chewed their way through obstacles, demolished structures blindly, swathed paths through unexpected distress, they too were at the brink of home. They squatted, back to back a moment, breathing hard. No audible command, no sign, no point that prod them forward, yet en masse they dove into the sea, into the deepest memory, into the recesses of submerged souls.

That was what happened and what will be? Singly, they will some day wade out of the water onto dry land, disperse, each in his own way along the beaten tracks from home to home, as vagabonds in a minor key, ballads long remembered, too soon forgot.

# Appendix One
# A Conversation with Roberta Kevelson

## William Pencak

When I visited Roberta Kevelson at her new home in Williamsburg, Virginia, in November, 1996, it was just as I had imagined it: an enchanted cottage in a forest. Here, surrounded by artwork gathered during her travels around the world to semiotic and philosophy conferences and her eclectic collection of books and manuscripts—including nearly everything that survives from the hand of Charles S. Peirce—she could retreat when she chose from the active intellectual and artistic life of her new community and continue to practice creatively the life of the mind for which "retirement" seems the most inappropriate term imaginable. She is Distinguished Professor of Philosophy Emerita—a distinction earned the old-fashioned way. Although she had lived in Williamsburg less than six months, she was already teaching philosophy and gardening in extension courses, planning more conferences and books, and taking courses on Puccini, among other things. And of course, she knew the best restaurants in town.

It was after breakfast at perhaps the most congenial of these, the Lodge, in front of a warm fireplace on a chilly autumn day, that I talked with Bobbie about her incredible career. (Much of what follows is a close paraphrase of what she actually said, with exact quotations so indicated.) She began by relating how after selling real estate, writing fiction and poetry, and participating in theater groups such as the Trinity Players of Providence, Rhode Island, she was a founding mother of the women's movement. "In the 1960s, except for Germaine Greer and a few others, there was no feminism in the academic sense, not even the word." The community college in Fall River, Massachusetts, where she lived, needed a director for a women's center that had yet to be formed. She "had a great desire to do something". The dean interviewed her, and asked her what she did. "I talked and I wrote," was the answer; that, plus "personality", landed her the job. The rest was history, and philosophy, and semiotics, and much, much more.

Bobbie explained how she created the women's center and, by extension, a good deal of the women's movement in Massachusetts, from scratch. She first went to the college president: the center needed a room, resources, a budget, and, most of all, a name: "a symbol of something which is alive." Next she went to the local newspaper and asked for a column—"the old-time editor laughed—but he gave me the column." Then she went to the local television stations and radio and asked for time—she got it. Finally, applying for federal grants under titles two and twenty, she obtained the first such funding for a women's center and got the community college to match it.

I asked what the women's center did. Fall River is a milltown. The population, predominantly Roman Catholic, is not well-to-do. Bobbie worked to get teachers in the health field to discuss planned parenthood and overcome religiously-based objections to abortion. This was not easy as there were few sympathetic (or women) doctors and no women surgeons in the area. "Consciousness raising" was the center's essential task. Before Bobbie stepped down, she was directing a staff of fifty people offering thirty-five courses ranging from English as a second language—Fall River has a large Portuguese immigrant community—to involving women in art, industry, and education. She secured assistance from the Council of Churches as well as the federal government.

Fall River was only the beginning. Drawing together women's organizations from all over Massachusetts under the name of "Sachem", an Indian term for council, Bobbie organized "The Woman Alone" conference. It was an enormous success and brought people from throughout the state to Fall River to discuss problems faced by different "women alone": homosexuals, single parents, non-married women, divorcees, and widows who chose not to remarry. This grass-roots conference put the regional, New England women's movement on the map. Out of her work at the women's center came her first book, *The Inverted Pyramid*. She had helped revitalize older women (and men) who no longer felt themselves a part of society by getting them to interpret headlines and write letters to the editors of newspapers.

Also in Fall River, Bobbie established a museum for this town of "mills, hills, and two dollar bills." Many of the Portuguese immigrant women who made up a sizeable portion of the town's population, although they worked and their husbands did not, had no sense of their own worth as human beings in a society dominated by machismo. There were at least five different Portuguese communities in Fall River from Lisbon, rural Portugal, Brazil, the Azores Islands, and Portuguese Africa. In an old candle factory, she laid the plans to set up a museum that included artifacts and descriptions pertinent to these women's lives as well as to the town's French-Canadian, English, and Polish women to instill in them a sense of their accomplishments as human beings.

Although she "had a wonderful time" at the women's center, Bobbie's work there prompted her to"take my own advice and go back to school." At first she went to Brown University's graduate school to study linguistics but was not happy: "no one was talking about meaning, it was all Chomsky and syntactic analysis." So she took a leave of absence and went to Cambridge, Massachusetts to study film at the Orson Welles Film School. She worked with a lot of young people, and learned about directing, operating cameras, editing, and animation. Why did she study film? "Peirce said that the process of thought is a motion picture process and I had to find out what he meant."

Bobbie had first discovered the philosopher Charles Sanders Peirce long before her days at Brown. A mathematics professor at Goddard College, where she had received her bachelor's degree, had helped her and other people who considered themselves mathematically blocked learn calculus by introducing them to Peirce's logic of relations. A course with noted linguist Roman Jakobson, visiting at Brown from Harvard, rekindled her interest in Peirce, with the result that she returned to Brown and later created her own graduate program at Brown in semiotics with Thomas Winner in Poetics and Robert Scholes in English as her principal professors. Her program required her to fulfill preliminary requirements from four departments. She did not ask for financial support to pursue her unique program, but Winner was delighted with her proposal and she received funding. She received her doctorate—the first in semiotics—in 1978. On the way, she published two more books: *Style, Symbolic*

*Language Structure, Syntactic Change* on the logic of questions and answers, and *Inlaws/Outlaws*, which deals with how the Robin Hood outlaw ballads reinforced the basis of English common law—a fundamental law above the vagaries of particular laws. This book invented and introduced the field of legal semiotics. Upon concluding her studies at Brown she spent a year at Yale as a post-doctoral fellow, meeting Rulon Wells, John Smith, Hillis Miller, and Edward Stankiewiecz. There she noticed that Umberto Eco was teaching a course in the Italian department; they exchanged ideas. Then followed a further post-doctoral year at Brown as University Research Fellow before her appointment at Penn State in 1981.

While she was studying in various fields, prior to taking her doctorate, Bobbie had decided to create her own: legal semiotics. The inspiration for this idea came from a sentence in Thomas A. Sebeok's book *Contributions to the Doctrine of Signs*, which suggested that someone should do something with law and semiotics. When she established the Semiotic Research Center at Penn State, she originally hoped to investigate this topic in conjunction with the semiotic centers at Texas Tech and Indiana Universities in a re-creation of Peirce's notion of a community of inquirers dedicated to discovering the truth. But "they didn't want to work with me; *they didn't want to play with me,"* she said, stressing as did Peirce the playful element of inquiry. (Only the late Max Fisch, who inaugurated and published the first several volumes of the Peirce Edition Project in Indianapolis, "was wonderful" in encouraging and facilitating her work.) So the Penn State Center for Semiotic Research began to sponsor on its own the annual Round Tables, which began in 1987. She joined with colleagues throughout the world, including Professor Bernard S. Jackson of the University of Liverpool—whose tribute is included in this volume—to co-sponsor the International Association for the Semiotics of Law. Proceedings of the Round Table have been published annually, and the International Association sponsors the *International Journal for the Semiotics of Law*, on whose editorial board she serves.

I asked Bobbie why she studied semiotics and believed in it. She replied that "the greatest thing about semiotics is the recognition that we communicate not in hierarchical fashion where an authority speaks downward but in a dialogic fashion among people who create a universe that is not finished, but open. What we take as a law or a fixed judgment is always provisional. We are open to the world; the self is a dynamic sign in play that continually creates something genuinely new. Semiotics can keep freedom alive—it is experimental and anti-authoritarian; it is never under anyone's control; there are no masters or slaves, only equals in relationships."

What troubles her most about semiotics is that people "have picked at signs in little pieces, like scavengers, without making an effort to understand the freedom it offers people, its anti-authoritarian nature." It has been distressing to her that "opportunists" have taken advantage of semiotics, "using it as a buzzword to do anything at all with the term 'sign' to make it more generally accessible. People can talk of signs—like Suzanne Langer and Ernst Cassirer, who are great thinkers about signs—but not semiotics. They need to get to the root of what semiotics really is, and then it is mind-blowing and radical, totally anti-authoritarian and open to freedom." Some people who are considered semioticians, like the French structuralists with their closed "semiotic squares" and "totalitarian" universe, are unfortunately grouped by some with Peirce and the dynamic, ever-changing world of his semiotics. But then, as Bobbie remarks, Peirce stated that only one person *almost* understood him—Josiah Royce. Far from being a realist, she insists, Peirce was an "objective idealist" who believed ideas can only be created through openness, spontaneity, and freedom.

Bobbie's teaching (for which she won the AMOCO Award for Outstanding Teaching that is annually awarded to one out of thousands of faculty at the numerous Penn State campuses) corresponds to her philosophy. "I am not there to give students anything. I am there to interact and get them to know that the way we can interact is through an idea, which is something you hold on to at both ends." She has taught an astonishing array of topics under the umbrella of standard introductory philosophy courses: logic; aesthetics; philosophy of law; ethics and moral values; social and political philosophy; maps; time; anarchism; invention and representation. She first learned that teaching ought to be the creative exploration of ideas rather than the perfunctory presentation of accumulated wisdom at Goddard College, a "counter-establishment" college where, in the early 1960s, "students were approached as adults by teachers who invited them to sit down and learn with them." Her first philosophy course was taught by an (Asian) Indian who had studied with Robert Frost which included gardening, wearing Indian clothes, eating Indian food, listening to Indian music, and incorporating the life of the mind into a way of life.

Besides the teachers at Goddard, Bobbie modeled her pedagogy on the poet David Cornel DeJong, whom she met in Providence simply by knocking on his door and telling him she needed some help with her writing and thinking. DeJong had escaped from the Puritanical region of Friesland in Holland to come to America to write; he founded some of the first little magazines which published short stories and poems by unknown as well as known writers. Bobbie brought him her writings every other week for more than six years: she joined his study group where people criticized each other's work without being destructive. One of her pieces, an experiment in the short story from this period, "Leeward Bound," is included in this collection.

More will be coming from Bobbie's prolific pen. She is completing a book on "Peirce's Pragmatism" to show that Peirce understood pragmatism not as a theory but as a process of experimentation in contrast to those "kidnapers" such as John Dewey and William James from whom he tried to keep the concept safe. She is also working on "Peirce: The Sign of the Gryphon" which will deal with Peirce's relation to mythology, language, and poetics, stressing the transformation of myth and its significance. She explains: "The Gryphon has been reduced in western legend to the fleur de lys. All that is left of the dragon slain by St. George is the three-pronged footprint. The imaginary grotesque has been reduced to a flower, just as in the modern world the fear of the unknown and the terrible has been reduced to science and commerce." But that reduction represents the shrinking of reality and is itself not true-to-life. Fortunately, "Peirce teaches us that the world is still magical through the logic of the possible."

Roberta Kevelson's life and the influence of her work is proof that ideas can indeed be magical and make a difference. Her numerous writings and the writings of those she has inspired demonstrate her contention that semiotics creates a chain-reaction of intellectual creativity which can transcend the disciplinary strait-jackets of the modern academic world. As traditional scholarship is not only proving inadequate to the needs of the human mind for mental and spiritual nourishment, but is under increasing threat from institutions that are only interested in ideas that manipulate things and people in order to make money, semiotics and its practitioners—who are by definition anti-authoritarian and anti-careerist since their work is usually ignored or despised instead of being rewarded—will become increasingly important in keeping alive the life of the mind. As one of the remnant who has resurrected Charles Sanders Peirce and his community of inquirers in the late-twentieth-century, Roberta Kevelson stands before us much as Peirce himself, the author of a vast array of essays and papers which can only become increasingly meaningful as the centuries roll on. For like Peirce about whom she has written more books than anyone else, she does not lay down "the truth," but offers a dazzling panoply of insights on all sorts of subjects that invites curious minds to join in the semiotic quest.

# Appendix Two

# The Achievements of Roberta Kevelson

## Education and Employment

Ph.D. in Semiotics, Brown University, 1978
Postdoctoral Fellow, Yale University, 1979–81
Research Associate, Brown University, 1980–81
Assistant Professor, The Pennsylvania State University, 1981; Professor, 1987; Distinguished Professor, 1988; Emerita, 1996

## Honors and Visiting Appointments

AMOCO Award for Outstanding Teaching, The Pennsylvania State University, 1986
Research Fellow, Princeton University, 1985–present
University Scholar, Cambridge University, 1986–present
Visiting Scholar, University of Virginia Law School, 1988–89
Visiting Scholar, College of William and Mary, Philosophy Department, 1991–present (in residence as of 1996)
Visiting Fellow in Law, University of Edinburgh, 1991–95
Visiting Scholar, University of New Mexico, 1992
Vice-President, Semiotic Society of America, 1994–95
President, Semiotic Society of America, 1995–96

## Administrative Positions

Director, Women's Center, Bristol Community College, 1972–74
President, Bristol Textile Museum, 1972–74
Director, Functional Writing Program, Brown University, 1973–75
Executive Director, Center for Semiotic Research in Law, Government, and Economics, The Pennsylvania State University, 1984–present
Member, Executive Board, Greater Philadelphia Philosophy Consortium, 1989–96

Member, Executive Board, International Association for Law and Semiotics, 1986–present

## Editorial Work

Editorial Board, *Journal of Philosophy and Rhetoric*

Editorial Board, *International Journal for Law and Semiotics*

Editor-in-Chief, series: *Law and Semiotics.* Plenum. 3 vols. 1987–89

Editor-in-Chief, series: *Law and the Human Sciences*. Peter Lang. 8 vols. to date

Editor-in-Chief, series: *Critic of Institutions*. Peter Lang. 11 vols. to date

Co-editor (with Marcel Danesi), series: *Semaphores and Signs*, St. Martin's Press.

## Publications

### 1960s

Numerous short stories, poems, and plays, published in various literary magazines such as *Forum* and *Southwest Review*

Assistance with editing and preparation of papers and writings of her teacher David Cornell DeJong for special collections at Brown University Library

Feature Op-ed column, *Fall River Herald News*

### 1976

*Style, Symbolic Language Structure, Syntactic Change,* Peter de Ridder, Lisse.

"Introduction to the Logic of Questions and Answers," *Brown Working Papers* 1.

### 1977

*The Inverted Pyramid,* Indiana University Press, with Peter de Ridder Press, Bloomington and Lisse.

*Inlaws/Outlaws*, Indiana University Press with Peter de Ridder Press, Bloomington and Lisse.

"A Restructure of Barthes' Readerly Text," 18 *Semiotica* 253–67.

"Introduction to the Logic of Questions and Answers," *Brown Working Papers* 2.

**1978**

"Reversals and Recognitions," 19 *Semiotica*, 29–58.

"Wittgenstein's Language Games as Systematic Metaphors," 19 *Semiotica*, 281–320.

**1980**

"Relations of Something to Nothing," 2 *Ars Semiotica,* 295–326.

**1981**

"Semiotics and the Art of Conversation," 32 *Semiotica*, 53–80.

**1982**

"Comparative Legal Cultures," 1 *American Journal of Semiotics*, 63–84.

"Peirce's Dialogism and Continuous Predicate," 18 *Transactions of the Charles S. Peirce Society*, 110–126.

"Legal Speech Acts: Decisions," *Linguistics and the Professions*, R. DiPietro, (ed.) Abex, New Jersey, 121–132.

"Semiotics and the Structures of Law," 35 *Semiotica*, 182–192.

"Peirce as Catalyst in Modern Legal Science: Consequences," *Semiotics 1980*. M. Lenhart and M. Herzfeld (eds.), Plenum, New York.

**1983**

"Peirce's Phenomenology and Solipsism," *Sign, Structure, and Function,* T. Winner et al. (eds.), Mouton, Amsterdam, 89-104.

"Francis Lieber and Legal Hermeneutics," *Semiotics 1981* M. Lenhart and J. Deely (eds.), Plenum, New York, 167-178.

"Time as Method in Charles S. Peirce," 2 *American Journal of Semiotics*, 267–276.

"Bridge Laws," evaluative review of Thomas A. Sebeok's *The Sign and Its Masters* (1978), 2 *American Journal of Semiotics*, 84–108.

"Charles Peirce and Legal Hermeneutics," *Abstracts, Vol. 4, IVR International Conference on Law and Social Philosophy*, Helsinki.

"Peirce's Method of Methods," *Abstracts, International Congress on Logic, Methodology, and Philosophy of Science*, Salzburg.

**1984**

"Semiotics in the United States," *The Semiotic Sphere,* T. Sebeok and J. Umiker-Sebeok (eds.), Plenum, New York, 519–554.

"Semiotics and Law," *Encyclopedic Dictionary of Semiotics*, T. Sebeok and J. Umiker-Sebeok (eds.), DeGruyter, Berlin, 438–43.

"Riddles, Legal Reasoning, and Peirce's Existential Graphs," 57 *Semiotica*, 197–223.

"Peirce's Speculative Rhetoric," 17 *Philosophy and Rhetoric*, 16–29.

**1985**

"Peirce's Philosophy of Signs and Legal Hermeneutics," *Man, Law and Forms of Life*, E. Bulygin et al. (ed.), D. Reidel, 125–35.

"Economic Justice," 213 *Semiotica Juridica,* 95–109.

"Causation in Law: A Semiotics Perspective," *Proceedings: Colloque International de Semiotique Juridique,* E. Landowski and D. Carzo (eds.), 71–94.

**1986**

"Trowing, Discovering, and the Flow of Invention: Peirce and Kant," *Proceedings of the Sixth International Kant Congress.* G. Funke and T. Seebohm (eds.), University Press of America, Lanham, MD, 553–568.

"How's of Why and Why's of How," *Proceedings of the Research Conference on Knowledge Seeking and Questioning,* 74 *Synthese,* 91–106.

"Prolegomena to a Comparative Legal Semiotics," *Frontiers in Semiotics* J. Deely et al. (eds.), Indiana University Press, Bloomington, 191–98.

"Property in Law and Semiotics," *Proceedings XII Congress of Philosophy of Law and Social Philosophy*. S. Panou (ed.), 125–36.

"Pragmatism and Paradox: The Deflection of John Dewey," *Proceedings of Conference on Signs and Transformation*, Munich, 1984.

"Semiotic Method and Legal Inquiry," 61 *Indiana Law Review*, 355–371.

"Toward a Global Perspective on Legal Semiotics," *Semiotics, Law and Social Science* (1985), 81-94; B. Jackson and D. Carzo (eds.); also in *Revue de Recherche Juridique: Droit Prospectif*, 95–109.

**1987**

*Charles S. Peirce's Method of Methods*, John Benjamins, Amsterdam.

*Law and Semiotics I* (ed.), Plenum, New York.

"Repugnancy and Paradox in Law: A Peircean Point of View," in *Semiotics and Law I.* R. Kevelson (ed.), Plenum, New York, 1–24; 239–282.

"Review of Round Table on Law and Semiotics," *The Semiotic Web 1986* T. Sebeok and J. Umiker-Sebeok (eds.), DeGruyter, Berlin.

"Representation in Law," *Recherches Semiotiques/Semiotic Inquiry*, Hans-Georg (ed.). Ruprecht, 187–206.

**1988**

*The Law as a System of Signs,* Plenum, New York.

*Law and Semiotics II.* (ed.), Plenum, New York.

"Peirce's Students on the Science of Value," Festschrift for Thomas G. Winner. A. Mandelker et al. (eds.), 22 *Canadian-American Slavic Studies*, 57–75.

"The New Realism and Lawlessness in Kaleidoscope," *Law and Semiotics II.* R. Kevelson (ed.), Plenum, New York, 189–208.

**1989**

*Law and Semiotics III.* (ed.), Plenum, New York.

"Pragmatic Method and Some Consequences," *Law and Semiotics II* (ed.) R. Kevelson, Plenum, New York, 1-12.

"Legal Things as Artwork," *Law and Semiotics III.* R. Kevelson (ed.). Plenum, New York, 193-210.

"Sinister Intent, Political Fallacy, and the Pearlizing of Value in Law," in *Laws and Rights*. V. Ferrari and C. Faralli (eds.), Dott. A. Guiffre Editions, Milan, 593–610.

**1990**

*Peirce, Paradox, Praxis: The Image, The Conflict, The Law*. Amsterdam: DeGruyter.

"Semiotics as Exploratory: Peirce's Art of the Possible," *Proceedings IASS 1989*. J. Delledalle (ed.), 1333–1341.

"Transactions and the Increase of Goods and Meaning: A Semiotics Approach," in special issue on Law and Economics, *Syracuse Law Review*. R. P. Malloy and R. Kevelson (eds.), 7–25.

"Tom Paine: Rights and Revolutions," 3 *International Journal for Semiotics of Law*, 169–186.

"Law and Semiotics," *Semiotics in the Individual Sciences*. Walter A. Koch (ed.), Brockmeyer, Bochum, I: 282–298.

**1991**

*Peirce and Law* (ed.), Semiotics and the Human Sciences Series, Peter Lang, New York and Bern.

*Action and Agency* (ed.), Semiotics and the Human Sciences Series, Peter Lang, New York and Bern.

"Peirce and Community: Public Opinion and the Legitimization of Value in Law," in *Peirce and Law* .R. Kevelson (ed.), Peter Lang, New York and Bern, 99–120.

"Legal Agency as Facsimile and Iconic Function: Authority, Power, Representation," in *Action and Agency*. R. Kevelson (ed.), Peter Lang, New York and Bern, 135–56.

"Confusion of Language in Legal Thought," *ASRP IVR 1991*. H. J. Koch and U. Neumann (eds.), Franz Steiner Verlag, Stuttgart, 143–155.

**1992**

*Law and the Human Sciences*. (ed.) Semiotics and the Human Sciences Series, Peter Lang, New York and Bern.

*Law and Aesthetics*. (ed.), Peter Lang, New York and Bern.

"Pragmatism, Utopic Constructions, Legal Myths," in *Law and the Human Sciences*. R. Kevelson (ed.), Peter Lang, New York, 193–218.

"Art of Discovery in Law," in *Law and Aesthetics*. R. Kevelson (ed.), Peter Lang, New York and Bern, 245-280.

**1993**

*Peirce's Aesthetics of Freedom,* Peter Lang, New York and Bern.

*Flux, Complexity, Illusion.* (ed.), Peter Lang, New York and Bern.

"A Peircean Approach to Human Rights," 6 *International Journal for the Semiotics of Law*, 71–88.

"Peirce and Conflict of Methods of Inquiry," *In Honor of Jerzy Pelc*, in press.

"Property as Rhetoric," *Cardozo Journal of Law and Literature*," 189–206.

"Aspects of Property in Law," in *Flux, Complexity, and Illusion*. R. Kevelson (ed.), Peter Lang, New York and Bern, 209–228.

"Public Opinion and Human Rights," in *Tracing the Semiotic Boundaries of Politics*. P. Ahonen (ed.), Indiana University Press, Bloomington, 159–174.

**1994**

*Codes and Customs* (ed.), Critic of Institutions Series , Peter Lang, New York and Bern.

*The Eyes of Justice* (ed.), Semiotics and the Human Sciences Series, Peter Lang, New York and Bern.

"Peirce at the Millennium," in *Codes and Customs*. R. Kevelson (ed.), Peter Lang, New York and Bern, 153–176.

"Lex Talionis," 7 *International Journal for the Semiotics of Law*, 155–170.

"Zero Sign and the Science of Justice," in *The Eyes of Justice*. R. Kevelson (ed,). Peter Lang, New York and Bern, 139–158.

**1995**

*Peirce, Science, Signs* (ed.), Semiotics and the Human Sciences Series, Peter Lang, New York and Bern.

*Conscience, Consensus, Crossroads in Law* (ed.), Semiotics and the Human Sciences Series, Peter Lang, New York and Bern.

*Spaces and Significations (ed.)* , Critic Series, Peter Lang, New York and Bern.

"Boyle's Lock'n'Key: Contract, Law and Peirce's Sign-Transaction," in *Conscience, Consensus, Crossroads in Law*. R. Kevelson (ed.), Peter Lang, New York and Bern, 163–180.

"Law at the Border," in *Spaces and Significations* . R. Kevelson (ed.), Peter Lang, New York and Bern, 167-180.

"Icons of Justice/Spirit of Laws," 8 *International Journal of the Semiotics of Law,* 227–239.

"Crises in International Law," *IVR Proceedings, Challenges to Law at the End of the XXth Century.* E. Pattaro (ed.). Milan.

**1996**

*Law and the Conflict of Ideologies.* (ed.), New York and Bern: Peter Lang.

"Semiotic Perspectives: An Ideological Conflict," in *Law and the Conflict of Ideologies*. R. Kevelson (ed.), Peter Lang, New York and Bern, 105-116

"Justice as Artifice and Sign," *Archiv für Rechts-und Sozialphilosophie* (ARJP), in *Law, Justice, and the State,* Franz Steiner Verlag, Stuttgart, 80-88.

"Eco and Dramatology," in *Reading Eco* (ed.), R. Capozzi, Indiana University Press, Bloomington, 196-209.

## Forthcoming in 1997 and later

"Codes, Crypts, Incantations: A Nether Peirce," *Symploke*.

*States, Citizens, Questions of Significance,* Semiotics and the Human Sciences Series (co-editor John Brigham), Peter Lang, New York and Bern.

*Peirce's Pragmatism*, Toronto: University of Toronto Press.

Immigrants and the New Anarchism: On Displaced Values," in *States, Citizens, and Questions of Significance.* R. Kevelson and J. Brigham (eds.).

"Peirce" and "Semiotics" entries in *The Philosophy of Law: An Encyclopedia.* C. Gray (ed.), Garland, New York.

*Revolutions, Institutions, Law,* Semiotics and the Human Sciences Series. (co-editor Joel Levin), Peter Lang, New York and Bern.

*Hi-fives: A Semiotics Manual*, Peter Lang, New York and Bern.

*Peirce and the Mark of the Gryphon*, St. Martin's Press, New York.

# Contributors

**John Brigham,** Professor of Political Science at the University of Massachusetts, Amherst, is the author of *Constitutional Language: An Interpretation of Judicial Decision* (1978); *Civil Liberties and American Democracy* (1984); *The Cult of the Court* (1987); *Property and the Politics of Entitlement* (1990). He hosted and edited the Proceedings of the Tenth Round Table sponsored by the Penn State Center for Semiotic Research (Peter Lang, 1997), the first not held at Penn State.

**Denis J. Brion**, Professor of Law at Washington and Lee University, is the author of *Essential Industry and the NIMBY Phenomenon* (1991) and articles in most of the Round Table Proceedings (see Kevelson bibliography) from 1987 to date.

**Marcel Danesi**, Professor and Director of the Program in Semiotics and Communications Theory at Victoria College, The University of Toronto, is the author of *Language Games in Italian* (1985), (with Tito Renzo) *Applied Psycholinguistics: An Introduction to the Psychology of Language and Learning* (1985), *Vico, Metaphor, and the Origins of Language* (1993), *Cool: The Signs and Meaning of Adolescence* (1994); *Vico and the Cognitive Science Enterprise* (1995).

**John Deely**, Professor of Philosophy at Loras College, has been Visiting Fulbright Professor at the Federal University of Minas Gerais in Brazil and the National Autonomous University of Mexico (UNAM). He was chosen the first Thomas A. Sebeok Fellow by the Semiotic Society of America, of whose proceedings (under the title *Semiotics* followed by the year) he has been the editor since 1983. (The series is now published by Peter Lang). Among his works are *Introducing Semiotic: Its History and Doctrine* (1982), *Basics of Semiotics* (1990), *New Beginnings: Early Modern Philosophy and Postmodern Thought* (1994), and the English translation of John Poinsot's *Tractatus de Signis* (1985).

**Rolando Gaete**, Professor of Law at South Bank University in London and Executive Secretary of the International Association for the Semiotics of Law, is a native of Chile whose defense of human rights compelled him to leave during the Pinochet era. His work is exemplified by *Human Rights and the Limits of Critical Reason* (1993).

**Robert Ginsberg**, Professor of Philosophy at the Delaware County Campus of the Pennsylvania State University, edits the series New Studies in Aesthetics for Peter Lang Publishing and the Value Inquiry Book Series for Rodopi Publishers. Formerly editor of *The Journal of Value Inquiry*, he has been elected President of the American Society for Value Inquiry. His writings include *A Casebook on the Declaration of Independence* (1967), *Welcome to Philosophy: A Handbook for Students* (1977), and the edited volume *The Philosopher as Writer: The Eighteenth Century* (1987).

**Bernard S. Jackson**, Queen Victoria Professor of Law at the University of Liverpool, is the author of *Theft in Early Judaism* (1972), *Essays in Jewish and Comparative Legal History* (1975), *Semiotics and Legal Theory* (1985), *Law, Fact, and Narrative Coherence* (1988), *Making Sense in Law* (1995), and *Making Sense in Jurisprudence* (1996).He is the founder and editor of Deborah Charles Publications, which specializes in legal semiotics.

**J. Ralph Lindgren**, Clara H. Stewardson Professor of Philosophy Emeritus at Lehigh University, is the author of *The Social Philosophy of Adam Smith* (1973), (with Nadine Taub) *The Law and Sex Discrimination* (1988, 2d ed. 1993), and editor of two other volumes in the Critic of Institutions Series for Peter Lang: *The Horizons of Justice* (1996); (with Jay Knaack) *Ritual and Semiotics* (1997).

**Robin Paul Malloy** is Professor of Law and Economics in the School of Law at Syracuse University. His writings include *Law and Economics: A Comparative Approach to Theory and Practice* (1990); *Planning for Serfdom: Legal Economic Discourse and Downtown Development* (1991);

(with Jerry Evensky) *Adam Smith and the Philosophy of Law and Economics* (1994).

**Hugh O'Donnell** teaches in the Department of Language and Media at Glasgow Caledonian University and is the author (with Neil Blain and Raymond Boyle) of *Sports and National Identity in the European Media* (1993).

**William Pencak**, Professor of History at the Pennsylvania State University, is the author or editor of thirteen books, mostly on the colonial and revolutionary history of the United States, but including *History, Signing In: Studies in History and Semiotics* (1993), *Worldmaking* (edited), both published by Peter Lang, and *The Conflict of Law and Justice in the Icelandic Sagas* (1996). He edits *Pennsylvania History* and serves as Associate Director of the Center for Semiotic Research at Penn State.

**Paul Ryan** has presented his design for an environmental television channel at the Museum of Modern Art, the First International EcoCity Conference, and the United Nations. His pioneering video art has been shown all over the world. NASA published his Earthscore Notational System. He has taught at SUNY New Paltz, the Visual Studies Workshop in Rochester, New York University, and Savannah College of Art and Design and the New School for Social Research, where he now teaches in the Graduate Communication Department. He has written *Cybernetics of the Sacred* (1973) and *Video Mind, Earth Mind* (Peter Lang, 1993), which contains a bibliography of his creative art and writings (pp. 411–420).

**William T. Scott**, Head of the Department of Language and Media at Glasgow Caledonian University, is author of *The Possibility of Communication* (1990) and articles in many volumes of the Round Table Proceedings.

**Thomas A. Sebeok** is Distinguished Professor Emeritus and Emeritus Director of the Research Center for Language and Semiotic Studies at Indiana University and Senior Fellow at the Institute for Advanced Study,

Colegium Budapest. He continues to serve as editor-in-chief of *Semiotica*. Former President of the Linguistic Society of America and the Semiotic Society of America (of which he was a principal founder and served as first Executive Director from 1976–1980), a bibliography of his writings and summary of his achievements fills the 144-page book, *Thomas A. Sebeok Bibliography: 1942–1995,* edited by John Deely (1995).

**Willem J. Witteveen** is Professor of Law at Tilburg University in The Netherlands. Besides many articles and edited collections, he has published *De retoriek in het recht: over retorica en interpretatie, staatsrecht en democratie* (1988) and *Het theater van de politiek: publieke retorica en de paspoortaffaire* (1992).

# Author Index

# Index of Subjects

# SEMIOTICS & THE HUMAN SCIENCES

*Edited by Roberta Kevelson*

This series, Semiotics and the Human Sciences, takes as its leading idea the Peircean assumption that human institutions, in theory and practice, are models and prototypes of the Theory of Signs, or Semiotics. The core of this Series is Law, and especially those concepts of the law which are central to all theories of signs, whether Peirce's, Greimasian, or various aspects of structural linguistics, Critical Theory, and similar outgrowths such as Postmodernism, Functionalism, and antipositivism. Included in the special topics developed in this series are Ideological Conflict, Value-making and Aesthetic Functions, Chaos Theory and theories of complex Systems. Just as semiotics presumes an underlying dialogic structure, one of its main focal areas is Legal Contract; others include Public Reason, Comparative Legal Cultures, problems of Paradox; Pluralistic Discourse and International Law. The Series is open to proposals in these and other related issues and topics, from many academic and professional perspectives. Collected Papers of the Round Tables on Law and Semiotics are a large part of this series, and serve as research tools.